W9-ACD-723

CONTENTS

To Sri
for his extraordinary friendship

Rajini Srikanth is Associate Professor of English at the University of Massachusetts, Boston. She is the coeditor (with Sunaina Maira) of *Contours of the Heart: South Asians Map North America* and (with Lavina Dhingra Shankar) of *A Part Yet Apart: South Asians in Asian America*.

Acknowledgments

THESE WORDS OF thanks are paltry, but they are heartfelt. Without the support and intellectual camaraderie of friends over these past several years, this book would have remained an unfulfilled aspiration. My deepest gratitude to Roshni Rustomji for launching me into the landscape of South Asian American writing and urging me to make it a subject of scholarly inquiry; Sunaina Maira, dear friend and first coeditor, for an unforgettable editing partnership in which literature became entwined with activism; Vijay Prashad for his pointed questions and valuable suggestions to sharpen my articulations and for the inspirational courage of his positions; Gautam Premnath for his astute and meticulous reading of my work, leading me to deepen and complicate my analysis; Lavina Shankar for joining me in challenging Asian American studies to consider seriously the position of South Asians; Gary Okihiro for underscoring for Lavina and me the validity of our endeavor; Sucheta Mazumdar for insisting on seeing the global picture—never losing sight of the Asia in Asian America—and for significantly enlarging my thinking; Esther Iwanaga for believing that we could do justice to the wide range of Asian American literary voices and for persuading me that *Bold Words* was a collection worth compiling; Min Song, for his thought-provoking observations about Korean American literature and for a valuable comparative perspective; Samir Dayal for the razor-keen intellectual challenges and deeply probing questions that spurred me to frame increasingly complex arguments; S. Shankar for his validation of my ideas when they were still in their very early stages; Leti Volpp for her generous spirit in exchanging scholarship and for the adventurousness of her thinking; Amitava Kumar, who, in sharing my love of Antjie Krog's *Country of My Skull*, reminded me of the pleasure of links that persist between friends who rarely see one another; Samina Najmi for our partnership in entering the field of whiteness studies and for her early and vital confidence that I could and would write this book; Amritjit Singh for opening up the world of scholars outside the United States and introducing me to researchers in Australia, India, Fiji, Sri Lanka, Malaysia, and South Africa; Raju Sivasankaran for his rigorous critical analysis and unrelenting focus on social justice; Aparna Sindhoor and John Mathew, fierce artists, for showing me the meaning of courage in performance; and Shona Ramaya for coaxing me to journey in new and unpredictable waters.

I am profoundly grateful to my colleagues in the English Department at the University of Massachusetts Boston for the warmth of their friendship, the nurturing atmosphere they provide, and the genuine and rigorous interest they take in my scholarship. Working among them is a unique pleasure. To my colleagues in the Asian American Studies Program, I owe deep and incalculable thanks for sustaining a vibrant environment that challenges conventional models of study.

And to my students at UMass Boston, whose perseverance and commitment to learning even as they work twenty to forty hours a week, raise families, care for parents, and participate in their neighborhoods, I turn in amazement—to learn how to defy fatigue and move the mind and muscles to think new thoughts and write the next page.

Lexington, MA
2004

ONE

Introduction

*Today I went to the post office. Across the river. Bags and bags—
hundreds of canvas bags—all undelivered mail. By chance I looked down
and there on the floor I saw this letter addressed to you. So I am
enclosing it. I hope it's from someone you are longing for news of.*

—AGHA SHAHID ALI, "DEAR SHAHID"

THIS BOOK GROWS out of the question, What is South Asian
American writing and what insights can it offer us about living
in the world at this particular moment of tense geopolitics and
interlinked economies? It is my conviction that reading this body of literature must be more than just an act of aesthetic or narrative pleasure.
Rather, it must be a *just* act—doing justice to the contexts from which
the writing emerges and challenging one's imagination to encounter the
texts with courage, humility, and daring. "The idea of America" in this
book's title signals not just an examination of South Asian American
writing within the context of North America, but also a discussion of
the global phenomena against which the idea of America emerges and
that so richly infuse a great deal of South Asian American writing.

South Asia comprises the seven countries of Bangladesh, Bhutan,
India, the Maldives, Nepal, Pakistan, and Sri Lanka. "South Asian
American" is a category that encompasses those individuals in the
United States and Canada whose ancestral origins lie in one or more of
these seven countries. For the purposes of this book, I limit the scope of
the term "America" to the United States and Canada, although I am

fully cognizant of the mission of the Organization of American States (OAS) to expand the term to include Latin America and the Caribbean—so that "America" may be understood as the America*s*. Quite apart from the need to work within a manageable framework, however, the decision to limit my study to South Asian American writers in North America is, I would propose, logical. The United States and Canada share a number of important traits that are relevant to this topic. Both countries occupy geographical regions that had large indigenous populations before the arrival of settlers from Europe. These settlers appeared in significant numbers at approximately the same time—the early seventeenth century—in both places, with similar attitudes toward the "wilderness" they encountered: it was theirs to claim.[1] Both the United States and Canada were populated through immigration, with the largest numbers of people in both countries coming initially from England (the French presence in Canada was largely concentrated in Quebec). Both nations adopted discriminatory immigration policies that restricted or excluded the entry of certain groups of people—Chinese, Japanese, and Indian, principally—and both nations either officially or unofficially adopted policies and passed legislation over the years that privileged those who were white-skinned. The immigration histories of South Asians are broadly similar in both countries.[2]

At the same time, there are critical differences between the two countries. There was no slavery in Canada. In the United States, up until the ethnic empowerment movements of the 1960s and 1970s, the various immigrant groups were encouraged to dissolve their specific characteristics in the melting pot of "American" identity; in Canada, the mosaic approach was more popular, and the diverse ethnic groups were encouraged to maintain their specific characteristics even as they lived side by side.[3] Beginning in the mid–nineteenth century, the United States pursued a vigorous expansionist policy against Mexico and Spain, acquiring Texas, the Philippines, Hawai`i, and Puerto Rico. In the twentieth century, the United States developed into a major military and economic power, and in the current historical moment, following the collapse of the Soviet Union and the Communist bloc, is the unchallenged superpower.

The South Asian American experience is one of diaspora.[4] One cannot discuss South Asian American literature without considering the numerous geographical locations this diaspora comprises—including the countries of South, East, Southeast, and West Asia, the Americas, Australia, and Africa—as well as the labor migrations, geopolitics, global economics, and war and peace that have driven it. Stuart Hall, in speaking of the black experience and its particular histories, observes that blacks have used their "bodies as canvases of representation."[5] One might justifiably speak of South Asians using the metaphor of space as the canvas of their representation. South Asian American writing is marked by "ways of living at home abroad or abroad at home—ways of inhabiting multiple spaces at once, of being different beings simultaneously, of seeing the larger picture stereoscopically with the smaller."[6] This body of writing offers both the pleasures and the complications of enlarged visions. I don't mean merely that South Asian American writing makes available to readers unfamiliar experiences and locations—although such an effect is a given, steeped as this literature is in evocations of the histories and geographies of many nations—but also that these texts at their best move the reader to consider why understanding the interconnectedness among nations and peoples matters, and how such understanding can be transported from the realm of literature into the material realm of politics and civic behavior.

As I have discussed elsewhere, not everyone subscribes wholeheartedly to the category "South Asian," thereby making the subcategory "South Asian American" a tenuous one to maintain.[7] It offers a convenient label, however, to signify individuals living in North America who trace their ancestry to one or more of the seven countries that comprise the geopolitical region known as South Asia. (The term "Indian subcontinent" is occasionally used to refer to South Asia, but it is not the preferred designation as it privileges one country over others.) The heterogeneity of South Asia (and therefore of South Asian America) has few parallels anywhere: every major religion is represented in healthy numbers, and more than twenty languages flourish in everyday use; cultural practices vary, not just across countries, but within countries, where language, food, customs, and dress can differ dramatically every few hundred kilometers; religious affiliations may not translate into cultural solidarity—for example, the Bangladeshis, although Muslim like the majority of Pakistanis, have more in common culturally and share a language with the Hindu Bengalis of India. South Asia and South Asian America are a pastiche of contradictions, correspondences, and unexpected linkages.

This discussion of the literature, then, is an effort to "muddy the waters" of our civic selves. You will not find here the linear logic of unimpassioned thought, the neat distinctions of cultural or national categories, or the precision of binaries. I offer these observations in the spirit of heteroglossia, seeking indulgence for the cacophony of analysis, narrative, remembrance, anger, and yearning that follow in these pages. The frame of my discussion is interdisciplinary, although I am always cognizant of the literary text and its function within this interdisciplinary architecture. It is not my intention that this architectural structure be symmetrical, that its various components be of similar proportions and of equal influence; in fact, at some level I hesitate to use the word "structure," because it carries with it a suggestion of fixity, of permanence. The structure I envision can be easily dismantled and a new one erected in its place. In explaining the theory and method of articulation, Hall says that "articulation" is

> the form of the connection that can make a unity of two different elements, under certain conditions. It is a linkage which is not necessary, determined, absolute and essential for all time. . . . The so called 'unity' of a discourse is really the articulation of different, distinct elements which can be rearticulated in different ways because they have no necessary 'belongingness'. The 'unity' which matters is a linkage between the articulated discourse and the social forces with which it can, under certain historical conditions, but need not necessarily, be connected.[8]

I write at a time of aggressive deployment of U.S. military power (though, admittedly, the late nineteenth century also saw an equivalent display of U.S. military and imperialistic might) and equally aggressive pursuit of terrorists. On the domestic front, an alarming erosion of civil liberties continues; in the sphere of foreign policy, U.S. self-interest dominates, and all other nations are being asked to put their self-interest in the service of the United States. This situation is not likely to change. In such a moment, I see South Asian American literature as providing the means to pull back from a close-up view of the United States to reveal a wider landscape of other nations and other peoples. Such enlargement of perspective is a moral responsibility, particularly in the twenty-first century, when no nation is an island unto itself. Thus, an articulation that facilitates connections between discourse and material object and between one type of discourse and another—in other words, that makes visible the ways in which we construct knowledge—is an appropriate mode for appreciating why we should care about the lives of others in our immediate communities and far away. I make no apologies for positioning a literary work as one text among many. I liken the interdisciplinary articulation I pursue here to the cosmopolitan consciousness of being at home abroad or abroad at home and of seeing the world "through kaleidoscope eyes."[9] Laura Kang's "trenchant interdisciplinarity" is a useful reminder of the disruptive possibilities of working across disciplines. She argues that, "[i]n its implication of both keenness and marginality, the 'trenchant' qualifier of interdisciplinarity signals an agonistic but nevertheless situated relation to prevailing disciplinary forms of knowledge formation and reproduction and their historical intimacies with tactics of political domination and social control."[10]

This book does not offer an exhaustive study of writing by South Asian authors in North America. It offers a very specific way of reading and thinking about the texts—as works of art that challenge rigid constructions of citizenship and overly narrow perspectives of location. My discussion seeks to examine the possibilities of a discourse that reconfigures emotional, ideological, political, and behavioral spaces so as to challenge prevailing trends of viewing the world within antipodal frameworks: national and transnational, individual and collective, insider and outsider. I use those literary texts that best illustrate my purpose; they include short fiction, novels, poetry, memoirs, essays, and plays. Writers as well known as Michael Ondaatje and Meena Alexander are discussed alongside newly published authors such as Sharbari Ahmed and Abha Dawesar. I omit certain writers altogether—the most noticeable being Rohinton Mistry—not because I don't consider their work pertinent to my purpose, but because the application of my strategy of reading to their works might prove repetitive and overdetermined.

Center-Stage Visibility of South Asian American Writing

The remarkable visibility that South Asian American writing enjoys today is the result of the cumulative impact of a number of historical and sociocultural forces. In the nineteenth century, Ralph Waldo Emerson and the Transcendentalists expressed a profound interest in Indian philosophy. In the years leading up to the overthrow of British colonialism in South Asia, Americans were keenly aware of the efforts of Indian independence leaders, and during the American Civil Rights movement, Martin Luther King, Jr., and other African American leaders were strongly influenced by the tactics of Mahatma Gandhi to oust the British from the Indian subcontinent. In the 1960s, the Beatles popularized and commercialized India as the site of their spiritual inspiration. India's role as the world's largest democracy and its early post-independence tilt to the USSR made the United States watchful of India's political and economic fortunes. Pakistan's strategic location between India and the USSR influenced U.S. foreign policy overtures to Pakistan during the Cold War. The emergence of Salman Rushdie in England as a formidable writer with his novel *Midnight's Children* (1980), with its vibrant and exuberant style of narration, placed writers of South Asian descent writing in English on the global literary map. The *fatwa* issued in 1989 by Iran's Ayatollah Khomeini against Rushdie for his novel *The Satanic Verses* (1988) brought to the author more publicity than any person could care for. More recently, Arundhati Roy's spectacular success in winning the Booker Prize in 1997 for her first novel, *The God of Small Things*, reinforced the keen global interest in South Asian writers living in South Asia and in other nations of the South Asian diaspora (England, Canada, the Caribbean, and the United States, in particular; other locations of the South Asian diaspora include Fiji, Australia, Kenya, South Africa, Uganda, Nigeria, Malaysia, Singapore, and Hong Kong). Finally, one cannot underestimate the U.S. reading public's enormous interest in and appetite for consuming "exotic" cultures—evidenced in the stupendous popularity of such novels as Arthur S. Golden's *Memoirs of a Geisha* (1997) or Amy Tan's *The Joy Luck Club* (1989).

The earliest South Asian American experience to receive literary treatment was that of the Indians (primarily Sikhs) who came to work on the farmlands of California's Imperial Valley in the early 1900s. Chitra Divakaruni's triptych of poems—"The Founding of Yuba City," "Yuba City Wedding," and "The Brides Come to Yuba City"— collected in *Leaving Yuba City* (1997) renders their hard labor as farmhands, captures their turbulent feelings as they married Mexican American women because immigration restrictions prevented them from bringing over brides from their villages in India, and portrays the eventual arrival of Sikh "picture brides" once some of the immigration restrictions were lifted.

In *Blood into Ink: South Asian and Middle Eastern Women Write War* (1994), Miriam Cooke and Roshni Rustomji-Kerns collect some of the poems and protest songs of these Punjabi farmers and their wives, giving us a glimpse into the transnationalism that operated in the early years of the twentieth century. These men and women, some of whom came directly from India, and others from British Columbia in Canada, formed a diasporic Indian network that extended along the West Coast all the way from the plains of California to the lumber camps and farms of Vancouver. They were instrumental in energizing North American support for the cause of Indian independence from British rule. Jane Singh details these early efforts at fighting colonialism and uncovers the newsletter—*Ghadr*—that was published to rally the diasporic community.[11]

Other pre-1965 South Asian diasporic experiences are recorded in memoirs by Dhan Gopal Mukerji, an early twentieth-century Indian American writer who gained visibility as a children's book author and commentator on life in India and Eastern philosophy; Dalip Singh Saund, the first U.S. Congressman of Asian American descent; and Ved Mehta, who came to the United States at the age of fourteen to enter a school for the blind in Arkansas and then went on to become a writer for the *New Yorker*. Mukerji's *Caste and Outcast*, first published in 1923, was reissued by Stanford University Press in 2002. Mukherji records the circumstances of his life in India before coming to the United States in the first part of his memoir, and, in the second, his varied experiences in California in the early decades of the 1900s as a student, farmhand, and factory worker. His memoir is a moving combination of exuberance and disillusionment. Saund's *Congressman from India*, published in 1960, displays an optimism that sounds extraordinarily naive to a contemporary audience made skeptical about "universal" access to the American dream despite the Civil Rights and multiculturalism movements. In his memoir, Saund willingly embraces the rhetoric of a democratic and fully participatory American society. Similarly, in *Sound-Shadows of the New World* (1986), Mehta celebrates both his own extraordinary achievement at having overcome the handicap of blindness, and the United States as having made possible such a transformation. The uncritical acceptance of dominant-culture assumptions about the construction of selfhood in these memoirs may contribute to their absence from ethnic studies discussions. (See Chapter 5 for a discussion of Saund's and Mehta's memoirs.)

Books of fiction, memoir, and poetry by South Asian American writers have proliferated in such quick succession from 1985 to the present that the overview provided here is by no means exhaustive. Five anthologies of South Asian American writing offer a wide array of writers and serve as good springboards into the literature: *Our Feet Walk the Sky: Women of the South Asian Diaspora* (1993); *Her Mother's Ashes and Other Stories by South Asian Women in Canada and the United States* (1994); *Her Mother's Ashes 2: More Stories by South Asian Women in Canada and the United States* (1998); *Living in America: Poetry and Fiction by South Asian American Writers* (1995); and the Before Columbus Foundation American Book Award winner *Contours of the Heart: South Asians Map North America* (1996), which features both first- and second-generation South Asian Americans.

Another relatively new and developing area is South Asian American theater. This genre is still in its very early stages, and its practitioners are negotiating the complex politics of securing performance space and making South Asian American bodies visible. There is, however, strong and vibrant work being written and performed, primarily by second-generation South Asian Americans. New York is a lively center of activity, and efforts are being made in Boston as well. Una Chaudhuri's point that playwrights and performers must "do representational justice to the complex realities of the diasporic experience, not only for . . . spectators but for . . . *subjects*," is well taken, and there is a growing sense in the South Asian American community that theater is a powerful medium in which to find a voice and use it.[12] Shishir Kurup's *Assimilation* (1994), Asif Mandavi's *Sakina's Restaurant* (1998), John Mathew's *Grave Affairs* (2001), Karthick Ramakrishnan and Jyoti Thottam's *Interrogations* (2002), and the steady stream of short South Asian American drama enacted at the Asian American Writers Workshop in New York City hold great promise for the future.

The present moment is a high point for South Asian American literature. Sohrab Homi Fracis's collection of short stories, *Ticket to Minto: Stories of India and America* (2001) won the 2001 Iowa Short Fiction Award. Akhil Sharma's novel *An Obedient Father* (2000) won the 2001 Hemingway Foundation/PEN Award. Jhumpa Lahiri's collection of short stories, *The Interpreter of Maladies* (1999), won the 2000 Pulitzer

Prize for fiction. Earlier "mainstream" endorsements of South Asian American writers include the National Book Critics Circle award for Bharati Mukherjee's collection *The Middleman and Other Stories* (1988), *Time* magazine's selection of Abraham Verghese's memoir *My Own Country: A Doctor's Story of a Town and Its People in the Age of AIDS* as one of its top four books for 1994, the PEN Oakland Josephine Miles Award for Chitra Divakaruni's short fiction collection *Arranged Marriage* (1995), the Barnard New Women Poets Prize for Reetika Vazirani's collection *White Elephants* (1996), and the Ainsfeld-Wolf Award for her poetry collection *World Hotel* (2002). I list these books and the awards they have won not to prove the "quality" of South Asian American writing, but rather to note that this recognition will likely boost sales of these books and consequently increase readership; therefore, it becomes imperative that this expanded readership engage with the multiple contexts within which South Asian American writing emerges. In what follows, I will attempt to provide an overview of these contexts.

On Literary Ground in South Asian America: The Realities and Possibilities

In his poem "Not Much Art," Sri Lankan American author Indran Amirthanayagam writes about the bombing of Jaffna, the stronghold of the Tamil rebels engaged in a fierce civil war with the government forces in Sri Lanka. But it is only the opening twelve lines of the poem that address themselves directly with images of the bombing. The rest of the poem (forty-seven lines) upbraids the United States for not caring enough about occurrences in Jaffna. The Americans see only a CNN report aired "in the post-midnight hour, / the scrambly witchy time / when Americans learn / the darknesses of dark lands." "[T]here isn't much art / in the bombing of Jaffna," but there also isn't much art in the indifference and self-indulgent, mind-numbing rituals with which Americans lead their lives, the poem suggests: "There isn't much art / in pill-taking / or the whiskey toothbrush // or 500 laps on one foot / to tire it out before working / the other foot to tire that out."[13] Amirthanayagam's accusation is echoed in the writings of other South Asian American authors, such as Amitav Ghosh, Meena Alexander, and Amitava Kumar, who write of the peril of our ignoring, as residents of the United States, the connectedness we share with inhabitants of other lands. These writers direct their efforts toward encouraging the creation and development of a reticulate consciousness—an awareness of oneself as part of an extensive network of the globe's inhabitants.

Vinay Dharwadker reminds us that this vision of oneself as part of a global community of fellow beings—a vision he equates with cosmopolitanism—was formulated in ancient society by the Buddhists (c. 500 B.C.) and the Stoics (330 B.C. to A.D. 200):

> As invented by the Buddhists and the Stoics, cosmopolitanism in antiquity is already a validation of inclusive, egalitarian heterogeneity, of the toleration of difference and otherness, of the equitable (re)distribution of resources and privileges, of the recognition of others' freedoms, of (comm)unity in diversity, or very simply, of the unqualified practice of fairness, kindness, and generosity. Instances like these suggest that for almost 2,500 years cosmopolitanism has continuously—though variably—aligned itself with what we now call universal human rights, equal opportunity, nondiscrimination, and social justice.[14]

Kwame Anthony Appiah offers a further dimension of cosmopolitanism, declaring that "while cosmopolitanism is indeed about seeing yourself as belonging to a world of fellows, the cosmopolitan's fellows are living lives in their own style, and the cosmopolitan rejoices in the fact that 'their' styles need not be 'ours.' Cosmopolitanism is, to reach a formula, universalism plus difference. . . . [I]t thinks nothing human alien, *but not because it imagines all humanity in its own image*."[15]

Amitav Ghosh's observation that "[t]o be different in a world of differences is irrevocably to belong" captures eloquently the condition of interdependent differences that characterizes the world.[16] Of the South Asian American writers featured in this study, Ghosh is perhaps the most attuned to the interconnected histories of nations. However, such a sensibility is present to some degree in almost all South Asian American writers—even those of the second generation, born and raised in the United States. It may be fair to say, therefore, that South Asian American writers' not insignificant contribution to American literature and to the American imagination is the delineation of narratives and spaces that enable the conception of a nation as simultaneously discrete *and* entwined within the fold of other nations.

In this tumultuous time of competing and conflicting memories, aspirations, and motivations, the writer's role is of undeniable importance. I would argue that we experience the world discursively, the force of visual images and the ubiquity of the media notwithstanding. The writer's delineation of the world, for better or for worse, conveys to us what we know, should know, can know, and cannot know. Walter Benjamin reminds us of the dangerous lure of the visual against which we must guard ourselves and implores us to turn to the written word to experience the world in its rich ambiguity and textured density.[17] In a system of global interdependencies and mass dissemination of visual images, an understanding of how language is deployed is critical to citizenship today. Language both introduces us to what we can know and demarcates for us what we cannot know. The spectacle of the visual gives us the false impression of knowing, but language reveals to us what cannot be known, by suggesting what lies outside the frame of the visual.

What we cannot know is equally important as what we should know. In knowing what we cannot know, we are perhaps made aware of the complexity of what we seek to know, and thus are reminded that we must approach it with necessary humility and a commitment to sustained engagement. Iain Chambers's remarks on art apply with undiminished force to literature. Talking about the special quality of art that makes it the ideal mode for the elaboration of "identity, subjectivity, and citizenship," Chambers notes "the necessary and disquieting alterity" of art:

> The aesthetics (and ethics) of disturbance that reveals a gap, an interval in the world, that signals a limit and establishes a transit, a passage elsewhere. In this space, which we could name with such a term as the sublime or the uncanny, the pedagogical languages of institutional identity, busily seeking to legitimate the narration of nation, citizenship, and cultural subjectivity, are interrupted by what refuses to make sense or speak in that prescribed way. . . . The art of the interruption, art as interruption, brings to light our prescribed state—its limits in time and space—while also opening the possibility of revisiting, reciting (in the sense of reworking), and resiting (in the sense of transporting) languages elsewhere. The prescribed is

overtaken by the inscription, by the event, artistic and ontological, that exceeds the grammar of expectancy and the semantics of institutional verdicts.[18]

The most satisfying South Asian American writing seeks to escape "the grammar of expectancy," both by presenting the reader with a complex landscape of indeterminate unpredictability and by challenging the reader to withhold summary explanation. For example, Amitava Kumar's exploration of the "text" of the passport sheds light on the ways in which it is possible to go beyond "the semantics of institutional verdicts." Kumar approaches the passport—one's badge of identity in a global world, one's proof of existence—as a kind of book. Two very different types of readers pour over this book, says Kumar: the immigrant and the immigration officer "seated at his desk with a gleaming badge on his uniform."[19] The officer does not, will not, permit himself the luxury of reading this passport imaginatively to plumb the anxieties and expectations of the immigrant who stands before him. He reads the passport strictly within the framework of institutional semantics and is therefore unable to fill the gaps in his knowledge of the complexity of the immigrant. He cannot know, for instance, that the immigrant may have spent his entire life savings to acquire this passport, or that he may have traveled many hundreds of kilometers from his village or town to the city where the U.S. consulate is located in the country of his birth. As long as the officer persists in restraining his imagination and adhering strictly to the dictates of prescribed language, the passport will yield no more than a mere surface glimpse of the man who waits patiently for the officer's dispensation. Kumar writes:

> The immigrant's reading of that book refers to an outside world that is more real. The officer is paid to make a connection only between the book and the person standing in front of him.
>
> The immigrant has a scar on his forehead at the very place his passport says that he does. For the officer this probably means that the man is not a fraud. For the immigrant, that scar is a reminder of his childhood friend in the village, the one whose younger sister he married last May. . . .
>
> The officer reads the name of the arrival's place of birth. He has never heard of it. The immigrant has spent all of the thirty-one years of his life in that village.[20]

In a 1988 essay, Gayatri Chakravorty Spivak notes that we read the world as text even when it is not immediately apparent that we do so. At the Riyadh University Center for Girls, where Spivak delivered a lecture titled "Literature and Life," she was asked by a student: "It's all very well to try to live like a book; but what if no one else is prepared to read? What if you are dismissed as an irresponsible dreamer?" Spivak gives the following answer:

> Everyone reads life and the world like a book. Even the so-called "illiterate." But especially the "leaders" of our society, the most "responsible" nondreamers: the politicians, the businessmen, the ones who make plans. Without the reading of the world as a book, there is no prediction, no planning, no taxes, no laws, no welfare, no war. . . . The world actually writes itself with the many-leveled unfixable intricacy and openness of a work of literature. If, through our study of literature, we can ourselves learn and teach others to read the world in the "proper" risky way, and to act upon that lesson, perhaps we literary people would not forever be such helpless victims.[21]

Spivak realizes, even as she insists on teaching others to read the world in the proper risky way, the difficulty of proposing such an attitude to women in Saudi Arabia, given the patriarchal repressiveness of its leaders. But her essay asserts the usefulness of literature as a mode of learning to engage with and force change in the world. Kumar notes, for instance, that the immigrant is reviled in language, but it is also in language—even a broken language—that the immigrant tells his story, and it is through "the swaggering banditry of language" that the immigrant can resist and threaten a mainstream America that denies him his humanity.[22]

Yet, one must balance the claim for language as an entryway into the deep crevices of experience with an acknowledgment of the limitations of a worldview that privileges the discursive. Pheng Cheah's scathing attack of Homi Bhabha for his exclusive immersion in the discursive space is worth keeping in mind. Criticizing the priority of the linguistic mode posited in Bhabha's *The Location of Culture*, Cheah remarks:

> The social is not coextensive with, or exhausted by, its symbolic dimensions.

. . . [T]he formation and deformation of group loyalty also involves political-organizational and economic forces such as law enforcement, the provision of welfare and other services by the state, and the establishment of a framework for the distribution and regulation of economic resources and capabilities to satisfy human needs. . . . [T]o be materially effective, emancipatory consciousness cannot subsist on linguistic dynamism or cultural-symbolic flux alone.[23]

Similarly, Elaine Scarry reminds us of the inadequacies of literary representation for "solving real-world problems."[24] Scarry's prognosis for the human imagination is bleak: "The human capacity to injure other people has always been much greater than its ability to imagine other people. Or perhaps we should say, *the human capacity to injure other people is very great precisely because our capacity to imagine other people is very small.*"[25] Although she grants authors a heightened capacity to represent the unfamiliar, she believes that the instances of literature's having effected noticeable change are painfully few: the two examples she provides are Harriet Beecher Stowe's *Uncle Tom's Cabin* (1852) and E. M. Forster's *A Passage to India* (1924). The former enabled the white population of the United States to imagine the "weight, solidity, [and] injurability" of the black population; the latter, "according to Stephen Spender, enabled the British population to begin to imagine India's population as independent."[26]

I was given convincing evidence of the disparity between a discursive interest in the condition of migrancy and the material reality of that condition in a conversation I had with a young Indian man (let us call him Ramesh) working in Kuwait. Ramesh is an employee of a South Asian airline with active traffic to Kuwait. He described the long working hours of his daily life and the lack of social outlets in a country that has a strict code of behavior regulating interaction between the sexes. Listening to him, I wondered how much worse, how much more constrained, the lives of migrant laborers (carpenters, plumbers, and welders, for example) and domestic servants from South Asia and other countries (the Philippines, primarily) were and asked him if he encountered these workers in his daily activities. The stories he told were heart-wrenching: young women pleading to be flown out of Kuwait because they couldn't take the conditions of their employment; the impossibility of their saving sufficient funds to cover their flight home; the sacrifice they committed for the sake of those back home. From time to time, one hears about maids raped by their male employers. (This abuse of domestic help is not specific to the Middle East; Indonesian maids in Malaysia are also subject to discrimination and abuse, and such cases are not uncommon in New York.) Human rights agencies may get involved in the more sensational cases of abuse, but there is no extended narrative of the lives of these migrant domestic workers and the day-to-day indignities they endure—seemingly trivial indignities, which as they accumulate gradually take on the psychological burden of a grievous iniquity.

I encouraged Ramesh to keep a journal recording the details of his life in Kuwait. He responded that he has no time to keep a journal. "It's late when I come back; then I have to cook for myself and I'm too tired to think of writing." The discursive, the symbolic, the narrative, could not emerge under the oppressive repetition of labor. And so, of course, one has to wonder to what extent globalism and transnationalism as themes in writing are inscribed by those who do not live the rhythms and realities of the less glamorous underside of such phenomena.

Yet, we cannot allow an admission of the limits of literature and language to become an excuse for civic despair and isolation. Taking on the rather formidable task of explaining literary interest and its value to civic life, Steven Knapp guides us through a carefully crafted argument that focuses specifically on literary texts. I quote him at some length so as to preserve the structure of his logical framework:

> [T]he moral benefit of literary interest lies not in any capacity to tell us which values are the right ones, but far more modestly, in the way it helps us find out what our evaluative dispositions *are*. Perhaps a complex [textual] scenario sets up a kind of experiment in which we test not the moral worth of one scenario against another one . . . , but the relative strengths of our own responses to the alternate scenarios. . . .
>
> A person who discovers, by reading literature, the conflicts, inconsistencies, and overdeterminations among her own dispositions is a person who can read herself as an instance of descriptive representation. She therefore encounters in herself an analogue of the predicament . . . in a descriptively representative legislature: how to choose a course of action without suppressing competing interests that all have a right to be registered in the same representational

space. . . . Here, . . . the Lockean account of free agency is especially illuminating. . . . Locke defines freedom solely in terms of the mind's capacity to suspend its decisions until it has had time to consider all its competing desires and their objects.[27]

There is no guarantee that every reader will bring to engagement with a text the kind of thoughtfulness and care that Knapp suggests is necessary to create in the reader's mind the capacity "to suspend its decisions until it has had time to consider all its competing desires and objects." But Knapp is interested in the *potential* of literature and language and, like Spivak, he urges us to consider the ways in which reading literature increases our self-consciousness about our own inconsistencies, and thus leads us to a critical reading of ourselves and our role in the world.

One of my concerns in this book is the act of *partial* reading, and I mean that in both senses of the word—as the biases with which we read, and as the ways in which those biases contribute to gaps in our understanding. Such gaps cause us to read texts only partially—that is, insufficiently, ignoring telling details in them. My discussion of South Asian American writing draws attention to some of the forces—political, economic, social, and cultural—contributing to such partial readings. I seek to uncover the possible reasons for partial readings and to suggest ways of recognizing, resisting, and perhaps overcoming them by engaging South Asian American writing within a web of interlocking events, phenomena, and attitudes that span a number of locations and historical periods. I do not wish to make grandiose claims for South Asian American writing. Rather, I wish to make clear the ways in which it is imperative for us to read these works with keen attention to the complexity and nuances of the South Asian American experience.

The First Caution: When Summary Judgment Becomes Bipolar Thinking

Amartya Sen, in an eloquent address given at the World Newspaper Congress in Belgium, May 26–29, 2002, argues with great dexterity against Samuel Huntington's "clash of civilizations" model and its attendant bipolar division of the world into an enlightened and scientific West versus a religious and traditional East. Evoking both the religious toleration of rulers such as the emperor Ashoka in the third century B.C. in India and the Mughal emperor Akbar (the latter's espousal of religious freedom was contemporaneous with the Inquisitions in Europe) and the impressive achievements in mathematics and science by medieval scholars in China, India, Persia, and the Arab world (contributions such as the concept of "algorithm," the technology for printing, and the understanding of the properties of the magnet), Sen objects on two fronts to the limited vision of Huntington's model:

> The deficiency of the clash thesis, I would argue, begins well before we get to the point of asking whether the disparate civilisations must clash. The problem begins with an impoverished vision of a singularly categorised world, divided into little boxes. . . .
>
> Second, civilisational categories are far from clear-cut, and the simulated history that goes with the thesis of clashing civilisations construct[s] a make-belief [sic] world of thoroughly hardened contrasts (partly by ignoring the heterogeneities within each culture) and also ignor[ing] historical interactions between them.[28]

Such a vision, Sen declares, makes it very easy for extremists in both camps to perpetuate and reinforce the supposed barriers between them. In the West, "[o]ften-repeated public rhetoric on the contrast between 'Western science' and 'non-Western cultures,' as well as crude civilisational classifications have tended to put science and mathematics well inside the basket of 'Western civilisation,' leaving other civilisations to mine their pride only in religious depths." Once the divisions are drawn in such a way, it becomes "very easy for the anti-Western activists, including religious fundamentalists and cultural militants, to secure leadership roles through focusing on those issues that separate the non-Western world from the West (such as religious beliefs, local customs and cultural specificities), rather than on those things that reflect positive global interactions running through history (including science, mathematics, literature, and so on)."[29]

Sen's call for a recognition and celebration of positive global interactions rather than "a dialectics of confrontation" comes at a critical moment in global geopolitics. His critique of bipolar thinking draws attention both to the convenience (and specious comfort) offered by such a model and the deprivations and diminishments that are likely to ensue if one adopts it. Keeping in mind Sen's impassioned call for an appreciation of the heterogeneity *within* supposedly discrete cultures and nations can help prepare us for a productive and fruitful engagement with South Asian American writing.

In 1995, *Amerasia Journal* published a special double issue that focused on theoretical models for Asian American studies. Of the many articles that examine the relative merit of different models (race and ethnic studies, postcolonialism, border theory, diaspora versus immigration), only one considers seriously theoretical models that are based in Asian philosophies. In "Asiacentrism and Asian American Studies," Paul Wong, Meera Manvi, and Takeo Hirota Wong call on Asian American scholars to tap into "[t]he immense theoretical and practical potential of the fusion between Eastern and Western theories and methods for the advancement of knowledge . . . recognized in such fields as comparative studies of spirituality, psychotherapy, medicine and some branches of science."[30] They point to the field of Afrocentrism, which turns to African ideologies to explain the black experience in America.

Thus far, however, the accepted theoretical paradigms in Asian American studies have their sources in France, Russia, and Germany, and now, with cultural studies, England. The many theoretical influences that have come to bear on Asian American studies in particular, and on ethnic and postcolonial studies in general, have had much to offer to a field of study that is rapidly becoming more textured, nuanced, and complicated in its positions. I have benefited from all these perspectives in my own work. But one "model" has proved surprisingly useful to me. I have been late to realize its value, supportive as I was of the determination of Asian Americanists to establish the field of Asian American studies as distinct from "area studies," which focused on countries in Asia, and to declare Asian American studies as an enterprise rooted in the *American* body politic by eschewing all association with "exotic" Asian philosophies. This model that I now embrace is suggested by a mythical story that has long fascinated me for its epistemological implications. The story appears to critique the limits and shortsightedness of a bipolar perspective and to imply that power lies in being able to think outside the either-or framework. I offer this mythical fragment with no small conflict, primarily on account of its Hindu identification, and particularly because I am not an actively practicing Hindu.[31] South Asia is home to Muslims, Christians, Buddhists, Sikhs, Zoroastrians, and Jews, in addition to Hindus, so in turning to a story from Hindu mythology, I don't wish to minimize the influence of multiple religions on my thinking. Perhaps the story has stayed with me because it seems so unmoored from any particular religion and portable across all boundaries.

This is how it goes: A certain demon wanted unlimited powers and so decided to pray long and hard to God. The sincerity of his worship so impressed God that He decided to grant the demon any wish that he desired. The demon asked for immortality, but God told him that immortality was reserved only for the divine and could not be granted to a human. Believing himself to be shrewd and capable of outsmarting God, the demon then rephrased his request as a set of conditions, thinking that by so doing he had anticipated and rendered void all the circumstances under which he could conceivably lose his life. "I wish to die neither on earth nor in heaven, neither indoors nor outdoors, neither in daylight nor in darkness, and to meet my death neither at the hands of man nor beast." God granted the demon his wish. Complacent in his supposed immortality, the demon renewed with increased vigor his campaign of terror and killing, bringing destruction upon those around him. One day, when he was warned by his God-fearing son that he would invite the wrath of God upon himself, the demon dismissed the power of God and flaunted the protection offered by the wish he had been granted. It was the hour of twilight, and at that instant, there emerged from a pillar in his palace, a creature that was half-human half-lion, who proceeded to lift the demon and carry him to the threshold of his home. There, between the indoors and outdoors, in the twilight (neither daylight nor darkness), the creature who was neither wholly human nor wholly beast lifted the demon off the ground and, holding him in the air (so that he was neither on earth nor in the heavens), tore the life out of him. Thus the demon authored his own death sentence, even as he arrogantly believed that he had envisioned and neutralized all possible scenarios that could defeat him. His bipolar thinking effectively put the chains on his imagination and led him to delineate a restricted reality based on the limited constructs of his consciousness.

The Second Caution:
Learning to Appreciate What Cannot Be Known

I turn now to a poem by Agha Shahid Ali, "Dear Shahid," an excerpt of which provides the epigraph to this chapter. The poem frames two narratives—an outer and an inner one. One possible way to read the poem is to note that it refuses to reveal its inner narrative, the center of the poem that presumably holds its most coveted missive. The poem's speaker, who lives in the war-torn land of Kashmir, records an intensely personal moment: on the floor of what looks like an abandoned or at least a nonfunctioning post office where hundreds of bags of mail lie undelivered, s/he discovers a letter addressed to a friend. In a gesture filled with hope and empathy, the speaker retrieves the letter and encloses it in a letter that s/he writes to the original addressee, the "Shahid" of the poem's title (the poet was known to his friends as Shahid). In this letter-within-a-letter format, we know what the first or outer framing letter—the poem itself—says, but it is the unopened enclosed letter that haunts us. The poem (the "outer" letter) tells of the violence in the speaker's homeland, from which Shahid is far removed. We read of the longing with which people wait for Shahid's return. But we are not permitted to read the enclosed letter—as if it holds a message too dear for strangers' eyes, too filled with significance for rapid consumption. Confronted by a barrier to the contents of the "inner" letter, the reader is challenged on the one hand to imagine what the contents of the letter *might* be (not *are*, because "are" is too definitive and does not admit of alternative explanations), and on the other to accept that there are some things that cannot be known, regardless of one's desire to know.

Rebecca Saunders notes that the Western tradition of hermeneutics "consistently depicts error, uncertainty, or absence of understanding as foreignness and treats that foreignness as a problem to be solved, a deviation to be disciplined."[32] Our strategies of reading and analysis also proceed from the notion that to be unable fully to explicate is somehow to be imperfect. When we read, therefore, we aim to render comprehensible, to bring into the realm of what is familiar, that which hitherto was unfamiliar and foreign. But if we are to read and study literatures of which we have inadequate knowledge of relevant social, historical, and political contexts—and cannot presume to come by such knowledge other than through sustained immersion either in the literature or in the material contexts from which that literature arises—then I submit that we must learn to operate as foreigners to the text—foregrounding the extent to which we cannot interpret or explicate the text and surmising from that gap, in that untranslatable zone, the vastness and complexity of what we seek to know.

I certainly don't mean to privilege willful ignorance of or to condone disinterest in the unfamiliar (and let me quickly dispel the notion that merely to be South Asian is to have some kind of inherited familiarity with or knowledge of the South Asian and South Asian American experience). Rather, what I am advocating is restraining the rush to explain and simplify the many complexities of the South Asian American experience. In this regard, Margaret Talbot's criticism of American multiculturalism is not without merit. Speaking about the declining interest among American students in studying foreign languages, Talbot says,

> There are plenty of reasons that Americans don't flock to language study, from geographic isolation to our traditional assimilationist credo to the widespread use of English. We don't have to! But if multiculturalism is not precisely to blame, it is odd that a movement so flamboyantly dedicated to the celebration of cultural diversity did so little to check our tendencies to cultural isolationism. In fact, it may have reinforced them, by lulling us into the sense that we were getting a resoundingly global education when all we were really getting was a little Arundhati Roy here, a little Toni Morrison there. . . . Multiculturalism was easy, whereas deep knowledge of another place, predicated as it usually is on linguistic competence, is hard.[33]

Not only do the majority of Americans shy away from acquiring competence in languages other than English, but they also exhibit a deep reluctance to gain historical competence in the experiences of nations other than the United States. And even in the case of the history of the United States there is a tendency to embrace only a very superficial rendering of it.

Appiah makes a crucial distinction between humanism and cosmopolitanism that is helpful in reading (and teaching literature) in an age of globalization: "The humanist requires us to put our differences aside; the cosmopolitan insists that it is the differences we bring to the table that make it rewarding to interact at all."[34] The humanist approach to reading and teaching literature in today's global age might be to look for commonalities as points of entry into a text; the cosmopolitan's approach to the text might be to identify gaps or seemingly insurmountable differences between the "shared culture" of the reader or student and "the culture implied in the text," and use these points as springboards for discussion. "The cosmopolitan celebrates the fact that there are *different* local human ways of being," Appiah observes.[35] Comfort with heterogeneity, I would argue, makes for a highly productive stance in the reading and teaching of literature from unfamiliar cultures. The dissonance between "our" way of being and knowing and "theirs" provides the impetus for making the attempt to step beyond our framework of understanding. That attempt may be unsuccessful, but it is my contention that an unsuccessful attempt can be of far greater value than a successful one. For it is only when we acknowledge that there are some chasms we cannot easily span, and yet continue in the effort to do so, that we achieve the true sense of understanding what it means to coexist in a world of disparate others.

Indeed, one of the criticisms of multicultural reading practices in the United States is that it has led to a kind of benign toleration of difference that is seen to be a laudable achievement in itself. There is no true appreciation for the myriad ways in which another is both different from and yet inextricably bound to oneself. Merely to say like Walt Whitman "I enclose multitudes" is not sufficient. One must consider how these domestic multitudes see themselves in relation to one another and to the global multitudes. Thomas McCarthy notes the complexity of "[r]econciling national diversity with cosmopolitan unity":

> The local "inside" is now increasingly linked with the global "outside." . . . The "inside" is also increasingly diverse. And there seems to be no halting this diversification short of violence, coercion, and repression. The growing heterogeneity of most populations makes any model of political community based on enthnocultural homogeneity or on forced assimilation to a hegemonic culture increasingly unsuitable as a normative model. The political-theoretical challenge it raises, is, rather, to think unity in diversity, to conceptualize forms of political integration that are sensitive to, compatible with, accommodating of varieties of difference.[36]

What appears to be common to most discussions of the relationship between patriotism/nationalism, on the one hand, and cosmopolitanism, on the other, is the basic premise that the dialectical tension between the two can be productive rather than destructive, salutary rather than harmful.

The Labor of Caring

Cultivating a cosmopolitan consciousness is hard work. For example, to engage meaningfully with the short story "Defend Yourself against Me" (1996) by Pakistani American writer Bapsi Sidhwa—so that one reads it with awareness of and sensitivity to its complex contexts—involves crossing a chasm of unfamiliarity.[37] Sidhwa appears to suggest that a meaningful relationship between people begins with a willingness to acknowledge each other's painful histories; such acknowledgement is particularly difficult when the parties involved have themselves been responsible for the tragedies. The narrative unfolds in Houston, Texas, but the events to which it refers and upon which the story climbs to its climax have their origins in India and Pakistan. What is particularly intriguing about this narrative is that while it presents the United States as the location in which certain troubled histories can be laid to rest and forgotten, it also, in the same breath, demands from the reader a knowledge of this erased history so as to enable the reader's full participation in the narrative's climax. The history that is both suppressed and surfaced is the partition in 1947 of the Indian subcontinent into two countries, India and Pakistan, and the butchery accompanying the double birth. Approximately 6 million people crossed the border between the two nations, and over half a million people lost their lives in horrific acts of violence that Hindus and Sikhs perpetrated on Muslims, and Muslims on Hindus and Sikhs.

The setting of the story is a dinner party in Houston. The guests have their origins in India and Pakistan, and they represent a wide range of South Asian ethnicities and religions—Hindu, Sikh, Muslim, Christian, and Parsi. There is no sign at this gathering of the hostilities that mark the relationship between India and Pakistan. An elderly Muslim woman, the host's mother, is visiting from Pakistan. The story's climax comes when two Sikh men—friends of the host—prostrate themselves on the threshold of his home attired in the most abject fashion and with their beards undone. They cry for forgiveness from the old Muslim woman (whom they have never met but about whose arrival they have been informed a few days ago) for the atrocities that their "fathers" committed against her and other Muslims in the partition riots of 1947. They refuse to rise, and when the mother screams to have them thrown out, they "[g]rasp[ ] her ankles [and] they lay their heads at her feet in the ancient gesture of surrender demanded of warriors" (419). First aghast at their gesture and shrieking that she can never forgive their grandfathers and fathers, the old woman ultimately relents in the face of their continued pleas and tells them that she forgave their fathers a long time ago, for how else could she have continued to live?[38]

The memory of Partition remains strong among many diasporic Indians and Pakistanis. People in both nations have inherited images of trauma—homes abandoned hurriedly, train rides made in terror, women raped, and families massacred. In recalling this tumultuous South Asian history within the context of a social event in Houston, Sidhwa underscores the promise of the United States as a site of rebirth, reconciliation, and forgiveness. However, she reminds the reader that some histories cannot entirely be discarded. That the two Sikh men feel compelled to seek absolution for the acts of their fathers may be read as Sidhwa's reminder that "responsibility" is not limited to geographical location or generational position. The young men insist on making the journey into the past and claiming its horrific deeds as theirs, believing perhaps that there can be no meaningful relationship between them and the old Muslim woman unless they bridge the chasm between Houston of the present moment and the Partition riots of 1947. They reject the polite and superficial conversations of a social gathering, refusing to cross the threshold of their host's home until they have called forth a painful history and inserted themselves into it. The narrator observes that their "blubbering" as they beg forgiveness "is unexpected, shocking, incongruous and melodramatic in this pragmatic and oil-rich corner of the western world" (416). It is precisely because they choose to inflect the easy comfort of pragmatism and material gain, shedding their usual bonhomie and confidence, with the searing issues of the past that the two Sikh men can be seen as embodying the attitude that Sidhwa may wish her readers to adopt: a willingness to engage deeply with the Partition distress of South Asia.

Sidhwa facilitates this journey, deftly supplying what the unfamiliar reader needs to know. The details range from quick summaries of major events—in the form of a history lesson—to delicate and lyrical explorations of personal pain. For instance, here is Sidhwa efficiently initiating the reader into the history:

> Lahore. Autumn 1948. Pakistan is a little over a year old. The Partition riots, the arson and slaughter, have subsided. The flood of refugees—12 million Muslims, Hindus, and Sikhs fleeing across borders that define India and Pakistan—has shrunk to a nervous trickle. Two gargantuan refugee camps have been set up on the outskirts of Lahore, at Walton and Badami Bagh. Bedraggled, carrying tin trunks, string-cloths and cloth bundles on their heads, the refugees swamp the city looking for work, setting up house on sidewalks and in parks—wherever they happen to be at sunset if they have wandered too far from the camps. (405)

Zooming in from this "wide-screen" depiction of the horror of Partition, Sidhwa's narrator, a writer teaching at the University of Houston, rests her eye on an intensely personal scene. A recollection from her childhood is set in motion by a man she meets at the party, and who she is convinced is the young refugee whose family had set up their belongings in the compound next to her home:

> A small boy, so extremely thin he looks like a brittle skeleton, is squatting a few feet away, concentrating on striking a marble lying in a notch in the dust. His skull-like face has dry, flaky patches, and two deep lines between his eyebrows that I have never before seen on a child. . . . The sun-charred little body is covered with scabs and wounds. . . . I see the improbable wound on the back of his cropped head. It is a raw and flaming scar, as if bone and flesh had been callously gouged out, and my compassion ties me to him. (407–8)

Almost fifty years later, it is this young boy's mother at whose feet the two Sikh men prostrate themselves and beg forgiveness. By immersing the reader in the trauma of Partition, Sidhwa succeeds in creating the backdrop necessary for an appreciation of the narrative's climactic moment.

But the story ends curiously and unexpectedly, widening out from the historically located Partition trauma to cast a net that pulls in the trauma of all womanhood—across all times and geographies. Driving home from the momentous party at which she has been witness to the reenactment of the memory of Partition, the narrator recalls the words of Bolivian poet Pedro Shimose, exhorting women to defend themselves against the relentless force of men—against fathers and the fathers of fathers and against all their patriarchal instruments of representation and socialization. Suddenly, Sidhwa's story becomes a feminist text, raising issues of abuse, objectification, and oppression. It invites an examination of the socialization of males, a comparative analysis of women's position in different countries, and the particular victimization of women during war. It goes from being a diasporic narrative of two South Asian American nationalities (Indian and Pakistani) to being a narrative in which readers are forced to confront difficult questions that have powerful relevance both inside and outside the United States.

But there is a question that gnaws at me: In pulling back to evoke the universal narrative of women suffering under the male impulse to war, does not Sidhwa too easily release the (non–South Asian) reader from a sustained engagement with the specifics of the pain of Partition—of the experiences of women and men of multiple ethnicities caught in the interplay of its forces? Does she not forsake the opportunity to encourage the reader to dwell on the meaning of that historic moment and its implications for the present? Does she not allow the reader to step outside the stream of history and enter, instead, the more familiar terrains of masculinity and femininity?

I confess that I don't know. There is no denying the power of Shimose's poem and its function of closing the narrative. There is also a breathtaking quality to Sidhwa's sweep, which, one could argue, enables the reader to empathize with the narrative's characters more readily now that s/he can see the events with the enlarged universalizing perspective. Therein lies the rub. How does an author render a very specific trauma so that readers who are unfamiliar with its particularities can still be powerfully affected by it? By going from the specific to the universal, does not an author minimize the specific trauma in question? Is it not the author's function to enable readers to enter into other persons' traumas and experience them as viscerally as possible given that these traumas are not theirs, rather than to enable readers to find points of similarity between these unfamiliar traumas and their own?

Sidhwa's ending presents several complications, and in doing so enables us to engage with the tricky issues of awareness, action, and change as they relate to the realm of trauma. I have already suggested that Shimose's poem facilitates the reader's exit from the subcontinental trauma of Partition and thus decreases the impact of a sustained immersion in that experience. But the poem raises other critical and not unrelated matters. Its speaker is male, and the poem captures a moment of extraordinary knowledge when he gives evidence of having realized that he and his kind are continual aggressors against women. His final plea is eloquent, calling on woman to defend herself against man. One could argue, of course, that the male speaker, self-aware as he is, characteristically places the responsibility for protecting herself upon the *woman*, suggesting that men cannot help themselves. There is no indication in the poem that men are capable of change, or even that they will attempt to change. Thus, even as the poem offers hope that the male voice understands the trauma of being a woman in a world shaped by the aggressive tendencies of men, it absolves men from having to do anything differently. At some level, this remarkable story lets the non–South Asian reader off the hook from a sustained immersion in the trauma of Partition and lets the male reader shift the burden of the responsibility for change upon women. The transference of trauma is incomplete, I would argue.

Traumas, Nations, and the Writer

If, following Sidhwa's trajectory of enlarging perspective, we were to move from considering the trauma of individuals to considering the trauma of nations, then I would suggest that only when nations appreciate each others' traumas and match their actions (foreign policies) accordingly will there be a likelihood of global cooperation. The World Conference Against Racism held in Durban, South Africa, from August 31 to September 7, 2001, illustrates the enormous difficulty that nations have in admitting their role in causing trauma. Some of the fiercest debates at the conference involved the call for recognition of the slave trade as a crime against humanity and an acknowledgment by former slave-holding nations of the trauma they perpetuated. Similarly, Korea continues to pressure Japan for a complete apology for Japan's use of Korean women as prostitutes for soldiers of the Imperial Army during World War II.[39]

For many nations, collective traumas can be points around which to shape national identity. For Israelis, it's the trauma of the Holocaust; for South Africans, apartheid; for Germans, Nazism; for Palestinians, the loss of their land; for Indians and Pakistanis, colonial rule and, for North Indians, in particular, and Pakistanis, the Partition; for Bangladeshis, the separation from West Pakistan and the bloody birth of a new nation; for Koreans, the colonization by Japan and the comfort women scandal; for Cambodians, the killing fields of the Khmer Rouge; for Sri Lankans, the continued civil war since the early 1980s. While any single nation's trauma is deeply embedded in the particularities of its own history, there is a critical need for other nations to engage with these specific traumas and understand how they came to be and how they might be averted in the future. A reticulate consciousness—cosmopolitanism as described by Dharwadker—begins perhaps in the appreciation of traumas other than one's own.

In this context the writer emerges as an indispensable figure. There is no denying that text is a primary conduit through which we encounter and internalize experiences outside our own. We often forget or take for granted that the writer enriches, deepens, and widens our understanding of complex situations. Antjie Krog is a case in point. An Afrikaner reporter for the South African Broadcasting Corporation (SABC), Krog was assigned to cover the hearings of the Truth and Reconciliation Commission (TRC). Krog is also a poet, and thus brings to her task of reporting a lyric sensibility and delicate sense of the potentialities of language. Her book *Country of My Skull* (1998) is both report and meditation, both information and heartfelt commentary. She writes not just as a reporter, but also as an Afrikaner woman who is slowly and painfully beginning to discover the hidden portions of her nation's history. Much of the book's impact comes from Krog's valiant journey toward making the traumas of apartheid's victims part of her flesh and bone, part of the crevices of her skull, as she says.

Krog's crossing of the chasm of race takes place within the geographical boundaries of one nation. The TRC's relative overall success, notwithstanding its numerous pitfalls, came from the overwhelming recognition by most South Africans that if they wished their nation to heal and move forward, they would have to undertake the excavation of thousands and thousands of hidden and silenced stories. Love of one's country set in motion and sustained this extraordinarily difficult cross-racial voyage into the most agonizing territories of trauma.

Harder to explain is Tony Kushner's motivation for writing the play *Homebody/Kabul*. True, Kushner is fiercely and unapologetically political in his art, but it is still surprising that the playwright focused such close attention on Afghanistan *before* September 11, 2001. The motivations for Kushner's pre–September 11 interest in Afghanistan reveal a fascinating portrait of a reticulate consciousness, of a deeply committed cosmopolitanism. Although he never visited Afghanistan, he was drawn to its "geopolitical plight." "I'd always been moved and disturbed both because of what the Soviet Union did there [invading Afghanistan in 1980]. . . . And then there was the American complicity in arming the mujahedeen and leading to a decade of slaughter."[40] In an October 2001 interview, Amy Barrett asked Kushner if his being gay and marginalized made him more empathetic to marginalized people in other countries where there were no laws to protect them. Kushner's answer explains his interest in other people's suffering but doesn't necessarily explain his particular interest in Afghanistan:

> Yeah, everybody has their own personal history, and you bring that with you when you address the world. And people who have suffered oppression can recognize oppression when it appears in very different context [sic]. And the question is, Can you recognize that you have been oppressed without turning yourself into a victim? Do you say, "No one has suffered like I have suffered"? Or do you say, "What I have learned from this situation is not my uniqueness but that suffering really is awful and people should not suffer"?[41]

Kushner's questions touch on issues of representation, especially in situations in which authors write about peoples and countries with whom and with which they have limited experience. I take these concerns up in greater detail in Chapter 4. In *Homebody/Kabul*, however, Kushner appears to have paid careful attention to getting the details right. In a *New York Times* article on Kushner, Peter Marks quotes an Afghan American:

"The play is written with so much attention to the small details," said Nisar Ahmad Zuri, an Afghan émigré who publishes a newspaper in Queens, Ayendah E-Afghan, for fellow exiles, and who helped Mr. Kushner translate scenes into the regional languages. It stunned him to discover, for example, a reference in the play to "Pashtunistan"—a long dreamed-of Pashtun nation incorporating parts of Afghanistan and Pakistan. "How this American writer knows this, it struck me like, 'Wow!,'" he said.[42]

Marks goes on to marvel that "the play is attuned to the historical and political realities of another part of the world to a degree that few American writers ever attempt."[43] Knowledge is, after all, predicated on desire, effort, and attitude—the desire to know, the effort made toward that end, and the attitude with which one conducts the exploration. There is no simple one-to-one correspondence between writing about that with which you are unfamiliar and the care you do or do not bring to that depiction. The same point may be made of writing about that which is known to you. Bharati Mukherjee's and Pico Iyer's writings present fascinating twists on precisely this relationship (see Chapter 4).

Kushner's oeuvre reminds us that his political vision is both intensely domestic *and* intensely global (for what is *Angels in America*, with its sharp critique of Reaganism, if not intensely domestic). It is the refusal to accept the binary opposition between national and international that marks Kushner as a cosmopolitan creature passionate about the knowledge of all nations. Bruce Robbins, in his discussion of the vein of cosmopolitanism in Michael Ondaatje's novel *The English Patient*, writes:

> The search for knowledge, which unites the explorers, is explicitly aligned with love and against nations: "We were German, English, Hungarian, African—all of us insignificant to [the desert tribes]. Gradually we became nationless. I came to hate nations. We are deformed by nation-states. . . ." We see a love story entangled in the classics, and the classics embedded in North African geography, archaeology, history—a full curriculum for "world studies" in an age when the line between Europe and non-Europe can no longer pretend to be coherent.[44]

Whether we think about cosmopolitanism and reticulate consciousness as powered by the eroticism of knowledge or grounded in the registers of empathy for suffering, what is clear is that, both intellectually and emotionally, one can arrive at a meaningful appreciation of the world as a network of interconnected peoples only through sustained hard work. I was discussing with a colleague the merits of including Arundhati Roy's long essay "The End of Imagination" in an anthology of nonfiction creative prose for use in college instruction.[45] What impresses me most about the essay is its combination of hard facts and emotional prose. Further, it raises the tremendously important issue of the role of the writer in society and the extent to which a writer can and should become the conscience of a people. "The End of Imagination" is Roy's cry of anguish and anger and despair at India's testing of nuclear capabilities in May 1998, which resulted in Pakistan's testing of its own nuclear program and the subsequent escalation of tensions in the region of South Asia.

My colleague, while admitting that the essay is brilliantly written, hesitated to introduce it to American college students. They would require too much background information to appreciate the essay fully, he claimed, and that would make it an impractical entry in the anthology. While acknowledging the validity of his observation that teaching the essay would be difficult, I wondered whether that was precisely why one ought to attempt the task. Both teacher and student would be challenged in the process, but both would, presumably, move closer to understanding international geopolitics—how the United States, Pakistan, China, and India are connected in an intricate web of alliances and counter-alliances and suspicions and interdependencies. Given the present heightened U.S. concern at the tension between India and Pakistan over Kashmir, and the anxiety that the hostilities could set in motion the deployment of nuclear missiles by either nation, one could make the case, it seems to me, that Roy's essay should be required reading.

If we think of the United States as always entwined with the experiences of other countries, then perhaps it will be easier for us to conceive of the nation as part of a global network of policies, aware that our actions have repercussions on the lives of peoples elsewhere and sensitive to the nature of these ramifications. September 11 has become the United States' trauma. We have forced the world to attend to our pain and our loss; it may be time for the United States to give the rest of the world the same measure of concern. We wish to know why the world hates us. Perhaps we should be asking why we seem to care so little for the rest of the world, or at any rate hold the world hostage to our political and economic interests.

A case in point is the proliferation of offshore call centers in India. Multinational corporations in Western countries realize substantial savings by routing their customer service calls—including help desk support, insurance claims, credit card processing, telemarketing, and retail purchases—to these centers thousands of miles away. India has a virtually unlimited labor pool that is significantly cheaper than those in Australia, Ireland, and the Philippines, locations once coveted by Western multinationals. In a surprising variation of the mobile transnational professional, these call centers are staffed by professionals who only "virtually" relocate themselves, physically remaining in their country of origin but living a kind of shadow life thousands of miles away. The call center employees—who typically are middle- and upper-middle-class Indians educated in schools where English is the medium of instruction—adopt American names, undergo intensive training in speaking with an "American" accent, and familiarize themselves with American popular culture, television, and sports. They even go so far as to study the street layout of certain cities in order to carry on meaningful conversations with their customers. The entire objective of this pretense is for customers at the other end of the line not to realize that they are talking with someone tens of thousands of miles away. For the offshore call center employee, the job is akin to taking on another persona.[46]

There are two rather vociferous reactions to the explosive growth of call centers in India. Arundhati Roy has called the practice "cultural abasement," speaking for those who believe that the Indians are prostituting themselves to American economic imperatives. A totally opposite view is that Indians are infinitely adaptable and are using this unique skill to their advantage. In either case, the offshore call centers demonstrate a one-way cultural transmission, reinforcing the global spread of American culture and practices, creating pseudo-Americans in locations far removed from the United States. Playwright Rustom Bharucha's criticism of the pressure placed upon the rest of the world to learn about the United States while people in the United States are never enjoined to learn about the other nations with whom they share the planet seems particularly apt in this instance.[47] Thus, not only do American economic interests take precedence over those of other nations, but also, in the service of these economic interests, cultural domination slips in. The offshore call centers demonstrate the formidable reach of the American narrative, with the employees undergoing the experience of acculturation without ever leaving their homelands.

Consider whether there would be any circumstances under which an individual in the United States would train him/herself to take on a South Asian or South Asian American persona. It seems unlikely, given the reality that there is no pressing need to do so. So it falls to South Asian American literature to supply the narratives and images that are compelling enough to make readers in the United States aware of the gaps in their consciousness, and intriguing enough to move them to fill these gaps by reading with care and living with vision.

The Idea of America

In case I should appear to be guilty of simplifying the complexity of the United States, let me hasten to say that the idea of America that I here describe is the one that most routinely informs U.S. foreign policy and frequently its domestic policy as well—namely, the idea of American *exceptionalism*. The brief outline of this idea that I give here by no means does justice to the many challenges to the official narrative of America that have originated from within the populace—from Native American writers, from slaves, from abolitionists, from women, from anti-imperialists, from anti-war protestors, from writers of color, from the working class. Thus, even as I speak of the idea of America, I want to acknowledge the overdetermined nature of the construct. Nevertheless, as a notion, it provides valuable insight into the beliefs of American decision-makers, and also sheds light on the beliefs of those in the United States who repeatedly invest these decision-makers with power.

In the preface to the 1855 first edition of *Leaves of Grass*, Walt Whitman wrote in resoundingly celebratory terms of the spirit of the United States:

> The United States themselves are the greatest poem. . . . Here at last is something in the doings of man that corresponds with the broadcast doings of the day and night. Here is not merely a nation but a teeming nation of nations.
>
> . . . Here is the hospitality which forever indicates heroes. . . . Here are the roughs and beards and space and ruggedness and nonchalance that the soul loves. . . . The largeness of nature or the nation were monstrous without a corresponding largeness and generosity of the spirit of the citizen.[48]

There is a certain element of wonder in Whitman's words—almost as though he cannot fathom why anyone would not share in his admiration for the country. I venture briefly into this terrain of the idea of America through Whitman because he both saw himself and was seen as the voice of the populace, the common American. His declarations, therefore, reflect a widely held and deeply embedded belief and pride in the country's uniqueness, at least among those who were not being victimized by the policies of the government—in other words, among white Americans.

The United States is not the only nation to have emerged from a group of people displaced from their original homeland or ancestral country—Canada, South Africa, and Australia are three other such nations. But those who came to New England (in contrast to those who landed in Jamestown, Virginia, or those who came to trade with the Indian tribes in what is today Canada) were distinguished by being armed with a religious mandate and the firm conviction that they were sent to do God's work. South Africa, on the other hand, began as a refuelling stop on the trade route between the Netherlands and Indonesia. The sailors' and merchants' reports of available farmland in the region around the Cape of Good Hope prompted the Boer farmers to arrive and stake their claims. The original impulse behind the Boer settlements in what is today South Africa was, therefore, material (as was the case for the Jamestown settlers) rather than religious. The British who followed the Dutch to South Africa also came for material reasons. Australia was begun primarily as a penal colony—hardly the sort of population that could or would espouse the support of God in their endeavor to survive. But in 1630, when John Winthrop, future governor of the Massachusetts Bay Colony, declared that he and his fellow passengers aboard the *Arbella* were to found "a city on a hill" for all the world to emulate and draw inspiration from, he was not being entirely hyperbolic. The idea of American exceptionalism—of the United States as a unique, an exceptional, nation—took root then, even though the republic itself would not come into being for more than a century.

A staunch conviction that God sanctioned their enterprise gave the New England Puritans the moral authority to declare the Native Americans obstacles in the way of God's work and to see their own attacks against the Indian populations as divinely ordained. Thus, William Bradford, governor of Plymouth Plantation, could declare with perfect equanimity that the massacre of four hundred Pequots during the Pequot War of 1637 indicated that God was on their side.[49] Dissenters such as Roger Williams who questioned Bradford's and Winthrop's reliance on divine signification were dismissed from the colonies and sent into exile. Early on, Williams cautioned against investing the events in the New World with divine significance. God's will could be not fathomed, he declared; therefore, to presume to see in the victories against the Indians the intervention of God was to commit the grave error of arrogance. Williams railed against the early Puritan leaders for what he called their "doctrine of persecution,"[50] but he was in the minority. Cotton Mather put the seal on the divine blessing of the Puritans' enterprise with his 1701 book *Magnalia Christi Americana*, or "the great achievements of Christ in America," in which he sought to revive what he perceived as the fading piety of the settlers by framing their efforts in New England in biblical terms. The actors in this history of the colonies were presented as biblical characters and the colonists as God's chosen people.

Benjamin Franklin, with his Enlightenment sensibilities, tempered somewhat the religious rhetoric so pervasive in the preceding generations; nevertheless, he, too, consolidated the idea of the exceptional American character as founded on reason, industry, and an eye for the practical. These qualities became enshrined in a credo, which was followed with as much fervor as a religious faith. What is perhaps most significant about Franklin's contribution to American exceptionalism is his belief in the ability of an individual—and, by extension, a nation—to succeed entirely independent of the aid and support of others.[51]

In the meantime, the Southern states, with their slave labor and plantation economy, became the country's dark id. Onto them were projected all the unfavorable impulses of the nation, as the South came to function as a convenient representation of all that was despicable in the American character. Although the industrialized North profited from the slave economy through its processing centers for the raw cotton harvested on the plantations, the South's entrenchment in its way of life enabled the North to persist in seeing itself as the moral arbiter of the nation.[52] The outcome of the Civil War added to this feeling; the Emancipation Proclamation of 1863 had the effect of recasting the war in moral terms, giving the Union soldiers the conviction that right was on their side and infusing them with a new vigor in the fight. In the westward expansion that followed the war, the aggressive displacement of numerous American Indian tribes was justified through the doctrine of manifest destiny, which was pursued with unshakable belief in its moral rectitude. The phrase "manifest destiny" was first used by John L. O'Sullivan in an 1845 article in *The Democratic Review*; he declared that it was the United States' manifest destiny, or obvious Providential right, to expand westward and claim the land for "the great experiment of liberty."

Exceptionalism, per se, is not necessarily a bad attitude for a people and a nation to assume. In fact, during times of national construction or reconstruction, it becomes an essential component of the national psyche. South Africa, for instance, needed to believe implicitly in its unique capacity to effect reconciliation between its citizens of color and the Afrikaners who had upheld apartheid. In the months immediately following the first democratic elections in 1994, the nation needed to see itself as a model for the world to emulate, particularly in the area of confronting and moving beyond its horrific racially divided past. Indeed, the Truth and Reconciliation Commission (TRC) convened in 1996 under the leadership of Archbishop Desmond Tutu provided South Africans with precisely such a claim to exceptionalism. Despite the many criticisms that white South Africans in particular launched against the TRC, it has come to be recognized as the model for any such commission. Thus, exceptionalism serves as a powerful ingredient of a national consciousness—particularly in times of transition.[53]

American exceptionalism has reasserted itself in the wake of the attacks of September 11, 2001. The United States was attacked, one public narrative goes, because there are some who do not like the American way of life; the nation's superpower status has drawn upon its citizens the envy and ire of less fortunate peoples, and so Americans have become a target. The U.S. response has been to rearticulate the country's exceptional founding principles—freedom, democracy, and the liberty to pursue one's life objectives without coercion—to reawaken in its citizens the idea of American exceptionalism and to take pride in this resurrected uniqueness. However, a different narrative has also emerged: one that seeks to understand to what extent the nation's single-minded tendency to pursue its agenda contributed to the climate that made it possible to mobilize a cadre of individuals willing to commit suicide in order to injure the United States. Those of this sentiment have chosen to undertake the task of re-imagining the United States as a nation among other nations and to consider how it may conduct its affairs, not as a unique and self-sufficient entity, but as a nation united with other nations in the achievement of commonly articulated goals.[54]

This brief characterization of the many discussions conducted in the months following September 11 and still being conducted is not, by any means, meant to simplify the complex geopolitical maneuvers undertaken by the many nations involved in routing the Taliban in Afghanistan. As an educator of South Asian descent living in the United States, and as one in the business of teaching American multiethnic literature, I cannot responsibly ignore the projections of South and Central Asia in the American imagination today and the extent to which such images affect the ways in which students engage with South Asian American writing. These regions of the world have been thrust into the American consciousness; the reports of what goes on there do not come, in Amirthanayagam's phrase, in the "scrambly witchy time," and so the American public has had to awaken to the knowledge of distant countries. Journalist Ahmed Rashid's book *Taliban* reached number one on the *New York Times* bestseller list. Readers are hungry for explanation. I would argue that readers are also keen to be given the tools to navigate their way through unfamiliar terrain. South Asian American writing recovers the connectedness of nations to Americans—it shows how isolation has rarely been a reality of world interaction, that even when the United States presented itself as a solitary beacon, there were other countries reinforcing the illumination it provided. In other words, what South Asian American writing brings to the idea of America is both the past memory and the future promise of connections with other lands.

The Centrifugal Histories of South Asian American Writing

The idea of America as a nation unto itself, separate from other countries, is at odds with the global sweep of much South Asian American writing. Long before the British colonial empire transported laborers from South Asia to far-flung regions of the globe (Guyana, Trinidad, Kenya, Uganda, South Africa, Fiji, and Malaysia, for example), making South Asians a widely diasporic people, India was joined in active commerce with a number of Middle Eastern and North African nations. Amitav Ghosh's ethnographic memoir/history/novel, *In an Antique Land*, is a fascinating weaving of two stories—that of Bomma, a twelfth-century Indian servant in the employ of Abraham Ben Yiju, a Jewish merchant from Tunisia who lived in India for several years and then ultimately returned to Egypt; and Ghosh himself, when he lived during the 1980s with local families in the towns of Lataifa and Nashawy, two towns in Egypt. Ghosh's skillful and fluid prose bleeds the conjectured details of Bomma's life into the fabric of his own current experiences with the men, women, and children of Lataifa and Nashawy. Paralleling Ghosh's deepening involvement in the lives of the people of these towns is his increasing penetration of the obscurity surrounding Bomma's existence. Ghosh had stumbled upon a reference to Bomma in the course of his doctoral research in social anthropology. In a library at Oxford he had first encountered the brief trace of a human life eight centuries ago. Now, in Egypt, the very same region in which Bomma's master ultimately settled, Ghosh refines his Arabic and Judeo-Arabic and attempts to read the medieval manuscripts in their original languages, in an effort to piece together fragments of references so as to create a reasonable narrative of Bomma's movements as he traveled from India to Aden, fulfilling his master's instructions of trade. At the same time, Ghosh witnesses the present-day movement of young men from Lataifa and Nashawy to Iraq, in their attempt to earn a living. The emotional drama of the twentieth-century narrative enriches our engagement with the desires, pleasures, and fears of the twelfth-century players. Bomma disappears into the dusty manuscripts of research libraries. The memoir ends soon after the Iraqi invasion of Kuwait in July 1990. Ghosh learns that Nabeel, one of the young men who left to work in Iraq, cannot be contacted; no one knows where he is or what has become of him in the mass exodus of people from Iraq. The last line of the memoir reads, "There was nothing to be seen except crowds: Nabeel had vanished into the anonymity of History" (353). But we know that Ghosh's memoir has rescued Nabeel from anonymity, just as it has resurrected Bomma from the confines of archival papers.

Beginning with an oblique reference to Bomma in a letter by merchant Khalaf ibn Ishaq (living in Aden) to his friend Ben Yiju (at the time in India), Ghosh recreates a finely textured medieval landscape. Aden, says Ghosh, is "that port which sits, like a fly on a funnel, on the precise point where the narrow spout of the Red Sea opens into the Indian Ocean."[55] The image of the funnel applies also to Ghosh's book, which flares out to show the flourishing Indian Ocean network of trade and commerce encompassing the western coast of India, Egypt, Yemen, Morocco, Tunisia, and other parts of the Middle East and North Africa. *In an Antique Land* shows that cosmopolitanism was alive and well in the Middle East, North Africa, and India during medieval times. Describing Mangalore and Calicut, two cities on the western coast of India at the time, Ghosh writes:

> The settlement of foreigners at Mangalore was by no means the largest or the most cosmopolitan on the coast: Calicut, a couple of hundred miles to the south, appears to have housed an even larger and more diverse merchant community. There were thirteen "Chinese" vessels in the harbour when Ibn Battuta's [a Moroccan traveler] ship docked there, and he reports that the city regularly had visitors from "China, Sumatra, Ceylon, the Maldives, Yemen, and Fars [Iran]." (242–43)

The cosmopolitanism of this Indian Ocean trade network was brought to a violent halt about three hundred years later, in 1500, two years after Portuguese explorer Vasco da Gama made his first voyage to India, landing at a small fishing village on the western coast. Ghosh recounts that Pedro Alvarez Cabral, who led a Portuguese fleet, arrived on the Malabar coast that year and

> delivered a letter from the king of Portugal to the Samudri . . . , the Hindu ruler of the city-state of Calicut, demanding that he expel all Muslims from his kingdom as they were enemies of the "Holy Faith." He met with a blank refusal; then as afterwards the Samudri steadfastly maintained that Calicut had always been open to every-one who wished to trade there—the Portuguese were welcome to as much pepper as they liked, so long as they bought it at cost price. The Portuguese fleet sailed away, but not before Calicut had been subjected to a two-day bombardment. A year or so later Vasco da Gama returned with another, much more powerful Portuguese fleet and demanded once again that all Muslim traders be expelled from Calicut. (286)

In 1509, the Portuguese triumphed over the regional rulers. Ghosh explains the defeat of the hastily assembled transcontinental fleet of the Muslim potentate of Gujarat, the Hindu ruler of Calicut, and the Sultan of Egypt as the inevitable outcome that attends "the rich confusions that accompany a culture of accommodation and compromise" (288).

In his writings, both in this work and elsewhere, Ghosh describes a robust transnational movement of peoples and goods at a time in history when one does not typically expect to find such a phenomenon.[56] The author's tremendously important work in excavating these instances of shared histories among geographically separated peoples provides a framework within which to understand the current manifestation of interest in globalization and transnationalism. It makes possible a complex response to these phenomena that is neither an outright criticism nor a euphoric celebration. Once asked about his fascination for narratives linked by travel across the Indian Ocean, Ghosh remarked that he is always interested in the ways that bodies of water provide networks of connection.

Traveling west from the Indian Ocean, we encounter a transatlantic connection in Bharati Mukherjee's novel *The Holder of the World*. Among the first South Asian American writers to gain widespread recognition in the United States, Mukherjee has been accused of duplicating and contributing to the mainstream stereotyping of South Asian Americans. This novel is remarkable, however, for its credible suggestion of an early seventeenth-century link between India, under the reign of Mughal emperor Aurangzeb, and the American colonies. Mukherjee charts the journey of one Hannah Easton, daughter of a Puritan woman, from America to England to India. In India, Hannah falls in love with an Indian king, has a child by him, and ultimately returns to New England to raise her child. Mukherjee boldly suggests that Hannah and her daughter might have been the models for Nathaniel Hawthorne's Hester Prynne and Pearl. I discuss the narrative strategies of *The Holder of the World* in greater detail in Chapter 4; here I wish to point out the daring association she makes between colonial America and Mughal-ruled India.

The Salem Maritime Historical Museum in Salem, Massachusetts, contains ample evidence of the active trade between the Massachusetts Colony and India and China. Quilts in the American colonies, for example, were profoundly influenced by patterns from India in the eighteenth and nineteenth centuries.[57] That there was much commerce between the two locations is often forgotten today.

A fascinating anecdote from the eighteenth century illustrates the complex international geopolitics of the time. It spans three continents (Asia, Europe, and North America) and four groups of people (Indians, French, and Americans, as well as their common enemy at the time, the English). Tipu Sultan, known as the Tiger of Mysore, was the Muslim ruler of this region of southern India from 1782 to 1799. He was a fierce opponent of the British, whose divide-and-rule strategy in India worked at setting the various maharajahs against one another. Tipu adopted a similar strategy in that he wooed the French and used them in his fight against the English. Consequently, a great many ambassadors from Tipu's court traveled to the court of Louis XIV to secure aid in their fight. Anecdotal history has it that in 1783, when Benjamin Franklin was in Paris to sign the Paris Peace Treaty, which officially ended the war between England and the United States, he received a bag of gold and a note from Tipu congratulating him on America's opposition to the British and wishing him well in the struggle. That Tipu was in close alliance with the French is extensively documented; that he actually addressed a note to Franklin is less certain, but it has the ring of truth, because Tipu was very encouraged by the French assistance to the Americans against the English and hoped they would do the same for him. This narrative reminds us of the ways in which the history of the United States is linked closely with the history of other nations, and that these linkages go far back in time.[58]

Rapidly, however, the newly formed republic turned inward and began to focus on itself. By 1831, when Alexis de Tocqueville visited the United States for nine months to study its penal system, he found ready evidence of the country's obsession with its own present moment and the continual refinement of the attributes of its democracy. The mid-nineteenth-century immigration from Germany and the northern European countries pressured the United States to articulate further its identity as a political and social entity. By the late 1800s—with the Civil War over and the westward expansion in full swing—the "presentness" of the United States had taken root firmly. There was pleasure in ahistoricity and rebirthing oneself. For this was a nation in which the imperatives of past lives could only hinder one. The consensual framework of

Americanizing oneself, so convincingly explicated by Werner Sollors in *Beyond Ethnicity: Consent and Descent in American Culture*, points to the creation of a new selfhood that rejects the ethnic bonds of the Old World and marks the entry into American culture.[59]

Dismantling Another Binary: Postcoloniality versus Ethnic Studies

When speaking about South Asian American writers, it is important to clarify the difference between postcoloniality and U.S.-based ethnicity. Scholars of ethnic studies in the United States have frequently expressed their frustration at the ascendancy of postcolonial studies in academia. It is their contention that the fascination with issues of postcoloniality enables a turning away from important work that is required within the U.S. body politic to ensure economic and social justice. Ethnic studies, they aver, forces attention onto conditions in the United States and onto the ways in which the nation's power structures disenfranchise certain populations within its borders. Critics of postcolonial studies say that while its practitioners focus critical attention on the legacy of imperialism and global colonialism, they do so at the expense of the urgent work that needs to be done *within* the United States.

Thus, a very crude differentiation between two rather broad areas of study could be framed in the following way: postcolonial studies requires an understanding of the *global* forces of neocolonialism and global capitalism that affect any single nation's economic, political, and social reality. Ethnic studies, while acknowledging the importance of understanding the forces at play beyond U.S. borders, is based on the idea that what is ultimately important is the reality within the nation state: the condition of people of color, the resources denied them, the opportunities withheld.

I would argue, however, that notwithstanding the convenience of delineating two areas of study for the purpose of sustained examination, to separate the two fields of inquiry is to fall into a dangerous trap of limited thinking that can have deleterious results. Not only will people be insufficiently apprised of the position of their country in the world of geopolitics (and that is an ignorance that the people of the United

States cannot afford to persist in, given the nation's long reach in world affairs), but also they will be unable to comprehend the many forces that bear upon domestic policy.[60]

In his provocative essay "Postcolonialism after W. E. B. Du Bois," Kenneth Mostern offers a persuasive reading of the parallels between Du Bois's primer of black consciousness and empowerment, *The Souls of Black Folk* (1903), and Homi Bhabha's take on the postcolonial condition, *The Location of Culture* (1994). Mostern finds "overlapping terminologies" in the two books, particularly in their discussions of "culture and psyches"—terms such as "doubling, ambivalence, hybridity, interdisciplaneity [*sic*], migration, and national art"—that justify reading Bhabha's book as a double of Du Bois's.[61] But the most telling point of Mostern's essay is his implicit call to scholars and activists to familiarize themselves with the complexity of Du Bois's thinking, rather than to see him only as the champion of blacks within the United States:

> If you've read one book by Du Bois, it is *The Souls of Black Folk*, and if you've read only *The Souls of Black Folk*, you've established him first of all as a writer about civil rights within the United States. . . . [T]hose who have followed Du Bois' subsequent career as a theoretician . . . have noted that he stopped conceiving of the politics of race as a U.S.–civil rights (and thus integration) issue within a decade of the publication of *Souls*, and began his lengthy career as a Pan-Africanist organizer and one of the United States' first anti-imperialists.[62]

Mostern insists that to appreciate fully the breadth and reach of Du Bois's efforts, one must attend to "his direct engagement with socialism after 1909, marxism after 1930, and [to] the anti-imperialist initiatives of which he is a part in 1940, that lead him to advocate African American autonomist politics in the U.S. context as a stage (specifiable in space and time) in a global socialist movement."[63] The value of Mostern's essay is that it encourages us to question the wisdom of separating projects of social justice within the nation from similar projects outside the nation. In practical terms, it may not always be possible to invest one's energy simultaneously in local and global issues; and yet, perhaps the singular value of avoiding the creation of a competitive relationship between the postcolonial and the ethnic is that it enables us to see how our partici-

pation as voters affects not only the towns in which we live but the larger world by which we are surrounded, and that the conditions of the
larger world eventually rebound to impinge on our local lives.

South Asian American writers who locate their narratives outside the
United States, and who bring into their images and narratives histories
and realities that have little to do with the United States, might at a fundamental level be characterized as "postcolonial." Their writings may
hint at forces that have been set in motion by colonialism, and which
now play themselves out in convoluted ways. I don't mean here to suggest that there is no reality prior to colonialism worth considering—far
from it, and in this regard I share Aijaz Ahmad's frustration at the privileging of the term "postcolonial." However, the forces of global capital,
the forces of global labor distribution, and the multiracial and multiethnic communities that have been created in different parts of the world
are the undeniable effects of colonialism. Therefore, to speak as though
our current realities have not been shaped by the pernicious structures
of colonialism on a global scale is to live with our eyes only half opened
and our ears only half attuned. Postcolonial writers keep us cognizant of
the effects of colonialism in the social, political, economic, or cultural
realm. South Asian American writers who focus primarily on the United
States—bringing us closer to the lives of its communities as they wres-
tle with conditions particular to the nation—may be called "ethnic," if
their work marks them as illuminating the cultural and social practices
of an identifiable social group with distinctive and shared cultural characteristics.

Certain writers are easily identified as one or the other: One could
call Ghosh, for example, "postcolonial," as will become clear in the discussion of his works in Chapter 2. So could Meena Alexander, Amitava
Kumar, and Bapsi Sidhwa. It is harder to place this label on Chitra
Divakaruni or Jhumpa Lahiri, who may perhaps be more readily identified as "ethnic." But I want specifically to avoid categorizing writers as
belonging to one camp or another and focus, instead, on reading their
works to determine what insights one might glean from them about
matters of individual dignity and civic justice.

In Chapter 2, "Transnational Homepages: Safety in Multiple Addresses,"
I explore how the United States becomes merely one of several sites of

emotional significance for many South Asian American writers. Though they live permanently in the United States, these authors reach beyond the boundaries of the U.S. nation-state to situate their narratives in places as diverse as Sri Lanka, Trinidad, the Sudan, Pakistan, India, Guyana, Canada, and Britain. In doing so, their works complicate ideas of citizenship and allegiance. They force us to encompass worlds outside the United States, to attend to lives other than our own, and to begin to see the interconnectedness of nations. Indran Amirthanayagam's poetry and Michael Ondaatje's novel *Anil's Ghost* zoom in on the natural beauty and the disfigurement from civil strife of Sri Lanka; Agha Shahid Ali (whose numerous collections include *A Nostalgist's Map of America* and *The Country Without a Post Office*), sings of Kashmir in his poetry, finding India "off the turnpike" of America. Meena Alexander's poetry and essays exhort us to care about the "worlds" beyond our own, to be outraged at the conditions that brutalize women on the battlefields of Bosnia, starve children in the ravaged cities of Iraq, exploit workers on the streets of India, racially profile African Americans in the prisons of the United States, and wound student protesters at Tiananmen Square. Amitav Ghosh sets his novel *The Calcutta Chromosome* only minimally in New York City before plunging us into the streets of Calcutta, where a hundred-year-old scientific discovery of how malaria is transmitted to humans becomes intertwined with a modern plot of mysterious and metaphysical dimensions. Ghosh's novel *The Glass Palace* pulls together nineteenth century Burma and India, resurrecting the links among South and Southeast Asia.

Chapter 3 ("Desire, Gender, and Sexuality") underscores the importance of resisting simple explanations of the culturally defined status of South Asian American females or males. The short stories of Tahira Naqvi and Jhumpa Lahiri in particular offer nuanced representations of gender relations in which motivations and behavior are remarkable for their unpredictability.

Among a section of the South Asian American community, overt sexuality and homoeroticism are frequently considered to be corrupting imports from Western thought. However, a vocal group of writers is illuminating the active sexuality of straight South Asian American women and men and giving voice to a rich homosexual and lesbian culture. Ginu Kamani points out that questions of sexuality and sexual orientation among South Asian Americans cannot be viewed solely in Western terms that focus on the *individual's* decision or actions; therefore, without an examination of family and community influences, the experiences of South Asian American gays and lesbians and sexually aware straight men and women cannot be adequately understood. Kamani's collection *Junglee Girl* revels in the sexuality of South Asian and South Asian American women. Sri Lankan Canadian author Shyam Selvadurai's debut novel, *Funny Boy*, is a coming-of-age story in which an adolescent boy acknowledges his homosexuality in the chaos and disruption of the explosive ethnic riots in Sri Lanka in 1983. Shani Mootoo epitomizes the multiple homeland experience of many South Asians. Born in Dublin, Ireland, and raised in Trinidad by her grandparents, who are descended from indentured laborers who came from India to Trinidad in the late 1800s, Mootoo now lives in Vancouver, Canada, and Brooklyn, New York. Her novel *Cereus Blooms at Night* disrupts the biological category of sex and locates ethics and morality in homosexual relationships. Questions of the "authentic" Indian, as well as the heterosexism of diasporic communities, emerge in her writings. Playwright Bina Sharif demands that we look at Muslim American women.

Most South Asian American writing focuses on South Asian American characters. While these representations provide critical visibility to the South Asian American experience, in Chapter 4 ("Writing What You're Not") I consider how the tendency to write within the bounds of one's own ethnicity, gender, race, or nationality might actually constrain the exercise of the imagination. At the same time, I take up the question of power and its effect in the context of writing outside the framework of one's experience. I address such matters as who can write *about* and *as* whom without being accused of appropriation. I engage these questions within the context of South Asian American writing and focus on authors who step out of the familiarity of their ethnicity, gender, or sexual orientation to write of that which they are not.

Pico Iyer's collections of travel essays complicate traditional notions of insider-outsider positions. Mukherjee's collection *The Middleman and Other Stories* and her novel *The Holder of the World* reveal an author who is skilled in portraying "others," but who resorts to reductive portrayals when depicting South Asian characters. Abraham Verghese's moving portrayal of the AIDS patients he treated as a doctor in the small town of Johnson City, Tennessee, is one cornerstone of this chapter. Verghese is both an insider and an outsider in the small Tennessee town in which he practices medicine, and it is this in–between position that gives him the strategic vantage point from which both to write about his AIDS patients without seeming voyeuristic and to help a community come to terms with its understanding of the epidemic and their sons who suffer from it. Tahira Naqvi's short story "Thank God for the Jews" offers a fascinating glimpse of how one can write responsibly about commonality and difference without trivializing the chasms between disparate groups. Naqvi quietly records the intersections between the culture of Pakistani Muslims and Jews living in Westchester County, and in so doing shows how it is possible to write engagingly about those from whom one is believed to be most distant. Abha Dawesar, an Indian American woman, writes with panache and sensitivity about two white bisexual men in *Miniplanner*. Michael Ondaatje lays claim to Canada as his own country by writing of its European immigrants in *In the Skin of a Lion*.

What is this land America in which characters live? In Chapter 5 ("The Idea of America") I focus on the many characteristics of the United States that emerge in a range of works. The best of these works eschew easy dichotomies between West and East and reject the typical oppositions of materialism/spiritualism, liberation/oppression, and modernism/tradition. How do we read these works in light of the heavy hand of anti-terrorist legislation such as the USA Patriot Act and its particular impact on the lives of South Asian Americans and Muslim Americans? Playwrights Shishir Kurup and Sharbari Ahmed create a United States that is chaotic and unpredictable, filled with paradoxes.

Whether from a small town or a big city, there is little predictability in the images of the United States that emerge in these works. In some texts, other people of color seem not to exist, or if they do, to exist as mere shadows. Why do some authors employ thematic and formal structures that foreground race in their works, while others seem to render it invisible? Why do Verghese's, Dalip Singh Saund's, and Ved Mehta's memoirs barely touch on race? If one were to read *only* South Asian American writing, what images of the United States would one have? And would those images represent the complexity of the nation?

Gaps remain in the literary representation of South Asian American experiences. Joan Jensen has written about the Indians who came to Salem, Massachusetts, in the mid-to-late eighteenth century on ships that plied in the trade between southern India and the United States. These ship hands jumped ship and disappeared into the African

American community of Salem. Their stories have never been fully elaborated, so it is up to the imaginative writer to trace their history in the vein of Ghosh's quest for the life of Bomma. Jensen also records the late-eighteenth-century manumission papers of Indian indentured laborers in Philadelphia, testifying to another early history that has not been explored. Other untold stories focus on issues of class and interactions of South Asian Americans with other groups of color.

The history of South Asian American literature is relatively recent; the creative energy of the immigrant generation and the rising number of second-generation writers in the United States promise to shape narratives and images about experiences as diverse as those of Bangladeshi cabdrivers in Washington, D.C., motel owners in the deep South, dot-com entrepreneurs in the Silicon Valley, and filmmakers in New York City. South Asian Americans, with their heterogeneous ethnic, linguistic, religious, national, and socioeconomic spaces, are ready to be imaginatively rendered in their myriad complexity.

TWO

Transnational Homepages: Safety in Multiple Addresses

IN THIS CHAPTER, I discuss the imaginative allure of geographies beyond the United States for South Asian American writers. Regardless of whether they are immigrants or U.S.-born, these writers make fluid and easy moves in their works between the United States and other locations as diverse as Bangladesh, India, Pakistan, Myanmar (Burma), Sri Lanka, Germany, and the Sudan. I attempt to trace the source of their wide-ranging longings and to address the implications of such a transnational sensibility for issues of belonging and citizenship. I want, especially, to resist the easy polarization of nationalism/patriotism against transnationalism and to explore, through South Asian American writing, the complex intersections between these two modes of being in the world.

The Indian American narrator of Jhumpa Lahiri's story "When Mr. Pirzada Came to Dine" plunges us at the outset into tumultuous events taking place thousands of miles away from the story's primary location, a university town north of Boston. She recalls that in the autumn of 1971, when she was ten years old, her parents and Mr. Pirzada, a scholar visiting from Dacca, spent every evening in their home in this university town urgently watching the television for news of what was happening halfway around the globe. We get a quick geopolitical lesson:

> Mr. Pirzada . . . came from Dacca, now the capital of Bangladesh, but then a part of Pakistan. That year Pakistan was engaged in civil war. The eastern frontier, where Dacca was located, was fighting for autonomy from the ruling regime in the west. In March, Dacca had been invaded, torched, and shelled by the Pakistani army. Teachers were dragged onto streets and shot, women dragged into barracks and raped. By the end of the summer, three hundred thousand people were said to have died. In Dacca, Mr. Pirzada had a three-story home, a lectureship in botany at the university, a wife of twenty years, and seven daughters between the ages of six and sixteen whose names all began with the letter A.[1]

Lahiri's story juxtaposes the United States against Pakistan and India (to where millions of refugees from the civil war in Pakistan fled); she interweaves the ritualistic American holiday of Halloween with the outbreak of war in South Asia in 1971 and the birth of the new nation of Bangladesh. A ten-year-old girl's understanding of friendship and loss unfolds against the televised images of disruption and chaos that signal the emergence of a new country.

Lahiri's narrator tells us how her interest in Pakistan, stimulated by Mr. Pirzada's regular visits and by seeing both him and her parents immersed in the politics of South Asia in 1971, was swiftly and efficiently suppressed by a grade-school teacher focused on educating her students about the intricacies of the American Revolution. The students are sent to the library to research different aspects of the Revolutionary War. The narrator easily locates the books she needs, but she cannot concentrate. Instead, she finds herself drawn to the section labeled "Asia," with books on "China, India, Indonesia, Korea," and eventually settles down with a book titled *Pakistan: A Land and Its People*. Absorbed in its contents, she does not notice her teacher approaching until a classmate warns her, and then she quickly tries to hide her transgression:

> I slammed the book shut, too loudly. Mrs. Kenyon emerged, the aroma of her perfume filling up the tiny aisle, and lifted the book by

the tip of its spine as if it were a hair clinging to my sweater. She glanced at the cover, then at me.

"Is this book a part of your report, Lilia?"

"No, Mrs. Kenyon."

"Then I see no reason to consult it," she said, replacing it in the slim gap on the shelf. "Do you?" (33)

Asian American writers—particularly South Asian, Filipino/a, Korean, and Vietnamese—do what Mrs. Kenyon cannot envision: they simultaneously engage the United States and other countries; process in parallel the history of the United States and the histories of other nations; and show that to turn one's attention to Pakistan, India, Bangladesh, Korea, the Philippines, or Vietnam is not necessarily to turn away from the United States. These nations all share the condition of being postcolonial, having won their independence from colonial powers in the mid-twentieth century. As a result, Americans who trace their roots to these areas exhibit interest in how their ancestral nations are faring in freedom and appear to be emotionally invested in following or contributing to the development of that freedom.

An Insurance Policy against Rejection

Asian Americans have a more urgent reason to exhibit interest in their ancestral nations, however: they never know when their membership in the United States will be called into question. In her eloquent and heartfelt essay "Home Is Where the *Han* Is," Elaine Kim writes of the sense of betrayal she felt when the outrage following the "not guilty" verdict for the four police officers who savagely beat Rodney King triggered a massive uprising in South Central Los Angeles in 1992. Those riots or uprising (depending on one's perspective of the mass disturbance) left Korean American merchants defenseless and resulted in damages to their property totaling $425 million. A Korean American born in the United States, Kim observes that her trust and faith in U.S. civic institutions and the solidarity she felt with other Americans of color were shaken to the core. Throughout the visible conflicts between Korean Americans and both African Americans and Latinos, the white community did nothing to acknowledge its central role in creating the landscape of inequity that fueled the hostilities other communities of color felt against Korean Americans. Kim delivers her outrage with scalpel-sharp precision:

> I was enraged when I overheard European Americans discussing the conflicts as if they were watching a dogfight or a boxing match. The situation reminded me of the Chinese film "Raise the Red Lantern," in which we never see the husband's face. We only hear his mellifluous voice as he benignly admonishes his four wives not to fight amongst themselves. He can afford to be kind and pleasant because the structure that pits his wives against each other is so firmly in place that he need never sully his hands or even raise his voice.[2]

Kim finds herself reassessing the position of Korean Americans in the nation's racial and civic landscape. Despite having always been aware of the tenuous nature of their acceptance into the fabric of U.S. sociopolitics, she is unprepared for the virulence that follows the publication of an article in *Newsweek* in which she takes the United States to task for its neglect of Korean history in schools, for its cavalier indifference to the democratic aspirations of the Korean people even while extolling and supporting similar goals for Lech Walesa and the Polish people, and for its dismissal of issues significant to Korean Americans. The hate mail Kim received from readers of the *Newsweek* article constitutes the most disturbing component of "Home Is Where the *Han* Is." Here are some representative responses:

> My stepfather and cousin risked their lives in the country where your father is buried to ensure the ideals of our country would remain. So don't expect to find a sympathetic ear for your pathetic whining. . . .

> You are dissatisfied with current school curricula that exclude Korea. Could it possibly be because Korea and Asia for that matter has [*sic*] not had . . . a noticeable impact on the shaping of Western culture, and Korea has had unfortunately little culture of its own? . . .

> Koreans' favorite means of execution is decapitation. . . . Ms. Kim, and others like her, came here to escape such injustice. Then they

whine at riots to which they have contributed by their own fanning of flames of discontent. (278–79)

These outbursts prove, in unmistakable terms, the fragility of Korean American—and, by extension, Asian American—acceptance within the U.S. body politic, and they reveal the hostility toward Asian Americans seething under the surface of mainstream America.

At a talk at Yale University in April 2002, Sreenath Sreenivasan, founder of the South Asian Journalists Association (SAJA), discussed the mainstream media's disregard of the abuse and racially motivated attacks suffered by many South Asians in the months following the September 11, 2001, attacks on the World Trade Center and the Pentagon (attacks in which as many as two hundred South Asians lost their lives). The media seem to have felt that in comparison to the deaths of thousands of individuals, the beatings and verbal harassment suffered by a few South Asians were hardly noteworthy. When Balbir Singh Sodhi, a fifty-two-year-old gas station owner in Mesa, Arizona, was fatally shot a few days after September 11 because his turban aligned him in the eyes of self-appointed "patriots" with the Taliban, South Asian American journalists called radio stations and news editors and asked that they run the story of Sodhi's racially motivated killing. The answer they received was that he was only *one* individual. Finally, one journalist realized that he would have to get rather dramatic with his request. So he asked an editor, "How many South Asian American deaths will it take before it becomes newsworthy enough for you to cover the killings?" That question appeared to jolt the editor out of his indifference. Perhaps it even motivated him to consider the possibility that his initial lack of interest may have stemmed from his inability to perceive the death of a South Asian American as the death of an American. Sreenivasan's comments confirm for Asian Americans their perpetual foreignness in the American imagination and consciousness. They are outsiders, regardless of the number of generations that their families have been in the United States, their dedication to the U.S. Armed Forces, or the number of flags they fly from their businesses and homes.

When Asian Americans *are* rendered visible, that visibility typically carries with it dangerous consequences. The case of Wen Ho Lee, a scientist imprisoned in 1992 for espionage but later cleared of all but one of the charges, illustrates the alacrity with which Asian Americans are seen as being involved in treasonous activities. From as early as the Chinese Exclusion Act of 1882, Asian Americans have been targeted for discriminatory treatment. There is, in short, no conceivable way to refute the overwhelming evidence that Asian Americans periodically become the target of racist attacks and are told to "go home."[3]

The internment of Japanese Americans during World War II, the killing of Vincent Chin, the beating death of Navroze Mody and vicious assault on Rishi Maharaj, the 1994 campaign finance scandal involving Chinese Americans, the incarceration of Wen Ho Lee, and the backlash against South Asian Americans and Arab Americans following September 11 make starkly clear to Asian Americans that their membership within the United States is a tenuous affair; regardless of how deep their roots may be in this country, there is always some doubt about the strength of their allegiance.[4] Being Asian American is no guarantee of being American. Certain groups are always seen to have transnational allegiances, or, as Kandice Chuh puts it, are forcibly "transnationed."[5] Such was the case with the Japanese Americans during World War II, and such is the case now with South Asian Americans and Arab Americans who have been indefinitely and secretly detained in connection with the "war on terror." Muslim Americans from certain countries—Pakistan, Iraq, Saudi Arabia, and Syria, for example—are automatically considered suspect because of their presumed loyalty to these other countries. Luis Francia observes that this awareness of one's shaky place within the U.S. body politic is reason enough for many Asian Americans to feel justified in retaining economic ties with ancestral homelands—through the purchase of real estate, primarily—and preserving memories of past histories and heritages in countries other than the United States.[6] That this insurance policy against rejection may be hollow and worthless—because the ancestral countries might be no more willing than the United States to acknowledge the diasporic descendants' legitimate membership—does not negate the intensity with which many Asian Americans engage in maintaining the double allegiance. Samina Najmi, in a talk given at Wheaton College in November 2001, shortly after the post–September 11 backlash against South Asian Americans, spoke powerfully as a Pakistani American of her resentment at being forcibly "uprooted" from "home," from a sense of safety and comfort: "I resent being cornered into feeling defensive about Islam or accountable for Pakistan's role in the . . . American war on Afghanistan. I resist feeling that I must have a gigantic American flag waving from my rooftop and car-top at all times, in order to prove my loyalty to America, while America feels no such loyalty to me."[7] Pakistani Americans have been one of the communities most adversely affected by the newly instated deportation drives of the Immigration and Naturalization Service, recently renamed the Bureau of Citizenship and Immigration Services (BCIS). Some Pakistani Americans who have been forced to return to Pakistan have little knowledge of Urdu or what it means to live anywhere other than in the United States.[8]

Both Here and over There
or Neither Here Nor There

In an earlier essay, I briefly articulate the two familiar yet fundamentally different perspectives of Frank Chin, on the one hand, and Lisa Lowe, on the other.[9] Chin has been emphatic in his insistence that the realm of Asian American literature should remain within the borders of the United States; for him, the hard labor of the Chinese railroad workers, the Filipino migrant farm and cannery workers, and the Japanese plantation workers earned these groups the right to claim American soil as theirs. He has held this position through changing political realities; while his 1970s U.S.-centric perspective is justifiable given the fervor of the Civil Rights movement of the 1960s and the ethnic empowerment movements that followed in its wake, Chin maintained his sights on America as the literary landscape of Asian American writing even into the 1990s, despite the fact that there were more foreign-born than American-born Asians in the United States at the time. His now famous 1974 statement—in the landmark anthology of Asian American literature *Aiiieeeee! An Anthology of Asian-American Writers*—that Asian American means "Filipino-, Chinese-, and Japanese-Americans, American born and raised,"[10] signals an almost obstinate refusal to expand his vision of Asian America. In 1991, when the same editorial collective of Frank Chin, Jeffrey Chan, Lawson Inada, and Shawn Wong published the *Big Aiiieeeee!*, they narrowed the focus of Asian American writing by subtitling this second collection *An Anthology of Chinese American and Japanese American Literature*. The *big* Aiiieeeee got *smaller*.

One could argue that in this later anthology Chin and his coeditors weren't attempting to collect Asian American literature, only the creative expressions of two specific Asian American groups. However, in calling this second collection the *Big Aiiieeeee!* they seem almost defiantly to be resurrecting the spirit of the first collection and, more importantly, to be suggesting that Chinese and Japanese Americans are the only truly authentic groups worthy of representing Asian Americans. That Filipinos are off the list—ousted from the privileged club, so to speak—may be in part due to the increased involvement by Filipino/a Americans in the efforts to end the fourteen-year dictatorship (1972–86) of President Ferdinand Marcos in the Philippines. Perhaps Chin saw such transnational or non-U.S.-focused behavior and literary production as disqualifying them from membership in Asian America.[11]

Lowe presents a diametrically opposite view. Her 1991 essay "Heterogeneity, Hybridity, Multiplicity: Marking Asian American Differences," first published in 1991, marks the articulation of a global perspective in Asian American studies, a widening understanding of the term "Asian American" to evoke landscapes and histories well beyond the United States:

> [C]ultures as different as Chinese, Japanese, Korean, Filipino, Indian, Vietnamese, Thai, or Cambodian—Asian Americans are born in the United States and born in Asia, of exclusively Asian parents and of mixed race, urban and rural, refugee and nonrefugee, fluent in English and non-English-speaking, . . . [T]he Asian-origin collectivity is unstable and changeable, with its cohesion complicated by intergenerationality, by various degrees of identification with and relation to a "homeland," and by different extents of assimilation to and distinction from "majority culture" in the United States.[12]

The debate among Asian Americanists is less focused today than ten years ago on the merits of a transnational perspective. This may be due to an increased understanding of the globalization of late twentieth-century and early twenty-first-century economics, as well as the continued migration of domestic, blue-collar, and white-collar labor from Asia to other parts of the world. Another contributing factor in the current political climate may be the precarious residency status of Cambodian, Pakistani, and Bangladeshi Americans, many of whom were deported in the backlash after September 11, 2001. In any case, most scholars and students in the field today seem to accept that Asian Americans have some degree of interest in, if not allegiance to, ancestral lands outside the United States. And yet there is anxiety about the extent to which such global or transnational interest can be misread by non–Asian Americans as a lack of commitment to the interests of the United States. In other words, one could argue that because Asian Americans are more readily deemed "foreign" than, say, Latinos and African Americans, they run the risk of further undermining their position as legitimate members of the U.S. body politic if they are seen to be attentive to the affairs of other nations.

Cynthia Sau-ling Wong's sharp critique of the turn to transnationalism and diaspora in Asian American studies in her 1995 essay "Denationalization Reconsidered: Asian American Cultural Criticism at a Theoretical Crossroads" points to another fallout of the field's de-centering of the United States. Many Asians in the United States bring their energies to social justice projects in their homelands or ancestral countries. Yet there is much social and political activism that needs to happen right here in the United States, she argues. Asian Americans who turn their attention to other locations devalue the remarkable struggle of the Asian American student strikers of the 1960s, who battled for the right of Asians in the United States to become full participants in the political and social landscape of the nation.[13]

Making a similar point, though in a slightly different context, Pheng Cheah reminds us that even in a time of expanding globalism and transnational mobility, any meaningful resistance to unjust social, economic, and political practices is only effective when grounded in local realities and the materiality of local conditions:

Proponents of a global civil society or an international public sphere that already exists independent of nation-states must gloss over the fact that we inhabit a decentralized political system in which global loyalty is thin, an ideal vision largely confined to activists and intellectuals. This means that in order to be effective at the level of political institutions or the popular masses, transnational networks have to work with and through the nation-state in order to transform it. They have to negotiate directly with the state in the hope of influencing its political morality and/or mobilize local support into popular national movements that press against the state.[14]

Cheah's discussion centers on the resurgence of cultural nationalisms among recently decolonized nations and the reluctance of these nations to embrace a cosmopolitan culture in the current moment of global imperatives. Globalism, Cheah asserts, has not brought with it an equitable distribution of resources among nations; neither is every nation equally influential in the arena of cultural influence. As long as such inequities exist, the nation-state, and in particular the postcolonial nation-state, will turn to assertions of cultural uniqueness to empower itself in resisting Western agencies and cultural manifestations, whether they be the International Monetary Fund (IMF), Coca Cola, or Valentine's Day. Ultimately, people can only effect policy changes at the level of the nation-state, not in some international realm. Cheah's discussion thus invites a careful reassessment of the importance of the nation-state in this time of global capitalism and transnational activist efforts such as Human Rights Watch, the Global AIDS Fund, or the International Criminal Court. The postcolonial nation-state, he observes, plays a central role in resisting the dictates of powerful Western economies and cultural disseminators. Every nation acts in self-interest, says Cheah; its decisions are predicated on self-preservation. Theoretically, that may be true; but in practice some nations adopt policies that appear to work against self-preservation. For instance, many nations adopt economic policies designed to benefit lending institutions—such as the World Bank and the IMF—rather than their own citizens.[15] Thus, while self-preservation may logically indicate attention to local urgencies, in reality, a nation may have little option but to consider someone else's urgencies—usually, those of the economic superpower. Thus local conditions are subordinated to the agenda of the global superpower.

In the United States, the situation is complicated because the nation's domestic or local interests are inextricably linked to its global ambitions. An outlay of $365 billion to finance the war in Iraq has disastrous effects on such domestic matters as public education and health insurance. The question is, How can the United States reconcile its domestic and global interests? And the question for this study is, How can the field of Asian American studies intervene at this geopolitical moment to ensure a complex understanding of the links between the local and the global, the domestic and the international? Both Cheah and Wong are right to insist that attention to local politics is the necessary first step in addressing both local *and* global injustices. Only when the global can be rendered in terms of the local will a nation-state take notice of edicts by international regulatory bodies. Cheah's focus is on postcolonial nations that feel compelled to reclaim power and economic self-sufficiency in this neocolonial age of global capitalism; Wong's focus is on disenfranchised groups *within* the United States who continue to face economic and political inequities. Both scholars offer a valuable corrective to the unexamined championing of transnational and global activism, drawing attention to its limits and the local material realities within which it can flounder. While I am mindful of Wong's caveat against a quick acceptance of transnationalism within Asian American writing, and while I agree wholeheartedly that attention to local politics is imperative to effect changes of governmental policy, I do not believe that a concern for homeland issues automatically results in indifference to U.S.-based social, economic, or political crises; it is entirely possible to be an activist on many fronts—in one's neighborhood, city, state, nation, and abroad. The group "Asians for Mumia," although principally concerned with protesting the unfair imprisonment on death row of African American reporter Mumia Abu-Jamal, is also deeply committed to fighting against exploitation and oppression in other parts of the world. "Asians for Mumia" includes both first-generation and U.S.-born Asian Americans.

Another example lies in the youth activism workshops started in the 1990s by immigrant and American-born South Asian Americans: YSS (Youth Solidarity Summer), based in New York City; and SASSY (South Asian Solidarity Seminar for Youth), which was started in Boston. These summer camps were launched largely by immigrant South Asians committed to encouraging activism among second-generation South Asian Americans. The focus of their activist politics is local (i.e., U.S.-based), but the attendees are also made to think critically about activism on a transnational scale. For example, Biju Mathew, a founding member of YSS and one of the principal organizers of the New York City taxicab drivers strike in May 1998, is also deeply invested in activist politics that relate to his birth country of India. Clearly, there are Asian Americans who are capable of practicing local and diasporic politics simultaneously.[16] Many Asians in the United States do not see a contradiction between the two. Roger Sanjek shows, for instance, that the Korean American Association of Mid-Queens (KAAMQ) is concerned both with creating linkages with African Americans in a nearby housing complex *and* mobilizing local Korean merchants to respond to crises in

South Korea—for example, raising money for victims of a flood.[17] Nirav Desai, executive director of the recently introduced journal *The Subcontinental*, notes that "U.S. policymaking in both the domestic and foreign arenas stands to gain from incorporating insights of the South Asian American community." He identifies domestic issues such as immigration, healthcare, and civil rights and then asserts that people of South Asian descent are ideally positioned "to help shape more informed foreign policies" because of the close ties that many of them retain with their ancestral homelands.[18]

Thus it becomes imperative to engage analytically with the trend toward diaspora and transnational issues in Asian American literature and thereby to understand the complex interaction between local and transnational concerns. Jinqi Ling's study of four "canonical" Asian American writers—Frank Chin, Louis Chu, Maxine Hong Kingston, and John Okada—is valuable in this regard. Not only does he historicize their writings to show how the narratives of claiming voice and space *in America* were necessary responses to social and political forces exerted on Asians in the United States at specific moments in time, but he also makes a convincing argument that despite their intense preoccupation with the images and treatment of Asians within the United States, these writers were by no means completely U.S.-centric. Ling declares that there is nothing inherently "domestic" about these early texts. I quote Ling at length because he introduces a thoughtful and necessary corrective to the binary perspective that has come to infect Asian American studies—a perspective in which a pre-1990s U.S.-centered narrative is pitted against a 1990s global, diasporic, and postcolonial articulation:

> [T]he representations of wartime internment of Japanese Americans described in *No-No Boy*, of the decay of Chinatown bachelor society portrayed in *Eat a Bowl of Tea*, of the strained encounter between Fred and his Chinese mother in the *Year of the Dragon*, and of the Chinese male immigrant laborers recruited to build America's Transcontinental Railroad in *China Men* are all deeply and unavoidably inflected with the authors' diasporic concerns and with their implicit commentary on America's imperial role in international power politics, a role that seriously affects the daily life of their characters. It is the critic . . . who, for contingent political reasons, tends to read rigidity into the "domestic" aspect of these works as a fixed par-

adigm or to misperceive the relative lack of textual maneuverability in them as a sign of their inherent failure to articulate differences ... rather than as an indication of their ironic commentary on America's inability to deliver its democratic promise to Asian immigrants and their American-born descendants in the period in question.[19]

Ling acknowledges that in teaching these canonical texts at this particular historical moment of intense globalization and cultural transnationalism, the "foregrounding of the international or diasporic dimensions of these texts is crucial," but like Wong he counsels prudence that "such a foregrounding should not be made either out of an underestimation of the difficulty of working through the social contradictions in Asian Americans' daily experiences, or out of the mistaken belief that a diasporic perspective is a necessarily advantageous critical position and therefore must be unconditionally emulated or reproduced."[20]

In this context, we should keep in mind the words of Sucheta Mazumdar, a historian with a global view who is also deeply committed to local action. Even as she calls for a vision that is cognizant of political forces outside the borders of the United States, Mazumdar is not blind to the need for a fiercely localized politics of action and knowledge of the history of local politics. She chastises South Asian Americans for being complacently ignorant of the involvement of Chinese, Japanese, Filipino, and African Americans in the Civil Rights movement and of the benefit South Asian Americans have derived from these earlier struggles. She is unsparing in her criticism:

> [F]or South Asian middle-class immigrants travelling the slippery road of upward mobility, it is easier to imitate the hegemonic culture of Anglo-EuroAmerica than explore other Asian cultures. After all, almost two hundred years of British colonialism have prepared us for this. So why bother to link up with all these other Asians when we can sit at the feet of the masters themselves? . . . Our temples, gurdwaras, jamatkhanas, mosques, and churches do not need to teach the history of Black struggles; one does not need to know the history of African America to be an engineer or a doctor.[21]

Mazumdar's mode of engagement with politics—interweaving the global with the local as the situation demands, responding to each crisis according to its particulars—is, ultimately, the type of nondoctrinaire approach that is likely to yield the most meaningful results. (See Chapter 4 for a discussion of Mazumdar's observations on ethnocentricity in South Asian American literature.)

Accompanying the turn of Asian American writing toward Asia is the expansion of the term "America" to its plural "Americas." The Inter-American dialogue of 1982 gave rise to the Organization of American States (OAS), a hemispheric body intent on establishing economic and political cooperation among the countries of the Americas—including the nations of the Caribbean, South America, and Central America, as well as Mexico, the United States, and Canada. The impulse behind the founding of the OAS—to underscore the links among the various nation-states of the Americas—is a shift from the intensely isolationist posture adopted by the United States during the Cold War years. The changing political and economic relationships among these countries are making available to Asians in the United States the complex narratives of the diasporic experiences of Asians in other parts of the American hemisphere. The multi-genre 1999 collection *Encounters: People of Asian Descent in the Americas*—which includes poems, oral histories, short fiction, and personal and critical essays—is based on this new vision.[22] The titles in this anthology are indicative of the wealth of richly nuanced stories. A representative list includes "Japanese Peruvians and Their Ethnic Encounters," "Phuri Sherpa: Nepal and Mexico in California," "Lessons from the Field: Being Chinese American in Panama," and "Land, Culture, and the Power of Money: Assimilation and Resistance of Okinawan Immigrants in Bolivia." The contributors have ancestries that defy predictable roots; their memories and heritage are kaleidoscopic. For example, Jan Lo Shinebourne was born and raised in Guyana but has lived in England since 1970. Her Chinese grandmother came from British Guyana, her grandfather was from Kashmir and step-grandfather from Delhi, and her mother is African Guyanese. She writes, "When I eat roast duck and Chinese greens at the Canton in London, I taste Indian duck in their Chinese duck, I taste Guyanese *calaloo* in Chinese greens. I am a Guyanese garden in my memory" (259).

Roshni Rustomji-Kerns observes in her editor's introduction to *Encounters* that one cannot approach the lives of these diasporic individuals from within traditional analytical/pedagogical frameworks. She asks: "How does one conceptualize being Asian in terms of religious and philosophical belief systems in a Latin American country if one's family publicly participates in the rituals of the Catholic Church (including baptizing all family members as Catholics and giving names that are considered Christian or western) but at home follows the rituals and tenets of Buddhism that the family had practiced in Asia?" (5).

The kind of intermingling of peoples and cultures that *Encounters* makes manifest underscores the limitations of the strictly compartmentalized multiculturalism practiced in the United States, where each ethnic group seems intensely preoccupied with its own experiences and where issues of authenticity surface constantly. Who is the real Asian American? The real African American? The real Latino/a? Increasingly, contemporary writing by Asians in the Americas deliberately rejects such constricting paradigms.

Rustomji's novel, *The Braided Tongue*, gives further evidence of such expanded sensibility. The narrative encompasses the United States, Mexico, and India. As a middle-aged woman, Katy Cooper, the novel's protagonist, discovers that she was born in Devinagar, India, and not, as she had supposed, in England, the land of her mother's birth. The novel charts her journey to the various locations of her father's life (her mother having mysteriously disappeared when Katy was very young) and records her gradually increasing awareness that the life she lived with her foster parents in New Hampshire (after her father's death), though perfectly satisfactory and comfortable, left her with many unanswered questions and unexplained memories. The trip to Devinagar sets in motion the process by which Katy comes to realize the myriad connections that her life has to other lives. In Devinagar, she learns from a newly discovered cousin that her "family name was not the English 'Cooper' but the Parsi 'Cooper' and that [Katy's] father was not a man from Europe who had spent a short time in India. He had been an Indian who had spent some time in England, returned to India, gone back to England and then gone to Mexico to try his fortune. He was a Freddy from Fareidun not Frederick."[23] Katy is introduced in Devinagar to a "terrifying labyrinth of relatives" (30). The phrase is an apt one to describe Katy's initial alarm at being told of the connections she has to the Mehtas and the Japanwallahs and the Chinese woman from Malaysia who is their common great-great grandmother. Katy's growth in the novel comes from her being able to envision the numerous branches of her family tree not just without fear but with eager interest. And the family she embraces is more than those related to her by blood. In fact, the novel ends in Oaxaca, the town in Mexico where her father died managing field hands for a British-owned farm. She is surrounded by friends and relatives, and in her contentment she declares, "Who needs . . . customs officials and border patrols, when we have a sari and stories and ghosts that travel around the world, back and forth, back and forth, Asia to the Americas, the Americas to Asia" (176).

(How) to Be a Better American

There is no easy way to describe the complexity of lives that oscillate between a U.S.-centered worldview and a transnational sensibility. This complexity might be rich or painful, intoxicating or enervating, but there is no denying that it requires emotional resilience. Even citizenship becomes a complicated question, because one may technically hold the citizenship of one country but be emotionally bound to another, or may feel equal allegiance to several countries or none to any country. Of course, these issues are not limited to Asian Americans: Irish Americans and Jewish Americans are also subject to similar imperatives.

Andrew X. Pham's 1999 memoir *Catfish and Mandala: A Two-Wheeled Voyage through the Landscape and Memory of Vietnam* reveals that there is no easy link between a search for roots and finding home.[24] In the opening pages, Pham, a Vietnamese American, relates an encounter with Tyle, a European American Vietnam veteran living in the deserts of Mexico. Pham initially steels himself against the hostility he expects will be directed at him when he tells the veteran that he is of Vietnamese descent. But, amazingly, Tyle offers him an eloquent apology instead: "Forgive me. Forgive me for what I have done to your people" (8). Pham is embarrassed, even stunned. He doesn't feel that he's a worthy recipient of such a moving and deeply felt declaration. Part of Pham's discomfort comes from his sense that he doesn't completely understand how Vietnam or its people have been devastated, how the war pulverized a society, and how people have reconstructed their lives in its aftermath. His journey to Vietnam is, in part, an attempt to fill those gaps in his understanding. Once there, Pham finds that he is frequently the butt of official harassment, the object of derision, and, at the same time, the coveted escapehatch for young women who beg him to marry them and take them to the United States. In a revealing outburst of frustration, Pham exclaims that he wants to flee the Vietnamese, "these wanting-wanting-wanting people" (102). At the end of his six-month bicycle journey through

Vietnam, Pham is ready to return, and, upon being asked what he will do when he returns to the United States, he says, "be a better American."

Pham has learned something about himself, and that knowledge presumably will help him negotiate the life he is about to re-enter in the United States. He has learned what it means to be viewed with a mixture of suspicion and envy, and, most importantly, he has learned humility: that his having escaped the poverty and hardship of Vietnam is merely the result of money and luck, that it is nothing more or less than the arbitrary working of fate. Vietnam, says Pham, has taught him never to delude himself: "every so often when I become really good at tricking myself, there is always that inevitable slap that shocks me out of my shell and prompts me to reassess everything" (327). He is eager to return to the United States, he says, eager for "the white, the black, the red, the brown faces of America . . .[for] their varied shapes, their tumultuous diversity, their idealistic search for racial equality, their bumbling but wonderful pioneering spirit" (337). There is a kind of ingenuous fervor about Pham's conceptualization of the United States here that is not unlike Carlos Bulosan's faith in America (discussed below), and one wonders whether both writers willfully ignore what they know to be its unpleasant realities. But Pham, like Bulosan, invokes the *ideal* of America, not its reality, and in this appeal it becomes clear that what both he and Bulosan celebrate is the nation's promise. It is a promise that they see with great clarity for having been elsewhere, for having witnessed another reality outside the United States. Inside the United States, the promise of the country becomes occluded by its injustices; outside the United States, one can see what it is capable of, what it can achieve. Perhaps, then, to be a better American means to challenge the nation to live up to its ideals, and that is what Pham intends to do when he returns: "Somewhere along the way, my search for roots has become my search for home—a place I know best even though there are those who would have me believe otherwise" (337).

Lest the split vision (with one eye on the United States and the other on the world beyond its borders) that scholars such as Mazumdar advocate be seen as an unattainable ideal, E. San Juan's reading of Carlos Bulosan's writing demonstrates that it is entirely possible. Bulosan came from the Philippines to the United States in 1931, when he was seventeen. In the essay "Unsettling Asian American Literature," I turn to San Juan's perceptive reading of Carlos Bulosan's writing to show that deep and abiding love for one's ancestral homeland (the Philippines) does not lead to an enervated commitment to one's adopted land. If anything, Bulosan can sometimes appear to be overly optimistic about the essential goodness of America, keeping faith in the nation's inner core of justice and equality. Informing this optimism is a fierce conviction that oppressed peoples around the world can draw inspiration from one another and mount powerful resistances against exploitation and fascism. As Juan points out, Bulosan was acutely aware of the connections among movements of resistance in different parts of the world. In his view, a spirit of irrepressible courage pervaded all these downtrodden people. Juan writes that in *America Is in the Heart* (1946), Bulosan's memoir of painful love to both the Philippines and the United States, he "pays homage to the grassroots initiative found, for example, in the 1931 uprising of peasants in Tayug, Pangasinan, which may be interpreted as an anticipatory emblem for the strikes of the multiethnic farm workers in Hawai`i and the West Coast."[25] Juan cautions against reading *America Is in the Heart* as a celebration of American individualism; he leads us to its message of solidarity and asks that we notice how Bulosan establishes links between the United States and the Philippines, giving evidence that in his consciousness the two are inextricable. For instance, in a letter to the wife of the famous Filipino writer and activist Salvador P. Lopez, who at the time was resisting the Japanese occupation of the Philippines, Bulosan writes, "America is not bound by geographical latitudes. America is not merely a land or an institution. America is in the hearts of men that died for freedom; it is also in the eyes of men that are building a new world."[26]

The transnational trajectory in Filipino/a American literature reveals itself in a deep ambivalence toward the cultural influences of the United States on the Philippines, as well as a resistance against all forms of colonization. Writing in English enables writers on both sides of the Pacific (Filipino/a and Filipino/a American) to express the rage that they would like the colonizer to hear—unmediated through translation.[27]

The World Unsettled:
The Long Arm of South Asian American Literature

As a body of literature, South Asian American writing encompasses large swaths of the world. Although located in the United States, South Asian

American writers train their memories and imaginations on other lands, other histories. The attention to landscapes outside the United States is not exclusively an attribute of the immigrant generation of South Asian American writers. American-born, second-generation South Asian American authors also exhibit a strong preoccupation with ancestral and diasporic homelands and in doing so necessitate a reconsideration of the notion of citizenship and national allegiance. Arjun Appadurai's assertion that for many South Asians around the world the several disparate locations of their life-experience function as "diasporic switching points" in a network of global citizenship, or that for South Asian Americans the United States is "one node in a . . . network of diasporas," is perhaps too glib in its implication that these individuals possess few ties to specific geographies and sites or exhibit no deep-seated commitments to particular civic spaces.[28] The sociocultural and political practices of diasporic South Asians belie both of these impressions. Yet, while Appadurai's language gives the unfortunate sense that South Asians animatedly cavort among the highways and byways of transnational existence, what can be said in his defense is that his description helps us appreciate the energy with which South Asian American writers portray worlds beyond the boundaries of the United States. The motivations for such portrayals vary widely, of course, ranging from nostalgia to historical interest to personal identity construction to exhortations for global social justice. The writers featured in this chapter—Jhumpa Lahiri, Agha Shahid Ali, Indran Amirthanayagam, Meena Alexander, Amitav Ghosh, Michael Ondaatje, and Sameer Parekh—are by no means the only practitioners of this extra-U.S. perspective, but their work most readily illuminates the range of impulses fueling the predisposition to embrace multiple topographies.

This yen is not a recent one, nor is it limited to South Asian American, Korean American, Vietnamese American, or Filipino/a American writers. Writing in the middle of the nineteenth century, Herman Melville located his works (*Typee*, *Omoo*, and *Moby Dick*, most famously) in lands far away from the North American continent. In the later part of the nineteenth century and into the twentieth, Henry James (in several of his novels, including *Portrait of a Lady*, *The Ambassadors*, *The American*, and *The Wings of the Dove*) placed American characters in Europe; Ernest Hemingway (in *The Sun Also Rises*, *For Whom the Bell Tolls*, *A Farewell to Arms*, and numerous stories set in Africa) continued the trend. Gertrude Stein's relationship to the United States was most complicated, perhaps best articulated in her frequently quoted statement: "America is my country and Paris is my home town." In the last decades of the twentieth century, Alice Walker sought landscapes external to the United States (particularly in *The Temple of My Familiar* and *Possessing the Secret of Joy*), and Oscar Hijuelos's novel *A Simple Habana Melody*, published in the early years of the twenty-first century, is set primarily in Cuba and secondarily in Europe.

Melville, James, Hemingway, and Stein, in particular, see the world outside through the eyes and consciousness of their American protagonists. What's beyond the United States is worth knowing because the American protagonist is there. Their protagonists' presence in those environments necessitates understanding these regions, because those extra-U.S. landscapes serve to enlighten the protagonists about themselves. The protagonists' inner core is American, with the quality of American-ness signified variously as innocence, artlessness, adventurousness, courage, candor, generosity, and moral righteousness. Those other locations provide the backdrop for the protagonists' heightened understanding of themselves as "American." Such understanding culminates in a rejection, modification, or acceptance of that appellation. That James, Hemingway, and Stein all spent considerable periods of time outside the United States gives further evidence that transnational allegiances have been commonplace throughout American literary history. American writers have not always felt it necessary to draw only on the social, cultural, political, or physical landscapes of the United States.

In South Asian American writing, the focus is not typically on an American protagonist who uses the backdrop of another country to reach self-knowledge. Rather there is the sense that this other world exists independent of the (American) protagonist's apprehension of it; sometimes there is no American protagonist, and the unfolding narrative or tapestry of images teems with a universe in which the United States and its residents are at best peripheral. South Asian American writers complicate the idea of place. In their writing, a location is both the site for the planting of roots and a launch pad from which to spring to other locations. This dialectic between the here and there, between the local and the global, forms the sphere of much South Asian American writing. The dialectic has the effect of both de-centering the United States in the consciousness of readers and illuminating the ways in which the lives of those who live there are inextricably linked with the lives of those who live elsewhere.

This looking beyond the borders of the United States can be impelled by various emotions—nostalgia, despair, deprivation, curiosity, adventurousness, and sense of moral responsibility that transcends national boundaries, to name a few. In the poems of Agha Shahid Ali and Indran Amirthanayagam, for example, nostalgia and despair seem to go hand in hand. Both poets call up their respective ancestral homelands (Kashmir for Ali, and Sri Lanka—previously known as Ceylon—for Amirthanayagam) in their writings, rescuing these war-torn lands from the oblivion of destruction and inscribing them on the map of their readers' consciousness. It is as though they wish to ensure that Kashmir and Sri Lanka not become disconnected from the lives of their readers. Thus, their poems weave nostalgia for a lost homeland with a fierce determination, born of despair, that Kashmir and Sri Lanka will not fall off the edge of the world's concern.

Ali Sees the World in His Rearview Mirror

Agha Shahid Ali's poem "Snow on the Desert" skillfully illustrates the complex relationship between the present moment in the United States and past moments in another land.[29] The poem begins with the speaker driving through a desert in Arizona. He evokes the landscape's long history by telling of the Native Americans who used the cacti there for making wine: "The Papagos place it in jars, // where the last of it softens, then darkens" (101). The speaker's understanding of the connection between people and location seems to be paramount. And then, suddenly, that rootedness in location is disrupted. Or perhaps it could more accurately be called a widening, an opening up, almost as if the speaker wishes to suggest that while the sense of history in the desert is rich, there are other histories that are equally significant. The speaker is transported from the Arizona desert to a concert auditorium in Delhi in 1971, where the sound of a singer's voice fills the room and connects the people: "It was perhaps during the Bangladesh War, / perhaps there were sirens, // air-raid warnings. / But the audience, hushed, did not stir. // The microphone was dead, but she went on / singing" (105). Four nations are linked in the poem—the United States, India, Bangladesh, and Pakistan. Perhaps two peoples are linked as well: the Native Americans in their beleaguered fight against the U.S. government and their long claim on the land, and the people of East Pakistan who sought independence from West Pakistan so that they could pursue their own destiny. The act of remembering allows him to meditate on loss and his ability to cope with it.

Other sights in the United States spark a similar retrieval of images with startling immediacy. The distance between two locations collapses, the one folds into the other. In the poem "In Search of Evanescence #3: When on Route 80 in Ohio," seeing the name of the Indian city "Calcutta" on an exit sign along the Ohio Turnpike evokes the memory of a bridge in Calcutta, and the numerous people who walk on the bridge become the countless cars on the highway. I have written elsewhere that the lines "India always exists / off the turnpikes / of America," while ostensibly minimizing the importance of India in relation to the United States, might in fact be read to opposite effect.[30] The real business of living in the United States goes on off its impersonal and rushed turnpikes—goes on, if you will, in the spaces where India lives, that is, among the United States' numerous immigrants, if one reads India as metonymic of all those who enter the United States from other lands.

Ali's poems record the consciousness in the act of leaping from an acute sensation of the local to an equally acute feeling about the transnational. His writing entwines the many strands of longing and desire as they relate to place(s). In "I See Chile in My Rearview Mirror," the act of driving through the desert toward Utah triggers images of all the lands south of the United States, almost as though in the mirages that appear in the desert the poet sees the other Americas that cannot be ignored:

> This dream of water—what does it harbor?
> I see Argentina and Paraguay
> under a curfew of glass, their colors
> breaking, like oil. The night in Uruguay
>
> is black salt. I'm driving toward Utah,
> keeping the entire hemisphere in view—
> Colombia vermilion, Brazil blue tar,
> some countries wiped clean of color: Peru
>
> is titanium white.[31]

Ali's poetic inspiration comes from, among other influences, Emily Dickinson. This doyenne of American poetry ironically is perhaps best known for her confinement to a single location. But Ali unmoors Dickinson, too, by showing that notwithstanding her legendary isolation and self-imposed seclusion, she could not help but be touched by a world outside, even if only rhetorically. Ali uses as an epigraph to one of his poems Dickinson's lines, "I'd bring them every flower that grows / From Amherst to Cashmere!"[32] Ali further strengthens the connections between Amherst and Kashmir, moving them out of the realm of the rhetorical to that of the flux of life. The speaker of his poem "Some Vision of the World Cashmere" is "here in Amherst" when the phone rings to tell him that his grandmother is dying. The phone rings in Amherst, but he "put[s] the phone down in Srinagar," once again telescoping two distant locations and erasing the boundaries between them. In the speaker's mind and memory, in the poet's language, worlds are yoked together.

The voice that asks in Ali's poem "The Correspondent," "When will the satellites / transmit my songs, carry Kashmir, aubades / always for dawns to stamp / *True!* across seas?"[33] sounds the call of the current age. It is as though the legitimacy and reality of an occurrence gain strength only when news of it is transmitted across space and made known to those far away. What is the weight of an event about which no one is informed? Is it not mere shadow, mere trace of fantasy? The importance of reporting—of retelling what has transpired—is used to great effect in William Faulkner's writing to create the sense of a complex and self-contained community of members whose lives impinge upon each other in innumerable ways. What Ali's speaker implies is that today the entire world is, or ought to be, a community, and that it is imperative for those who live in one part of the world to know of what happens to those who live in other realms. In this global community, the protagonist is the news correspondent. He brings footage of Sarajevo to Kashmir. His local counterpart in the Kashmir of which Ali writes is the boatman who steers the floating post office on the canals of the region. The occupants of the houseboats await his arrival, knowing that he will bring them word from others and will carry their words out to others "through the tense waters" (53). A central sentiment that emerges in these poems is one of desired connections—among different peoples, among different lands—across time.

In "A Footnote to History," a poem that epitomizes the wide historical and geographical net cast by much South Asian American writing,

Ali recalls the journey of gypsies from India to Europe a thousand years ago.[34] The poem's speaker, standing on the banks of the Indus river, laments: "For ten centuries / they sent no word" (69). Now, as he looks at the river's waves, he feels the gypsies' voices reaching him, "demanding/ [he] memorize their / ancient and recent / journeys in / caravans ambushed by / forests on fire" (70). Ali's poems underscore another salient feature of South Asian American writing: the notion that it is impossible to discard the multiple historical sediments and the expanding spatial realms contained in the construction of individual identities.

Sri Lanka as an Ever Present Reality

Indran Amirthanayagam, as I point out in Chapter 1, does not want Sri Lanka (known previously as Ceylon) to be reduced to televised images that are beamed into American homes. He wants to evoke his homeland (Amrithanayagam was born in Sri Lanka in 1960 and came to the United States in his early teens) and give it history, substance, and purpose. He wants the American viewer to invest him/herself in what happens in Jaffna. You may, he says, "punch your eyes out / blindfold them / and tear the cloth off, // and in the white dark / fling the balls out," but you cannot hold at bay the images that invade your dreams as you sleep.[35]

Amirthanayagam wants to express his rage at what the civil war is doing to his birth country; he wants to share that rage and that sadness with his readers so that they, too, will know of and care about a land and a people that are being held hostage to hostility. The poems in his 1993 collection *The Elephants of Reckoning* shout, weep, sing, and reflect. They are an evocation and expression of the beauty of a country, of the destruction of that beauty, of the endurance of a people, and of sorrow that any people should be called on to display such endurance.

Amirthanayagam's interest in Sri Lanka is matched by his passion for Mexico. He is fluent in Spanish, with two collections of poetry published in the language. An employee of the U.S. Foreign Service, he has worked in Chennai (in southern India) and in Mexico City. Amirthanayagam's foreign service work and writings represent a fluid movement among many cultures and locations. Writing in an essay "How Politics Becomes Language," Amirthanayagam speaks of precisely this movement:

> As it turns out, these elephants [he's speaking of his collection *The Elephants of Reckoning*] were awarded the Paterson Poetry Prize in

New Jersey in 1994. How honored and accepted I felt in the birth-place of William Carlos Williams and Allen Ginsberg, in the nurs-ing streams of the Paterson Falls, of American speech and American poetry in the tradition of Walt Whitman. Here I had brought my elephants, my crows, lorries, betel, songbirds, cranes and kingfishers, my hoopoes. Here, in the great American democracy, near the Lady who takes in the tired and hungry, my own language was stamped with a kind of approval. Unfortunately, the audience was rather thin on prize-giving day. And soon after, I fled into other languages, French and Spanish, into a diplomatic career that forced me to keep cultivating a floating garden, a raft made of fine steel alloys, unbreakable, but always at sea between continents, between lan-guages and loves.[36]

In *The Elephants of Reckoning*, he sets himself the task of remember-ing what's important about the country he left behind: "Ceylon days, what's left, / I'm trying to gather essences" (62). The moments of pleas-ure are rendered with exquisite longing in the poem "Be Rude, Boy, Again," in which the speaker addresses a companion and asks, "Shall we take a sea-bath, friend / then burn the salt off / devouring hot prawns // . . . Shall we swing high / over the palms in Ceylon / cut off a king coconut // snap it on a stone / spoon the sweet flesh / belly in belly out, my friend" (16).

But reality intrudes. Sri Lanka is in the grip of a decades-long civil war between the separatist Tamils (who are the minority and are demanding their own autonomous state) and the Sinhalese-led govern-ment. Young boys and girls have been recruited by the militant Tamil organization, the Liberation Tigers of Tamil Eelam, to sacrifice their lives in the service of independence. (For more on this civil war, see the dis-cussion below on Ondaatje's novel *Anil's Ghost* and also the discussion in Chapter 3 on Shyam Selvadurai's *Funny Boy*). Amirthanayagam records the horrors of the civil war in "Ceylon." The poem ends with a powerful litany:

> (Pity the poor lion,
> pity the poor tiger,
> the cobra, the elephant,
> the fish and fowl
> the birds and beasts

who see their jungle cut down
to build huts
for knife throwers guns
bombs rapists
thieves of every color

who come to drink the milk
and eat the bread
of young boys and girls
who've always been told,

when the beggar comes
give something, give something you like
like your life.) (55)

That the litany is enclosed in parentheses may signify that pity is largely absent from the circumstances in Sri Lanka, that the perspective of those who feel pity is relegated to an aside, an incidental insertion. Or, conversely, if we are to subscribe to Helen Cixous's notion that parenthetical assertions mark sites of intervention, sites of rupture in utterances, the parentheses in this instance may indicate that the core of the poem—anything worth knowing or feeling—lies in this apparent aside (See my analysis in Chapter 3 of how the epilogue in *Funny Boy* serves a similar central function.) The other curious image in the poem is that of the "beggar." Amirthanayagam may be likening nation and ethnicity to a beggar, a figure who pleads for our allegiance, who exhorts us to look his/her way. Seen in this light, the poem could be read as a critique of nationalism and ethnic affiliation.

Amirthanayagam warns the prospective tourist in "Words for the Sri Lanka Tourist Office" that although Sri Lanka is still a beautiful place, "just remember here everywhere // there is only man burning / and woman burning // here everywhere // in shallow graves / in deep graves / floating out of salt water/ washing down the sands" (13). He asks what these dead are saying, but the poem offers no answers. In fact, the poem ends with the speaker addressing the birds, the animals, the monsoon of Sri Lanka and asking if they are going to sing. It seems that only Nature in Sri Lanka has the means to create the semblance of a tourist spot. The people cannot.

Poems of hope leaven the despair at Sri Lankan's violent turbulence. In "Star over Jaffna," Amirthanayagam declares: "The fishermen will fix / the holes left by bombs / and ride their boats out / in the bay, and catch / fat prawns under the starry night" (53). "After the Monsoon" closes with this Edenic image of harmony and coexistence: "For a minute, the Sinha lion licks / the Tamil tiger's face on a bed / draped by plantain leaves" (63). Significantly, these are the last lines of the collection. Yet, Amirthanayagam's is no idle or idealistic hope. His recent poem "Elegy for Neelan Tiruvechalam," lamenting the assassination of a man fiercely committed to the cessation of hostilities in the Sri Lankan civil war reminds us that Amrithanayagam is fully aware of the grim reality of the Sri Lankan political landscape.[37]

Anil and the Corpse of the Nation: Ondaatje's Global Forensics Expert

Michael Ondaatje's novel *Anil's Ghost*, though located in Sri Lanka, seems particularly relevant to the current debate about the roles of various groups likely to participate in the reconstruction of post-Saddam Iraq. (See Chapter 1 for a discussion of how Ondaatje and other South Asians living in Canada enlarge and complicate the South Asian American literary landscape.) Among the issues that emerge in *Anil's Ghost* are the relationship of the diasporic individual to the ancestral homeland, the role of the diasporic woman in the construction of nationhood, the relationship between national sovereignty and international law, and the intervention of an international agency in the internal affairs of a state. Finally, the novel also raises the issue of narrative perspective itself: does Ondaatje's portrayal of the Sri Lankan situation do adequate justice to the particularities of the conflict there, or is his treatment of violence and civil war generalized, as though he wished readers to consider the futility of violence per se and not necessarily the specific tragedy of the Sri Lankan civil war?

The novel, although informed by the conflict in Sri Lanka, does not inform its readers about the complexities of this decades-long battle—specifically, the motivations of the various parties and the power structures operating within and between the several groups involved. A brief author's note that opens the novel is the only political framing Ondaatje provides for the events of the book:

From the mid-1980s to the early 1990s, Sri Lanka was in a crisis that involved three essential groups: the government, the antigovernment insurgents in the south and the separatist guerrillas in the north. Both the insurgents and separatists had declared war on the government. Eventually, in response, legal and illegal government squads were known to have been sent out to hunt down the separatists and the insurgents.

This explanation is never adequately deepened or complicated, leading Qadri Ismail to characterize the novel as "a flippant gesture towards Sri Lanka." Amitav Ghosh makes a similar assessment, when he says that the novel doesn't do much for him because it doesn't address the substantive issues of the political conflict in Sri Lanka.[38]

However, its very weakness—Ondaatje's treatment of the political situation in generalized rather than specific terms—makes *Anil's Ghost* a useful text to engage amid the geopolitics of the present moment. How can an abstract idealism—a belief in the principles of freedom and democracy, for example—be intertwined with a solid understanding of and sensitivity to complicating local factors that may cause the "agent" bringing these supposedly universal ideals to be viewed with suspicion? How can an intervening outside force—whether a foreign government or an international agency—recognize the power and reality of conflicting emotions in the people whose land it enters? For Americans, whether immigrants or their American-born daughters and sons, these ought to be urgent question, particularly in light of the United States' aspirations to direct the geopolitics of the Middle East, South America, South Asia, and Southeast Asia. A fundamental issue to consider is the extent to which a diasporic "son" or "daughter" is viewed as an insider or outsider by those in the ancestral homeland and the extent to which such "returning" individuals are welcomed or trusted. Although *Anil's Ghost* does not provide adequate or sustained treatment of these questions, the fact that the text evokes them gives it value. There are other reasons, as well, to engage this novel: Ondaatje's writing is spare and finely honed; there is almost no artificiality of sentiment, and even the most horrific acts of violence are rendered in prose that forces readers to go past their initial shock to consider how the raw and brutal reality of the acts they have been made to witness are shaped by the hand of a craftsman skilled in the art of language. Ondaatje's prose impresses upon the reader the role of the artist in both recording and providing the vehicle for transcending the violent event.

Anil's Ghost was published in 2000. Reading it today, in light of the U.S. entry into Iraq, with the stated objective of liberating the Iraqi people, one finds that the novel lays out useful psychological and political terrain. At the present moment, with the dictatorship of Saddam Hussein dismantled, many Iraqis who were in exile have eagerly returned to their homeland to take an active part in the rebuilding of their nation. Iraqis that remained in Iraq and endured persecution at the hands of Hussein's government bristle at the suggestion that those who left should have a greater say than those that stayed behind. The dynamics among the various ethno-religious groups—Shiites, Sunnis, and Kurds—and between the returning exiles and Iraqi residents is likely to be complex and result in an unpredictable postwar political and social scenario. Intersecting with this volatile cast of players are the U.S. military and State Department, and even between these two actors there remains the unresolved question of who will have a greater role as "overseer" or facilitator of the reconstruction. Further, Iraqi Americans are perceived by Iraqi exiles in Britain to have an unfair advantage in securing key positions in the interim administrative government. And then, what of the interaction between the U.S. contingent (whether from the Pentagon or the State Department) and the various groups of Iraqis? These are not idle questions, because depending on which Iraqi group(s) secure(s) power, the neighboring Syrians and Iranians could have a lesser or greater role to play in post-Saddam Iraq. The United States very likely will want to keep the influence that Iran and Syria have on Iraq to a minimum. Iraq is a country without a blueprint for the future, and powers outside are busy drafting a plan. The United Nations is calling for a strong role for itself, but U.S. Secretary of Defense Donald Rumsfeld, Vice President Dick Cheney, National Security Advisor Condoleezza Rice, and many Republican senators are loath to allow the United Nations any part at all. Researchers and scholars of international politics and global policy point to the critical necessity of envisioning and maintaining a delicate balance between external "help" and internal actors.[39] There is danger in an external party interfering too much; on the other hand, an external party's intervention may be absolutely critical to resolving deep conflicts among many diverse indigenous groups.

To what extent Iraq will be permitted to exercise its own sovereignty as a nation (however feeble its identity as a discrete country might be
at this present time) amidst the avid interest in its affairs exhibited by
multiple external powers is an issue that will, in the weeks and months
ahead, take on varying shapes. Iraq's predicament establishes beyond a
doubt that nations cannot exist in isolation; the countries of the world
are regulated by a "supranational" system of power in which domestic
considerations are subordinated to the dictates of international law.
Michael Hardt and Antonio Negri label this state of affairs—unique to
recent decades—as the manifestation of Empire.[40] Although they avoid
identifying the command center of this Empire as the United States (and
one can only attribute their reluctance to their having developed their
argument in the years between the 1991 Gulf War and the United
Nations' 1997 intervention in Bosnia, antedating the presidency of
George W. Bush, the events of September 11, and the stalemate between
the United Nations Security Council and the United States over the
decision to invade Iraq), their characterization of the power of Empire—
its ubiquitous presence and its global reach—is immensely useful in
appreciating the tensions that can arise between independent nation-
states and the directives of international bodies. They observe, "The new
paradigm is both system and hierarchy, centralized construction of norms
and far-reaching production of legitimacy, spread out over world space"
(13). They note that Empire's power lies in its ability to "exhaust[ ] historical time, suspend[ ] history, and summon[ ] the past and future within its own ethical order. In other words, Empire presents its order as
permanent, eternal, and necessary" (11). Nations are subjected to the will
of "supranational subjects that . . . intervene in the name of any type of
emergency and superior ethical principles. What stands behind this
intervention is not a just a permanent state of emergency and exception,
but a permanent state of emergency and exception justified by *the appeal
to essential values of justice*" (18).

Sri Lanka is a nation torn by internal conflicts. Caught in the grip of
a civil war that has escalated steadily since the early 1980s, it has worked
with outside mediators (primarily the Norwegians) several times in an
attempt to move beyond fragile cease-fires. The Tamil minority in the
north and east wants to establish a separate state where it can be free
from what it sees as the persecution and discrimination by the Sinhala
majority; the Sinhala majority in the south and west is fiercely opposed

to a separate Tamil state or autonomous region, which it believes will establish links with the populous Indian state of Tamilnadu and thereby become a formidable opponent. The Muslims (who are part of the Tamil minority) find themselves without any safe location: they are discriminated against both by the Sinhala majority and the Tamil Hindus. The Tamil Tigers, the militant arm of the Tamil separatists, are considered to be highly skilled in the tactics of guerilla warfare. They have used suicide bombings with devastating effectiveness on several occasions—assassinating Sinhala leaders, Tamil moderates, and the Indian prime minister Rajiv Gandhi. Sri Lanka is an island nation, but its Tamil diaspora is far flung and constitutes a virtual "global" nation through the active use of the internet web site www.tamileelam.org.

In an age of globalization, the finality of exile is mitigated by the possibility of return—even if only temporarily—to the original home or nation. Even if physical return is prevented by legal and political barriers, the daily dissemination of information about the homeland through global conduits of news delivery (the internet being the most efficient in this regard) permits exiles to monitor continuously the pulse of the land they left behind. In this context, *Anil's Ghost* can be read as both a postcolonial author's readiness to confront the terrible truth about his ancestral nation and his effort to imagine the conditions for its reabsorption into the international geopolitical fold. Anil Tissera, the eponymous protagonist, is an anthropologist in forensic medicine working for an international human rights organization. Her partner in Sri Lanka is Sarath Diyasena, an archaeologist. He represents the force of excavation—the unearthing of the terrible past; she is the agent of analysis, the global professional who will give to the human remains found at burial sites the meaning that they now lack.

Anil is young, and in her youth she embodies hope. At the same time, she is an outsider, a diasporic individual from whom the innermost secrets of the nation will always be concealed. Ondaatje infuses in her the exile's conflicted feelings about the land from which she is removed. My interest here is in the intersections between exile and return as embodied by Anil, and in how Ondaatje treats these intersections against the backdrop of globalization, manifested in the novel by the intervention of an international human rights agency. Within this context, two important questions emerge: What is the nature of the exile's influence over the homeland? And what impact does the postcolonial writer have

both on the nation-state's perception of itself and on the exile community's construction of the homeland?

Jayadeva Uyangoda observes that "[s]ince the early 1980s, the everyday experience in Sri Lanka has centered on violence, destruction,
hatred, and moral commitment to enmity. An overbearing sense of
uncertainty and anxiety translates into violence as well as fear of violence. Engulfed in so much violence, Sri Lanka is not a normal society;
it is a shell-shocked society."[41] He believes that the depth of distrust
among the various parties is so intense that outside intervention is necessary to move them toward meaningful discussion. Yet, Uyangoda cautions, outside mediation can only yield results if it occurs at the right
time and is founded on the external players' complex understanding of
the ways in which they are likely to be manipulated by the internal players. Uyangoda's caveats are echoed by others working in the field of
international human rights.[42]

Ismail has delivered a scathing critique of Ondaatje's Sinhala cen-
trism in this novel. I would argue that Ghosh's comment that the novel
fails to engage with the complexities of the ethnic positions in the conflict comes closer to explaining the gap at the center of the novel.
Ondaatje presents a generalized landscape of violence without sufficient
attention to the country's immensely tangled ethno-politics. I'm not
suggesting that the reader requires a history lesson detailing every Sri
Lankan government's contribution and response to the civil war or the
emergence and development of the Tamil Tigers and the JVP (Janatha
Vimukthi Peramuna—People's Liberation Front—the largest socialist
party in Sri Lanka) as counter-government forces, but some grounding
in the intense ethnicization of Sri Lankan politics would help, if only to
gain a richer understanding of the novel's characters. In some ways,
Ondaatje is guilty of offering a bird's-eye view of the conditions in Sri
Lanka. Perhaps a better way of putting it might be to say that when he
swoops down for a closer look, his vision is so tightly trained on one particular object that he does not notice the features of the ground immediately surrounding the object in question. He is guilty both of too general and too narrow a perspective. And maybe that is the curse of being
an outsider, or an occasional insider—that one cannot know where one
should stand and what one should see. Gamini, the *medicins sans fron-
tier*-type character in the book, voices a criticism of the Western visitor
to Asia that might provide some insight to Ondaatje's inability to mod-

ulate his vision to accommodate multiple urgencies, to look in multiple crevices of reality:

> American movies, English books—remember how they all end? . . . The American or the Englishman gets on a plane and leaves. That's it. The camera leaves with him. He looks out the window at Mombasa or Vietnam or Jakarta, someplace now he can look at through the clouds. The tired hero. A couple of words to the girl beside him. He's going home. So the war, to all purposes, is over. That's enough reality for the West. It's probably the last two years of Western political writing. Go home. Write a book. Hit the circuit. (285–86)

Is Ondaatje being self-critical about his endeavor, ironic about his book? He too is culpable, guilty of temporary concern, ultimately headed for somewhere else. And is he suggesting that despite the depth of his interest, his engagement with the complexities of the situation on the ground is necessarily limited because he is, after all, a visitor? Yet, Ondaatje does not wholly concede the insider's advantage over the outsider. The last brief section of the novel is titled "Distance," and in it Ondaatje presents a powerful tension between the Buddha's distant gaze and the artist's close and careful examination of material. While the statue of the new Buddha (over a hundred feet high) with its freshly painted eyes can "witness figures only from a great distance" (306), Ananda, the sculptor and artist who paints the statue's eyes, witnesses with his "human sight . . . the smallest approach of a bird, every flick of its wing" (307). But Ananda, perched on the ladder he has ascended to paint the Buddha's eyes, can also see things at a great distance—"a hundred-mile storm coming down off the mountains near Gonagola and skirting the plains" (307), and he realizes the seduction of this long-distance vision. And though he is ultimately brought back to the closer reality by the touch of his nephew's hand—"this sweet touch from the world," Ondaatje calls it—the tension between distance and proximity informs the final paragraphs of the book. And despite Ondaatje's inability to negotiate this tension and find the appropriate perspective—the various intermediate positions between the distant and close views—one has to grant that he recognizes the artist's responsibility to work in the continuum between the two extremes. The diasporic writer is always in an awkward position with respect to the ancestral land. The writer seeks to re-create the homeland of his/her memories, usually those preceding the rupture or traumatic departure. In the case of homelands that have changed dramatically since departure (for example, Vietnam, Cambodia, and Sri Lanka), the writer may find it difficult to acknowledge that his/her knowledge of current realities is no better than that of a stranger. In fact, if anything, the writer's desire to revisit, both literally and metaphorically, the homeland of memory may impede the ability to understand new complexities. Ondaatje's failure of perspective—if one may be permitted so harsh a word—is paralleled by Anil's youthful naiveté about the role she can play in Sri Lanka as a forensics expert. She is not entirely certain about her motivations for returning to Sri Lanka in this position as international professional, applying desultorily (or so she says) for the job when it is posted by the human rights organization's office in Geneva. One suspects that Sri Lanka is an unresolved problem for her; both her parents were killed in a car crash there while she was away studying in England. There is, technically, nothing for her to return to—no pull of family or ancestral property—and so one can only attribute her somewhat undefined desire as part curiosity, part nostalgia, part apprehension, part idealism. The idealism is, in some ways, the safest attitude: it is intricately bound to the kind of work she does, it allows her to look forward rather than backward, and it gives her a sense of control. But Sri Lanka, as Ondaatje demonstrates, does not suffer idealists lightly.

The novel opens with a brief description of the forensic medical team's work in Guatemala. The men and women of Guatemala watch the team's activities with keen interest, believing that they will at last discover what happened to loved ones who disappeared. One afternoon, when Anil returns from lunch to the burial site, she finds a woman sitting in a grave meditating over the remains of two bodies, perhaps those of her husband and brother. Anil is so moved by the woman's posture that she never forgets "the grief of love in that shoulder" (6). I would argue that this is the image Anil carries with her as affirmation of the work she does—as one who brings hope into the lives of those who seem to have no reason to hope. Anil does not see herself in any grandiose terms as the discoverer of truth—she is far too intelligent and cynical for that. In addition, she has had the experience of investigative work being rendered void, when all the documents and data that she and her team collected in the Congo were confiscated so that they had to leave the country with nothing at all. But she is motivated by a trace of idealism in the value of the forensics expertise she brings and in its humanitarian and moral dimension.

Such idealism is misplaced in the ethno-political world of Sri Lanka. Anil's framework of expertise is forged in a transnational context—as part of an international agency. The working tenets of her labor transcend the particularities of national histories. The human rights organization for which she works believes in the theoretical application of its principles uniformly across nations, in the hope that each nation will accept the fundamental abstractions of full disclosure and truth. Anil's gradual acceptance of the specificities of the conditions in Sri Lanka forms one arc of the narrative trajectory of this novel. What begins as an intellectual project—her professional desire to uncover the truth through the study of bones—becomes, over time, a means of emotionally reconnecting to Sri Lanka. She starts out as a global citizen and ends up feeling herself sufficiently a part of Sri Lanka to say, at a briefing to government officials, "'I think you murdered hundreds of us'" (272). It is almost as though she is giving a citizen's evidence. But the crossover is not entirely complete. She still sees herself as the representative of an international organization, a human rights group that is answerable to no state authority, only to a universal code of law. Not only does she not wholly relinquish her connections to the world outside Sri Lanka, but also she is not permitted to do so by those who consider themselves to be more genuinely Sri Lankan. And it is as a global citizen that she escapes with her life, if not her dignity.

Anil's Ghost does not privilege the Sri Lankan insider or the Sri Lankan outsider. Anil is humiliated. Gamini, the doctor who worries only about saving lives and not about the politics of his nation, and who declares somewhat self-righteously that he loves his country as no outsider can, must experience the brutal harshness of his brother's murder at the hands of the state. Gamini is most intimately connected to the violence in which this nation is engulfed, but he cares little about the principles underlying it or the ideas behind it. To him the unit of compassion, the measure of humanity is, ultimately, the individual. He "turned away from every person who stood up for a war. Or the principle of one's land, or pride of ownership, or even personal rights. All of those motives ended up somehow in the arms of careless power. One was no worse and no better than the enemy" (119). And yet Ondaatje, in having Gamini confront the murder of his brother, may be suggesting that a focus exclusively on the individual is, ultimately, myopic because one cannot divorce the individual's life from the political context in which he lives. In fact, Gamini's unwillingness to recognize the legitimacy of personal rights is problematic, both because it is at odds with his commitment to the individual and because it allows him to ignore the state's complicity in assaulting personal rights. Thus, while Gamini's doctoring is certainly presented in elevated terms—because he does save lives, after all—his apolitical and non-interrogative stance is not offered as a model. His love of country is shown to be misguided, a kind of blindness.

In Sarath's case, blindness takes the form of turning to the past, refusing to immerse oneself in the urgencies of the present. "There's no hope of affixing blame" (17), he tells Anil, and takes refuge in the claim that he is "just an archaeologist." Anil rightly surmises that "[m]ost of what Sarath wished to know was in some way linked to the past. . . . [H]e found the social world around him irrelevant. His desire . . . was to write a book someday about a city in the south of the island that no longer existed. Not a wall of it remained, but he wanted to tell the story of that place. It would emerge out of this dark trade with the earth, his knowledge of the region in chronicles—its medieval business routes, its presence as a favorite monsoon town of a certain king, as revealed in poems that celebrated the city's daily life" (29–30). Sarath is juxtaposed against his mentor, the famous Palipana, who, at the height of his fame was "the main force of a pragmatic Sinhala movement," but is now living in discredited exile in the forest, blind, and cared for by a niece. In the novel, archaeology, if it is rooted only in a preoccupation with the past, is shown to be a rather ineffectual response to the urgencies of the present.

However, Sarath, for a brief interlude, becomes infected with Anil's desire to make sense of the present, and he tells the skeptical Palipana, "You have reconstructed eras simply by looking at runes. You've used artists to re-create scenes from just paint fragments. So. We have a skull. We need someone to re-create what he might have looked like. One way to discover *when* he was twenty-eight [Anil has determined through forensic analysis the age of the skeleton] is to have someone identify him" (96). Ultimately, he finds himself in the most delicate and tragic of positions—having to go through the charade of discrediting Anil in public as a means to save her life and perhaps his as well, but nevertheless becoming a victim of the government's fury at what it believes is his complicity in her investigation.

Ultimately *Anil Ghost* reveals the futility of international intervention when the conditions within a nation are not conducive to it. Anil represents the unbending moral principle of truth as a universal abstraction, unbound from context. However, as those who study and participate in truth commissions emphasize repeatedly, unless international agents enter nations with a sophisticated understanding of the way "truth" is perceived and received in specific national contexts, the pursuit of truth will always fail. "There were dangers in handing truth to an unsafe city around you," Sarath meditates, acknowledging that Sri Lanka is perhaps not quite ready for full disclosure. "As an archaeologist Sarath believed in truth as a principle. That is, he would have given his life for the truth if the truth were of any use" (157), the narrator tells us. Ironically, that is indeed what Sarath does. His murder uncovers the truth that Sri Lanka is not quite ready for the truth. "The country existed in a rocking self-burying motion": the image that comes to mind is of a deranged person, hugging himself, rhythmically locked within his own reality. Sri Lanka, the novel suggests, must turn outward, must learn to balance its internal truths with the larger universal truth.

Moral Indignation for the Near and the Far

Meena Alexander's work is engaged in exploring a similar relationship between the internal and the external: the individual's moral responsibility to herself and to the communities within which she lives. How does one read Alexander? One cannot imbibe her without feeling a sense of being wrenched out of a comfortable location—she thrusts glimpses of other worlds into our eyes and zone of consciousness. She does this in a way that does not transport us out of our own realities into those others; rather she creates the effect of having two disparate realities running side by side—as though we perceive with a split consciousness separate components that we must reconcile and yet know that we cannot. Perhaps the precise nature of her poetry and prose is that she creates discomfort and seeks to evoke the impossibility of ever being able to bring the multiple realities of our lives into harmonious coexistence.

The weight of Alexander's writing is burdensome. Her prose does not intoxicate with the magic of being transported from place to place in a whirlwind of global exposure. It does not carry with it the pleasure enclosed in Appadurai's phrase "diasporic switching points" or the hopeful celebration of differences that a cosmopolitan writer such as Appiah invites and welcomes. But like those who celebrate what lies beyond the borders of individual nation-states, and those who envision shared communities beyond the enclosure of specific geopolitical locations, Alexander declares the necessity for a global awareness—for a sensibility that is acutely troubled both by what happens on the streets of the city in which one lives and behind barbed wires in the refugee camps of a war-torn country like Bosnia. In her collection *The Illiterate Heart*, she writes, "Someone will swim farther and farther from what she feels is the shore."[43] That someone is herself, and she invites her readers to do the same—to venture out into the unknown.

"We must always return / to poems for news of the world / or perish for the lack" are the opening lines of Alexander's poem "News of the World."[44] Later in the same poem, the speaker says, "In Cambodia I carried / my mother's head in a sack / and ran three days and nights / through a rice field" (27). One could argue that Alexander's concern for all suffering, her rendering of injustice in numerous locations worldwide, flattens the differences among these discrete oppressions and inequities. But one could just as easily argue that her cognizance of these numerous miseries and torments on the global landscape indicates a sensibility that cares enough to traverse the chasms of difference that separate one nation from another, one people from another. In a powerful tribute to the slain youth of China making their stand for democracy at Tiananmen Square, Alexander writes, "the young of Tiananmen. / From a far country I sing // As blood swallowed them whole / they became our blood."[45]

Alexander's writings do not allow us to turn away. She takes us from location to location, thrusting injustices into our eyes, into our ears, forcing us to attend:

> I think of Bensonhurst in Brooklyn, of Jersey City and the racist murders there. In Jersey City an Indian man was beaten to death, Indian women who wore saris or buttus were stoned by skinheads. I think of Hyderabad, Meerut, Delhi, Bhagalpur, and the communal riots and murders in those cities, as well as in the countryside of India. . . . I think of the terrible bombardment of Iraq during the Gulf War, the

countless quick and slow deaths, the massacres of children from on high under the gleaming aegis of the latest fighter-bombers.[46]

In Alexander's vision, a literature born in the United States is a literature that must of necessity evoke other locations.[47] A war in Iraq affects not only the Iraqis and the Americans who fight there but also the migrant workers who come to Iraq and Kuwait from Palestinian camps, from Kerala in India, and from northern Africa to earn a decent living and support families in their homelands. All these lives are disrupted. (See Chapter 5 for a further discussion of Alexander's work.)

In a poem that appears to be a response to the first Gulf War, "Estrangement Becomes the Mark of the Eagle," Alexander suggests that the United States' only connection to other nations is through the act of war. Otherwise, the eagle's mark is one of estrangement. She describes the destruction accompanying the Gulf War: "Mesopotamia's largess under tanks / and the colonels of Texas and Florida / with cockatoo feathers in their caps / and the young lads of Oregon torn from their pillows / bent under bombs, grenades, gas masks / and the young lads of Kuwait beheaded in the sand." She juxtaposes this devastation against the indifference of those who orchestrate it: "men well trained to the purchase of power / knot water bottles, burst cans of shaving cream / spent condoms, to the rear ends of jeeps and race / at the crack of dawn, at the bitten end of our century / through Broadway, through narrow desert tracks."[48] Through this disturbing juxtaposition, Alexander exhorts us to care. In the essay "Translating Violence," Alexander once again shows how she seeks continuously and relentlessly to link the local with the external, the United States with other nations. She speaks of Maya Angelou's poem delivered at Clinton's 1993 presidential inauguration:

Maya Angelou spoke with lyric intensity of the mixed multitudes of America, the living whose voices and bodies cry out for change. . . . On the inside back page of the newspaper that carried the text of Angelou's poem, I read of Iraqi children dying from spent shells spat out by American missiles. The spirit of Angelou's fierce compassion forces me back into the desolation of the actual—radioactive shells mimicking nature, contortion that the innocence of childhood could never decipher.[49]

Alexander has lived in and partakes of the histories of many nations—India, the Sudan, England, the United States—and her consciousness ranges the world over. Is it possible to do justice to the multidimensionality of her sensibility? By now, the phrase "a woman cracked by multiple migrations" has become so clichéd in talking about her that it is merely a formulaic epithet that glosses over the complexity of her histories. And while her lamentations about not being able to locate herself in one place—because her vision is always intercepted by scenes from multiple locations—can sometimes border on excessive and, therefore, artificial despair, Alexander's value lies in her being able to pack her words with the contours of many lives and geographies.

In a remarkable image, she conveys what it is to be a migrant creature of the world: "I am at home on the road that bumps a little as it passes the old wharf, where at dawn the fishermen crowd, laying out their wares, crying out the prices of shrimp, catfish, swordfish, parrotfish, sardines, soles, hot, houseless soles dredged from the mothering sea."[50] Several tropes come together in this passage: the road as movement, but also as home; the sea as eclectic, as embracing infinite variety; the fish in their diversity as mankind. Finally, the play on "sole" (to evoke "soul") reveals that Alexander's "soul" seeks solace amidst myriad others. Alexander's is not the globalism of economics, of breathless travel, or of professional consulting. Hers is the globalism of outrage, of moral indignation, of social justice, of compassion for those others like us who are also a part of this world.

Parenthetical Aside: Literary Discourse and the Task of Unmooring the Conscience in a Global Economy

(An April 15, 2001, front-page story in the *New York Times* informs us: "For the most part, it is the wretched of the earth who do the world's tailoring. Made in Bangladesh competes with Made in Honduras, Made in the Philippines, Made in Macao, Made in Any Steamy Reservoir of Third World Unemployment: those places where plentiful labor lacks the leverage to command high pay, and the most pitiful thing about the jobs is how hard it is to get them." The article continues with a full-page spread on page 10, complete with photographs of some sweatshop workers in Bangladesh.

I am reminded by this story of the frustration and helplessness that my students in the mid-1990s expressed when I introduced them to the song "Are My Hands Clean?" by Bernice Johnson Reagon, showing how their act of purchasing a garment was inextricably linked to the lives of people thousands of miles away living in conditions that they perhaps could not even imagine. "What can we do?" they asked. "Isn't it better that we buy these clothes rather than boycott them? If we don't buy the clothes, then the declining sales will lead to the closing of garment factories and the people won't have any jobs at all. This way they at least have some kind of employment."

As I consider their responses today, I think about the role of literature. I am, after all, a teacher of literature, someone who revels in the rise and swoop of words, who can taste the sound of letters on her tongue and can grasp the shifting contours of topographies come alive in the stringing together of language. But there I was, teaching about labor, women's labor, the politics of global capital, the structural adjustment programs forced on Third World countries that borrow money from the World Bank and IMF. I had traveled, it seems, a long way from literature, a long way from the injunctions for good writing—solid grounding in place, deep roots in location.

Yet, questions of global capitalism are now routinely discussed by literary critics such as Rey Chow, Pheng Cheah, Bruce Robbins, and R. Radhakrishnan.[51] The discursive realm is continuously informed by the economic and the material. Given this reality, a literature as global in its reach as South Asian American writing can only be enriched by an understanding of the economic and political practices that link South Asia with the United States. Thus, an article such as the one about sweatshop workers in Bangladesh performs the critical function of unmooring the reader. It occurs to me that this is what I have been engaged in as a pedagogical practice: cutting students loose from whatever holds them in place and casting them out to wander. And in doing so, I hope I am making them better readers and writers of literature. As the United States is displaced from the center of their consciousness and conscience to make room for other regions of the globe, perhaps they will find in themselves a fierce desire to see those other places and other peoples with "kaleidoscope eyes." The writer of the South Asian diaspora, says Alexander, "is haunted by the radical nature of dislocation, not singular, but multiple, given the world as it comes to us now—not just in the dailiness of our lives, waking up, walking down a winter street, setting down 50¢ for a newspaper, but in the manifold figurations of knowledge, through CNN, faxes, E-mail, the visible buying and selling of multinational corporations, the invisible telephone lines that link New York with Delhi or Tiruvella."[52])

The Sheer Intoxication of Global Knowledge

In Chapter 1, I referred to Bruce Robbins's analysis of Michael Ondaatje's novel *The English Patient* as a paean to the pleasures of global knowledge, a knowledge that "is explicitly aligned with love and against nations."[53] I spoke of the eroticism of knowledge that transcends national boundaries. Amitav Ghosh's novel *The Calcutta Chromosome* (1995) exemplifies this eroticism of transnational knowledge. Spanning three periods (the late nineteenth century, 1995, and the early twenty-first century) and numerous locations (New York, Baltimore, Calcutta, Secunderabad, Renupur) Ghosh's novel tells a gripping story of the scientific discovery of how malaria gets transmitted. The novel doubles as a grand Victorian novel—with its vast cast of characters and plot twists—and a work of science fiction.

Following September 11, the discourse comparing the supposedly opposed civilizations of East and West seems to be confined to the domains of the cultural and the religious: modernity versus tradition, Islam versus Judeo-Christianity. In this context, *The Calcutta Chromosome* provides an alluring alternative by taking us into the realm of scientific inquiry. At the same time, it doesn't gloss over the impact of colonialism on questions of credit for scientific discovery. The cosmopolitanism and transnationalism of *The Calcutta Chromosome* manifest themselves as an intoxication with and a reveling in the collaboration of several individuals across different continents, all in pursuit of the answer to the problem of how malaria is transmitted.[54] The cast of characters is numerous: scientists working in the Johns Hopkins Medical Center labs in the late 1800s, British civil servants in the Indian Medical Service during late-nineteenth-century colonial rule in India, French scientists, and Indian lab assistants who have more insight into the scientific process than their colonial rulers. Interestingly, it is only in India that the effort involves a woman, and she emerges as the one who holds the key to how the discovery will eventually unfold. In Ghosh's telling of the tale, it is the Indian woman who orchestrates the moves of Ronald Ross, the Englishman who is ultimately credited with making the scientific breakthrough, for which he wins the Nobel Prize in 1902.

The narrative of the transnational links among scientists and the sometimes sequential and sometimes serendipitous movements toward the final objective is from time to time delivered in the breathless and excited voice of an Indian American man, Murugan, a self-appointed malaria expert and Ronald Ross enthusiast. Murugan's interest in the subject reaches its height in the latter part of the twentieth century— 1995, to be precise; he lives in the United States but asks his employer to send him to Calcutta, where Ross performed his final experiments in the late nineteenth century. Murugan claims to know everything there is to know about Ross's life for the five hundred days that he was focused on malaria research. I quote Murugan at some length to give the flavor of his dizzyingly rapid and excitable narration. He is explaining to Antar, the Egyptian American data processor who works for the same firm as Murugan, the circumstances under which Ross decided to take up malaria research:

There he is: he's at an age when most scientists start checking their pension funds; he knows sweet fuck all about malaria (or anything else); he's sitting out in the boonies somewhere where they never even heard of a lab; he hasn't set hands on a microscope since he left medical school; he's got a job in this dinky little outfit, the Indian Medical Service, which gets a couple of copies of *Lancet* and nothing else, . . . But our Ronnie doesn't give a shit: he gets out of bed one sunny day in Secunderabad or wherever and says to himself in his funny little English accent, "Dear me, I don't know what I'm going to do with myself today, think I'll go and solve the scientific puzzle of the century, kill a few hours." Never mind all the heavy hitters who're out there in the ballpark. Forget about Laveran, forget about Robert Koch, the German, who's just blown into town after doing a number on typhoid; forget about the Russian duo, Danilewsky and Romanowsky, who've been waltzing with this bug since when young Ronald was shitting himself in his crib; forget about the Italians who've got a whole goddam pasta factory working on malaria; forget about W. G. MacCallum out in Baltimore, who's skating on the edge of a real breakthrough . . . ; forget about the Italian government, the French government, the US government, who've all got a shit-load of money out there chasing malaria; forget about them all. They don't even see Ronnie coming until he's ready to stop the clocks.[55]

The volatility with which Murugan makes the links, follows inferences, and pursues leads provides the novel with its swirls and eddies as it
rushes between the 1800s, 1995, and the early twenty-first century. This
is a novel that combines mystery, science fiction, and a good old-
fashioned, highly satisfying ghost story. In characteristic Ghosh style, the
novel reveals the links among nations and peoples; the point is hard to
miss—what is of import in the world cannot be attributed to the efforts
of one nation or one person. Learning about malaria's transmission to
humans required the effort of many scientists, doctors, and ordinary citizens, even if they did not all know that they contributed to the discovery
for which Ross was ultimately honored. In *In an Antique Land*, Ghosh
shows us transnationalism and cosmopolitanism in the world of twelfth-
century trade (see Chapter 1); in *The Calcutta Chromosome*, we see the
same phenomena in the realm of scientific discovery and medicine.

In his most recent novel, *The Glass Palace* (2001), Ghosh provides a
panoramic view of the connections between South and Southeast Asia,
setting his novel in Burma (present-day Myanmar), Malaysia, and India,
and spanning a period from 1885 to 1996. *The Glass Palace* is a saga; it
begins with the British occupation of Burma and ends in Myanmar, more
than a hundred years later. Four generations of the family of Rajkumar
Raha feature in the narrative. Rajkumar is an orphaned Indian boy in
Burma when the book opens; the story follows his passion for a maid in
the Burmese queen's entourage; his pursuit of her to India where the king
and queen are in exile following the British takeover of Burma; his return
as a married man to Burma to set up a flourishing teak business; his purchase of a rubber plantation in Malaysia shortly before the outbreak of
World War I; and, finally, his return to India in his old age. Woven into this
narrative are the narratives of the Japanese invasion of Malaysia during
World War II and the Indian struggle for independence.

As a boy and, later, as a businessman, Rajkumar is advised and nur-
tured by Saya John, a part-Chinese businessman. Saya John reveals to
Rajkumar the complicated lives of people who have lived in many places
and are shaped by many influences. When Rajkumar, upon first meeting
Saya John, expresses surprise at Saya John's knowledge of Hindi, Saya
John explains:

> I learnt as a child, . . . for I am, like you, an orphan, a foundling. I
> was brought up by Catholic priests in a town called Malacca [in

Malaysia]. These men were from everywhere—Portugal, Macao, Goa. They gave me my name. . . . They spoke many languages, those priests, and from the Goans I learnt a few Indian words. When I was old enough to work I went to Singapore, where I was for a while an orderly in a military hospital. The soldiers there were mostly Indians, and they asked me this very question: how is that you, who look Chinese and carry a Christian name, can speak our language?[56]

The King of Burma, as his ship is getting ready to sail away to India where he will remain in exile, ponders the impact of the British empire on the peoples it colonizes and whose lives it uproots: "What vast, what incomprehensible power, to move people in such huge numbers from one place to another—emperors, kings, farmers, dockworkers, soldiers, coolies, policemen. Why? Why this furious movement—people taken from one place to another, to pull rickshaws, to sit blind in exile?" (43–44).

The Glass Palace is a rich novel in which the United States figures not at all. Rather, the United States exists on the sidelines, as the place in which Saya John's son Matthew finds his wife. One might wonder whether the work could even strictly be called South Asian *American*; Ghosh lives in New York, but does that fact alone warrant the inclusion of this novel in a discussion of South Asian American literature? This is not a novel that oscillates between the United States and other locations, or that shows the geopolitical relationship between the United States and other part(s) of the world. It is, as London-based writer Salil Tripathi says, a novel that links Burma, India, and Malaysia, a novel that makes visible histories that have hitherto remained unrecorded: "Of all the Indian experiences overseas, none is more harrowing than that of plantation workers. They were lured by promises of riches that were certainly not attainable in one lifetime. Mr. Ghosh recalls a saying common among Tamil plantation workers in Malaya: They believe that every rubber tree in Malaya is paid with an Indian life. Until now, virtually no one has dramatized their lives."[57]

While the novel has huge relevance to the British reading public as a view into the ramifications of its empire, what does it do for the American reading public? There is no definitive answer to that question. In the final analysis, one must return to the knowledge continuum that has Bruce Robbins at one end and Meena Alexander at the other. *The Glass Palace* can be seen as providing either the intoxication or the moral responsibility of knowledge. The novel itself may hold the clue to its value: Saya John reads in the *Straits Times* (published in Singapore) of the June 1914 assassination of the Grand Duke Franz Ferdinand in Sarajevo. He points the item out to his son, Matthew, and to Rajkumar. The narrator observes:

> No more than anyone else in the world did either of them have any inkling that the killing in Sarajevo would spark a world war. Nor did they know that rubber would be a vital strategic material in this conflict, that in Germany the discarding of materials made of rubber would become an offense punishable by law; that submarines would be sent overseas to smuggle rubber; that the commodity would come to be valued more than ever before, increasing their wealth [Matthew and Rajkumar's] beyond their most extravagant dreams. (173)

Whether for the sake of knowledge alone or for the purpose of understanding how our lives, unbeknownst to us, are always implicated in the lives and actions of others, reading about what lies outside the United States is a responsibility of citizenship, whether national or global.

For a Second Generation: The Faith of Passport, the Reality of Skin

Second-generation South Asian American author Sameer Parekh's first novel, *Stealing the Ambassador* (2002), is an engaging book, although unevenly so, that holds moments of quiet but penetrating insight. Parekh lays out many of the oppositions discussed in this chapter. The novel opens with a story of the narrator Rajiv's grandfather planning and carrying out the bombing of a railway bridge in British India. It closes with a letter written by Rajiv's father, a year or two after he arrives in the United States, to his father (the explosives expert) explaining why he wishes to stay a while longer in the United States even though he has completed his engineering degree and has several promising job offers from firms in India. This closing letter takes us back to the optimism and hope of the immigrant generation. In between these two ends of the novel, the narrative shifts skillfully from New Jersey to Gujarat in India, where the narrator has gone to visit his grandparents.

In the course of the novel, the father moves from an eager belief in the "magic" of the United States to a disillusionment with its racism. Rajiv, the U.S.-born child, however, will not believe that the problem lies with his birth country; instead he chooses to attribute the disconnectedness his father feels from the United States to his father's own ineptness. Gradually, Rajiv learns to see the truth of his father's bitter observation that "[y]our skin will always argue with your passport."[58] Ultimately, Rajiv acknowledges his confusion: "I'm unsure how to choose now, tomorrow, allegiances, nations, between loves which refuse to reconcile themselves" (270).

In the closing lines of his letter justifying his desire not to rush home to India right away, Rajiv's father writes: "When something remarkable does not happen in the laboratory, or in my classes, something magical occurs all the same. I know what you are thinking, that the novelty of the new is something that can only entertain for a short while. I know this. So let me stay in this place, let me take this job for two or three years, and when I find it has grown uninteresting, as you know it must, I will come home" (274). That Parekh ends with the father's voice, the immigrant's yearning for the United States, is revealing. It is as though, second generation though he is, he wishes to see anew with the eyes of a newcomer the promise of America. But he weaves in a caution. The juxtaposing of the "magical" with the "uninteresting" says it all. Although "uninteresting" is an innocuous word to describe the suddenness with which the United States can turn on its own residents, I would argue that it masks a deeper apprehension, one that the writer has chosen not to verbalize. Notice that "home" is elsewhere. Through Rajiv's father, Parekh has left the door open for a notion of home outside the United States. The insurance policy against rejection (see above) is in operation.

In the early nineteenth century, James Fenimore Cooper was writing a self-consciously American literature, an articulation that derived its images and themes from the New rather than the Old World. His tales of the American wilderness and the contact between the Native Americans and whites focused the imagination of Americans on scenes in their immediate rather than ancestral world. In the late nineteenth century, the American realism championed by William Dean Howells gave rise to authors who brought their imaginations to bear on the experience of a nation recovering from the Civil War and confronting the sudden rise of industrialism and material wealth and the corresponding expansion of commerce on a global scale. This was when the United States entered into world politics with the Spanish-American War and the subsequent colonization of the Philippines. In looking at the literature that flourished during this period, Thomas Peyser asks, "How did the pressures of globalization stimulate the formation of American national culture?"[59] In his view, globalism provided the impetus for Americans to ask the question, "Who are we?" because they found themselves becoming implicated in other territories among other peoples.

The same question remains today, a century later, both because the United States is now overtly and covertly involved in the economy, culture, and politics of many nations—Iraq, Israel, the Balkans, Korea, Japan, Mexico, India, Pakistan, and Malaysia, to name a few—and because it is logistically easier to live a global life and maintain a global consciousness, given the technological advances that have made possible the creation of transnational networks. Asian American literature poses the same question of Asians in the United States: Who are we? All Asians in the United States—first- through fifth-generation—must engage urgently with the question because the label "foreigner" is so readily applied to them, necessitating on their part a constant assessment of where they feel most at home and most welcome, and because they are enlisted to serve the interests of global capitalism—their foreigner status paradoxically marking them as particularly well equipped to bolster U.S. economic penetration of Asian markets and iron out cross-cultural management-labor interactions. Evelyn Hu-DeHart cautions Asian Americans to be alert to the ways in which they are used in this fashion.[60] Two writers of Indian origin—V. S. Naipaul and Meena Alexander—have titled their personal reflections *The Enigma of Arrival* (1988) and *The Shock of Arrival* (1996), respectively. Both writers ponder the meaning of their presence in their current physical locations—England and the United States, respectively—and speculate on the nature of their emotional belonging. Both words—"enigma" and "shock"—contain multiple connotative possibilities and confer on "arrival" a corresponding semantic ambiguity. The best that one could ask of a nuanced response to (South) Asian American literature is that it strive to spotlight and engage with the enigmas and shocks of arrivals and departures, and that it reject the seductive comfort of a localized and self-satisfied complacency.

THREE

Desire, Gender, and Sexuality

I N HER 1996 BOOK *The Invisibles: A Tale of the Eunuchs of India*, Zia Jaffrey explains her fascination for the Hijras (variously identified as eunuchs, cross-dressers, and hermaphrodites) of India, whom she encounters for the first time when they arrive as uninvited guests to a wedding she attends in Delhi:

> They were like the shadows and the critics of society. Everything about them suggested paradox; they were not men, nor were they women; they were not invited to perform, but neither were they uninvited; they carried the instruments of song, but made no pretense of being able to sing; they blessed the bride and groom, but through a stream of insults; they were considered a nuisance, even extortionists, and yet they were deemed lucky; they were paid not to perform, but to leave everyone in peace; they partook of the rights of passage that they themselves were incapable of—marriage and birth.[1]

Because it highlights the allure of paradox and indeterminacy, this passage serves as a useful starting point for a discussion of issues of gender and sexuality as they occupy the consciousness of South Asian American writers. Jaffrey revels in the contradictions of the Hijra community's position in the Indian social fabric and concedes that she may never understand the exact nature of their lives, sexual identities, sexual behavior, and whether they are to be considered victims or villains or both or neither. In contrast, the general Western view of South Asian gender and sexuality is overdetermined by Orientalist perceptions of women in non-Western cultures as occupying rigidly and prescriptively constructed lives with little opportunity for the exercise of individual desires. The related assumption is that everything to be known about South Asian sexuality is already visible, and that what one reads, hears, or sees is to be taken literally. Repressed women, domineering men, female feticide, loveless marriages, crude and unsophisticated sexual desire: the litany is fairly predictable.[2] Therefore, in this chapter, I seek to focus on those South Asian American texts that muddy the apparent transparency of representations of gender and sexuality—that make turbid the lens through which we read these matters of hetero- and homoerotic desire, sexism, patriarchy, feminism, identity, and marriage. I do not privilege obfuscation for the mere sake of intellectual puzzle-solving; rather, I resort to it in the hope that it will lead ultimately to an appreciation of the complex interplay of multiple forces in experiences involving sex, gender, and desire.

The preceding chapters have examined in different ways the diasporic construction of identity and selfhood. Jaffrey was born in the United States and raised here primarily; like many diasporic individuals and their descendants, she is keenly interested in learning about the social and cultural details of her ancestral country. (See Chapter 2 for a discussion of this impulse.) She stumbles upon the Hijras during a trip she makes to study ancient philosophy in India, keen "to travel invisibly, to see the country, to come to know it objectively, anonymously, without reliance on family, caste, or color."[3] Her unplanned interest in the Hijras causes her to reassess all of these aims, because she finds that she cannot begin to gather details about them without the help of many people. Her desire for invisibility, too, is thwarted: she is hypervisible for two reasons—as an obvious visitor from the United States and as an individual making inquiries about a group of people seldom discussed by Indians.

Her decision to research the Hijras seems to stem from a desire to create for herself a particular kind of Indian-ness and an equally particular kind of American-ness. That Jaffrey chooses to focus on a group of individuals who are rarely the subject of public discourse in India perhaps enables her to feel that she is revealing India to the Indians who live there, thus becoming the "familiar stranger" who can claim a legitimate space in the ancestral country because she has charted a certain unfamiliar territory within it. (See below for a similar impulse underlying Ginu Kamani's interviews of social workers who raise AIDS awareness within the MSM community.) Although Jaffrey's book is riddled with problems of representation (among the most annoying are the author's use of innovative spellings to render the Indian pronunciation of English and her judgment that the voices of some of the Hijras grate on her ears), it is valuable for what it reveals about one young woman's effort to see a facet of her ancestral homeland that is largely invisible. Details about the Hijra community emerge through a ricocheting of various perspectives—police officials, well-connected family friends, members of the Hijra enclaves who have chosen to leave, and the Hijras themselves.[4] As an American, Jaffrey feels that perhaps she can overturn some of the common assumptions that the West holds about sexuality and gender relations in South Asia; she can take pleasure in complicating a simplistic portrait and pride in having widened the perspective of her American compatriots.

The poet Lloyd Schwartz, in extolling the work of an up-and-coming fiction writer, notes, "He flirts with but ultimately avoids the cliché."[5] This assessment offers a fruitful way of thinking about the creative work of South Asian American writers in the territory of gender relations and sexuality. How do or *can* these writers avoid the trap and lure of clichéd portrayals of South Asian women and men? How do these writers work in a climate of such assumptions as "non-Western women are situated within cultural contexts that require their subordination"?[6] This type of idea has currency not only among Western audiences but also among non-Western audiences who have sought to erase the histories of feminist activism in their own cultures. Legal scholar Leti Volpp's meticulous objections to such a preconception reject binary modes of thinking that "identify sexual violence in immigrant of color and Third World communities as cultural, while failing to recognize the cultural aspects of sexual violence affecting mainstream white women" (1189). Volpp bases her critique on the foundational work of such feminist scholars as Inderpal Grewal, Caren Kaplan, and Chandra Talpade

Mohanty, and she cautions that by positioning "other" women as perennial victims, one "denies their potential to be understood as emancipatory subjects." Such an attitude also "diverts one's gaze from the sexism
indigenous to United States culture and politics" (1205). She exhorts
Western feminists "to examine the importance of Christian fundamentalism within the United States and its effect on the lives of millions of
women around the world through funding and development that structure reproductive practices and politics," noting that "President George
W. Bush, as the first substantive action of his presidency, . . . issued an
executive order barring United States aid for overseas programs that support abortion through surgery, counseling, or lobbying" (1207). As a legal
theorist, Volpp is well placed to demonstrate the reductiveness of law and
public policy in their treatment of immigrant groups and people of
color. Volpp's immersion in the writings of feminists of color and cultural
and literary theorists, particularly in the context of analyzing case law as
it relates to women, reminds us that the law is, after all, a type of text
requiring an exercise of interpretation. Her various articles drawing
attention to the intersections between mainstream U.S. perceptions of
immigrant cultures and case law illuminate the enormous gap in legal
practitioners' appreciation for the nuances and complexities of the experiences of immigrant communities of color, particularly the women.
Misapplications of the law are often preceded by superficial or erroneous
readings of complex realities.[7]

I do not wish to make any facile link between thoughtful and careful
reading of literary texts, on the one hand, and the appreciation of nuance
and complexity, on the other; nor will I rehearse here the argument I
made in Chapter 1 for the particular value of literary texts in a time of
sociopolitical crisis. I will note, however, that the writers discussed in this
chapter cover a wide range of depictions of South Asian American experiences of gender and sexuality. Therefore, in reading them I *encourage* a
suspension of quick judgment and perfunctory understanding. I emphasize "encourage," because no text can be guaranteed a reading that does
full justice to its many facets. One can merely hope for such an outcome.
As is my approach in other chapters, I do not offer an exhaustive study of
the authors featured here; the works I select are, in my opinion, best suit-
ed to represent the authors' boldness of vision and strategy. The challenges
of these texts are not located exclusively in questions of homosexual
desire or transgender/transsexual identity; they also challenge the more

conventional contexts of heterosocial relationships and family dynamics, and I address these areas as well. Finally, I also touch on embedded provocations that are insufficiently developed—that is, points in the text where the authors come close to following "safe" trajectories.

Inversions, Transformations, Re-creations

Shani Mootoo's disruptions of the categories of sexuality, nationality, and ethnicity are effected with humor, anger, and, at the same time, a deep sensitivity for her characters. The title of one of her short stories—"The Upside-Downness of the World as It Unfolds"—reveals the attitude that permeates her writing: question everything, take nothing for granted. Mootoo is an intriguing figure for a number of reasons, not the least of which is the pastiche of cultural influences that have shaped her as someone born in Ireland, raised in Trinidad, and resident in Canada since the age of nineteen. As of 2004, she was dividing her time between Vancouver, British Columbia, and Brooklyn, New York. Mootoo's experiences and writing span the Americas. She is poet, fiction writer, and visual artist. Her life, like her fiction, emphasizes the porosity of boundaries.

In Mootoo's novel *Cereus Blooms at Night*, a child, born as a girl, gradually "becomes" a boy and grows into adulthood believing himself to be a man, despite his female reproductive anatomy. Mootoo's disruption of gender boundaries is a principal component of her strategy to unsettle all easily accepted categories of understanding and experience. Hers is a formulation of the world that continuously loosens foundations and questions normativity. Her adventurous navigation of the controversial domain of gender and sexuality is characteristic of the challenge issued by South Asian American writers to restrictive constructions.

Lantanacamara, Mootoo's fictional island in the Caribbean, is a postcolonial location, like Trinidad, where Mootoo was raised. Trinidad's population comprises, for the most part, Africans, Indians (from India), Chinese, and Lebanese, with the two largest groups being the Afro and Indo Caribbeans. Indigenous peoples speaking the Carib and Arawakan languages lived there prior to the arrival of the Europeans in the fifteenth century. The Spaniards transported slaves from Africa to the Caribbean and other parts of South America to work on the sugarcane plantations. The British took control of Trinidad from the Spaniards in 1797 and, in the latter part of the nineteenth century, brought to the workforce indentured laborers from India and, in smaller numbers, from China. The colonial history of the Caribbean in the novel, however, comes to us in the context of missionary work and is focused almost exclusively on the Indo Caribbean community (a focus I discuss later). The novel is set in the town of Paradise, where Chandin Ramchandin, son of an Indian indentured laborer, is plucked from his household during his preadolescent years and groomed into being an Indian Christian who will carry the word of God to his people. Chandin experiences all the self-loathing and repulsion of his background that are symptomatic of emotional and mental colonization (a condition that Fanon so compellingly discusses in *Black Skin White Masks*). And yet, his change from a hopeful young man, eager and earnest to do what he has been trained for, to a raging, abusive husband and father is attributed not so much to the repercussions of colonial and racial subordination as it is to insecure masculinity. Chandin's wife, Sarah, like him selected from among the other young girls of the Indian laborer class to receive the benefits of a Christian and colonial education, elopes with Lavinia Thoroughly, the daughter of the missionary couple by whom both Chandin and Sarah were selected to be introduced to the missionary life. Lesbian desire explodes into Chandin's life, disrupting his plans for the future and dismantling his home. His descent into cruelty—particularly his sexual abuse of his two daughters, Mala and Asha—takes place with amazing rapidity.

Mootoo is unrelenting in her portrayal of Chandin. Moreover, she offers no alternative model of positive masculinity outside the realm of homosocial desire. Ambrose Mohanty, the man in whom Mala becomes interested, emerges briefly as the promise of a caring and sensitive male figure. But his development in that direction stops when he is unable to get past the revulsion he feels on discovering that Mala has been sexually abused by her father. At the moment of his failure of purpose—the very moment at which Mala most needs his trust and support—Ambrose is overcome by a "feeling shame for her and for himself—as though he had been betrayed by Mala, and at the same time wrestling with the notion that she could not possibly, not conceivably have been agreeable to intimacies with her father. In that instant of hesitation he so distanced himself from Mala that, like an outside observer, he saw the world as he had known and dreamed it suddenly come undone" (227–28). This terrible act of incestuous sexual abuse haunts the novel's time-present, and the overgrown dilapidated rotting structure of the Ramchandin house embodies the horrific mystery at its core. The home as the site of belonging and stability is particularly laden with meaning for the displaced or diasporic individual. The home at the center of this novel is a trap, not a haven; perhaps Mootoo warns us against the too ready allure of home as the site of comfort and refuge. The Ramchandin abode takes on the dimensions of a gothic dwelling of horrors, but unlike the gothic convention that plays with exaggerated horrors for the purposes of titillation, this home is the site of searing pain.[8]

Against this backdrop, Mootoo posits a homosocial and homoerotic alternate reality. The narrator, Tyler, who unfolds the story of Mala Ramchandin—now a demented and aging woman ordered by the court to be moved to the Paradise Alms House, in which the narrator works as a nurse—weaves in the expression of his homosexuality. Although there is the usual tittering by the other employees of the Paradise Alms House at the narrator's "difference," there is also a kind of "live-and-let-live" attitude about his kind of desire. Undoubtedly, such an ethos can be attributed in no small part to the narrator's presentation of Lantanacamara as a place hospitable to, even encouraging of, homo-eroticism and transgendered identities. It is in this context that the story of Otoh Mohanty emerges, and it is here that Mootoo displays in full measure her engagement with the task of interrogating even the biological category of sex.

Otoh Mohanty is born a girl—Ambrosia. We learn that "[b]y the time Ambrosia was five, her parents were embroiled in their marital problems to the exclusion of all else, including their child. They hardly noticed that their daughter was transforming herself into their son" (109). Over time, "[h]ours of mind-dulling exercise streamlined Ambrosia into an angular, hard-bodied creature and tampered with the flow of whatever hormonal juices defined him." The transformation from female to male is so perfect "that even the nurse and doctor who attended the birth, on seeing him later, marvelled at their carelessness in having declared him a girl" (110).

As if this transgendered transformation were not sufficient to mark Ambrosia as a noteworthy character, Mootoo invests him with yet another significant quality:

Ambrosia's obviously vivid imagination gave him both the ability to imagine many sides of a dilemma (and if it weren't already a dilemma, of turning it into one) and the vexing inability to make up his mind. Ever since the days of early high school, where he excelled in thinking but not in doing, this trait of weighing "on the one hand" with "but on the other" earned him a name change. He began, though through no choice of his own, to be called Otoh-boto, shortened in time to Otoh, a nickname to which he still answered. (110)

Perhaps not surprisingly, given Mootoo's vision for the novel, Otoh's "vexing inability to make up his mind" is not, ultimately, rendered as a shortcoming. In fact, Otoh is the only character in the book who displays the moral courage to save Mala from imprisonment or worse. The reader is given every reason to believe that he destroys the evidence that would have mistakenly labeled Mala a murderer, when in fact she had been defending herself from unimaginable abuse. Perhaps we are meant to understand that Otoh's tendency to weigh multiple sides of an issue, while contributing to "a vexing inability to make up his mind" on most occasions, may in fact be that component of his character that, at critical moments, reinforces his actions with the inner core of ethical responsibility.

Otoh is a nexus of opposites: Mootoo (through her narrator) celebrates his ability to examine opposing sides of an issue and thereby refrain from unthinking action; his embodiment of sexual duality is also presented not as an aberration but as a normal phenomenon. In the process, Lantanacamara becomes the radical site of fluid categories, a place where the unfixable is accepted and accommodated with idyllic casualness. Otoh's mother, Elsie, declares that his situation is not unusual and urges him to consider carefully before he commits to his female lover Mavis, who wishes to marry him. Elsie's advice to him that he take the time to decide whether to choose a man or a woman as a sexual partner is astonishing, given that she has exhibited no other extraordinary characteristics. That so ordinary a person should hold such unexpectedly radical views is what marks Lantanacamara as an unusually hospitable place for those who occupy no comfortable categories of sexual identity.[9] Elsie declares,

[E]very village in this place have a handful of people like you. And it is not easy to tell who is who. How many people here know about

you, eh? I does watch over the banister and wonder if who I see is
really what I see. Look here, what I want to ask you is, you sure
Mavis is a woman? I not asking you to tell me your business, but I
just want as a mother to advise you to make sure she is what you
want. Is a woman you want? . . . What you want? In a case like yours,
you just have to know, careful-careful, what you really want. (238)

Elsie further normalizes her son's situation by equating it with a recognizable and commonly occurring motivation: "almost everybody in
this place wish they could be somebody or something else. That is the
story of life here in Lantanacamara" (238).

One could argue that Tyler, the narrator, is not to be trusted, that he
would have reason to present Lantanacamara as accepting of homoeroticism and transsexual identities. The very rarity of such an attitude of tolerance gives to the setting an element of fantasy. However, there is also
this to consider: Lantanacamara is home to a terrible secret—the abuse
suffered by Mala at her father's hands and the repercussions of that abuse.
At the center of the novel, the cruelty of Chandin Ramchandin underscores that the town of Paradise is no paradise. Yet, the fire which burns
down the Ramchandin house, and along with it Chandin's remains,
seems to mark a break from the horrific past and the promise of a future
on the island that will by and large be welcoming and inclusive of all
types of desire. The final pages are explicit in their anticipation of a
meaningful relationship between Tyler and Otoh Mohanty, who, one
must assume, has taken his mother's advice to consider carefully his
choice of mate and has decided that he doesn't want a woman but a
man. Tyler's narration of that moment is packed with sensual detail. Otoh
has just been planting cuttings of the cereus flower on the grounds of the
Paradise Alms House. Tyler says,

When he stood up, I reached over to brush the soil off the knees of
his pants. I felt the form of his shapely leg and when be braced himself, I heard him catch his breath. He too was stirring. I got up, my
legs unstable, and walked as best I could throughout the garden,
picking a bouquet of shrimp bush, lilac, rose bay and flame ixora. I
presented the arrangement to Otty. He deliberately cupped my
hands and held them to his chest. With practised elegance I mois-
tened my lips and continued to stare at him. (248)

Otoh and Tyler, Ambrose Mohanty and Mala Ramchandin: the one pair is young, the other old. Ambrose and Mala are reunited only in their old age and as a result of Otoh's and Tyler's actions. Mootoo is perhaps suggesting that heterosexuality discourages the taking of risks and through its in-built attitude of caution inhibits the timely seizing of opportunities for pleasure and fulfillment. I don't mean to polarize heterosexuality and homosexuality at opposite ends of the continuum of caution and daring. However, there is a decided difference between how boldly Sarah Ramchandin and Lavinia Thoroughly seize their moment of opportunity despite the tremendous odds against them and the reluctance Ambrose displays to support Mala in her moment of greatest need. Ambrose has frittered away the best part of his life unable to be with Mala because of his inability at a critical moment to get past the hesitation he felt when he wondered "if and how to get help, . . . [and] thought that a call for help would expose the shameful goings-on in the house, to which he had become connected" (228). Even when the discovery of Chandin's skeleton threatens Mala with imprisonment, Ambrose cannot bring himself to act. Otoh is exasperated at his father's lack of resolve: "Why don't you do something? You just going to let them take she so?" (187), he demands of his father. In the end, it is Otoh who decisively sets fire to the house and so burns the evidence that most certainly would have convicted Mala. When it matters, Otoh, despite his name, does not vacillate. The same determination informs his relationship with Tyler. Otoh and Tyler plunge into their desire for each other, and one expects that they will spend many fruitful years in exploring and developing their relationship. Transsexualism and homoeroticism provide in this novel the milieu of stability and normalcy, the spirit of ethical compassion.

Mootoo might be faulted for portraying sex change as easily and painlessly achieved. Anne Fausto-Sterling, Dierdre McCloskey, Diep Khan Tran, Sheila Kirk, and other researchers, doctors, and individuals who have contemplated or undergone sex-change operations have recorded the deep emotional conflict attending the process— including the feeling of dissatisfaction of being in one's body, the constant emotional despair of knowing that one has been socialized into the wrong gender, the fear of making known one's desire for a sex change, surgical procedures, the hormonal regimen that must be strictly followed, and all the postoperative physiological and psychological trauma.[10] Otoh's breezily simple transformation might even be considered a trivialization of the process. By contrast, Mootoo's presentation in the novel of Chandin's change from Hindu brown-skinned boy to Christian brown-skinned boy desperately imitating and attempting to please his white missionary foster family is imbued with deep pain.[11] That these two transformations should be so differently rendered is, admittedly, curious. Perhaps Mootoo wishes to suggest that Chandin's transformation is forced, not self-initiated, and therefore can never be free from pain; Otoh's, on the other hand, is motivated by inner desire and is, therefore, ultimately pleasurable. Nevertheless, Mootoo's oeuvre as a whole presents no simplistic oppositions. She does not offer an outright disparagement of heterosexuality or a blanket condemnation of maleness. She provides, instead, a thoughtful examination of the shifting dynamics in situations where concerns of gender and sexuality predominate.

Cereus is curiously silent about the African presence. Given the parallel histories of the Indians and Africans in Trinidad and other parts of the Caribbean, the absence of black characters in Lantanacamara cries out for explanation. Anthropologist Viranjani Munasinghe, literary critic Shalini Puri, and historian Vijay Prashad, among others, discuss the tensions between and intersections of the Afro and Indo Trinidadian communities.[12] Puri, in particular, focuses on the figure of the "dougla," the multiracial person of African and Indian parentage. The dougla is seen by the Indian and African orthodoxies as the dangerous site of sexual and racial mingling. (The fear is less pronounced in the Afro Trinidadian community, which, as all three writers point out, is not as concerned with cultural and racial purity as is the Indo Trinidadian community. This difference in attitude toward cultural and racial preservation is historically determined—grounded in strategies of division orchestrated by the British colonizers—and is also an outgrowth of "Hindu notions of caste endogamy."[13]) Precisely because the figure of the dougla arouses such anxiety around issues of sexuality and racial intermingling, Puri believes that it serves as the potential site for "the disruption of notions of racial purity . . . , and a dougla poetics could provide a vocabulary for disallowed racial identities," offering a way to reframe race and gender relations.[14] Mootoo's reframing encompasses gender and sexuality, not race. One could argue that an exclusive focus on sexuality is not in itself problematic. However, in the context of Indo and Afro Trinidadian relations, where sexuality is so intertwined with race, Mootoo's lack of

attention to race raises the question of whether her project of challenging sexual categories is compromised. The novel is compelling in its
characterization, plotting, and thematic treatment of gender/sexuality.
Perhaps Mootoo's tightly constructed field of action is less a failing or
oversight on her part than a decision to offer us a zoom shot rather than
a wide-angle perspective.

By contrast, one of her most delightful short stories—"Out on Main
Street"—places sexuality within a broader canvas.[15] I have written elsewhere about this story, calling attention to its exposure of the heterosexism of diasporic South Asian communities and their preoccupation
with authentic identities.[16] Mootoo undercuts all restrictive sentiments
through her wry narrator—a lesbian from Trinidad, now living in
Canada—whose utterances spare no one: not the Indian Trinidadians
who hunger for connection to their 150-year-old Indian roots, adhering
to the customs and traditions without fully understanding their significance (and the narrator doesn't exempt herself from this shortcoming);
not the Indian Canadians smug in their sense of themselves as genuine
Indians because they speak one or more Indian language and know the
specific names of various Indian desserts; not the heterosexual Indian
Canadian women who disapprove of the lesbians in their community;
not herself, for being possessive about her partner, Janet, and reacting
with exaggerated jealousy when a man finds Janet attractive and gives
her his attention.

In this piece, Mootoo succeeds in unsettling her readers' orientations
and creating a fluid and continuously unpredictable topography of com-
prehension. Part of the reason that the narrator is so effective is that she
faithfully records the flux of emotions she experiences, following the
swerves and curves of her changing feelings with seeming abandon.
"Going for a outing with mih Janet on Main Street ain't easy!" (48), the
narrator declares. It isn't easy because she must negotiate the maelstrom
of emotions she knows she will experience—potential embarrassment at
Janet's using the wrong term for Indian desserts; the narrator's fragile
sense of being an authentic or genuine Indian shattered by the smug
Indians on Main Street; the jealousy she expects to feel when men ogle
the seductively clad Janet; and the delight she takes in her disruption of
their comfort, evident in her description of their reaction to her: "And
den is a whole other story when dey see me with mih crew cut and mih
blue jeans tuck inside mih jim-boots. Walking next to Janet, who so

femme dat she redundant, tend to make me look like a gender dey forget to classify" (48). The mischief in her tone is endearing rather than malicious or sinister. We're swept along with her narrative because she has a sense of humor about herself, in addition to her good-natured ridiculing of the heterosexist world: "[D]e women dem embarrass fuh so to watch me in mih eye, like dey fraid I will jump up and try to kiss dem, or make a pass at dem. Yuh know, sometimes, I wonder if I ain't mad enough to do it just for a little bacchanal, nah!" (48).

The story begins with a question: "Janet and me?" (45). The narrative that follows this question could be read in one of three ways: (a) as the answer to the implicit question, "Do you want to know about Janet and me?" (b) as providing the clues to solving the puzzle—"Let's see if you understand about Janet and me"—implied in the opening question; or (c) as a challenge the narrator sets herself: "Will I be able to tell the story of Janet and myself?" The story she tells is wide ranging. It begins with a quick history of the Indo-Trinidadian experience of diaspora under colonial rule and the conversion to Christianity of many members of the community. From there, it moves to Canada and engages the issue of authenticity—that is, Who is the real Indian? It offers a glimpse into the daily challenges of discrimination endured by the Indian Canadian community. And finally it comments on the heterosexism of diasporic Indian communities. It is as though Mootoo wishes to underscore that the story of two Indo-Trinidadian Canadian lesbians is not just the narrowly defined narrative of their personal relationship, but also a narrative that encompasses many diverse forces. Thus, desire is not just personal; it is shaped in myriad ways by the world around it.

Desire Monger

Desire as complicated by social and cultural forces: this is the terrain of Ginu Kamani, who describes herself, somewhat in jest, as a "desire monger."[17] Her writings are marked by the simultaneous foregrounding of desire and the sociocultural world in which it occurs. Using as springboard a publisher's explanation for rejecting one of her stories, Kamani articulates the distinction she makes between desire in the American (Western) world and in the South Asian world. The publisher in question (specializing in erotica) wrote that although she was "enthusiastic" about Kamani's writing, she didn't think that it followed "the well-defined erotic formula of seduction–climax–denouement." Kamani continues, "She also hinted strongly that there were too many family members crowding my stories, and that I'd do better concentrating on the lovers alone." In response, Kamani arrives at the following conclusion: "In American culture, individual sexuality has now evolved to a place where, more often than not, the desirable ideal of sexuality is opposed to pleasure-less repression. But in other cultures, including South Asian, individual sexuality is still rigorously opposed to family control, and pleasure/repression are tertiary topics at best."[18]

At first blush, Kamani's statement may seem to essentialize both American and South Asian cultures and confirm the mainstream impression that in non-Western cultures women are forbidden from expressing sexual desire for pleasure alone. But Kamani's stories offer no such predictable scenarios. Her women do not wallow in the misery of repression. Rather, her writing is distinguished by the presence of feisty women on the verge of entering or actively exploring sexuality. Anger, too, is abundant. Kamani observes, "At some level, perhaps all of us are better equipped to deal with women resigned to their misery, ensconced in silent suffering, rather than those who show their anger without remorse."[19] Writing beyond this expectation and zone of security, Kamani treats with compelling effect the anger seething in Daya, the protagonist of her story "Just Between Indians."

Daya wishes to isolate herself from the irritating and interfering Indians who seem always to intrude into her life in attempts to find her a marriage partner. Her frustration at the lack of respect for her privacy echoes the publisher's reaction that "too many family members crowd" Kamani's stories. While Kamani is sympathetic to Daya's need to distance herself from unwanted family attention and gives ample play to the expression of her sexual desire, she does not allow Daya the satisfaction of feeling that the interfering community is categorically to be disdained. Part of this story's genius lies in its skillful juxtaposing of Daya's anger against the equally complicated and unresolved emotions of its two other protagonists: the brothers Ranjan and Sahil, who are trying to exorcise the painful memory of their mother's suicide. Daya is continuously shown to be reductive in her responses to the two brothers, because she cannot see past her own summary dismissal of all Indian men. For instance, she accuses Ranjan of seeking a marriage partner simply to fulfill his sexual desire in a socially accepted fashion:

> "Your brother tells me you want to marry. Why? . . . Why don't you just pay a prostitute?"

> Ranjan stared unhappily at his empty plate. "That's cruel. . . . I was actually engaged for quite a while. I loved her. But . . . she changed her mind. Terrible mess, actually. So I'm . . . I'm forced to look again."[20]

In her cruelty, Daya appears as a child, unable to modulate her emotions, unable to think beyond herself. And yet, the story's structure provides her this space. It is as though in some way Kamani concedes the truth of the notion that self-centeredness is essential to the exploration and fulfillment of sexual desire.

Ultimately, however, Daya is the victim of her own self-absorption. In a brilliant and startling conflation of thanatos and eros, Kamani forces upon Daya the realization that the bed on which she so ardently and satisfyingly has made love to Sahil is the same one in which his mother committed suicide many years ago. Predictably, Daya, believing herself to be the victim of a cruel joke, is enraged that she has been made to endure such gross manipulation. Her first reaction is to throw the equivalent of a temper tantrum and try to telephone her mother. Later, however, riding a bus in Manhattan, she shifts to grief and finally to understanding:

> *How many women had been condemned to that bed?* Daya felt numb with grief. She waited for the familiar anger to rise through her once again, but the memories of the previous night were still locked in her groin, glowing like coals. . . . She felt his gentle hands on her face. And it was then that she understood. He'd had to do it. In some strange way, it had broken the spell that hung over him. (181)

A word of caution here. It is easy to read this passage as Kamani's capitulation to the image of the empathetic female or as the wayward Daya finally returning to the essentialized sensitivity of her gender. And such a danger would be strong were it not for two things that mitigate (though not entirely dispel) it: one, Kamani's use of the fairy tale convention in the phrase "broken the spell" serves not to reinforce the image of the helpless and passive female (which Daya certainly is not), but precisely to invert such a construction. It is Daya who has broken the spell in whose thrall Sahil has been held. And though one could argue that Sahil has used her for his own ends, Daya's real pleasure in the sex they share makes it difficult to read her as a mere instrument of Sahil's desire. *Her* desire is equally instrumental in initiating their lovemaking.

Perhaps the only way to do justice to the complexity of what takes place on that bed is to see it as an instance of mutual manipulation. Sahil, one could argue, is released from the spell of his mother's death at the same time that Daya is released from her imprisonment within self-absorbed anger. They have both enjoyed their sexual union, and now they are both free from whatever held them captive. Desire, in this instance, has not turned them toward an immersion in each other; rather, it has enabled them to move outward, to embrace the world beyond their bodies and their emotional preoccupations.

The story closes with the joyous image of an exuberant hot dog vendor who insists on trying to identify Daya's nationality: "You are Greek? . . . Armenian? Turkish? Palestinian? . . . You are Lebanese? Egyptian? Iraqi? Come, come, I feed you!" (181–82). Feed her he does, with his reminder that there is a rich world outside herself of which she is a part—a world teeming with a multitude of peoples. She responds to the vendor's final peremptory question—"Woman, . . . where are you from?"—by saying, "Isn't it *obvious* that I'm Indian?" (182), thereby indicating that she no longer feels it necessary to isolate herself from her ethno-national community, that she can comfortably claim membership in it. Note, however, that this realization of her identity comes in the chance encounter with a complete stranger, a person who offers her an abundance of nationalities to claim as her own. Daya's willingness to declare herself Indian perhaps startles even herself, because it is an identification she has actively avoided in the past. The hot dog vendor, who emerges suddenly at the close of the story, completes Daya's re-entry into the world outside herself. Kamani has effected a delicate balance between sexual desire and community belonging, and has shown the multiple facets of an angry South Asian woman.

Kamani's tendency to "flirt[ ] with but ultimately avoid[ ] the cliché" is once again evident in a curious and illustrative piece titled "The Goddess of Sleep." In this story, as in "Just Between Indians," she juxtaposes sensuality and sexual expression with death/sleep. It's a curious text because Kamani comes dangerously close to exoticizing and romanticizing the poverty of street life in the cities of India. It's illustrative because in this extremely short story she continues her insistence that a person's sexual desire cannot be separated from the messiness of living. Steven, a white American, is fascinated by his Indian lover's capacity to fall blissfully asleep even amidst chaos and noise: "She was a genius at sleep. In her own bed she excelled at slumber, but even in unfamiliar locations she rested peacefully, suffering marginally if at all. He marveled at this uncanny ability to surrender her body to the abyss."[21] Visiting India with her, he finds an entire nation skilled at the art of sleeping: "On the pavements outside where taxi drivers pushed and shoved for access to passengers, prone bodies lay dissolved in rhythmic breathing, oblivious to those stepping over them. The uncomplicated abundance of sleep brought hot tears of envy to his eyes." His lover explains, "We're trained in this kind of chaos. We have no choice but to make lullabies of this vitality" (261). Ultimately, Steven leaves his lover, seduced by the world outside:

> He felt a yearning to lose himself in the dense crowds, to be ogled by the dark-eyed stares and the impulsive reaching for his skin. He liked the sensation of locking his gaze with every passing individual, of being endlessly consumed by the quizzical masses, of emotionally recharging through the powerful call and response expressed in a look, in a smile, in a posture that invited "Show Me." (263)

This passage is both perceptive and problematic. Through the sensuality of her description of Steven's experience of a crowded Indian city, Kamani expands our understanding of desire. It is not only what one might feel for a single other being—the need to meld one's body with that chosen other—but also a need one feels to be entwined with all humanity, to experience the sensuality of contact with multitudes of people. Certainly, it is not at all uncommon to hear visitors from South Asia yearn, after having had their fill of the peace and quiet of the suburban United States, for the hustle and bustle of the urban streets of their home countries, to feel connected to other human beings. In a larger context, one might speak of the allure of urban geographies, the ways in which they serve the basic human need to belong even as they hold within them the potential to become spaces of alienation.[22] The seductiveness of the urban street that Kamani describes is in marked contrast to the fear and loathing expressed by modernist architects such as Le Corbusier, who observed in 1930 that "the street wears us out. When all is said and done, we have to admit it disgusts us."[23] Le Corbusier's perspective was challenged by Dr. Maurice de Fleury, who, writing in the same journal in which Le Corbusier expounded his vision of a new Paris, rejected the connection between urban life and pathological emotional disorders. De Fleury asserted about the city and its streets that "[t]hese external stimuli, which from all sides assail us, are like a bath of vital energy. They play for us, at our behest, the beneficent role of military music which relieves the step of the tired soldier, or the orchestra whose rhythmic accents unleash the muscular strength of dancers. Let us not fear urban life too much."[24]

Kamani sensualizes the city street. This is a text that intertwines desire and the body in the urban landscape; in this sense, it re-creates the shift that Anthony Vidler traces from a nineteenth-century notion of space as an a priori entity, independent of the mind's apprehension of it, to a twentieth-century entanglement of space with emotion, in which space became a "psychical internalization."[25] In "The Goddess of Sleep," Steven is rejuvenated by the crowds of the city:

> Dark eyes twinkled and flashed, hands touched him casually, ascertaining his corporeal nature. A feeling of deep benevolence descended on the American as he fielded inquiries on a vast array of topics. Even as he spoke, individuals thrust out their hands to be shaken, savoring the feel of having gone palm to palm with him. Others ran fingers down the crease of his pants and over the fine leather artistry of his Italian shoes. The crowd closed in on him with effortless coagulation. His skin tingled with waves of contact. His body filled with unfathomable well-being. (262)

The multitude of bodies in Kamani's story, one should note, "come alive" at night. While Steven's lover sleeps deeply, the crowds outside move. One could speculate that Steven transfers his desire for the body of his lover onto the bodies in the crowd. The crowd consumes him even as he longs to be consumed by it, engulfed in its collective desire for him. However, it is critical to keep in mind that the story unfolds from Steven's perspective; thus, the perception of the crowd's desire for him most likely stems from his own sense of difference as an outsider, his own desirability as the Other. In the words "individuals . . . savoring the feel of having gone palm to palm with him" and "[o]thers ran fingers down the crease of his pants," one is perhaps made to see how Steven projects onto those in the crowd his own tendency to objectify the Other.

There is a certain voyeuristic quality to Steven's longing for the crowd, and herein lies the one problem of this story. Kamani's lack of ironic distance from Steven's longing for the contact of street life is risky in that it subordinates the realities and exigencies of the street dwellers' lives to Steven's need for spiritual rejuvenation. It brings Kamani to teeter on the precipice of Western romanticization of the material harshness of poverty and survival. Arjun Appardurai's description of the deprivation of Mumbai street dwellers provides a necessary counterpart to Steven's perception of the crowd (Kamani spends considerable amounts of time in Mumbai); at the same time, Appadurai offers a glimpse into the particular allure of sleep when he notes that for the street dwellers "home is anywhere you can sleep. And sleep is in fact the sole form of secure being. It is one of the few states in which—though usually entirely in public—there is respite from work, from harassment, from eviction. Sleeping bodies are to be found everywhere in Bombay and indeed at all times. . . . Public sleeping is a technique of necessity for those who can be at home only in their bodies."[26]

It is not unequivocally clear, however, that Kamani slips down the precipice of romanticizing the crowds on the street. The closing lines of the story read: "Steven gazed a long last time at his sleeping Goddess and knew that this was no longer where he belonged. He got up and slipped out the doors and into the beckoning human stream" (263). That Steven rejects his *Goddess* (an exoticized and deified image of the non-Western woman) for the human stream suggests that he will probably avoid a reductive and worshipful relationship with the unfamiliar world outside. Thus, although Kamani comes dangerously close to suggesting that the crowded and noisy Indian streets are spaces of spiritual renewal, one could say with some justification that she ultimately stops short of such a problematic construction.

Kamani is a bold explorer of the realm of desire. She is constantly challenging herself to enter, both literally and metaphorically, complicated spaces of sensuality. One of her most adventurous texts is a play that she co-authored with Filipino American writer Joel Barraquiel Tan. Titled "The Cure" (Kamani has also written an unrelated short story by the same title), this play deals with the dark humor employed by caregivers working with HIV-infected populations and AIDS patients. Michele Janette observed that a staged reading of the play at the Kansas State University on March 7, 2001, left members of the audience almost speechless, so radical is the play's use of humor and shock in the context of AIDS.[27]

As part of her exploration of desire both in the United States and India, Kamani collected hundreds of hours of interviews with non-governmental organization (NGO) workers in India who discuss sexual health issues with homosexual men. Kamani's article in *MAN'S World* fulfills several functions. First, like Jaffrey's study of the Hijra community, it discloses a hidden portion of Indian society and in doing so lays bare for readers in India a hitherto unknown aspect of their national sexual landscape. Second, it celebrates NGOs in India that do critical work in the face of enormous governmental obstacles. Third, in pointing out that the most visible of these NGOs is led by a woman, the article calls attention to the resourcefulness and progressive health politics of South Asian women. Fourth, the knowledge that Kamani gains from her interviews enriches the comparative framework within which she understands the challenges that AIDS social workers face in the United States. Finally, Kamani learns to question the applicability of Western terminologies of same-sex desire to individuals in South Asia and those of South Asian descent in the United States. (That such interrogation is critical was made evident to me in a discussion that followed a performance of three plays on homosexuality in India, staged at Wellesley College in April 2003. Several South Asian Americans both in the audience and among the cast observed that they were uncomfortable with the imposition of Western words such as "lesbian," "butch," and "dyke" to characterize their behavior.) I include a lengthy excerpt from Kamani's interview of one of the sexual health workers, Anjali Gopalan, in India, to show the depth of Kamani's engagement with the difficult forces surrounding the expression of certain kinds of desire:

An early experience doing MSM [men having sex with men] outreach work taught Gopalan an invaluable lesson: "I used to meet a
very macho, masculine-looking, 6'4" man every Sunday in the park.
After I got to know him, I said it must be hard for him to be homosexual. He jumped up saying, 'Do I look like a *chhukka* to you? What
proof do you want of my maleness? My wife has just given birth to
a son. What more do you want?' Then he continued: 'What is a
man? A man is someone who is not a woman. *Aurat na-mard hai.* [A
woman is someone who is not a man] *Aurat ko kya kiya jata hai?*
[What is done to a woman?] *Aurat ki to li jati hai.* [The woman gets
taken] *Mein jab yaahan aata hoon, mein ladkon ka sirf leta hoon.* [When
I come here, I'm only taking the boys] *Ladkon ka leta hoon, woh na-
mard hai, isliye aurat hain.* [I'm taking from the boys, who're not men,
therefore they're women]' I thought, Oh dear, no wonder prevention is not working. How on earth could I have imagined in my
wildest dreams that a man who is actually having sex with a boy, is
rationalizing by saying that this is a woman."[28]

Gopalan learns that her outreach will succeed only if she is able to
rethink her assumptions about the language surrounding same-sex
desire. Because outreach is critical to prevention and cure of AIDS and
other sexually transmitted diseases, Gopalan underscores the importance
of keeping one's categories of knowledge fluid. "Prevention cannot happen if people don't feel good about themselves, if they don't feel accepted," she says.[29] The man quoted above could only be reached once
Gopalan accepted his language of self-affirmation and then began to
work from there.

Kamani's writing challenges readers to move out of the comfort
zone. There are two principal reasons for paying attention to her. First,
in her "mission" to uncover the interstices of desire, Kamani is able to
portray with sensitivity the complications of each person's position. In
the passage above, for example, she is attentive both to the sexual health
worker and to the "client" with whom the worker is attempting to make
contact. Second, her interest in desire is also always an interest in the
social and cultural forces affecting the manifestation of desire in any
given time and place. The erotic is wrested out of the realm of the private and placed within the domain of the public.

Sexual Awakening and Ethnonational Identity

The same could be said of the Sri Lankan Canadian author Shyam
Selvadurai's debut novel *Funny Boy* (1994), which offers a skillful
entwining of sexuality and national politics. His novel is set in Sri Lanka,
in the years preceding the 1983 riots that mark the onset of the civil war
between the minority Tamils and the majority Sinhalese. Sri Lanka has
been very much in the news since the United States' declaration of global war on terrorism, and much has been made of the Tamil Tigers' superior skills in terrorist tactics. Selvadurai's principal focus in the novel is
on young Arjie (Arjun) Chelvaratnam, an adolescent upper-class Tamil
boy on the verge of becoming conscious of his sexual orientation. Arjie
is known to be "funny," to prefer the games of girls, in fact to demand
to dress as the bride in one such game. The engaging Arjie constructs a
retrospective narrative, looking back as an adult at his childhood and
youth. He weaves a rich backdrop of the ethnic and political tensions
prevalent in Sri Lanka such that the linear movement of the narrative,
which traces Arjie's growth from ages seven to fourteen, is illuminated
by the complex sociopolitical milieu of the nation. For instance, by getting involved in his aunt Radha's trysts with her Sinhala lover, Arjie
begins to understand the near impossibility of making a cross-ethnic
romantic alliance; he realizes the danger of the hostilities between the
Tamils and the Sinhalese when his mother's lover, Daryl, is killed while
investigating reports of torture and terror in Jaffna; and he is shaken into
acknowledging the influence of the Tamil Tigers when he learns that
Jegan, the supervisor of his father's hotel, once belonged to the separatist
group. Of the children in the family, Arjie appears to have been the closest to Radha Aunty, Daryl, and Jegan: he is Radha Aunty's and Jegan's
confidant and his mother's companion in her visits to Daryl. One could
conclude, therefore, that his political education occurs in the context of
intimate relationships.

The novel's most compelling juxtaposition of politics and sexuality
occurs at the boys' school, Victoria Academy, where Arjie's father sends
him to begin ninth grade in the hope that he will develop into a "regular"
boy. It is here that Arjie becomes fully conscious of his sexuality when he
makes friends with Shehan, and it is here as well that he takes an overtly political stand. The principal of Victoria Academy, Abeysinghe, is
engaged in a dispute with the vice principal, Lokubandara. The vice

principal is a political appointee and therefore has more power than the principal, who is popularly known by the boys as "Black Tie." Lokubandara wants to change the name of the school from Victoria Academy, with its reminder of British dominance, to that of a Buddhist priest and to make the institution a Buddhist school, excluding all Tamils. Black Tie, although a Buddhist and a Sinhala himself, wants the school to remain secular, to be for all races and religions.

In the midst of this political dispute, Arjie and Shehan discover their attraction for one another and the pleasure of homoerotic desire. Shehan is the constant target of Black Tie's punishments, enduring kneeling on the floor for several hours a day and being caned. Arjie, who is found to have good elocution, is chosen by Black Tie to recite two poems— "Vitae Lampada" and "The Best School of All"—at the upcoming prize-giving ceremony of the school. Arjie, too, becomes the recipient of Black Tie's cruelties, whenever he stumbles at the recitation, in the days leading up to the ceremony. On the verge of refusing to be burdened with the responsibility of the recitation, Arjie is coaxed by the teacher Sunderalingam (a Tamil) to persist with the task, so as to save the school from becoming a Buddhist institution. Listening to Sunderalingam's reminder of the dispute between Black Tie and Lokubandara and his explanation of why it is critical that Black Tie not lose the battle, Arjie begins to comprehend the significance of his being chosen to recite the poems:

> It seemed that the chief guest at the prize-giving . . . would be a minister of the cabinet, who, it was rumored, was next in line for the presidency. This minister was an old boy of the Victoria Academy and was the principal's last hope. "Vitae Lampada" and "The Best School of All" were two poems that the minister liked and knew very well because he had won the All Island Poetry Recital Contest with them. Black Tie would be creating his speech around those poems, and he would appeal to the minister and the other old boys to prevent the school from altering. It was hoped that the poems would remind the minister of his schooldays and he would take some action. (240–41)

Arjie is thus invested with the power to rescue the school from becoming the victim of ethnic politics. Despite the fact that a victory for

Black Tie in his dispute with Lokubandara would benefit the Tamils, Arjie chooses not to cooperate. His decision is based entirely on his anger at Black Tie's cruelty to Shehan, Arjie's newfound friend and lover. He devises a "diabolical plan" and resolves that instead of

> trying to get out of reciting the poems, [he] would do them. But [he] would do them wrong. Confuse them, jumble lines, take entire stanzas from one poem and place them in the other until the poems were rendered senseless. Black Tie, who Mr. Sunderalingam said would write a speech based on these poems, would be forced to make a speech that made no sense. His attempt to win the cabinet minister to his side would fail, he would lose the battle to Lokubandara, be forced to resign, and that would solve things for Shehan. (270–71)

One could argue that Arjie is too young to have made a self-consciously political decision. As an adolescent, his attention is focused on his evolving sexual orientation; therefore, to read politics into his actions is perhaps to oversignify them. There is certainly validity to such a view, but *Funny Boy*, though ostensibly about Arjie's youth and emerging sexual orientation, also pays significant attention to the growing ethnic tensions that will soon erupt into the riots of 1983, in which Tamils were attacked and their homes burned. That Selvadurai chooses to dwell on these political and ethnic realities even as he sensitively explores Arjie's emotional and intellectual growth demonstrates that he sees Arjie's sexual coming-of age as inextricable from Sri Lanka's realization of its own fractured nationhood. In fact, immediately after Arjie's "disastrous" recitation of the poems and his explanation to Shehan—"I did it for you, . . . I couldn't bear to see you suffer anymore" (277)—the novel ostensibly ends. What follows is titled "Riot Journal: An Epilogue." Although the epilogue, in terms of its structural location, functions as an afterthought, as being outside the novel's principal concerns, its deeply disturbing contents—the attack on Tamil businesses, homes, and people; an angry mob's brutal act of burning alive Arjie's grandparents in their car; the Chelvaratnam family's decision to leave for Canada; and their recognition of the Tamils' precarious position in Sri Lanka—belie such a peripheral positioning. I would argue that Selvadurai perhaps wishes us to rethink the marginal location of the epilogue and to see it instead as critical to the narrative. The appearance of marginality is itself called into question—almost as though we are being asked to consider the possibility that the marginal can be the site of real understanding. (Gary Okihiro makes a similar argument when he asserts that marginal groups have been the truest upholders of the American Constitution.[30]) It is in the epilogue that Arjie comes to realize that the difference between his and Shehan's ethnicities does matter in the context of Sri Lankan politics: "as I listened to him talk, something occurred to me that I had never really been conscious of before—Shehan was Sinhalese and I was not. This awareness did not change my feelings for him, it was simply there, like a thin translucent screen through which I watched him" (295). Thus, while the novel's "formal" closure inscribes the romantic and apolitical discovery of two young men's attraction for each other, the epilogue shatters that apolitical union and introduces the inexorable impact of the world of politics on matters of sexual desire.

Gayatri Gopinath and M. Jacqui Alexander both speak to the connection between matters of sexuality and matters of nationhood. Gopinath's essay "Funny Boys and Girls" discusses the ways in which gays and lesbians "queer" the nation, by establishing bonds that extend beyond the physical borders of South Asian nations to create a sense of queer South Asian transnational citizenship. Many queers, Gopinath writes, are not welcome as full citizens in their countries of residence; thus, this transnational citizenship constitutes a necessary locus of belonging.[31] In the case of the Tamils, who are largely scattered in France, Canada, Germany, Australia, and the United States, the diaspora functions as a virtual nation. (I am not attempting a specious analogy between the queer South Asian diaspora and the Tamil diaspora, merely pointing to their common transnational condition.)

Alexander notes that sexuality is, in fact, central to the construction of the nation: "Erotic autonomy signals danger to the heterosexual family and to the nation. And because loyalty to the nation as citizen is perennially colonized within reproduction and heterosexuality, erotic autonomy brings with it the potential of undoing the nation entirely, a possible charge of irresponsible citizenship or no citizenship at all."[32] Thus, to read *Funny Boy* as a political novel of ethno-nationalism is not to eclipse the sexual coming-of-age narrative that is undoubtedly central to it; rather, to approach it with a willingness to engage sexuality within the context of national politics is to enrich our understanding of the connections between individuals and the systemic structures within which they live. In this connection, Monique Truong's novel *The Book of Salt* (2002) provides a confirmation of the link between queerness and fragility of belonging—either in the nation or at home. The novel's homosexual Vietnamese protagonist, Binh, leaves home and nation to escape his father's wrath at his son's sexuality. Although the rejection by family is primary, it is contained within the larger rejection of eviction from nation.

Publicizing the Body

Performance artists have contributed to the increased visibility of the South Asian American body in significant ways since the early 1990s. Although Uday Shankar and his dance troupe were stage presences in the United States as early as the first decade of the twentieth century, it was not until the 1990s that South Asian American artists could be seen on stage performing in roles other than as cultural ambassadors.[33] I don't mean to undermine the importance of performers who transmit dance and other traditional cultural art forms; they fill a critical function by demonstrating the complexity and richness of their cultural heritage. However, such performances of culture also "fix" the performing bodies in certain ways, freeze them as occupants of unchanging roles. But cultural performances need not always reinforce fixed roles. For example, Matthew Bourne's largely male production of Tchaikovsky's ballet *Swan Lake* gives to a classical ballet the energy of a contemporary narrative framework and choreographic interpretation. In a similar fashion, South Asian American dancer Aparna Sindhoor uses the elements of the traditional Indian dance form of *bharatnatyam* to shape the South Asian female body not as a vehicle of tradition but as instrument of change and social protest.

In July 1998, in Amherst, Massachusetts, Sindhoor and Purva Bedi performed a stage adaptation of Chitra Divakaruni's short story "Clothes." Commissioned by New World Theater director at the time, Roberta Uno, long an advocate of women playwrights of color, this collaboration marked the successful confluence of a South Asian American writer and performing artists. Their performance drew attention to both the problematic and transformative potential of the South Asian body and the South Asian community's narratives on the American stage: problematic because, at some level, Divakaruni's story reinforces stereotypical notions of the South Asian woman—oppressed in her ancestral land, liberated in the West; transformative because Sindhoor's rendition of the female character is charged with an erotic power not frequently seen in the South Asian female body on the Western stage. Sindhoor's project attempts to recover the erotic in South Asian dance tradition and to infuse it with contemporary politics.

Una Chaudhari underscores the unique power of the stage: "Putting its material into play again and again, from rehearsal to rehearsal and then from night to night, the theater is a space of creative reinscription, a space where meaning . . . is not merely made, but remade, negotiated out of silence, stasis, and incomprehension."[34] Not only do the performers make meaning over and over again and in the process strengthen their understanding of their bodies and the relationship between their bodies and the world at large, but the audience also partakes actively in this process of discovery. Because the South Asian female body has been so pervasively codified in the West as victimized—through the media's fascination with female infanticide, arranged marriage, dowry deaths (when brides are burned for having brought insufficient dowry to their husbands' homes), and Islamic dress codes—the act of staging the body in ways that suggest alternate realities provides a necessary intervention. The corporeality of the actors on stage forces the audience members to confront their own reactions to female bodies of color. As Josephine Lee says in her treatise on Asian American drama, "The theater does not let us forget that questions of racial difference concern our most basic gut reactions, experiences, and sensations."[35] Precisely because staged performance engages the viewer's visceral reactions, it has the potential to effect a more total disruption of stereotypical and reductive perspectives than does a written text.

Bina Sharif's monologue "Afghan Woman" and her multicast play *Democracy in Islam* are cases in point. "Afghan Woman" is a lengthy monologue performed entirely in burqa, the fully enclosing body and face covering that women wear over their clothes. The audience never sees the actor out of the burqa and therefore does not see her eyes or her mouth. Yet, the actor's words take the audience through the full register of emotions—attack, sorrow, rage, accusation, bitterness, joy, and despair. The robed Afghan woman becomes more than just a symbol of oppression or tradition: instead she emerges as a fully realized individual who challenges the viewers' silence toward and complacency in the perpetuation of her predicament.[36]

It might be argued that the corporeality of the female body on stage draws attention to and reinforces gendered codes about the body and underscores the biological essentialism of being a woman. Such an argument might have particular force in the case of "Afghan Woman," with its extended presentation of a fully robed woman, long the visual symbol of Islam's "backwardness" in the eyes of non-Muslims. But Deborah Geis's analysis of female performers offers the counterview that one way to subvert such a patriarchal and masculine reading of the female body is to invest it with a textual presence that suggests subjectivities beyond that of the essentialized female. The speaking subject, Geis argues, undercuts the gendered subjectivity of her body and enables her to project multivalent and multivocal subjectivities. In addition, Geis believes that the monologue is a particularly empowering medium for women because it literally involves "seizing the word" or sets up conditions under which the word runs away from the body.[37] The disjuncture between the "trapped" corporeality of the robed woman and the unchecked release of her lengthy utterance creates a Brechtian space of disruption and change. As Elin Diamond points out, "If feminist theory sees the body as culturally mapped and gendered, Brechtian historicization insists that this body is not a fixed essence but a site of struggle and change." Diamond explains the female performer's deployment of Brecht's technique of gestus as, "a gesture, a word, an action, a tableau by which, separately or in series, the social attitudes encoded in the playtext become visible to the spectator." This Brechtian-feminist body, according to Diamond, is "available for both analysis and identification, paradoxically within representation while refusing its fixity."[38] Thus, the monologue and the presence of the robed Afghan woman make clear to the viewer/listener that the woman is aware of being gazed upon, that she is fully cognizant of the ways in which she is being read as visual text. Watching her on stage is an oddly discomforting experience in which one is both compelled by the words she speaks at the same time that one has the strong urge to see the face beneath the burqa.

Sharif's more recent play *Democracy in Islam*, performed in New York in December 2002, continues this Brechtian trend. Here, Sharif features a South Asian Muslim family in New York and charts the changes in their lives after the events of September 11, 2001. The mother, Fauzia, is divorced and lives with her daughter, Najma, and two sons, Imran and Kamran. Najma is a lesbian and is gradually beginning to get involved in social and political causes through the influence of her partner, Noor, and because she can see the ways in which being Muslim is tantamount to being branded a terrorist or abettor. Kamran, too, a young man who was perfectly content with being American in the past, now finds himself being drawn toward Islam because he realizes that he will never be fully accepted as American by the larger society. Imran actively denies his Muslim upbringing and is engaged to Mary, a white American.

Fauzia is the play's most complex character—irreverent, charming, confrontational, and wise. One of the most memorable scenes involves Fauzia making a few extra dollars by posing as a model for an art class. Sprawled in her chair, scantily clad, her legs splayed, and her arms and torso arranged provocatively, she mocks both herself and the artists who rely on her body for the study of their craft. There is no one else on stage, only Fauzia. Her figure becomes both the object of our voyeurism and the site at which that voyeurism gets disrupted. This disruption takes place because in mocking the artists who "feed" upon her body Sharif mocks the audience as well.

That said, I would argue that the closing scene of Sharif's play partially undercuts the efforts she has made to complicate how one views the body of the South Asian female, and the Muslim female in particular. The play has shown us Najma and Noor's physically erotic relationship and Fauzia's bold use of her body. In addition, the three women's lines are charged with disruptive energy, not permitting the viewer any easy grasp of the Muslim female—for example, a particularly lively exchange between Najma and Noor on the conflict between Sunni and Shia Muslims (Najma is Sunni and Noor is Shia) reveals the fissures within Islam and shows that even this homoerotic relationship between two independent Muslim women is not free from the entanglements of the nuances of Islamic belief. Yet, at the end, Fauzia dons the traditional Muslim headscarf and makes a conscious choice to enter the spiritual space of Islam. The act of covering herself takes place in silence. It is a powerful moment—our eyes are focused on her transformation from being seductively clad to modestly robed. One wonders why Sharif leaves us with this image. What does Fauzia's turn to Islam—a space that she has avoided in the past, preferring to live her life without the constraints of religious dictates—signify? An obvious response would be to conclude that Sharif has opted for the clichéd ending of the prodigal Muslim woman returning to the comfort and security of her religion, that both the playwright and her character have unequivocally declared their allegiance to a once-rejected faith. Such a reading would not be entirely inaccurate.

Nevertheless, the ending of *Democracy in Islam* does not altogether foreclose alternate readings. Fauzia is not a woman who can be coerced into doing anything—that much has been made clear by the script. Therefore, her actions at the end can perhaps be seen as an active choice—a gesture of defiance at a world that has reconstructed her sons as dangerous threats (and the play has provided continual articulations of such rhetoric). Sharif herself has pointed to *choice* as an important motive for taking the veil. Although she never wore a veil growing up in Pakistan, she observes that many women in Afghanistan choose to continue wearing the burqa, and in some parts of Pakistan more women are also choosing now to cover themselves. What is most important is "the freedom of choice."[39] Thus, the Westernized Fauzia of the early part of the play can be construed as having unthinkingly aped the ways of the West, and the Fauzia of the end of the play as having consciously opted for another mode of living. However, what saves the play from being a facile celebration of this "return" to Islam by Fauzia is that the audience is given no indication whether her choice leads to future happiness. What is clear is that, given the circumstances surrounding the family—the extreme suspicion toward and alienation of all Muslims—the *emotionally logical* choice (and I use the phrase in full awareness of its contradictory nature) is to turn to a cultural space in which one is likely to be welcomed.

Leila Ahmed provides a comprehensive historical account of the way in which the veil has become for non-Muslims the symbol of Islamic oppression of women. She contends that the focus on the veil has diverted attention from what ought to constitute the real discussion of the status of women in Islam—that is, their rights to education, property, health care, and so on. Unfortunately, the Western colonialist project in Islamic countries invested the veil with all the evil attributes of Islam. Therefore, those who advocated resistance to colonialism used it as a potent symbol of defiance.[40] Ahmed is quick to point out that hers is not an effort to defend Islam against the charge of androcentrism; rather, she hopes that non-Muslims will look beyond the veil to the urgent issues at hand:

> Because of this history of struggle around it, the veil is now pregnant with meanings. As item of clothing, however, the veil itself and whether it is worn are about as relevant to substantive matters of women's rights as the social prescription of one or another item of clothing is to Western women's struggles over substantive issues. When items of clothing—be it bloomers or bras—have briefly figured as focuses of contention and symbols of feminist struggle in Western societies, it was at least Western feminist women who were responsible for identifying the item in question as significant and defining it as a site of struggle and not, as has sadly been the case with respect to the veil for Muslim women, colonial and patriarchal men . . . who declared it important to feminist struggle.[41]

The gaps between white feminists and feminists of color have, of course, been well explored by scholars such as Audre Lord, Inderpal Grewal, Chandra Mohanty, Rey Chow, and M. Jacqui Alexander, among others. What is surprising is that despite the long and extensive discussions emphasizing the pitfalls of constructing "woman" as a universal category, there appears to be a fundamental inability on the part of many white feminists to acknowledge that struggles against patriarchy can take different forms in different sociocultural contexts. This inability has a direct impact on the ways in which actions by women of color and Third World women get read—and such misreadings carry over into the encounter with fictional and poetic texts.

Reading through/into the Indignities

There is anger in Amitava Kumar's critique of Chitra Divakaruni's short story "Ultrasound," but it is not the anger of a wounded South Asian American male incensed that he and his gender are made to look bad.[42] His anger is born from the suggestion in Divakaruni's story that India is a place where female fetuses are routinely aborted while the United States is the land of enlightened appreciation of boys *and* girls. Yet, even as he rails against the polarized presentation of East and West in Divakaruni's story, Kumar acknowledges that the practice of female feticide is rampant in India. What he bristles at are the erasures and silences in Divakaruni's story, the unexplored elements that would complicate the picture and reveal the interconnections between East and West that show the extent to which the West abets elsewhere the practices that it abhors at home.

One cannot hold the Western world accountable for every ill of the Eastern world, however convenient that may be. And yet, I admit to a sense of beleaguered fatigue whenever I read in the Western media of oppressed women in the developing world, of megalomaniac patriarchal figures, of medieval codes of sexuality and justice. I want, like Zora Neale Hurston, to believe that we don't have to write always for the man or against the man or in explanation to the man, even as I understand that it's naive to believe that South Asian American authors write only for their own communities. The U.S. publishing industry is not controlled by South Asian Americans (Sonny Mehta of Knopf is the exception), so it's more than likely that the decisions made there reflect the biases of the mainstream reading public. Given this situation, I choose to work with a split vision—one eye on South Asian American readers, inviting them to probe their views on gender and sexuality, and the other eye on readers from other ethnic groups, urging them to examine their own easy branding of gender and sexuality practices within South Asia and South Asian America as "backward" and "barbaric."

Kumar's distaste for the messages he detects in "Ultrasound" appears to encompass three areas: Divakaruni's silence about fearless women activists in South Asia; her Indian American narrator's smug self-satisfaction at her progressiveness, which she sees as being in stark contrast to the submissiveness of her cousin in India who fears that she will have to abort her female fetus; and the narrator's (and, Kumar suggests, Divakaruni's) reliance on a CBS *60 Minutes* program for information "'about the increasing popularity of amniocentesis in India.'" Kumar's attack is searing: "Is feminism American? Did the narrator in Divakaruni's story, even if her knowledge of women in India was to be limited to the *60 Minutes* segment, have no knowledge of Indian feminists? Could she not have noticed the outspoken activism of Brinda Karat, the charismatic Communist leader of the women's organization Janwadi Mahila Samiti? *On that very show!*" [43] I think of Kumar's reaction as I read a July 23, 2002, story in the *New York Times*. "Losing Spouse, and Maybe a Country: Dependents of 9/11 Victim Search for Ways to Stay in the U.S." tells of an Indian woman whose husband died in the attack on the World Trade Center towers, where he worked as a computer technician for a U.S. company. Ganesh Ladkat was one of tens of thousands of programmers and computer professionals from South Asia (primarily India) who are hired by U.S. companies at rates far below those paid to local computer workers. These imported software technicians work long hours, because they see their stint in the United States either as a way of amassing quick money with which to return to India or as an entry into the U.S. job market and perhaps permanent residency. The widowed Sonia Gawas, also trained as a computer technician, awaits the U.S. government's decision about her right to remain in the country now that her husband, on whose visa she came here, is dead. The government, says the story, "is taking a lenient approach to enforcement" of the law requiring dependents of foreigners killed on September 11 to leave when their visas expire or on September 10, 2002, whichever is the later date (Gawas's visa was due to expire in April 2004). But a bill introduced by Senator Jon Corzine (D-NJ) proposes that dependents of foreign victims be granted American citizenship. We learn that Gawas wants to stay in the United States and has enrolled in courses at Rutgers University to improve her chances for employment. Toward the end of the article, we read, "She does not want to return to India, where she said widows are shunned, forbidden to remarry, and believed to be cursed."[44]

The article leaves me conflicted. On the one hand, I am glad that there's a story about a South Asian victim, because the majority of articles have surprisingly ignored the losses of this community, despite the fact that more than two hundred South Asians lost their lives in the towers, and that many of the medical staff who came to help in the aftermath of the attack were South Asian in descent. So I welcome the coverage, even though it's on page 20 of the newspaper. On the other hand, the story doesn't acknowledge that there are other South Asian American victims, so Gawas's situation is presented as one of a kind. Her story gradually unfolds as evidence of the fairness of the U.S. government, which is trying very hard to acknowledge the pain and suffering of families that have lost loved ones, even when members of these families are not U.S. citizens. As I read the paragraphs in the article that tell of the government's efforts to be magnanimously accommodating, I also hear the echo of another narrative (one that is absent in this version)—the roundup of hundreds of South Asian Americans on suspicion of terrorism and their summary detention in jails with no access to lawyers. Then, at the end of the article I find that Gawas has deemed India to be a hostile place for widows. She is right, of course, but she is also wrong. Like all broad characterizations of peoples, cultures, and nations, specific details are omitted. In a country as diverse as India, the details are particularly important. The sentiment about widows is by no means monolithic, nor is the view of widow remarriage. Region, class, rural versus urban location, caste, the widow's economic independence, and religion all affect the social climate in which a widow lives. Therefore, while I acknowledge in the main the validity of Gawas's description of India in the context of widowhood, I cannot help but hope for a few complicating sentences that hint at other realities. Newspapers are driven by word count; thus, while it may be unrealistic to expect protracted discussions of complex subjects, precision of language and analytical complexity are not mutually exclusive.

Widowhood in India as a fate to be avoided at all costs is the theme of another Divakaruni story, "Clothes." The protagonist has lost her husband violently to a shooting at the 7-Eleven store where he worked the late-night shift. The relatively new bride resolves that she will not return to India because she doesn't wish to submit to the indignities of widowhood and a life of service to her parents-in-law: "That's when I know I cannot go back. I don't know yet how I'll manage, here in this new, dangerous land. I only know I must. Because all over India, at this very moment, widows in white saris are bowing their veiled heads, serving tea to in-laws. Doves with cut-off wings" (32). She is determined to stay in the United States and to don the new clothes that have been the symbol of her evolving liberation and individual aspiration: "The thought is like an unexpected, intimate gift. I tilt my chin, readying myself for the arguments of the coming weeks, the remonstrations. In the mirror a woman holds my gaze, . . . her eyes apprehensive yet steady. She wears a blouse and skirt the color of almonds" (32).

I've always been troubled by this story, despite its illumination of a little explored aspect of the South Asian American immigrant experience—the dangers of running a convenience store. Moreover, Divakaruni writes with a fine poetic eye, and she ably conveys the eager imagination of the new bride as she envisions the physical layout of the store that she has never seen. Besides, this is a narrative in which the Indian American male is sketched with sensitivity and nuance—he is trying to balance the obligation he feels to look after his parents with his awareness of his wife's desire to be more than just a daughter-in-law. But "Clothes" leaves me troubled because it, too, sets up the inevitable dichotomy of oppressive East and liberating West.

Yet, there might be another way of reading "Clothes"; and it is Meena Alexander who leads us to this alternate space. The most obvious analysis of the wife's desire to remain in the United States is to see it as her choosing the freedom afforded by the West. A less obvious treatment of the decision would be to focus on the violence that drastically alters her life. When her husband becomes the victim of violence, she, too, could become a secondary victim by having her future possibilities curtailed. "[T]his new dangerous land" is how she refers to the United States. The juxtaposition of "new" and "dangerous" suggests that the narrator links danger with beginnings. Violence has now created possibilities by destroying what was familiar to her—marriage and dependency. I don't mean to minimize the horror of violence by suggesting that within every act of violence lies opportunity. Rather, I want to echo Alexander's observation that women frequently react to violence in unexpected ways, by refusing to succumb to total despair. These refusals to be psychologically demolished by violence are evident not just in the West but in other parts of the world as well. In times when physical, social, or cultural givens are destroyed, is not one "freed" to articulate new ways of being, to shape new lives? In her preface to the collection *Blood into Ink*, Alexander notes:

> [T]he radical disruption of life in the war zone permits an escape from the strict feminine mold of ordinary life and opens up explosive possibilities of freedom. . . .
>
> What becomes of so-called "normalcy"? How shall we continue to cross the street, wash vegetables, bring our children home from school, approach our lovers, bury our dead? . . . The contortions of the everyday caused by multiple forms of violence—bombardments, mass shootings, curfews, riots, rapes, the forced exodus of civilians—when crystallized into art, reveal not merely the extreme, enforced condition but also the hidden structures of a world previously taken for granted, a world in which women have not always been at ease.[45]

East and West need not be seen only as oppositions of culture, as though each space represented an unchanging set of circumstances. Rather, it is possible to look for other forces impinging on the decision by Divakaruni's protagonist to stay in the United States. The violent loss of someone dear derails the mind, sets it moving in a new direction. Understanding the potential for self-regeneration at moments of extreme chaos and social disintegration allows one to see in her decision not to return to India the recognition that she has lost all that was meaningful and ordered. She can shape her life now in the way she desires. And if that reshaping is more creative, less unencumbered in the West, it is because there are fewer systems of support that come into play, fewer networks of family and friends to whom one could turn. Thus, there is both liberation and isolation in her situation. I acknowledge that this alternate reading of the ending of "Clothes" might appear defensive, a rush to soften the impression of India as inhospitable to female ambition. But I offer it merely to show that there may be something to be gained from withholding quick explanations and, instead, probing a situation for more than seems immediately apparent.

In 1996, when I was teaching an introductory course in women's studies at a university in the American Northeast, I screened the film *When Women Unite: The Story of an Uprising*, directed by Nata Duvvury and Shabnam Virmani. This documentary film tells of the amazing strength and solidarity of women in the Nellore district of Andhra Pradesh (a state in southern India), an area that includes more than three hundred villages. These women set in motion a movement spanning hundreds of villages to resist the sale of the state-supplied liquor, arrack. Arrack, which the men consume, destroys family structures and threatens to undermine the stability of people's lives. The women determine that they must do something to change the situation after a man disoriented by alcohol beats to death his wife when she tries to stop him from violating their daughter. The village women decide that they have been silent for too long and resolve that they will bring control into their lives. These rural and largely illiterate women take on the formidable forces of government and a male-dominated system of alcohol manufacture and distribution with remarkable success. In 1995, after four years of protest and uprising, the sale of arrack was banned by the government of Andhra Pradesh. Students at the wealthy private institution at which I taught this course were struck by the power of these women, whom they had typically thought of as being unable to break free from patriarchal systems of oppression. Many students expressed to me that this was the one film that truly consolidated their faith in collective action. I felt no small sense of satisfaction in the fact that they had found evidence of successful female empowerment and resistance in a region of the world in which women are typically seen as submissive and without agency. What is also interesting about *When Women Unite* is that it does not paint men as being inherently evil. The film's nuanced representation of the village men shows them to be as much victims of corrupt government structures as are the women. The women fight not just for themselves, but also for the preservation of their families. Among the most memorable images from the film are those in which women and men unite in powerful processions against injustice.

It is precisely the absence of such stories from the consciousness of readers in the West that many South Asian Americans lament. The mother-daughter team of Shamita Das Dasgupta and Sayantani Dasgupta direct their criticism not only at white feminists but also at the South Asian communities, in general, and the Indian American community, in particular, which they see as pervaded by patriarchal structures. In their jointly written essay "Bringing Up Baby," they question the ethnocentrism of white feminists' belief that "motherhood implies a lack of mobility, an unbreakable chain to home and hearth, and powerless self-sacrifice," while, by contrast, being feminist means "being what you want to be," with no concern for one's family or community.[46] But their sharpest barbs are reserved for the patriarchs of their own communities, to whom they say, "Neither feminism nor activism are alien to our culture—they are nested within our heritage" (194). They also deplore the role fashioned for diasporic women in which "[m]others socializ[e] their daughters within prescribed roles, and a daughter [learns] to be 'a good Indian girl . . . who does not date, is shy and delicate, and marries an Indian man of her parents' choosing'" (191).

Nalini Natarajan observes that the anxiety of the diasporic male may explain the fierce patriarchy of diasporic communities.[47] (See below for a discussion of how traditional gender roles get transmitted and enacted even in the second-generation offspring of these immigrant communities.) In an earlier essay, I wrote that the "'cultural' woman is a necessary presence. She enables the displaced and dislocated male to go out into the complicated world of economic and social challenge because she provides him with the stability of home and roots in an alien landscape. In other words, she makes it possible for the male to locate himself, to define himself, within the space she inhabits."[48] Thus, women frequently become complicit in their own subjugation in diasporic communities, but their acquiescence is not a simple matter of reenacting traditions of submission carried over from ancestral homelands that devalue the status of women. I argue that "when the woman accompanies her male partner into diaspora, she witnesses for herself the many causes of his anxiety. Her empathy for his anxiety may influence her to accommodate to his demand, expectation, or desire for her predictability" (155). Without condoning the patriarchy of diasporic communities, it is, I believe, possible to engage in a complex analysis of the many reasons for displays of male dominance in diasporic settings. Das Dasgupta and Dasgupta make the telling point that Indian American men forget the active tradition of assertive women in South Asian history. It is as though they begin to label resistance and independence as Western modes of behavior, and in doing so replicate the specious contrast between West and East in terms of women's outspokenness. Thus, they reinforce the Western world's conception of South Asian gender relations as hopelessly skewed in favor of men.

The Homecoming of the South Asian (American) Male

Saleem Peeradina's poem "Sisters" offers a valuable counter-perspective to the predominant cultural stereotype by presenting a South Asian American male who celebrates his daughter's defiance:

> On bad days
> I shout her down, immediately
> regretting my words.
> But even as she retreats
> into a simmering silence, she stands her ground
> knowing me to be unfair. Secretly,
> I rejoice at the lesson never intended
> but so well learnt: how to overcome
> fathers, real and imaginary.[49]

Peeradina writes with moving complexity about South Asian males' relationships with women. His collection of poems *Group Portrait* is a sensitive exploration of husband and wife, father and daughters, son and mother. In "Homecoming," the speaker tells of his rambunctious daughters and their claim on his time and attention when he returns home from work every day. The poem closes with the father's deep-felt hope that his daughters' souls

> like big milky swans
> taking off from the ribbed water,
> may free their feet from his clay
> and soar into their dreams of sky. (16)

His poem "Ode to Her Legs," which initially indulges the male fantasy of unabashedly viewing exposed female limbs, turns at the end into a call to men to care about and for women's legs not for their sensual appeal but for the labor they have endured:

> So, let her stretch out and place her feet
> In your hands. Everyday. After all, she has lavished
> Attention and care, devotedly tending your feet every night.
>
> Which you have taken as your birthright
> Citing scripture and myth in your defense.
> Well, here is your service manual: Stroke and press those legs.[50]

Although the poem reinforces the idealized image of the selflessly serving female, "lavish[ing] / Attention and care, devotedly tending [his] feet every night," one is also surprised at the starkness and lack of ornament in the closing line. In a direct command, the male reader is told of his obligation. Peeradina speaks from a decidedly male position; yet, his poetry is marked by a noticeable attempt to shift perspective. Gautam Premnath is unwilling to concede this point, however. He believes that the poem's speaker "assumes the subservience of the female" and that this subservience functions as the "precondition for the magnanimous reciprocation" displayed in the closing lines by the male voice. If I were to grant the validity of this analysis, I would add only that the ironic play in the title leaves open the possibility of seeing the poem either as a genuine attempt by an as yet insufficiently sensitized male to undo his own sexist limitations or as the male's good-humored admission of his intention yet inability to escape his patriarchal cast of mind.[51]

Precisely such complicated negotiations characterize the gender relations in Tahira Naqvi's and Jhumpa Lahiri's works. Both writers exhibit great sensitivity and nuance in their depictions of the partnerships and conflicts between South Asian women and men, Naqvi for Pakistanis and Pakistani Americans and Lahiri for Indian Americans. Naqvi's two collections of stories—one set in Pakistan and the other in the United States—exhibit subtle but significant differences in the degree to which the male is an integral part of the story. In the collection of Pakistan stories, *Attar of Roses*, the protagonists are sometimes male, sometimes female, and there is always a rich interaction between the sexes. In the U.S.-based collection, *Dying in a Strange Country*, the narratives largely revolve around female protagonists, with the men forming a faint backdrop. There is a kind of gentle infantilizing of the South Asian American male, a suggestion that he doesn't think through the intricacies and ramifications of situations and blissfully goes through life as though there were nothing to worry about. Naqvi's Pakistani American men could be seen as revealing a slightly different component of the anxious diasporic male about whom Natarajan writes. They appear to reinforce the vulnerability of the diasporic male who needs caring for because the world outside is largely so hostile to him.

Three stories from *Attar of Roses* in particular reveal that gender relations in Pakistan defy easy assumptions about the exercise of patriarchal power or the repression of women. In "Love in an Election Year," romance and the arrangements for a marriage take place against the backdrop of the first run by Benazir Bhutto, daughter of a prominent political family, for prime minister of Pakistan. The story's narrator tells us that Bhutto "has a notion she will win" even though the religious leaders, the mullahs, "their hands lifted ominously, their eyes glinting passionately, are up in arms because, as they see it, a woman cannot, and if they can help it, will not, hold executive office" (1). In those opening lines, two contradictory strains of thought are intertwined. One is the pronouncement, delivered with precious little fanfare, of a woman's belief that she can win the most powerful office in the country (not a sentiment that any woman, however powerful, can realistically hold in the United States, notwithstanding, or perhaps because of, Elizabeth

Dole's short-lived candidacy for the presidency in 1998). Pakistan is a Muslim nation (though founded with a secular vision) in which the patriarchal religious leaders exercise a fair measure of power. Thus, Bhutto's confidence ought to be remarkable, but the narrator's presentation of the matter is noteworthy for its tone of normalcy. The second idea is the more predictable, from a Western perspective: the mullahs are determined that a woman will not be leader. But the reader is not allowed to settle comfortably into that mode of thinking, not permitted the predictable reading of Islamic religious leaders constraining a woman's aspirations. Though Bhutto's move is characterized as "brazen," there is nothing in the narrator's presentation to suggest that it is abnormal, unwise, dangerous, or futile. Instead, she refers back to the early years of Pakistan's existence as a nation and observes that Bhutto reminds her of Fatima Jinnah, "another woman who had . . . wished to be the president of the country her brother had helped found." The narrator, who was fifteen years old at the time, remarks that in those days "the *mullahs* hadn't been given a voice yet" (1). In that simple sentence, the narrator speaks volumes—the power of the religious leaders is not automatic within Islamic nations; on the contrary, they attain ascendancy because some people give them the opportunity to do so.[52]

"Love in an Election Year" is not primarily about politics, but the story draws parallels between choosing a leader and choosing a life partner in marriage. The narrator is enlisted by a twenty-one-year-old female relative, Baji Sughra, to be the go-between in a clandestine love affair that Baji is having with Javed Bhai. Eventually, however, Baji abandons Javed for a "sensible match" arranged by her parents. The narrator, although disappointed that the romance does not culminate in marriage, understands the pressure that leads Baji to accede to marriage with a man with whom she is not in love. But in her adolescent fantasy, she believes that Baji still loves Javed and will remember him. In an interesting juxtaposition, Naqvi places Baji's distraught reaction to her parents' arranging of her marriage alongside Fatima Jinnah's loss to General Ayub Khan in the 1965 election. It is as though Naqvi is suggesting that in choosing a leader a nation frequently fails to exercise vision and opts instead for the familiar, just as a woman weighs too cautiously perhaps the merits of the man she decides to marry.

Twenty-three years later, in 1988, the year of Benazir Bhutto's first run for prime minister, the narrator visits Baji Sughra, who has become "fat and dour" and whines about her lack of domestic help. When asked if she is rooting for Bhutto, Baji contemptuously dismisses Bhutto as being "too much in love with that horrible husband of hers, that playboy" and of wanting the impossible: "she wants too much. Just think, you can either be a good wife and mother or a good leader. And she wants to be all three" (17). The narrator, appalled at Baji's crass criticism of Bhutto, reflects on Fatimah Jinnah's defeat: "I thought about Fatima Jinnah. One could say the country at that time was young. That Fatima Jinnah was old and weary. That she reminded people too much of a past that needed to be put aside so the country could move forward unfettered. That democracy was a word with enormously complicated and rather foreign connotations. And so she didn't win" (17). Remembering that defeat and listening to Baji Sughra's inane objections to Bhutto, the narrator asks, "Do you ever think about Javed Bhai?" That line closes the story. With it, Naqvi indicates that while the narrator understands, though does not agree with, the nation's rejection of Fatima Jinnah in 1965 and Baji's rejection of Javed for the spouse of her parents' choice, she is clearly aware of the dangers of erasing from one's consciousness all traces of idealism and impracticality. Does Naqvi wish to suggest that if the people once again allow themselves to be ruled by practical considerations rather than taking a risk and voting for the brazen Bhutto, then Pakistan will become a nation of no consequence, a wasted and bitter land, in the same way that Baji Sughra has forgotten what it means to dream?[53] "Love in an Election Year" is a sophisticated intertwining of the personal realm with the public political realm. In an understated style, Naqvi focuses on the microcosm of a fifteen-year old's awakening understanding of romance and marriage and succeeds in evoking from within that personal space the macrocosm of national politics.

Most of the other stories in *Attar of Roses* offer penetrating insights into the domestic space. Distinguished by their nuanced presentation of the relationship between men and women, the stories belie reductive understandings of gender roles in Islamic societies. "A Man of Integrity" is, at one level, a humorous commentary on gender relations and, at another level, a profoundly sad assessment of the routine and mundane patterns of behavior into which marriage can settle. A successful doctor, Sami, receives a letter at his office from an anonymous female who makes the daring proposition to be his companion:

For a strange woman to be writing to a man, especially one who is married, is beyond the bounds of good behavior, I agree, but I have written to you after much thought. This is not the act of a thoughtless, insensitive woman. For a whole year I have wondered what to do. Can I be candid? You seem like a lonely man. You stay long hours in your clinic, even when you have no patients. Why do you not go home to your wife, your two children? I do not wish to be rude, but I think you are running from them. Perhaps you need a friend. Perhaps I can be your friend. Is it possible that we meet somewhere? (122)

At first, the doctor is extremely discomfited, believing that the letter has been sent by someone who wishes to trap and discredit him. But gradually, as more letters arrive at regular intervals and are eventually supplanted by phone calls, he begins to anticipate these communications somewhat eagerly. A strong sense of guilt accompanies the excitement, because he considers himself a man of integrity and has never been unfaithful to his wife, Zaheen, a sophisticated and intelligent woman. One day, when Sami stays home nursing a cold and searches for tissues, he discovers the by-now-familiar envelope in his wife's dresser drawer. Panic grips him. The letter writer, he believes, has betrayed him by sending a letter to his home. Why has his wife said nothing? As he lifts the envelope, his wife enters the room: "The envelope fluttered to the floor from his hand like the last eddying leaf broken off from a bare-limbed, autumn tree. He noted that a look of astonishment spread over her face like a slow blush" (135). In those final moments of the story, as the doctor wonders why his wife has chosen not to question him about the letter, it becomes apparent to us, *though not to him*, that she is the letter writer and caller. (There is no cheap last-minute surprise in this dramatically ironic scene, since the author has already hinted as much when, during one phone call, the doctor reflects that the laugh at the other end of the line is vaguely familiar.) The doctor's obtuseness in not realizing that his wife is the letter writer is apparent in his puzzlement at why "she had not planned on telling him about the letter" (135). The narrative's closing line offers no simple resolution to the obvious chasm in their marriage: "One hand firmly on the doorknob, she returned his gaze silently, without flinching, her face suddenly pale, her eyes brimming with tears of accusation" (135). But there is no doubting the author's suggestion of a wealth of possible outcomes, even though it is clear that Zaheen is creative and imaginative and Sami is not. Both characters are sketched with sensitive complexity: he is no inconsiderate monster, and she no suffering victim. That she has a sense of humor and daring is evident in her posing as a woman of mystery pursuing her husband. His silence surrounding the letters and phone calls comes across as a peccadillo, not an unforgivable transgression. There is enough in the story to suggest that obtuse though he might be in the main, the doctor will ultimately understand and appreciate Zaheen's wit and intelligence.

A slightly different situation prevails in "The Notebook." In some ways, the relationship in the story appears to fulfill the conditions for a strongly patriarchal marriage, with the male protagonist portrayed as an abusive husband, who both physically and mentally attempts to control his wife, berating her for what he believes is her barrenness. However, Naqvi is clever in her manipulation of this stereotype of the abusive husband. First, although the female protagonist is given a name, Salma, the man is referred to only as "her husband." Second, it is with the same notebook in which her husband has ordered her to maintain an accurate and strict household budget that Salma claims her agency. Thus, from within the master's house and using the master's resources, Salma asserts her independence and, moreover, appears to take over the house.

The story traces Salma's gradual resistance to her husband through the medium of poetry and creative expression. For a short while, Salma diligently keeps the day-to-day accounts. But then she begins to copy into the notebook couplets and verses that she had cut out of magazines before her marriage. This act of inscribing the poems into the notebook gives her great pleasure. In fact, the narrator quite explicitly indicates that writing the poems is Salma's way of claiming space, of seizing territory, as it were:

> First she tore out the accounts, neatly, so the binding on the inside did not appear disfigured. She didn't want to keep anything, not even a jagged edge, no matter how tiny, to remind her of what once been in this notebook. Then, . . . she painstakingly transferred to the notebook every word from those crushed and faded pages which still exuded a fragrance of the turmeric and rose attar mixture which she had vigorously rubbed into her skin on the eve of her wedding. (54)

In a short while, Salma exhausts her supply of magazine cuttings and becomes restless. Gradually she awakens to the creativity within her and begins to compose her own poems. They excite her, almost to the point of arousal: "Strung together in rhythms, they left her trembling and fearful, for she did not understand where they came from, or why. There was a time, when, just as her husband pulled her shirt up and threw himself on her, she closed her eyes and two couplets flitted in, glided around her, as if they were garlands of cambeli, of red roses" (55).

Writing poetry becomes her constant outlet: when her husband hits her, she takes up the notebook and composes a poem; when she is cooking, the notebook claims her primary attention. One day, her husband discovers the notebook and, predictably, is enraged. He accuses her of writing the words for another man and begins to tear the pages out of the notebook: "'You slut!' Her husband ripped the pages into shreds, calling her names, swearing until his face was bathed in sweat. The veins in his neck swelled and pulsed. Finally, throwing the notebook at her so that it fell in her lap like a wounded bird, he wiped sweat from his forehead and raised a fist. 'You barren slut!'" (59).

Salma's response is to declare, "I'm not barren," and to warn him, "[I]f you hit me today, I will open that door and walk out into the gulley and you will never see my face again" (59). That it is her writing that has given her courage is unequivocally clear: "Words formed a screen before her eyes, like rain coming down in a sheet of moisture on a windy day. Walking past him, she stooped to pick up, one by one, the torn, crumpled, soiled pages, and placed them between the cracked, twisted covers of the notebook" (59). Secure in this courage, with the "notebook snug under her arm," Salma steps out into the courtyard and beckons to the vegetable vendor, asking if he has fresh cauliflower.

What is significant about this final image is the author's juxtaposing of the notebook—the symbol and instrument of Salma's independence, daring, and creativity—with her call to the vegetable vendor. It is not that Naqvi chooses as her final image the domestic Salma, but rather that the domestic Salma draws upon the courage of the creative Salma to bring forth a fearless Salma *within* the domestic sphere. The notebook has allowed Salma to infuse the domestic space—hitherto a region of oppression—with her control. Thus, rather than escaping the master's house, she transforms it into her domain, bringing it within the purview of her desires. Naqvi skillfully avoids the bipolar trap: she shows that it is possible to wield control from within the domestic space, and that a woman's independence from prescribed gender roles need not be measured in terms of her distance from the domestic or from her husband.

Naqvi's stories set in Pakistan give texture and density to the issue of gender relations. Her stories set in the United States—in the collection *Dying in a Strange Country*—are less concerned with the interaction between men and women than with the ways in which cultural mores from Pakistan get transformed or adapted in the United States. The female presence is predominant in these stories, underscoring the accepted contention in diaspora studies that "women become the bearers of cultural tradition" in diasporic communities. But Naqvi's diasporic women are, for the most part, inventive, not slaves to rigidly defined traditions that they feel compelled to preserve. (See Chapter 4 for a discussion of Naqvi's masterful story "Thank God for the Jews.")

Several stories in *Dying in a Strange Country* feature female protagonists who return to Pakistan on vacation after being in the United States. In these narratives, the United States hovers as a distant presence, its influence on the visitors strong without being overwhelming. One of the most thought-provoking pieces is the final story, "Lost in the Marketplace," which is set entirely in Lahore, Pakistan. The protagonist is Farwa, a young Pakistani American woman on holiday and, at the same time, looking for a marriage partner—much to the consternation of her roommate, Jeanne, in Connecticut, who is appalled that Farwa would submit to such a "primitive" custom. At a social gathering in Lahore where she is supposed to be assessing Sajjad, a Pakistani doctor, as a possible husband, Farwa's interest is caught by another man, Ata'ullah, whom she finds startlingly handsome. When she is told that he comes from a community that knows nothing about women's rights and does not permit him to marry anyone from the outside, she envisions him "on a horse, blazing a trail in the Sindh desert, his beloved behind him, clasping his waist with both arms, her head resting against his back as he flees from his tyrannical tribesmen" (129). The Orientalism and exoticism of the image indicate that the protagonist has absorbed sufficiently the Western media's understanding of and attitude toward those who look like Ata'ullah: "a fierce little beard that's blacker than any black [the protagonist has] ever seen and his mustache zooms across his lips and disappears into the sides of the beard without a trace. He's wearing a long white kurta with a shalwar and carelessly draped around his lean shoulders is a voluminous black shawl" (127–28).

The next time Farwa sees Ata'ullah she is at the marketplace with her female relatives. He has a woman companion, clad in chador, her face veiled except for the rectangle of her eyes. Farwa observes: "This is not how I had imagined him. He's incongruous among these mundane surroundings—a bazaar, women fingering fabric, buying shoes, eating chaat. Standing like a watchman next to a fully veiled woman in a busy section of the cloth market while she shops for chenille, he's curiously out of place. Not once had I imagined him anywhere else except in the desert, on a horseback, the wind gusting through his long dark hair" (134–35). Farwa's subsequent thoughts show that she is attempting to differentiate, attempting to tease out specificities from the monolithic representation of Pakistani men that she has doubtless imbibed from living in the United States: "And would I also wear a veil if he and I were together in public? Suddenly I think of Sajjad, the doctor with . . . his heart a wide open space where any young Pakistani American girl could fit easily, and fear clutches at my heart. What if I was alone here, and lost?" (135).

They lose Ata'ullah and his companion in the crowded marketplace, and Farwa's final thoughts are a fitting conclusion to the collection: "Lahore is a marketplace, I think . . . I'm constantly giving something of myself to it when I'm here, and I take something away each time. I'm never now what I was a minute ago. It changes me, makes me a stranger to myself" (135). The notion that Lahore is a marketplace can be read both as an Orientalist perspective and as a view that emerges from a deep appreciation of the Pakistani milieu. As an Orientalist point of view, it carries the undertone of commodification and purchase—Lahore is a place where wares can be had and transactions entered into. The entire globe is rich for tapping, ripe for mining, and Lahore is a wealth of heterogeneity and unexpected discoveries—replete with the pleasures of a mix of diverse possibilities. But what saves this portrayal of Lahore from an unequivocally Orientalist cast is that Farwa is not just *taking* something from Lahore, but also "constantly giving something of [her]self to it." Farwa is changed, both because she perhaps recognizes what is important about choosing one's life partner, but also because she realizes her own tendencies to stereotype. She sees herself as she sees a stranger, as someone who comes with her Americanized views and hastily categorizes the men she meets in the marketplace of marriage as the brash one, the benevolent one, the blazing one. Lahore has taught her to be skeptical of too-ready labels and to leave herself open to the inexplicabilities of people and life. As the closing story of Naqvi's U.S.-based collection, such a sentiment is remarkably fitting.

Although Farwa appears to be a young, second-generation Pakistani American raised primarily in the United States, this is not typically the age group with which Naqvi concerns herself in her U.S.-located stories. That generation is more the domain of Jhumpa Lahiri.

The Young and the Restless of South Asian America

While the stories in Lahiri's collection *The Interpreter of Maladies* are not exclusively about the children of immigrant Indian Americans, a number of them address the experiences of Indian Americans born and raised in the United States. In doing so, Lahiri offers a glimpse of a world that is fast becoming the focus of scholars and creative artists alike.[54]

One of the most fascinating and complex studies of second-generation South Asian Americans is Sunaina Maira's examination of club culture among Indian Americans in New York. Encompassing issues such as nostalgia for the home country, desire to embody an Americanized "cool," performance of ethnicity, authenticity of ethnic image, gender relations, and sexuality, Maira's *Desis in the House* offers a rich discussion of the ways in which second-generation Indian American men and women embody and enact what appear to be many conflicting tendencies. Club culture, she points out, both encourages the performance of alluring and seductive "vampishness" among Indian American women *and* requires a reproduction of the ethnicized chaste Indian woman. For the men, the restrictions are perhaps less severe, but they, too, find themselves negotiating between a sexy masculinity defined by "gangsta" machismo, on the one hand, and the stable masculinity of the upwardly mobile and well-dressed professional, on the other. Maira eschews reductive explanations of second-generation behavior that see it either as simplistic reproductions of immigrant-generation nostalgia or as rebellious acting out against parental strictures. The second-generation, she notes, simultaneously embraces *and* rejects the expectations of the immigrant generation in the context of gender roles, sexuality, and success: "The dichotomy of 'Indian' and 'American' is not absolute, for ultimately these second-generation youth belong to both cultural fields and demonstrate the blurred boundaries between them" (177). The Indian American party and dance scene and its sampling of hip hop, Maira says, is the space in which these second-generation youth craft and maintain the delicate balance between performing their ethnicity by socializing with their ethnic peers in this uniquely Indian American subculture and creating a hybrid space in which they "reinterpret[ ] Indian and musical and dance traditions through the rituals of American pop culture" (42–43).

While Lahiri's stories do not specifically address the youth culture of which Maira writes or deal with protagonists in their late teens or early twenties (the predominant age range of Maira's study), the negotiation between paradoxical impulses that characterizes the youth of Maira's research provides a useful backdrop against which to focus on the thirty-something men and women of Lahiri's stories. A knowledge of the ways in which the young women of Maira's study skillfully perform *and* subvert expected gender roles enables a nuanced reading of Lahiri's female characters, who share the middle- and upper-middle-class background of the younger women. It is not difficult to imagine the women, and men, of Lahiri's stories "A Temporary Matter," "This Blessed House," and "The Interpreter of Maladies" (the latter two are discussed in Chapter 5) as having in their twenties frequented the clubs of Maira's study.

In "A Temporary Matter," a young Indian American couple find in the darkness (resulting from the scheduled 8 to 9 P.M. cut off of electricity by the utility company to conduct repairs) the opportunity to disclose their never-revealed thoughts about one another. Their marriage has not been particularly intimate since their first child was stillborn six months ago, and they have been rather mechanically going about their separate routines, relating to each other only in the most superficial way.

Shoba works as a proofreader in a publishing company in Boston; Shukumar is a graduate student writing his dissertation. It is Shoba's idea to begin this truth-telling, because it reminds her of the game she used to play as a child during power failures on visits to her grandmother's house in India. She begins the "exchange of confessions," and, gradually, over the course of four nights, while they sit for an hour in the dark, they reveal things about themselves that trace the deepest grains of their rela-

tionship. Shoba confesses that when Shukumar's mother came to visit
them, she lied about having to stay late at work one evening; instead she
had gone out for a martini with a co-worker. Shukumar discloses that
he hadn't really lost the sweater-vest Shoba bought him for their third
wedding anniversary "but had exchanged it for cash at Filene's, and that
he had gotten drunk alone in the middle of the day at a hotel bar" (18).
In the darkness, in this manner, they begin to feel their way back to the
intimacy they once had in their three-year-old marriage:

> They were able to talk to each other again. The third night after
> supper they'd sat together on the sofa, and once it was dark he
> began kissing her awkwardly on her forehead and her face, and
> though it was dark he closed his eyes, and knew that she did, too.
> The fourth night they walked carefully upstairs, to bed, feeling
> together for the final step with their feet before the landing, and
> making love with a desperation they had forgotten. She wept with-
> out sound, and whispered his name, and traced his eyebrows with
> her finger in the dark. (19–20)

A notice from the electric company informs them, on the fifth day,
that the line has been repaired ahead of schedule so there will be no cut
off that evening. Shukumar is disappointed. After dinner that night, with
the lights on, Shoba announces that she is moving out, that she has found
an apartment close to work and needs some time to herself.

The story unfolds largely through Shukumar's perspective, despite its
third-person narrative voice. The reader learns that Shukumar was "sickened, knowing that she had spent these past evenings preparing for a life
without him. He was relieved and yet he was sickened. This was what
she'd been trying to tell him for the past four evenings. This was the
point of her game" (21). Deeply hurt, Shukumar reveals to Shoba the
one thing that he had promised himself he would always spare her
knowledge of because she had so much wanted it to be a surprise: the
sex of their stillborn child. With calculated pointedness, knowing that he
is almost certainly causing Shoba immense sorrow, he declares, "'Our
baby was a boy. . . . His skin was more red than brown. He had black hair
on his head. He weighed almost five pounds. His fingers were curled
shut, just like yours in the night'" (22).

"A Temporary Matter" is a deftly constructed and deeply layered story about the gradual erosion of meaningful interaction between two people who were once in love. Nothing in the narrative marks their experience as specifically South Asian American—what happens to them has little to do with their upbringing. This could be a story about *any* young, educated, middle-class and urbanized couple. It doesn't call attention to itself as a tale of ethnic particularity, despite Shukumar's and Shoba's having first met at a recital of Bengali poets in Cambridge, or Shoba's frequent visits to India as a child and Shukumar's rare visits there, or the fact that Shukumar's dissertation is on agrarian revolts in India. If their coming together in marriage is a result of their shared ethnic heritage, that fact is never given prominent play. The circumstances of their childhood, youth, and pre-marriage adulthood are related with an air of casual confidence in the *normalcy* of the South Asian American presence on the American landscape. But precisely because it takes for granted that there is nothing out of the ordinary in how Shoba and Shukumar have grown up in the United States—with India a constant reality in their consciousnesses—"A Temporary Matter" functions as a powerful announcement of the coming-of-age of the second generation of South Asian Americans. It's an announcement intended both for the in-group and the out-group: to South Asian Americans it says, "This is the life that some of us will lead here—we will mature, find professions, choose our partners, suffer our losses, and take up the thread of our lives and carry on." To non–South Asian Americans, it says, "We are here, and this is who we are in all our complexity and nuance."

Lahiri presents Shoba and Shukumar as finely individuated characters with richly developed traits. As a narrative on gender relations, the story offers no predictable behaviors. Shoba is the efficient proofreader; Shukumar, the doctoral student still struggling to finish his dissertation at thirty-five. In their three years of marriage, the time preceding the stillbirth of their child had been warm and intimate, with both reveling in their discovery of each other's personalities. One can cull no simple theory of gender roles in the context of South Asian American ethnicity from their interactions with each other. They feel no need to "perform" their ethnicity, nor do they feel it necessary to assert their assimilation into the U.S. social fabric. They appear comfortable with both their Indian-ness and their American-ness, because they make no issue of either. Thus, as the opening story of *The Interpreter of Maladies*, "A Temporary Matter" makes a strong stand for the voices of second generation South Asian Americans as an integral part of the social fabric of the United States.

Empty Spaces

I close this chapter with a reference to two women—Bhairavi Desai and Monami Maulik—who are not writers, but who are bold in their imaginings. Desai works in an area that is almost exclusively the purview of males. She organizes taxicab drivers in New York City to fight for labor rights—to demand decent working conditions, to refuse to endure their sweatshop on wheels. Desai's efforts have persuaded immigrant male taxicab drivers to sign up for membership in the New York Taxi Workers Alliance (NYTWA). Desai has become something of a celebrity among young South Asian Americans eager to feel that they are contributing to the cause of social justice. In her public statements, she makes light of her gender, although she has been a fierce advocate of women's rights, having cut her activist teeth at Manavi, an organization for battered women started in New Jersey.[55]

Monami Maulik is one of the founding members of Desis Rising Up and Moving (DRUM), a community activist organization whose work in the past two years has come to focus on the post–September 11 detainees—primarily Muslim men, many of whom are from South Asian nations—being held without access to legal counsel.[56] The implementation of the USA Patriot Act has made political activism much more dangerous, especially among the families of detainees, and their reluctance to speak up is directly related to the arbitrariness of arrests of Muslim men.

For both women, gender is incidental to the work they do; yet their being women is most noticeable in the context of the activist work they perform—Desai in the midst of taxicab drivers, Maulik in behalf of the male detainees. In closing this chapter with them, my aim is not to deflect attention from literary expression or to undercut its importance to understanding the South Asian American experience. But Desai and Maulik serve to uncover the gaps in the South Asian American literary landscape. As far as I know, there are no comparable figures to be found in South Asian American poetry, fiction, drama, or memoir—no portraits of young working-class women skilled at challenging unjust systems of power and comfortable with moving in and out of the gendered spaces of their organizing. Theirs is a narrative waiting to be told imaginatively for a number of reasons. It forces us to engage with class heterogeneity in the South Asian American community. It also offers an instance of a particular kind of generational reversal so frequently seen in immigrant communities, where the children quickly become adept in the English language and the ways of American official bureaucracy and begin to serve as mentors and advisors to their parents.[57] In the case of Desai and Maulik, their expertise as native-born Americans is not confined to the boundaries of their home but extends outward into the community, thereby making their influence as young women a matter of no small significance. Desai and Maulik serve not just as *explicators* of the American system to the communities in which they organize, but also as agents who challenge the failures in the system and thereby test the limits of democratic protest. They embolden those whom they serve to challenge the shortcomings of the status quo and to protest the current inequities. In order to do so, the taxicab drivers and the families of detainees must take a crash course in political activism in the American context. (Gautam Premnath rightly observes that many South Asian immigrants bring homegrown traditions of protest, which are retooled for and adapted to the new setting.)[58] Desai and Maulik, on the frontlines, present a complex image of the South Asian woman both to the South Asian American and the non–South Asian American communities. Their actions, their words, their presence all serve to warn us of the futility of stereotypical reductions and, instead, to promise the gratification of rich understandings.

FOUR

Writing What You're Not: Limits and Possibilities of the Insider Imperative

Writing, in a way, is listening to the others' language and reading with the others' eyes. The more ears I am able to hear with, the farther I am able to see the plurality of meaning and the less I lend myself to the illusion of a single message.

—TRINH T. MINH-HA, *WOMAN, NATIVE, OTHER*

TO PUT IT BLUNTLY, who can write *about* and *as* whom and not invite accusations of appropriation? Can a black man write in the voice of a black woman with impunity? Can a brown woman write about a black man? About a white man? Can a Muslim woman write about a Jewish man? Speak in his voice? Can a Muslim man speak for a white Christian woman? Can an Indian American Hindu take on the voice of a Pakistani American Muslim? The permutations are endless. And under what conditions, if any, can the white man—who has written *as* everyone, *of* everyone—enter the consciousness of other races, of women, and not appear to be insensitive, arrogant, or just plain misguided? Although I don't pretend to have satisfactory answers, I want to engage these questions within the context of South Asian American writing, to dwell on those occasions when its authors endeavor to "listen[ ] to the others' language and read[ ] with the others' eyes." My invocation of Trinh Minh-ha is an acknowledgment that such a discussion can never be dissociated from considerations of power.[1]

In the afterword to the collection of South Asian American/Canadian fiction, poetry, essays, and photography *Contours of the Heart*

(1996), Sucheta Mazumdar offers a provocative critique. While she acknowledges the pleasure of encountering these narratives and representations of the South Asian presence in North America, she questions the preoccupation with ethnic identity that lies at their base. She rather pointedly characterizes the narratives as "self-indulgent" and asks, "[D]oes my identity have to be constructed by what I have inherited and not by what I have struggled to make of myself? Am I doubly doomed by my genes and my country of ancestral origin? Or do politics that struggle for social change, for social justice for all—not just the people with whom one may share a certain ancestral affinity—matter at all?"[2] In this chapter, I take up the questions embedded in her critique and consider works by South Asian American writers that tell of the experiences of non–South Asians, with a particular view to examining these texts for the questions they raise about their representation of these "others." Ultimately, I am interested in what such writing, which resists containment within the field of South Asian experiences, may reveal about the capacity of South Asians to engage with the lives of "others."

I take on this task with no small degree of apprehension, given the explosive political debate that has frequently been sparked by the efforts of writers who step outside their own ethnic or racial categories and write about whom they are not. Theoretically, the creative imagination has the entire field of human experience at its disposal. Practically, the exercise of this creative imagination is intertwined with sociopolitical and economic forces. Postcolonial and ethnic studies scholars have established convincingly the power dynamics underlying representations of racial and ethnic minorities the world over. Racial and ethnic groups that have been dominated for centuries invariably have been represented in ways that deny their full complexity as humans and contribute to their continued subjugation in all facets of life. Social and political forces that emerged to resist and overturn these dominations set in motion artistic phenomena that have both liberated and confined the creative imagination of artists of these hitherto oppressed groups.

Writers of color have flexed their creative imaginations and reveled in portraying the previously undocumented experiences of their peoples.[3] We now have a rich American literature that encompasses the writings of all ethnic and racial groups, giving evidence of the heterogeneity of our lives. However, these various ethnic literatures have set out on their own separate paths, as it were—Asian Americans writing about Asian

Americans, African Americans writing about African Americans, and so on. And even these discrete ethnoracial groups contain further distinctions that artists, by and large, seem to observe. For example, as Mazumdar points out, within South Asian American writing, Indian Americans typically write about Indians and Indian Americans, Pakistani Americans about Pakistanis and Pakistani Americans, and so on, further constricting the domain of creative endeavor.

Like Mazumdar, Christopher Fan worries about what he sees as "the redundancy of explicitly Asian themes in APA [Asian Pacific American] literature" and believes that such a redundancy is "a bankrupt and counterproductive subversive strategy . . . which ultimately performs a disservice to the project of liberating the APA community."[4] Reminding us of the controversy surrounding the publication of James Baldwin's *Giovanni's Room*, Fan declares that in writing that book Baldwin struck a powerful blow against the racist publishing industry and liberated the African American writer's creative imagination from being fettered strictly to African American characters and themes. Fan hopes that Asian American writers will liberate themselves in the same way: "The thematic liberation of APA literature will lead to the political liberation of the APA community. APA writers must not participate in the reinforcement of the oppositions that have organized our oppressive society and given birth to the racist vocabulary Baldwin speaks of. The fight is for America, not Asian America."[5]

Mazumdar and Fan are both aware of the critical work that South Asian American and Asian American writers have performed for their communities by opening up new landscapes of experience for the American reading public. In fact, Mazumdar acknowledges that reading the poems and narratives in *Contours of the Heart* is deeply comforting. Therefore, their critiques are all the more imperative to heed. They both point to the ultimate political limitations of ethno-particular writing: the impossibility of breaking down institutional structures of racism that thrive on keeping people divided from one another by emphasizing their differences in the guise of "celebrating diversity." In this context, it is useful to remember Gayatri Spivak's oft-quoted articulation of the need for a posture of "strategic essentialism" that, even while serving to mobilize groups around clearly defined criteria of belonging (race, gender, ethnicity, or sexual orientation), must nevertheless be prevented from hardening into the only mode of resistance and activism:

Just as "The personal is political" became, finally, in our personalist ideology, "Only the personal is political," in the same way, the strategic use of essentialism became a kind of carte blanche for being an essentialist when one wanted to be. Strategy went out the window. . . .What is useful for political intervention is to keep questions of collective agency right in front of one's nose, and to be very careful to realize that what makes collective agency possible is rational, established discourse, and . . . the only way to work with collective agency is to teach a persistent critique of collective agency at the same time. You cannot not want it and at the same time you do a critique of it. It is the persistent critique of what one cannot not want.[6]

I embark on this discussion of South Asian American writing that eschews an ethno-specific focus with full cognizance of the dangerous ground on which I am treading, specifically with reference to the ethics of responsible representation .The controversies accompanying the publication of William Styron's *The Confessions of Nat Turner* and Forrest Carter's *The Education of Little Tree* and the awarding of a Pulitzer Prize to Robert Olen Butler for his story collection *Good Scent from a Strange Mountain* give ample evidence that when European American writers depict the experiences of and speak in the voices of people of color, their works are seldom received without consideration of questions of power (see below for Monique Truong's critique of Butler).[7] Readers of color are wont to consider these writings closely to determine the degree of responsibility exercised by their white authors. Any trace of glibness in the crossing of the racial or ethnic or cultural line tends to inauthenticate the work, marking it as yet another instance of white appropriation of the voices of people of color.

However, reductive representations are by no means the shortcoming of white writers alone; writers of color frequently fall into the same mode even when narrating the experiences of those within their own racial or ethnic group, let alone characters from other groups of color. Socioeconomic class, religion, and gender can present seemingly insurmountable barriers. For example, one of the strongest criticisms among South Asian readers of Bharati Mukherjee's works is that her characters reproduce dominant-culture stereotypes. Chitra Divakaruni has not infrequently been questioned about her unflattering depiction of the

Indian American male. Lois Ann Yamanaka has been accused of perpet-
uating stereotypes about the Filipino Hawaiian male and has even had a
literary award revoked for one such depiction (see below for further discussion of Yamanaka). Thus, being a writer of color is no guarantee of
heightened attention to the complexities of characterization. A writer
wields power, and that power frequently is deployed in ways that do not
please certain groups of readers. The exercise of imaginative power is the
issue at hand.

Mazumdar's agenda is clear: a politics based on ethnicity is, she
believes, doomed to failure because it eventually becomes reduced to a
claustrophobic concern with questions of cultural authenticity—who is
the more authentic Indian American or Pakistani American or African
American? This preoccupation prevents one from feeling outrage at economic and social injustice unless it is directed against those who share
one's racial, ethnic, national, gender, religious, or any other identifiable
affiliation or category. Her call is simple: inform yourself of the conditions under which your own group and others live and understand how
you are *all* implicated in the complicated forces of regional, national, and
global politics. Hers is a daunting challenge for she exhorts us all to go
beyond the comfortable boundaries of the familiar—either in terms of
race, class, ethnicity, or national origin—and engage with peoples outside our immediate circles of concern.

Mazumdar is a historian with a wide scope. When she talks of the
Chinese or Indians in the United States, her consciousness expands to
encompass the political and economic forces that set in motion labor
movements of the nineteenth century resulting in the dispersal of hundreds of thousands of workers from China and the Indian subcontinent
to places as diverse as Fiji, the United States, Canada, Guyana, Trinidad,
and Panama.[8] No group can understand its position in any location, she
insists, without understanding the interplay of power and economics,
across several geographies and over the course of years, that created the
conditions in which the group now finds itself in a particular location,
such as the United States or Canada. She cautions us against simplistic
articulations of ethnic, class, and national membership.

This kind of expansive vision is not easy to maintain and can seem
rather artificial in the face of a powerful yearning "to belong" to a group
in which one's membership requires no explanation. In a talk that she
gave at the University of Massachusetts, Amherst, in December 1999,

Mazumdar challenged the newly established certificate program in Asian American Studies there to consider the changing relationships over time between the different countries in Asia and the United States and to consider the effect of these changes on U.S. citizens and residents of Asian descent. The reminder to instructors and administrators launching the program of the need to articulate a broad framework for the study of Asians in the United States was more than just a rhetorical flourish. Today's students become tomorrow's researchers, teachers, public servants, and civic participants; the kinds of understanding they bring to questions of citizenship and public policy are likely to have a significant effect on the quality of the lives of Asians in the United States. Mazumdar's afterword in *Contours* reminds us of the types of frameworks to avoid:

> Asian American Studies with its pathetic eagerness to prove its American origins and disdain for learning about Asian history, has proved incapable of disentangling how colonialism has warped its own world view. For the second- and third- and fourth-generation Asian Americans, mostly of Chinese American and Japanese American origin, who emerged as the progenitors of the Asian American movement in the late 1960s, "Asia" was easily and readily identified with the homeland of their parents [and grand- and great-grandparents]. Radical politics did not translate into radical rethinking of national-origin categories; there was no perceived need to redefine the "Asia" in Asian American, or to reach out to strange black and brown peoples.[9]

Can the United States See with Others' Eyes, Hear with Others' Ears? Or, How Do We Avoid Essentializing Those Whom We Wish to Know?

A mindset such as the one Mazumdar urges us to adopt in order "to reach out to strange . . . peoples" requires an appreciation for the long view—both past and future. It is a sensibility that is particularly relevant today, and the exhortation to achieve it should by no means be directed specifically at South Asian Americans. It behooves the entire civic body of the United States to begin to grapple with the histories and narratives of peoples we deem unfamiliar. In the months and years following the attacks on the World Trade Center towers and the Pentagon, the United States is slowly beginning to realize that it can no longer continue to see itself as independent of other nations or see its actions as self-contained in certain geographies and within certain time periods. There are repercussions to most decisions, and some of these repercussions are by no means trivial and may manifest themselves after many decades. Having armed Osama Bin Laden and his Al Qaeda network during the Soviet occupation of Afghanistan in the 1980s, and also having armed Iraq during its hostilities with Iran in 1980–88, the United States has been faced with having to contain its own offspring, so to speak.

Historians, political scientists, and commentators in the United States are struggling to understand precisely why their nation seems so misunderstood by other peoples. Stanley Hoffman argues in "America Goes Backward" that it is time for the United States to recognize that it belongs to a world community, and that if it wishes to preserve its liberties and prosperity, then it must be willing to create the conditions that enable the growth of such liberties and prosperity in other parts of the world. Hoffman observes that "[t]he anti-Americanism on the rise throughout the world is not just hostility toward the most powerful nation, or based on the old clichés of the left and the right; nor is it only envy or hatred of our values. It is, more often than not, a resentment of double standards and double talk, of crass ignorance and arrogance, of wrong assumptions and dubious policies." That means, of course, that we should not support oppressive regimes simply because we see them as favorable to our national interest. Jack Beatty of WBUR's "On Point Radio" shares the sentiment, noting that nationalism is perhaps not the path to world humanity.[10]

Social commentator Shelby Steele voices another perspective. He notes that American and Western cultures represent the pinnacle of civilization's development. Certain peoples of the world (Africans and Arabs) have been cut off—as a result of colonialism and discrimination—from the normal trajectory of development toward these ideals. So when they throw off the shackles of colonialism and free themselves from conquest, they are thrust suddenly into the conditions of a free and open society for which they are unprepared. They therefore find themselves enormously fearful of this wealth of choices and so retaliate against the force that they perceive to be the source of their confusion.[11]

There is nothing inherently wrong with professing a view such as Steele's, but it does become an impediment if one wishes to understand how peoples outside this conceptual framework (in which the United States is seen as embodying the acme of a civic society's achievement) might construct and respond to the United States. In a provocative essay on Western anthropology, Deborah Gewertz and Frederick Errington take up the much-debated Eurocentrism of Western fieldworkers, but they do not do so merely to reiterate the danger and injustice that the resulting reductive portrayals and inaccurate analyses pose for those observed. The unexpected turn of their essay lies in their contention that "misrepresentation of the 'other' contribute[s] to the misrepresentation of ourselves."[12] If the United States sees the rest of the world as backward, poor, oppressed, dependent, chaotic, imprisoned, manipulated, or unable to take charge, then by comparison it imagines itself to be what those other nations are not. Self-delusion in itself may not be an alarming trait, but when it contributes to complacency and self-satisfaction, then the robustness and viability of a democracy are undermined. An implicit faith in the health of the political and civic system prevents Americans from examining the ways in which certain fundamental changes are urgently needed in their own social and political processes. The United States is at a historical moment of great import: either it can use the current crisis to step outside of its own system of knowing and apprehending the world long enough to attempt another way of viewing global conditions, or it can become further entrenched in its own worldview as a gesture of defiance against those who would wish it harm.

When individuals and groups have broken out of familiar and comfortable perspectives and ventured into new territories of knowledge it has usually been a matter of survival. I am reminded of Nelson Mandela's careful study of the Afrikaans language and culture as a means of understanding his oppressors, the Afrikaners. His immersion in the Afrikaner's way of viewing the world was critical preparation for the time when he knew he would be called upon to negotiate with Afrikaner leaders to create a new democratic South Africa. Perhaps the Mandela analogy is not entirely valid in the context of the United States. The United States may not believe that its survival is dependent on other nations, and so its government officials and broader citizenry may be unwilling to make those pioneering journeys into the hearts and minds of the people of different nations. Or, conversely, the United States may wish to reconstruct other nations in its own image as a way of addressing the problem of being misunderstood. It should be apparent, however, that isolationism as a political stance is not a viable option when even our allies of the North Atlantic Treaty Organization find our positions untenable (for example, refusal to endorse the Kyoto agreement on climate control, rejection of an International Criminal Court, or reluctance to pressure Israel to return to its pre-1967 borders). But the United States has the military and economic might to persist in its belief that it can, indeed, hold strong to its policy positions and thrive as a nation. That, at any rate, appears to be the prevalent view of the political leadership today. Whether or not the citizenry shares this perspective is yet to be determined with any certainty, although the opinion polls seem to suggest that they do.

I would argue, however, that our "survival" as a nation depends on our being able to step outside ourselves and envision how it might be to live elsewhere in the world. By survival, I don't mean our continued presence as a nation; rather, I mean our ability to live without constant fear of being attacked, of being sabotaged in our day-to-day lives. As I discussed in Chapter 1, coexistence in a global sense is more urgent today than ever before. If the United States is to coexist with other nations in some sort of uneasy yet relatively stable alliance, then it probably will have to learn to see with multiple eyes and through multiple consciousnesses. And this will be no easy task for a nation that has long had the luxury of seeing only itself even when it is not looking in the mirror.

It may seem that I have moved a long way from talking about South Asian American literature, from taking up Mazumdar's challenge to writers of South Asian descent in the United States to expand the sphere of their creative endeavors. I would argue, however, that a digression to consider the situation of the United States after the September 11 attacks is actually very pertinent to questions concerning the exercise of the creative imagination. How do we imagine the condition of others? How do we do justice to the complexity of their lives? How do we re-create the nuances of their day-to-day activities? And, most importantly, how do we invest them with the same multitude and paradox of emotions that we know ourselves to possess. Or, to put it another way, how do we avoid essentializing those whom we wish to know?

Moving Closer But Not Too Close

Philosophically, it is not always desirable to seek commonality with those whom we seek to describe. That kind of quest runs the risk of force-fitting their distinctiveness within ours, of giving the impression that without these points of similarity there would be no way we could begin to depict those who are different from us. Characterizations of sameness and difference are beset with complications. The danger in portraying someone as being fundamentally different is that it can lead to difficulty in empathizing with that person or understanding the motivations for his/her actions. At the same time, *not* acknowledging fundamental dissimilarities may lead to committing an equal disservice, since the group that we wish to portray may take pride in its difference from us.

A short story by Tahira Naqvi helps illustrate the dynamic of this contradiction of similarity versus dissimilarity as it operates in a cross-ethnic cross-cultural representation.[13] "Thank God for the Jews" is set in a Connecticut town and tells the story of a Pakistani American woman, Zenab, who is anxiously trying to procure *halal* meat—meat that has been killed in a religiously prescribed fashion—for an older visitor who is an observant Muslim. It is the height of winter and too dangerous for Zenab to make the trip to New York City, which is where she normally purchases the meat from the halal butcher.

The time is the 1980s, and the news on television one evening is about the conflict in the Middle East: "An Israeli school bus had been bombed. Its carcass sat forlornly on a hill; some children had been killed, some injured. . . . The camera moved with sudden abruptness to another scene . . . [a]n Arab village in ruins. Nearly all the houses had been demolished, the survivors of the attack moving in slow motion like wandering spirits." Zenab notices among these survivors "[a]n old woman whose face looked oddly familiar, squatted before a crumbled hollowed-out dwelling . . . cr[ying] without restraint, her mouth hanging open in a grotesque caricature of a smile" (22). That old woman, she realizes, reminds her of the orthodox guest whose impending visit is causing her such consternation. "Saddened by loss and despair, all old women look the same," Zenab muses.

The news over, she is once again confronted by the dietary problem at hand and is close to panic that she will not be able to meet her obligations to her guest. She calls a resourceful friend who has often helped her during previous emergencies, and once again the friend comes to the rescue. "What about kosher? . . . You see, all their meat is prepared just like ours. They recite God's name before slaughtering the animal and bleed the animal afterward" (26). The friend directs her to the kosher section at the supermarket.

This story was first anthologized in the collection *Imagining America* (1991); presumably the editors included it for its fascinating juxtaposition in the United States of two religious groups that elsewhere in the world are in deep conflict. And there is, indeed, something reassuring about being shown this glimpse of an intersection of two cultures—Islamic and Jewish—that are otherwise always depicted in opposition to one another. But Naqvi has said that at certain readings of the story, Jewish members in the audience have felt affronted by what they consider to be the trivializing of the conflict between the two cultures. I would argue, however, that what is particularly brilliant in Naqvi's treatment of the situation is precisely that she does not romanticize the simple shared dietary prescription. The presentation of similarity—the Jews prepare their meat like the Pakistanis (Muslims), and so in the United States going to a Jewish deli is the equivalent of going to the halal butcher—is skillfully balanced against the stark reminder of the deep hostility between the Jewish state of Israel and its Muslim neighbors. That the protagonist voices her sense of kinship with the old woman who is left homeless by the Israeli bombing bears out even more forcefully that Zenab's visit to the Jewish deli will be an act of convenience only, not one necessitating a fundamental alteration of her worldview.

In this narrative, Naqvi has succeeded in juxtaposing sameness and difference—neither romanticizing the one nor glossing over the other. And it is through this delicately balanced representation—articulating a possible connection between two cultures while never letting us forget the fragility of that link—that she pulls off the complicated feat of cross-cultural representation while preserving all the nuances of that portrayal.

Vivek Bald's eloquent narration (the text of which is included in *Contours of the Heart*) to his documentary film *Taxi-vala / Auto-biography* raises similar issues with other types of crossings. Bald, the offspring of a Pakistani mother and Australian father, tells of his eagerness to document the work of cabdrivers in New York City, more than 50 percent of whom are of South Asian origin. He is, however, fully aware of the disparities between him and the cabdrivers and is anxious not to minimize these gaps. Almost James Agee-like[14] in his agonizing, Bald declares his unresolved misgivings about the project:

> [T]here's a tense silence as I sit with the camera in my hands—the camera my parents bought me. I won't admit that while my mother and Ahmed [a cabdriver] share a birthplace, Ahmed and I may not share anything at all. Or that my few words of Urdu, because they're spoken here in New York, don't suddenly make us part of the same community. As I start to shoot, I want to believe that we're connected, though we grew up in different nations, religions, histories, and here in New York, we're separated by a taximeter and a plexiglass partition.[15]

It is not social class alone that separates Bald from Ahmed and other cabdrivers; additional differences intervene, not the least of which is the suspicion of African Americans on the part of some drivers. But even in his narration of this difference, Bald offers a rich and multilayered presentation. In one instance, he refrains from challenging the obvious racism of a driver named Aziz, who, in the presence of Bald's black girlfriend Kym, declares that he will date any type of woman but a black woman, because "he cannot trust black women" (71). Chastened by his own silence in that situation, Bald speaks up later during a conversation he has with Saleem, a cabdriver who has become Bald's friend and political ally. They are talking "about the 'right' which many cabdrivers are demanding to refuse to stop for passengers they think look dangerous" (71–72). Bald informs us that "Saleem has long opposed this 'right of refusal,' saying that it's a racist measure which drivers would aim at African Americans and Latinos" (72). Thinking that he has a like-minded companion in Saleem, Bald tells him about "different friends of color who, no matter what time of day, no matter what their age, dress, or physical appearance, have all been passed by empty yellow-cabs" (72). Saleem responds by exploding in anger and underscoring to Bald the unbridgeable chasm between them: "He [Saleem] says I'm in no place to speak. He says I can stand behind my camera or sit comfortably at my desk and call him and his friends racist, but until I drive a cab on the streets seven days a week to support my family, I don't know a thing" (72). Bald's narration treads carefully through the terrain of commonality and difference. That he desires to understand viscerally the lives the cabdrivers lead is apparent; that he is wary of easy identifications gives his narration a rich texture.

Bald, like Agee, exhibits a painful "guilt of privilege." Entering the world of the cabdrivers may be Bald's way of acquiring what he calls "a badge of brownness." Bald, a biracial individual, wonders at the ease with which he overlooks or passes over his identification with the lineage of his white father. We never quite understand what lures Bald to the cabdrivers' hard life; it may lie in the tantalizing nearness-and-distance of their identity and experience from his own. The documentary mode gives him the illusion of being an insider even if it paradoxically makes him aware of his outsider status. Saleem's outburst tells us that Bald's film is a search for a similarity, for belonging, that is likely to elude the filmmaker. By calling it *Taxi-vala/Auto-biography*, Bald acknowledges that the film is a double voicing, as much about himself as it is about the cabdrivers. However, he is fundamentally honest about the ways in which his foray into the cabdrivers' economic and discursive space in a search for insiderness is ultimately thwarted. He doesn't try to bridge the chasms because he comes to realize that they are too wide.

Held Hostage by the Long Shadow of Anthropology

The complicated terrain of the insider-outsider antithesis has become increasingly nuanced over the years. The academic discipline that has given this topic the most attention is anthropology, and the colonial legacy of the discipline has, not surprisingly, made it a ready target of postcolonial critique. The rich debates that have arisen over anthropological fieldwork have demonstrated the limitations of the insider-outsider polarity and advanced instead the view of a continuum in which one's position as insider or outsider is fluid rather than fixed, contextual rather than absolute.

In his 1997 book *Routes*, James Clifford offers a valuable overview of changes over the last three decades in the notion of what constitutes legitimate anthropological research and what can be accepted as the "field" or site of research.[16] Traditional expectations necessitated that the anthropologist go to a location distant from Western academic centers and immerse her/himself for extended periods of time (usually several months of uninterrupted stay) in the study of unfamiliar peoples. Over the years that model has been challenged, and today one frequently finds a non-Western anthropologist returning to a known location and observing/studying a not entirely unfamiliar people. One also finds anthropologists making numerous short visits to a relatively nearby research site—as in the case of anthropologist Karen McCarthy Brown, who traveled regularly from her home in Manhattan to Brooklyn to study a voudou priestess there.

One of the non-Western feminist anthropologists Clifford cites, Kamala Visweswaran, speaks of the importance of doing "homework" as a necessary condition of responsible fieldwork. Visweswaran's "homework" is the preparation and self-scrutiny that an anthropologist must engage in so as to negotiate the insider-outsider continuum with integrity. "Speaking from a place where one is not, where location and locution are tightly bound by a distant imaginary, is, of course, the normative practice of anthropology," observes Visweswaran of the traditional edicts of the discipline. "'Anthropology in reverse' then means speaking from the place one is located, to specify our sites of enunciation as 'home.'"[17]

Anthropology's colonialist heritage has invited a healthy critique and interrogation of its methodological practices and assumptions. Such scrutiny has resulted in a much needed overhaul of the discipline, particularly of the component that required the participant-observer researcher to assume a removed and distanced voice when analyzing observations and reporting findings. Patti Lather addresses the issues of authority and voice in the context of her ethnographic work with women living with HIV/AIDS. She identifies her methodology as emanating from the new ethnography, which "grew out of a literary turn in the 1980s with concerns of 'textuality, disciplinary history, critical modes of reflexivity, and the critique of realist practices of representation.' What George Marcus has termed 'messy texts' announces the new: partial and fluid epistemological and cultural assumptions, fragmented writing styles, and troubled notions of ethnographic legitimacy."[18]

The idea of "messy texts"—that is, articulations that have embedded within them critiques of their own legitimacy, in other words, that deconstruct themselves—marks the new ethnography.[19] I find this idea useful in examining the authorial approaches that writers take to the task of representing dissimilar others. Today, the field has enriched itself by creating discursive spaces for the anthropologist to articulate her/his own subjectivity as it impinges on peoples and practices being studied. These discursive spaces or "sites of enunciation" have let the air out of the ponderous and oppressive weight of "objective" presentation of data.

Clifford's brief survey of anthropology's research debates provides at least one significant contrast between anthropological research/interpretation and literary writing: anthropology has encouraged inquiry into and study of the unfamiliar; by contrast, literature, particularly in the post–Civil Rights movement and postcolonial era of the last forty years, has encouraged precisely the opposite. Authors are urged to write about what they have witnessed or lived. The experiential or testimonial imperative reigns supreme. Among people of color, the colonial legacy of anthropology casts its long shadow on literature, such that the reception of any piece of imaginative writing is tinged with questions of representational authenticity and exercise of power. Readers of color in particular demand from literature a glimpse into the "sites of enunciation" of those writers who venture out of their immediately apparent racial, ethnic, gender, and sexual orientation frameworks. In the genre of the memoir, these sites of enunciation can be explicit and visible—as they are in Abraham Verghese's *My Own Country* or Pico Iyer's collection of travel essays *Video Night in Kathmandu*; in other forms of writing, such as Abha Dawesar's novel *Miniplanner* or Vikram Seth's novel in sonnet form, *Golden Gate*, they are not so immediately apparent.

Seeing Like the Other: As Though One's Life Depended on It (Some examples from European American Literature)

There is no denying the sheer dramatic force of writing that grows out of lived experience. The testimonial perspective makes for powerful insider accounts that bear the automatic stamp of legitimacy and authenticity: captivity narratives, slave narratives, accounts of being forcibly boarded in American Indian schools at the end of the nineteenth century, Depression-era working-class narratives, prison journals. And because many of these utterances are by groups and individuals who have long been disenfranchised and denied the power to represent themselves, the very existence of these writings is occasion for celebration and reason enough for guarding against the appropriation of these experiences by writers from dominant groups.

But guarding against appropriation need not mean outright prohibition. I would argue that the landscape of American literature is given more contour and texture when there is opportunity for interplay among writings—such as the ricocheting among Frederick Douglass's *Narrative* (1845), Harriet Beecher Stowe's *Uncle Tom's Cabin* (1852), and Douglass's *The Heroic Slave* (1853); or, to take a more contemporary example, the possibility of reading Robert Olen Butler's *A Good Scent from a Strange Mountain* (1992) against the anthology *Watermark: Vietnamese American Poetry and Prose* (1998). In both *Uncle Tom's Cabin* and *A Good Scent*, the writers venture into territory in which their authority is called into question. Stowe was roundly criticized by Southern readers for having no first-hand knowledge of plantation life and for representing it with particular Northern bias. In addition, later generations of black readers would reject her portrayal of the character Tom for being too subservient and accepting of hardship. Rather than dismissing the book for its various flaws—as generations of critics have done—it is actually more useful to position it within the counterpoints and correctives provided by Douglass's *Narrative* and *The Heroic Slave* so as to bring the books into "conversation" with one another.

The same can be said of Butler's collection, notwithstanding Monique Truong's intelligent and scathing attack against it, in which she accuses Butler of a "blatant act of textual 'yellow face.'"[20] Truong excoriates Butler for "appropriat[ing] and assum[ing] the first-person voice(s) and identities of fifteen, different Vietnamese Americans, including both male and female, to tell their 'own' stories of life as a refugee and a newly settled inhabitant of southern Louisiana" (76). She sees Butler's text as a continuation of the practice by non–Asian American interviewers of "manipulating and maneuvering [the] textual form and content" of oral histories and thereby removing and replacing "the authorial agency of the Vietnamese American literary voice" (77). There is undeniable legitimacy to her assertion that Butler's text is "a finalizing step in the removal and replacement of the authorial agency of the Vietnamese American literary voice" (83). Nevertheless, I would insist that his collection be read and taught. But, and this is where I throw in my support for Truong, reading it in isolation perpetuates the notion that Vietnamese voices can only "emanate" through Butler's act of ventriloquism. Reading *A Good Scent* along with other texts by Vietnamese American writers enables a discussion of responsibility, sensitivity, and skill in the deployment of the imagination. Such discussion leads us to consider the complexity of issues embedded in a white man's imaginative rendering of a person or community of color and the extent to which a position of dominance may contribute to an inability to imagine in (subordinate) others complexity of thought and action.

The complexity of motivations leading one to seek connection across seemingly unbridgeable chasms can be glimpsed in one of the earliest testimonial accounts in American literature: the seventeenth-century captivity narrative of Mary Rowlandson. Rowlandson was taken from her home in Lancaster, Massachusetts, in 1675 by the Wampanoag Indians and lived among them for three months before she was returned to the Puritan settlers. Her account of the captivity is instructive for two reasons. Forced to depend on the Indians for her survival, Rowlandson grudgingly finds much to value in their way of life, and her narrative is punctuated by descriptions of their many kindnesses to her. In addition, her account, like other captivity narratives that followed it in subsequent decades, provides fertile ground for a study of the fluidity of insider-outsider positions. Typically, the captives entered the tribe as outsiders and saw themselves as such in the early days of their captivity. Their view of Native American ways was, at this point, harshly critical. They saw the cultural practices of their captors as being far removed from their own Christian and "civilized" ways. Over time, however, they adapted to the ways of the tribe, if principally for the purpose of survival, and in that quasi-insider position were able to appreciate aspects of Native American life that eluded their understanding as outsiders. Upon their release from captivity, they once again adopted an outsider's perspective in order to report their ordeal in terms that would be acceptable to the white community among whom they had to live. However, interwoven into the post-captivity negative portrayal of the Native American tribes can be found glimpses of a sympathetic insider's voice, or at least a voice that skillfully negotiates the continuum ranging from complete identity with a Native American world view to complete dissociation from such a perspective.[21]

When Imperfection Is Desired: Crossing Race and Gender and the Case of Anna Deavere Smith

Complicating the insider-outsider dichotomy and *embodying* that complication on stage is African American playwright and solo performer Anna Deavere Smith. She speaks eloquently of the need to trouble these categories: "Many of us who work in race relations do so from the point of view of our own ethnicity. This very fact inhibits our ability to hear more voices than those that are closest to us in proximity. Few people speak a language about race that is not their own. If more of us could actually speak from another point of view, like speaking another language, we could accelerate the flow of ideas."[22]

In creating her performances, Smith interviews many individuals and records their responses. Then, as part of her solo performance, she reiterates their words on stage, bringing them to life in her body and voice. For Smith, this stepping outside of herself to inhabit the mind and voice of another human being is a critical step in crossing the boundaries that exist between individuals. In putting together her play *Twilight: Los Angeles, 1992*, she interviewed many people who were either directly or peripherally involved in the Los Angeles uprising following the first verdict acquitting four policemen of beating Rodney King. One of the interviewees is Twilight, a gang member in L.A., and what he says is particularly relevant in the context of this discussion, because he articulates the *desire* to step outside himself: "I can't forever dwell in darkness, / I can't forever dwell in the idea, / of just identifying with people like me and understanding me and mine."[23]

Smith's process of reenacting the perspectives of the various players in a situation gives her, she says, a new language to talk about the complex reality of race relations in the United States. She is under no illusions about the limitations of theater in forging new civic ties among groups in conflict, but she does believe that if individuals took it upon themselves to enter the consciousness of others unlike themselves and to try to see the world through their eyes, then we would come closer to a dialogue that matters. One of Smith's most memorable performances in *Twilight* is her embodiment of Young-Soon Han, a Korean American woman whose liquor store was burned to the ground during the uprising. Smith says that her portrayal of Young-Soon Han is one of the most important things she has ever done. I would argue that because there are so few opportunities to portray Asian American realities on stage or in any other form of visual media (notwithstanding the growth of a healthy Asian American theater movement), there is a sense in which such an embodiment can be seen as a pioneering moment. That Asian Americans are hungry for their stories to be heard is demonstrated by their response to Smith when she set out to do interviews for *Twilight*: whereas the African Americans in South Central Los Angeles were suspicious of her arrival, believing her to be an outsider coming in to exploit their narrative, Korean American students, by contrast, sought her out because "they wanted to make sure that [she] heard what had happened in and to their community."[24] Relationships between blacks and Korean Americans were particularly strained during the 1980s and 1990s, with a complicated terrain of power relations—economic power lying with the Korean Americans, but the power of comfort in one's location lying with the African Americans. In this context, Smith's portrayal of Young-Soon Han offers a compelling example of the crossing of racial/ethnic boundaries in the service of interethnic understanding. I have seen both a stage performance and a television adaptation of *Twilight*, and on both occasions I have been struck by the force and complexity of Smith's enacting and voicing of Young-Soon Han's rage, frustration, and deep sadness.

Yet, Smith is not offering some simplistic theory of the actor losing herself in the physicality of the person she portrays—in fact, she is very clear that what she does is mimicry, an *almost like*, an *almost but not quite there* rendition of the individual she represents. Jonathan Kalb's assessment of Smith's performances is astute in its explanation of the power of these "imperfect" portrayals:

> Her impressions weren't entirely convincing by the standards of fourth-wall realism, and they weren't meant to be. She built the characterizations around penetrating enlargements of isolated traits and mannerisms, but the fact that she was always visible beneath the intensely studied character surfaces was what gave the pieces their strangely persuasive texture. The ever-changing split in her persona assured spectators of the constant presence of a discerning editorial eye and a selective framing hand.[25]

The audience witnesses the process by which her body undergoes the necessary changes to accommodate to the new character she inhabits. Thus, her body on stage paradoxically serves the dual purpose of both erasing the difference between herself and the person she portrays and simultaneously calling attention to that difference. The dissonance that the audience witnesses—that of watching an African American woman temporarily take on the characteristics of someone differently racialized and differently gendered—opens up a valuable space in which each spectator can contemplate the possibility of an "imperfect" transformation into another bodied subjectivity. "Imperfections" of literary representation can serve a similar purpose. If the author's sincerity and honest effort at crossing boundaries is evident in the text— as it is, for example, in Bald's narrative—then the imperfect crossing suggests to readers that they, too, can hazard the attempt.

Hutzpah with Humility: Responsible Crossing

In theory, words are at liberty to range over all experience, to render anything, any person, any event.[26] Undoubtedly, there are all kinds of political implications in launching one's imagination to follow these routes. But let's consider what we would learn if we paid attention to the politics of imagining and *then* gave our syllables free rein and encouraged them to wander. There is real strength in writing from within the space that one knows best—one is most likely (though there is no guarantee) in such a case to shape a complex representation of people and the environment—but there is also an often unacknowledged benefit to entering spaces that one does not know and learning about them as though one's life depended on it.

In this regard, Naheed Islam's "project" is instructive.[27] Islam sought to explore how one becomes coded racially in the United States and what reactions one invites upon oneself as a result of being "marked" and perceived as belonging to a certain racial group. Islam, who is of Bangladeshi descent, wanted to better understand the experiences of her closest friend, Frances Winddance Twine, and also to build coalitions with other African Americans. She describes how people's behavior to and perceptions of her changed dramatically the minute she had her hair done in corn rows and thereby became coded as black. Islam's willingness to step outside herself and enter viscerally into a different social/psychological/cultural space is not that different from the writer's act of imagining characters and creating settings unfamiliar to him/herself and of investing those imaginings with emotional depth and accuracy. Of course, there's a certain degree of hutzpah and arrogance in believing that you can enter into a life that is far removed from your own—in fact, the act of literary creation is itself infused with hutzpah. But when a writer ventures into unfamiliar territory in a manner that is cognizant of the multidimensionality and density of that territory, then that writer can provide for readers a means of engaging meaningfully with the unknown and the unfamiliar. Hutzpah with humility—paradoxical as it may sound—is possible; a writer can couple the hutzpah of creative energy and skill with the humility of acknowledging and suggesting the many layers and unknowable depths of the unfamiliar.

Other factors besides attitude come into play, however. According to Clifford, one of the fundamental distinctions between an anthropologist and a travel writer—even an excellent travel writer—is that the anthropologist spends an extended period of time in the company of those about whom he writes.[28] That sustained contact gives the anthropologist a breadth and depth of exposure that allows for meaningful insight. While the value of a lengthy encounter is obvious, I would also suggest that time often becomes the red herring in a discussion about responsible representation. There is no strict correspondence between a lengthy stay and a nuanced portrayal. Anna Deavere Smith's interviews with the individuals she portrays typically last no more than an hour. I grant that the situations under which she conducts the interviews are not typical: they take place after crises, and Smith is very clear that her interviewees have the "will to speak."[29] One could argue that Smith does not, in the strictest sense, interpret her subjects; she merely provides the means by which their voices can be heard. The subjects interpret themselves, so to speak, and their power is never compromised because they supply the words that reveal who they are. This is not the place to enter into a prolonged discussion of performance theory, but Smith is by no means stripped of all interpretive license.

Trinh Minh-ha eloquently makes the point that lengthy contact can give to the anthropologist a false sense of confidence. She is highly critical of the "anthropologist-nativist who seeks to perforate meaning by forcing his entry into the Other's personal realm [and] undertakes the desperate task of filling in all the fissures that would reveal the emptiness of knowledge." The "object" of study, says Minh-ha, may not wish to be known, may desire "opacity" and show "reticence in sharing its intimacy with a stranger." According to Minh-ha, "Trying to find the other by defining otherness or by explaining the other through laws and generalities is, as Zen says, like beating the moon with a pole or scratching an itching foot from the outside of a shoe."[30] In a not unconnected vein, Dayanita Singh, who photographs female sexual workers in Bombay, does not take candid photographs of the women, despite having spent a great deal of time in their company and developed close relationships with them. "I let them create the pose and present themselves as they would like to," she says. "This way, they have the power to decide how they want to be seen by the viewer."[31]

In the sections that follow, I take up four South Asian American writers—Pico Iyer, Abraham Verghese, Bharati Mukherjee, and Abha Dewasar—for the insights their works offer into questions of representing dissimilar "others." The length and mode of their engagement with those about whom they write differ: Iyer is a travel writer, Verghese a physician-memoirist, and Mukherjee and Dawesar fiction writers.

On a Continuum of Knowing

Iyer, in his 1991 collection of travel essays *Video Night in Kathmandu: And Other Reports from the Not-So-Far East*—which records impressions of his travels in Bali, Tibet, Nepal, China, the Philippines, Burma, Hong Kong, India, Thailand, and Japan—makes scrupulously clear that he is no authority on the places about which he writes. In fact, quite the opposite is the case, he says: "I speak not a word of any of their languages and I have never formally studied any Asian culture. Nor did I try—except in India and Japan—to consult local experts (a job best left to other experts). . . . Instead, I let myself be led by circumstance. . . . Instead of seeking out information, I let it find me" (24). The only particular qualification he brings to his travel writing is "a boyhood that schooled [him] in expatriation." Iyer details this "training":

For more than a decade while I was growing up, I spent eight months a year at a boarding school in England and four months at

home in California—in an Indian household. . . . Nowhere was
home, and everywhere. Thus, for example, when I was seventeen, I
spent a long summer traveling around India, returned to England in
the autumn for a final term at school, devoted my winter to working as a busboy in a Mexican restaurant in Southern California and
then spent the spring traveling by bus with a school friend from San
Diego through Central America and across Colombia, Ecuador and
Peru to Bolivia, before hopping back to Miami through Brazil,
Suriname and West Indies, and Greyhounding it back to the West
Coast. . . . I do not know whether such experiences sharpened my
instincts for traveling, but I hope that they taught me a little about
how much to trust, and when to doubt, first impressions. (24–25)

It is worth noting that Iyer, at least in this collection of essays, chalks
out "first impressions" as his realm of interpretation. As thoughtful readers and scholars, everything in our bones cries out against first impressions. We seek the long study, the deep engagement, and so typically we
eschew the superficial knowledge gleaned from "first impressions."
Being a writer for *Time* magazine also puts Iyer at some disadvantage
with those readers who disdain the simplified and U.S.-centric picture
of the world most frequently found in its pages. Further, one might
argue that Iyer is complicit in the Orientalist perspective evident in
Time. Iyer's own academic training has been in Western centers of learning (English public school and Oxford), places whose histories are
steeped in the colonialist project.

    Yet, it is not so easy to dismiss Iyer. His essays are intriguing precise-
ly because they challenge us to tease through simple dichotomies of
insider/outsider, Eastern/Western, cultural imperialist/cultural victim.
He takes us into places of understanding that yield more than casual
insights, and there is a quality about his observations that simultaneously evokes the flat stone skipping lightly over the surface of the water *and*
the deep waters beneath. His writings do not permit us to settle easily
into any one position; they show how "mistakes can, in their way, be as
revealing as epiphanies, and even a wrong impression may say as much
about a place as a right one" (28).

    Take Iyer's essay on Bali, the Indian Ocean "island paradise" in the
country of Indonesia. This essay contains all the turns and contradictions
that occur in much of his writing. On the one hand, his response to Bali

is uncomfortably akin to that of the Australian sun-seekers who come looking for an Edenic paradise; he seems to partake of their wide-eyed wonder and intoxicated delight at this pleasure haven. On the other hand, there is a sharp critique of such an attitude. Thus, on the same page we find two antithetical passages—one extolling the beauties of Bali's inhabitants in language dripping with Orientalist exoticism, the other offering a pointed analysis of Bali's allurements. Here is the first:

> Bali offered all the amenities of Eden. Its regally graceful people dwelt in a lush Rousseauesque garden of snakes and tropical flowers. Young girls, careless of their loveliness, bathed in running streams, wore scarlet hibiscus in their hair and silken sarongs around their supple bodies; the soft-eyed local men seemed likewise gods of good health, dazzling smiles offsetting the flowers they tucked behind their ears. In Bali, even old women were slender creatures who moved with a dancer's easy grace. (31)

But we read this passage against the backdrop of an earlier passage in which he characterizes Bali as "the most pestered" (30) of islands and informs us that "a race of charmed spirits still danced in its temples, and a crush of foreigners kept pushing their way in for a view. Tourism hung around Bali like chains around a mermaid" (31). Granted, the image of the mermaid, with its evocation of the magical and the seductively feminine, is problematic, but "crush of foreigners . . . pushing their way in for a view" is unequivocally sharp-edged in its criticism of those who would use this mermaid for their pleasures.

Among the more penetrating yet unsettling of Iyer's insights about Bali is that it is a place that offers up its rewards too easily. It's unsettling because one cannot but wonder whether Iyer's perception of Bali's easy comfort comes from his comfortable position as tourist. It may appear to the visitor that there is no hardship associated with living in Bali, but can the residents of the island honestly say the same? But then Iyer elaborates with a comparison, and in doing so complicates the initial articulation:

> At least, so I thought, the trekkers in Nepal had to hike and suffer for their uplifting highs; even the tourist in Burma or Tibet had to tilt against the crazily spinning windmills of a socialist bureaucracy

before he could collect his epiphanies. But the visitor to Bali was handed a gift-wrapped parcel of paradise the minute he arrived. After that, he had only to lie back and let the idyll present itself to him, demanding nothing in return. (48)

Yet, this insight, too, is offered from the vantage point of the tourist. One still gets the impression that Iyer does not "see" the residents of Bali and that he writes as though the only people worth watching are those who, like him, come to visit the island.

A powerful illness gives Iyer the opportunity to dwell on the complex unknowability of a place that is more than just an answer to a tourist's yearning. Yet, note that even in this engagement with Bali and the country of which it is a part, Iyer swings between a Western-centric perspective and a point of view that hints at the limitations of the Western mindset:

And as I lay alone in the dark, I began to think about the secrecy of this whole mysterious land, a secrecy so deep that it seemed like sorcery. Indonesia is the fifth-largest country in the world, exceeded in population only by the three superpowers and India, home to more people than South Korea, the Philippines, Thailand, Hong Kong, and Nepal combined. But how often was it heard from? . . . Indonesia was far and away the largest Islamic nation in the world, with *twice* as many Muslims as Iran, Iraq, Syria and Saudi Arabia combined. Yet even in Muslim Java there seemed to be few mosques, the mythology was Hindu and its most famous monument (Borobudur) was Buddhist. What was driving this place and why did it shy away from the headlines? . . . What was going on here? And what were these beautiful people weaving behind the screens of their eerie shadow plays? (57–58)

There is much that we cannot know about Bali, Iyer says, but that is because Bali will not allow itself to be read, has no interest in making the headlines of the Western press. One detects both frustration and admiration in Iyer's response to Bali's refusal to "open" itself to his understanding.

One might justifiably wonder whether reading Iyer illuminates anything of worth about the limits and possibilities of nuanced representation. Do his voice and vision not seem too compromised by privilege and Western blessing? Perhaps. Still, I would be unwilling to cast him off. Iyer's brown skin does put him in a slightly different position from a white-skinned tourist in the places he visits. He is perceived differently, but, more to the point, people respond to him differently. Iyer's works are particularly relevant to the growing second generation of Asian Americans who make their way back to ancestral homelands in an effort to learn about the ethos of their identities. These second-generation Asian Americans return as privileged tourists armed with no small cluster of the types of Western preconceptions that weave their way through Iyer's writings. Andrew X. Pham's *Catfish and Mandala* is a case in point. In this travel memoir, Pham, a California-based Vietnamese American in his twenties, takes a bicycle journey through Vietnam. His extreme discomfort at the poverty and official corruption he encounters there and his trepidation at being cajoled into trying "adventurous" foods such as snake heart indicate that his sensibility is more non-Vietnamese than he is at first willing to acknowledge.[32]

Iyer's writing, particularly his *The Lady and the Monk* (1991), might be profitably read against David Mura's memoir *Turning Japanese* (1991). Mura, a Sansei poet, goes to Japan, the land of his grandparents, on a U.S./Japan Creative Artist Exchange Fellowship. Prior to his visit, Mura had never been particularly interested in Japanese culture, having been raised by his Nisei parents to be as American as possible. The year that he spends in Japan gives him the opportunity to realize the extent to which he is and isn't a part of a country in which he looks like most people but cannot speak the language adequately or understand the subtlety of its customs.[33]

Iyer is attracted to Japan in a rather ineffable way. He finds that it evokes in him the deeply comforting memories of a childhood in England. In fact, Iyer's meditations on the similarities between the English and the Japanese are quite perspicacious:

> There were many features of Japan that might have reminded me of England: the small villages set amidst rich green hills, all scaled with a cozy modesty; the self-enclosure of an island apart from the world, not open to sea and light, as tropical islands are, but huddled in upon itself [. . .] ; a sense of polite aloofness, a coolness enforced by courtesies and a language built on shadows; even the sense of the immovable hierarchy that made both countries seem like giant Old Boys Clubs.[34]

And so it is that Iyer, in the fall of 1987, resolves to spend an extended period of time in Japan to put to the test "the vision [he] had always
cherished of living simply and alone, in some foreign land, unknown. . .
. A life alone was the closest thing to faith I knew, and a life of
Thoreauvian quiet seemed most practicable abroad. Japan, besides,
seemed the ideal site for such an exercise in solitude, not only because
its polished courtesies kept the foreigner out as surely as its closed doors,
but also because its social norms were as unfathomable to me, and as
alien, as the woods around Walden Pond" (7–8).

Iyer's stay in Japan is, however, anything but solitary. Before long, he
becomes romantically involved with a married woman, Sachiko, and in
exploring the growth of their relationship Iyer reveals how much of
Japan will always be inaccessible to him:

> By now, Sachiko and I were bypassing language altogether very
> often. . . .
>
> The Japanese, of course, had long prided themselves on their abil-
> ity to communicate without words (in part, no doubt, because this
> served to bind the tribe together and so keep aliens out); . . . they
> enshrined the Buddhist ideal of speaking through actions more than
> words. And Sachiko, living her life in subtitles now, and resolving
> herself into the simplicity of a haiku, was, without trying, teaching
> me gradually to see a little below the surface and grow more atten-
> tive to the small print of the world. (324–25)

Of course, one could object to the Orientalism of his presentation of
Sachiko as "living her life in subtitles . . . and resolving herself into the
simplicity of a haiku," but Iyer doesn't allow for such an easy reading. In
almost the next breath, he tells us that he has far to go before he can
master the fine art of paying attention to the small print of the world.
Presented by Sachiko with "chocolates wrapped in a stylish green
pouch," Iyer tears open the packet and wolfs down the chocolate, only
to learn later that "the present was not, in fact, the candies but the bag,"
and that "ever since the Heian period, giving someone a present
wrapped in a bag of spinach-green had been the most eloquent way of
giving him one's heart," because the Japanese word for spinach "was a
homonym for their word for 'secret love'" (325).

What makes Iyer's writing so rewarding is his acute consciousness of the impossibility of fixing boundaries of insider/outsider-ness. He is scrupulous in reminding his readers, at almost every turn, that he can claim no special insider's privilege in any part of the world, but that this limitation in no way ought to disqualify him from attempting to meet the world with sharpened hearing and heightened vision. In fact, his recognition of his tenuous status everywhere enables him, he says, "to live a little above parochialisms." Iyer "exult[s] in the fact that [he] can see everywhere with a flexible eye" (*The Global Soul*, 24). (Let's not forget, however, that a flexible eye is also one that is perhaps most likely to take a bird's-eye view aerial photograph rather than a time-delayed exposure; see my analysis of Ondaatje's narrative perspective in *Anil's Ghost* in Chapter 2.) Reading Iyer calls for an alertness to the quick swoops of his language from generalizations to sudden specifics, from surface descriptions to piercing particulars.

There are two major differences between Iyer, on the one hand, and Pham and Mura, on the other, and it is critical that any intertextual discussion of their works keep these differences in mind. Pham and Mura visit and write about the country of their ethnic heritage, whereas Iyer's journeys span the entire globe. Pham and Mura write from their positions as Vietnamese American and Japanese American, respectively; Iyer writes as a "Global Soul . . . falling between all categories" (*The Global Soul*, 23): "The country [India] where people look like me is the one where I can't speak the language, the country [England] where people sound like me is a place where I look highly alien, and the country [Japan] where people live like me is the most foreign space of all" (24).

So if Iyer doesn't see himself as Indian American, why bother to discuss him at all in this chapter on South Asian American writing? Do I not, by including him, privilege his ethnic identity by birth even when he makes no overt claims to such an identity? (He is not, however, averse to being interviewed by ethnic publications that feature him as an Indian American or South Asian American writer.) I include Iyer because his travel writing and lifestyle force us to consider the limits of ethnic and geographical location, even as they provoke us to confront the implications of the kind of mobility that his life embodies:

A lack of affiliation may mean a lack of accountability, and forming a sense of commitment can be hard without a sense of community.

Displacement can encourage the wrong kinds of distance, and if the nationalism we see sparking up around the globe arises from too narrow and fixed a sense of loyalty, the internationalism that's coming to birth may reflect too roaming and undefined a sense of belonging. The Global Soul may see so many sides of every question that he never settles on a firm conviction; he may grow so used to giving back a different self according to his environment that he loses sight of who he is when nobody's around. (*The Global Soul*, 24–25)

Thus, Iyer himself seems to pose the question, "Where do you stand?" How can one be a responsible Global Soul, leading a life of ethical commitment to humankind, even as one doesn't live long enough in any one place to understand the dimensions of local urgencies or the extent to which one's involvement in them affects the environmental, political, social, or economic landscape of the place? That he is an outsider everywhere is a status he accepts; that this perennial outsider-ness renders his observations weightless is not something he will concede—nor should he.

Iyer rejects the easy authority of experiential knowledge that his South Asian ancestry confers upon him in this age of multiculturalism and the privileging of roots. He speaks of his discomfort with writing about India. He's supposed to know about India, he says, simply because his parents are Indian, but he doesn't really know much about it at all. When he writes about it, he's expected to bring the perspicuity of insider knowledge, but he doesn't have any claim to such information. He's as much a stranger in India as he is anywhere else. In fact, Iyer feels freed to journey to and write about remote corners of the globe in a way that he doesn't about India, simply because no expectations are placed on him. He is free to construct those other locations as a thoughtful, sophisticated travel writer, not as a cultural expert. Being considered an expert can, therefore, be a disadvantage if it inhibits one from approaching one's supposed area of expertise for fear that one cannot live up to this assumed expertise.[35]

On-the-Job Insiderism

In contrast to Iyer, who claims no location as his own (despite his increasing fondness for Japan), Abraham Verghese makes a convincing case in his memoir for calling the region of the United States where he practiced medicine in the 1980s as his own country. The title of Verghese's memoir, *My Own Country: A Doctor's Story of a Town and Its People in the Age of AIDS*, sets the stage for our reception of this work as an enmeshed narrative of a doctor, a town, and an epidemic. (I discuss this work further in Chapter 5 in the context of the trope of journey.) That Verghese does not draw attention to his Indian American ethnicity in the title may mean that he wishes to downplay its impact on his experiences as a doctor. This is a memoir that focuses on doctoring, not on identity. Yet, Verghese uses the platforms of medicine and AIDS to complicate issues of belonging, acceptance, and home. By telling the story of the small Tennessee town of Johnson City through the lives of its AIDS patients, Verghese widens the scope of South Asian American writing beyond the boundaries of ethnicity. The memoir plays in fascinating ways with insider/outsider positions and challenges the reader to reorient preconceptions of these notions.

The urgency of AIDS as a national health care imperative certainly had much to do with the book's instantaneous success, but there is much more to Verghese's memoir. His approach to questions of insider/outsider-ness require us to think about these concepts in multiple ways. Verghese is an outsider in this small town in Tennessee in more ways than one: he is most obviously an outsider to the majority white community; he is also an outsider to the many other South Asian doctors who live and practice there, both by virtue of his religion (he is Christian, whereas the other South Asian doctors are predominantly Hindu) and by virtue of his being more Westernized—a guitar playing, nightclub-frequenting, beer-drinking doctor. As the book progresses, he also becomes increasingly an outsider in his marriage, as his wife becomes less and less willing to go along with his escalating involvement with AIDS patients. But Verghese is also the ultimate insider: he knows the most intimate secrets of some of the town residents—he knows which of them is gay, he knows which of them is infected, he knows which of them most likely will not survive. The intimacy that he establishes with his patients and their families is remarkable for the way in which it leads us to see how the town gradually begins to accept the sons that once felt they had to move away because they were gay. I have written elsewhere about Verghese's manipulation of his "outsiderness" to become the ultimate insider.[36] The AIDS patients, he believes, reveal their secrets to him because they see him as being equally peripheral to the social fabric of their community, and therefore nonthreatening—that is, not likely to condemn or judge them.

Although Verghese's memoir centers on what it means for his patients to be gay and dying of AIDS in a small Southern town, it also elaborates a zone of contact between South Asian Americans and other Americans. It is Verghese's elaborate exploration of this zone that makes the book compelling for non–South Asian and South Asian readers alike. In fact, doctors of South Asian descent see this book as offering compelling evidence of their presence and value in the United States. The memoir shows that these doctors often go to small towns in remote places, where they are frequently the only non-white residents. They become valued members of the community because they fulfill a critical function. Verghese's memoir, by focusing on individuals outside the South Asian American community, paradoxically functions to illuminate and value the South Asian American experience.[37]

Even in rural Johnson City, Verghese encounters other Indian and Pakistani American doctors who, like him, have eschewed the cities. It is in his presentation of these doctors that Verghese is at his most problematic, providing evidence that there is no guarantee that writers who choose to depict individuals similar to themselves will do so with complexity. His portrayal of himself as a foreign doctor who understands how to speak and behave in the mainstream U.S. social landscape brings him dangerously close to inviting upon himself the label of ingratiating informant for the majority culture. His depiction of a Dr. Aziz is especially troubling, reinforcing the link between foreignness and crassness. It is one of the few moments in the book in which Verghese sounds like V. S. Naipaul (particularly in Naipaul's *India: A Wounded Civilization*) in his condemnation of the non-Western individual as unsophisticated and uncivilized:

> Dr. Aziz . . . hailed from a village outside Karachi. Despite going to medical school in the city, he had retained all his country ways. . . . He spoke with a thick guttural accent, pronouncing "system" as "shishtem" and "thirty" as "durty" and "zero" as "jeero," putting the burden of figuring out what he was saying onto the nurses. . . . When he ate in the cafeteria, it was with his mouth open and with loud smacking noises. Had he been approachable, someone might have instructed him on what was considered good manners in America.

...A nurse, stepping into a staff bathroom that Aziz had just emerged from, called after him and to everyone in earshot, "Did you never learn to raise the seat before you pee? Or at least wipe it clean? Were you brought up in a pig sty?" (40–41)

Verghese's especially harsh depiction of Aziz may signal his apprehension that he, too, might be aligned with this "uncouth" foreigner. If that is the case, then one expects from Verghese some criticism of the majority culture's tendency to generalize and essentialize. Unfortunately, we do not get an ironic perspective on the hospital staff. Aziz is Pakistani and Muslim; could Verghese, as an Indian Christian, be guilty of finding in his colleague an easy target of ridicule and contempt?[38]

The memoir offers a more nuanced depiction of the other Indian American doctors in the region. Here, too, however, Verghese tells us of his skill in being able to glide easily between two worlds, "the parochial world of Indians in America, and the secular world of east Tennessee." For Indian parties, his wife at the time (he is now divorced and remarried) "wore a sari and [they] completely immersed [them]selves in a familiar and affectionate culture in which [they] had their definite place as the juniormost couple; but at night [they] could don jeans and boots and go line dancing at the Sea Horse on West Walnut or listen to blues at the Down House" (23). But Verghese is not dismissive of those Indians who choose to fraternize only with other Indians; he himself repeatedly returns to these Indian-only gatherings, revealing his comfort with the crowd and reveling in his role as the enfant terrible who encourages the children of his staid Indian American friends to take up AIDS medicine with all its unknowns and frustrations. One could say of this posture that it allows him to pose as the fearless and pioneering adventurer, willing to forego the comforts and security of cardiology or pulmonary medicine. Verghese is not unaware of this tendency of his to perform the role of courageous soldier—he recognizes that his draw to AIDS medicine feeds, in a sense, his "pride of the front-rank soldier" (67).

Verghese appears to be entirely comfortable in establishing a parallel between his own outsider status and that of the gay men who are his patients. In the following passage, Verghese goes through several positions; in probing his comparison, it becomes apparent that while he appears to understand the complexity of otherness for gay men, he trivializes the otherness of immigrants and diasporics:

As I got to know more gay men, I became curious about their life
stories, keen to compare their stories with mine. There was an obvious parallel: society considered them alien and much of their life was
spent faking conformity; in my case my Green Card labeled me a
"resident alien." New immigrants expend a great deal of effort trying to fit in: learning the language, losing the accent, picking up the
rituals of Monday Night Football and Happy Hour. Gay men, in
order to avoid conflict, had also become experts at blending in,
camouflaging themselves, but at a great cost to their spirit. By contrast, my adaptation had been voluntary, even joyful: from the time I
was born I lacked a country I could speak of as home. My survival
had depended on a chameleonlike adaptability, taking on the rituals
of the place I found myself to be in: Africa, India, Boston, Johnson
City. I felt as if I was always reinventing myself, discovering who I
was. My latest reincarnation, here in Johnson City, was my happiest
so far. (51)

Verghese's intoxication at repeatedly reincarnating and reinventing
himself is somewhat disingenuous, and in this it echoes Carmen
Wickramagamage's readings of the novels of another well-known immigrant writer from India, Bharati Mukherjee. Mukherjee has been repeatedly criticized by several South Asian American scholars for romanticizing the immigrant experience and for failing to see the ways in which
many diasporics and immigrants are not permitted to reinvent themselves and are always already positioned in various categories of otherness and outsider-ness. Wickramagamage, however, offers a sympathetic
reading of Mukherjee, describing "relocation as a positive act," an opportunity to cast off the cultural and social restrictions of the homeland and
remake oneself.[39] Verghese, in the passage quoted above, reveals a similar sensibility. What he does not acknowledge is that, as a Westernized
Christian and middle-class professional, it is infinitely more possible for
him to remake himself and adapt to the majority culture than it would
be for a non-Westernized, non-Christian, working-class immigrant.

Perhaps part of Verghese's appeal as a confidant to his AIDS patients
is that he is, like them, both inside and outside the mainstream. Verghese's
nuanced awareness of his homosexual patients' outsider-ness stands in
marked contrast to his glib rendition of an immigrant's position. Thus, a
sensitive and textured portrayal need not always be tied to insider status.

Verghese's ability to render the full complexity of the AIDS patients' emotions comes from the care and attention he devotes to their lives precisely because he is aware of his difference from them and seeks to understand that which he is not. He is careful not to invite upon himself the charge of voyeurism. Despite his knowledge of these men as patients—and in this realm he is the expert, the insider—what makes the memoir so compelling is Verghese's engagement with his AIDS patients as individuals in their capacities as sons, siblings, and partners, as well as his own growing understanding of who he is as a man, as a father, as a husband.

Going to the Edge of the Unfamiliar

In her bold and adventurous first novel *Miniplanner*, Abha Dawesar writes from the perspective of a white bisexual male in his mid-twenties. Despite its hectic pace, *Miniplanner* partially succeeds in getting readers past its surface preoccupation with sexual liaisons to engaging with the protagonist's deeper emotions and desires. Dawesar is a young South Asian American woman who, like the protagonist, worked on Wall Street during the time that she was writing the novel. The idea for the book came from a curious practice that she noticed at her firm: new male recruits were taken to a strip club as a form of induction. Intrigued, she decided to go on one of these "visits" and so found herself with the material for the opening scene of her novel. At first, she had not intended for the protagonist to be bisexual, she says, but that element just seemed to flow once she started writing.

When asked how she managed to write about the white male bisexual experience with credibility, Dawesar said that she showed drafts of her writing to several gay friends to ensure that she wasn't being reductive in her characterizations and descriptions.[40] Somewhat ironically, she bestows great care in her depictions of the gay and bisexual males in her narrative. The two most complex characterizations in the book are of the protagonist, André, and his lover and boss, Nathan. All the other characters are thinly developed. Perhaps like Mukherjee (see below), Dawesar may have taken great pains to guard against superficiality in her portrayals of those characters with whom she initially has the least in common. The result is a novel that from time to time offers us sensitive and memorable moments. Take, for instance, the passage in which André, having discovered that a female worker with whom he has had a one-night stand is pregnant—and having gotten over his initial panic—imagines the pleasures of being a father:

> I'd take him to the woods and teach him how to play sports, I'd talk to him about things in the world that really mattered. . . . I would name him Camille. He could then decide if he would be a boy Camille or a girl Camille. . . . I wouldn't give in to living with her [the mother of his child]. This was New York at the beginning of the new millennium. The kid wouldn't be ostracized for not being the son of married parents. He wouldn't be teased because his father was a fag. No one would really call him a bastard. All the other kinds would probably think he was really hip for having a name like Camille and having a gay dad.
>
> I could feel lumps in my throat as I imagined him grow up a little and ask me why his mother and I weren't married. . . .
>
> He wouldn't ask me all this because he wanted me to be married—he would ask me this to know why I had been inconsistent. I would have to explain how I got a woman pregnant if I really liked men. (214–15)

Dawesar's attempts at crossing lines of race, gender, and sexual orientation are gritty. That the novel focuses predominantly on sex may bring on her the charge of having reduced the gay and bisexual relationship to one dimension. To an extent, the charge might be valid. But Dawesar does succeed in conveying the sense of a strong bond between André and Nathan that transcends sex, as becomes evident in Nathan's complex reaction when he discovers that André has also been sleeping with Nathan's wife. Initially outraged and deeply hurt, Nathan ultimately realizes that his love for André is too powerful to leave them permanently separated.

Enlarged Politics: Reaching beyond Ethnicity

Cynthia Sau-ling Wong is among the few critics who have recognized that Bharati Mukherjee very early on engaged the issue of U.S. military involvement in Asia and that this involvement affects the lives of her characters. Whatever her shortcomings, there is no denying that Mukherjee's vision is vast, that she sees the interconnectedness between nations and follows the repercussions of actions in one sphere of the globe upon peoples in another. She was writing with this mindset well before the notions of transnationalism and globalism gained currency. As Wong observes, "Mukherjee is perhaps the first Asian American writer to exhibit a full awareness of the global context of contemporary Asian immigration: she deconstructs cultural clichés, looks beyond the push-pull between two nations to acknowledge the reality of the world economic system, and sets her tales against a background of intertwined, transnational economic activities and mass uprootings caused by proxy wars in the Third World.[41]

In her award-winning collection *The Middleman and Other Stories*, Mukherjee does not limit herself to writing about the South Asian experience. Four of the eleven stories give us glimpses into other worlds. The title story, "The Middleman," takes us to Central America, to "a moldering spread deep in Mayan country" (1), and tells of the experiences of a man who is perhaps originally from Baghdad—but who gets mistaken for Israeli, Arab, and Indian—and who makes his living somehow by entangling himself with Texans who flee the Securities and Exchange Commission. In "Orbiting," an Italian American woman named Renata deals with the problem of introducing her Afghan lover Roashan to her family at Thanksgiving dinner. "Fathering" is the story of a white Vietnam veteran's struggle to quell the traumatic horrors that beset his Amerasian daughter, Eng, who lives with him and his wife. In "Fighting for the Rebound," an American man from Atlanta finds himself inexplicably attracted to a woman from the Philippines.

It is in "Orbiting" that Mukherjee gives the strongest evidence both of her ability to cross ethnic boundaries skillfully and of her awareness of the complexities of the world outside the United States. *The Middleman and Other Stories* was published in 1988, so Mukherjee deserves credit for being attuned even at that early date to what the Russian presence in Afghanistan was doing to lives there. Here, the Italian American Renata tells us how Ro (Roashan) explains his life to her family:

[H]e's holding forth on the Soviet menace in Kabul. Brent [Renata's brother-in-law] may actually have an idea where Afghanistan is, in a general way, but Dad is lost. . . . He [Roashan] talks of this "so-called leader," this "criminal" named Babrak Karmal and I hear other buzz-words like Kandahar and Pamir, words that might have been Polish to me a month ago, and I can see even Brent is slightly embarrassed. It's his first exposure to Third World passion. He thought only Americans had informed political opinion—other people staged coups out of spite and misery. It's an unwelcome revelation to him that a reasonably educated man like Ro would die for things that he, Brent, has never heard of and would rather laugh about. (73–74)

Earlier, Roashan has told Renata about his cousin Abdul, detained in jail on an immigration violation and on the verge of being deported to Afghanistan. Abdul knows he will be tortured upon his return, so he plans on going on a hunger strike. Roashan wants to dissuade him. Renata's response to this information is eerily ironic, given the state of domestic and global politics in 2004, more than fifteen years after "Orbiting" was published: " 'A hunger strike! God!' When I'm with Ro I feel I am look-ing at America through the wrong end of a telescope. He makes it sound like a police state, with sudden raids, papers, detention centers, deporta-tions, and torture and death waiting in the wings. I'm not a political per-son. Last fall I wore the Ferraro button because she's woman and Italian" (66). It seems as though Mukherjee here is subtly pointing to the limited vision that results from a politics that focuses only on narrow boundaries of identification—in Renata's case, gender and ethnicity.

In speaking favorably of Mukherjee's forays into lives other than those of South Asians, I don't mean to suggest that her characterizations are always unproblematic. Mukherjee has drawn much heat for her por-trayal of South Asians, in particular. Her novel *Jasmine* is the most Orientalist of her works in its depiction of South Asian men and women (the protagonist Jasmine is exoticized and the other South Asian women are portrayed as mere ciphers) and in its polarization of the West as the land of liberation and the East as the land of oppression. Inderpal Grewal and other South Asian American scholars have been trenchant in their criticism of Mukherjee for such portrayals.[42] Complicating the recep-tion of her writing among South Asian Americans is a September 22, 1996, essay she published in the *New York Times*, in which she compares herself to her sister Mira and describes their lives in the United States as "two ways of belonging." Of course, Bharati's way is presented as being bolder, because it involves the daring though traumatic act of self-transformation. Bharati's critique of her sister Mira is that despite having lived in the United States for more than thirty years, Mira retains her Indian citizenship and dreams of retiring in India. "My sister is an expatriate, professionally generous and creative, socially courteous and gracious, and that's as far as her Americanization can go. She is here to maintain an identity, not to transform it," Mukherjee writes.[43] And in that assessment one can detect her disdain for those who do not venture—artistically socially, culturally, or politically—out of the comfort and security of familiar identity zones.

Mukherjee's assessment of her sister may help explain her own predilection for writing narratives depicting the lives of non–South Asian Americans. It is as though by writing about the experiences of non–South Asian Americans she inserts herself into the lives of all the American peoples and in doing so claims their voices as her own. At one level it is a rather arrogant move; on another level, however, it is a rather desperate move, signaling a yearning to belong.

The Holder of the World: Literary Chutzpah

When Mukherjee's novel *The Holder of the World* was published in 1993, Kwame Anthony Appiah, writing in the *New York Times Book Review*, called it a bold reworking of Nathaniel Hawthorne's *Scarlet Letter*.[44] In the text, Mukherjee asserts that her heroine, Hannah Easton, provided the model for Hawthorne's Hester Prynne, and thus boldly inserts herself into the American literary canon. There is much that makes *The Holder of the World* an unusual text. Set in the late 1600s, the novel encompasses three continents—North America, Europe, and Asia—and records the adventures of a *female* traveler. Hannah Easton is orphaned when her mother, a New England widow, is "taken captive" by a Nipmuc Indian in August of 1675 (more, later, on Mukherjee's brilliant rendering of this event). From this moment on, Hannah comes into the care of another family—Robert and Susanna Fitch—in the Massachusetts Bay Colony, and moves with them to Salem. She eventually marries a smooth-talking English seafarer and journeys to England. From there, she goes to the southwestern coast of India, where her husband, now in the employ of the East India Company, gets involved in piracy and is killed. Hannah becomes the lover of a Hindu king, gets pregnant, and returns to New England when her lover is killed in battle with the Mughal emperor Aurangzeb, ruler of India at the time. These events are narrated by a twentieth-century woman who, while searching for information on her ancestors, discovers her connection with Hannah in the dusty rooms of a Salem museum through paintings and other possessions believed to have belonged to the Salem Bibi (the name Hannah is given in India). This rather bare outline does scant justice to the sweep of the novel: the large period of time encompassed, the imaginative re-creation of the ethos of the seventeenth-century, and the impressive wealth of characters. Mukherjee's command as a writer is unmistakable.[45]

However, that command does not extend evenly through the book. Mukherjee is less successful in her depictions of the Indian characters than she is for the Western characters. The book can be seen as having two parts—one set in America and England and the other in India. The New England and England chapters are rich with complex and nuanced characterization; the India chapters suffer from flat portrayals. It is as though Mukherjee sees and hears with greater acuity when she conceives of her Western characters. I would argue that she takes special care to avoid any hint of superficiality in those areas in which her authority is most likely to be called into question or challenged.

As a result, the depictions of Puritan life are masterful. Two instances, in particular, stand out. The first is the "capture" of Hannah's mother, Rebecca Easton, by a Nipmuc warrior when Hannah is five years old. In Mukherjee's creation of this event, the Nipmuc Indian is presented as Rebecca's lover and the capture as Rebecca's willing departure from the world of the Puritans. Her voluntary escape is staged to look like a violent abduction:

> The lover, now painted and feathered as befits a warrior, comes to woo her one last time. And Rebecca surprises him. Reading Hannah's eyes, she stands slowly and turns, facing the window without surprise or terror. She stands on a reed rug by the window . . . and peels her white radiant body out of the Puritan widow's somber bodice and skirt as a viper sheds skin before wriggling into the brush. Her body is thick, strong, the flesh streaked and bruised, trussed with undergarments.

The Nipmuc enters the cabin, suddenly immense in his full battle regalia. He cradles the whimpering Easton hound in his arm.

Rebecca scoops Hannah out of her bed, clasps her and weeps as
though the child were dead. The Nipmuc jerks his arm, the hound
lurches, and a spume of blood leaps from his arms across the table. He
swabs Rebecca's old garments in the blood, smears them with his feet
over the floor, stabs holes in the cloth as they darken with blood, then
hands her something new and Indian and clean to wear. (29)

The reason for the ruse is clear: to protect Hannah and ensure that
she is well cared for after the mother's "death." Mukherjee writes: "Had
[Hannah] been perceived the daughter of a fornicator, not the offspring
of an upright widow, no family would have taken her in" (30).

That Mukherjee has absorbed the ethos of Puritan New England is
evident in the images and language she uses—for example, the simile of
Rebecca shedding her "widow's somber bodice and skirt as a viper sheds
skin before wriggling into the brush," or the label "fornicator" with
which Rebecca would be branded were it known that she had willingly accompanied the Nipmuc warrior. Stronger proof of Mukherjee's
immersion in the Puritan psyche can be found in a letter that Hannah's
foster-father, Robert Fitch, writes to a William Pynchon in response to
his request for Hannah's hand in marriage for his son. Hannah has by this
time distinguished herself for her fine needlework and embroidery, but
this skill has also given rise to no small apprehension on the part of her
foster parents, for they see it as a flirting with ornamentation and luxury and fear that she is being tempted by excess. I quote at some length
from Fitch's letter to Pynchon to demonstrate how completely
Mukherjee has plumbed the Puritan sensibility:

It is the Ghost's teaching and there is nothing She has learned from my
Goodwife or the Salem Congregation that causes her Fingers to be so infected, that so pollutes her Eye with infamous design, to make of the plain and
simple Necessities that might cover the shame of Nakedness in Man and
Woman a Proud and Unseemly Decorativeness, as Unneeded as Paints and
feathers on a sauvage.

Allow me, my dear Pynchon, to spare your Son the Agonie we have
known, and such can never be known by Those who have but Commercial

Intercourse with Her; if the Angel of Death marks His Brides not with the
Pain of physical Suffering, but is made known through Disruption of the
Humours, Infections of the Very Soul, then we have been Warned of His evil
Intent to claim Her as His Bride, and we shall Warn others in our Turn.
(58–59; italics in original)

Hannah rejects this restrictive environment when she marries Gabriel Legge, an English seafarer. "Nothing in colonial society had demonstrated its unalienable claim on her affection," Mukherjee writes. "Nothing in English society or among recently arrived Englishmen excited her contempt. The English, like her husband, seemed vastly more exciting and knowledgeable and appreciative than the men of Salem; . . . And England itself, though it might be an exhausted force, as colonists liked to think, still compelled a fascinated study" (73).

The sections set in India are not as compelling, unfortunately. Mukherjee appears to accept the expertise conferred on her with regard to South Asia and so does not do the hard work of rendering that territory with textured and finessed appreciation for its contradictions and irresolutions. We get predictably Orientalist descriptions of Englishmen who fall prey to the heat of India, and whose sexual energies become so insatiable in this environment that they have to turn to taking an Indian mistress or "bibi": "a healthy young black girl, a native woman in Black Town, or some servant of the English or a slave of one of the Muslim nawabs, or a girl of low morals still living in a mud hut with a widowed mother who could be counted on to look the other way" (131). In her defense, Hannah is "exasperated" by the attitude of the other English wives; they accept the inevitability of their husbands' infidelities and caution Hannah that she must never "confront" her husband's bibi, must "never acknowledge her" (131). One could argue that *no one* is sketched with any nuance in these accounts—the Englishwomen, the Englishmen, and the Indians all are given predictable lines to utter, predictable roles to play, in the grand narrative of East meets West. The problem with such an argument is that it does not address the question of why Mukherjee fails to present us with Indian characters of the same depth as her English/Puritan characters. The one Indian character that has any significant role to play—Bhagmati, the woman who works in Hannah and Gabriel's home—serves merely as the backdrop against which Hannah's daring and courage display themselves. Bhagmati was the mistress of Henry Hedges, the dead Englishman in whose home Hannah and Gabriel now live. Her identity is always linked to serving someone, and the novel's final portrait of her is as a woman who, when asked by Hannah to accompany her to England, refuses to go because "she couldn't conceive of England without Hedges. She preferred to keep his shrine alive, to walk the parapets in his clothes" (224). Mukherjee seems not to be able to give to Bhagmati the depth and complexity that she bestows on Hannah.

However, the novel's true achievement is Mukherjee's claim to the position of America's literary ancestor by declaring that Hannah provided Hawthorne with the model for Hester Prynne in *The Scarlet Letter*. In Mukherjee's reworking, Hannah, her mother Rebecca, and Hannah's illegitimate child by her Indian lover live together after Hannah returns to Salem. Here, Hannah is known as White Pearl and her daughter, Black Pearl. Mukherjee boldly wrests authority from Hawthorne:

> Joseph Hathorne, a boy of ten, "My doleful young Joseph," White Pearl called him in her letters, son of the witchcraft judge, John Hathorne, was only nine years old when Pearl returned with her baby and her mother, and he seemed to have found in her company, doing odd jobs, running errands, a corrective to the orthodoxy of his household. He even went to sea, driven from the taint of Salem, drawn by the stories of the China and India trade that White Pearl related as she sewed. His great-grandson, Nathaniel Hawthorne, was born in Salem in 1804. (285)

Thus, Mukherjee inserts herself into America's literary tradition not as an immigrant writer but as the source of what "many call [America's] greatest work" (286). In doing so, she links India with American letters, giving notice that even a nation's literary landscape may be shaped by influences from afar. *The Holder of the World* does to American literature what the story of Tipu Sultan's gift to Benjamin Franklin (see Chapter 1) does to the American Revolution. Mukherjee's willingness to step outside the bounds of ethno-specific writing facilitates her effort to seek links among peoples and nations. That she does not depict diverse peoples with equal care—or, oddly that her lack of care seems more often than not to affect detrimentally her portrayals of South Asian characters—should not blind us to the boldness of her venture. I speak as no apologist for Mukherjee; however, at the same time, I desist from an outright rejection or condemnation of her work. In *The Middleman and Other Stories* and *The Holder of the World*, Mukherjee gives evidence of the breadth of her imagination.

A Gap of Love: Ondaatje's In the Skin of A Lion

Just as Mukherjee boldly inserts herself into the canonical literary history of the United States, Michael Ondaatje seizes the landscape of Canada's European immigrants. Most famous for his 1992 novel *The English Patient*, Ondaatje has never restricted himself to writing about South Asians. *The English Patient* dwells on four dissimilar individuals (an English pilot/spy, a Canadian nurse, an Italian Canadian "thief," and a Sikh sapper) caught in an odd cocoon of friendship in an Italian villa during the final days of World War II. The collection of poetry that won him the Canadian Governor General's Award, *The Collected Works of Billy the Kid* (1970), constructs the complex persona of a Wild West outlaw. In *Coming through Slaughter* (1976), he recreates early twentieth-century New Orleans and crafts a semi-biographical text about Buddy Bolden, cornet player and jazz pioneer. *In The Skin of a Lion* (1987) uncovers the experiences of immigrants from Macedonia, Finland, Greece, and Italy who labored to give to Canada its economic strength. Ondaatje's writings encompass North America and the world.

The title *In the Skin of a Lion* comes from the Mesopotamian *Epic of Gilgamesh*, one of the oldest known narratives (Gilgamesh, king of Uruk, lived sometime between 2750 and 2500 B.C.). One of the two epigraphs to Ondaatje's novel is from the Gilgamesh text: "The joyful will stoop with sorrow, and when you have gone to the earth I will let my hair grow long for your sake, I will wander through the wilderness in the skin of a lion." Among other things, the *Epic of Gilgamesh* is the story of the great friendship between Gilgamesh and Enkidu. When Enkidu dies, Gilgamesh is inconsolable, wandering through the wilderness and plains in search of purpose. The depth of Gilgamesh's grief at the loss of Enkidu dominates the epic once Enkidu has died.[46] The second epigraph to the novel, from John Berger, is a variation on the theme of deep friendship to which the first epigraph alludes: "Never again will a single story be told as though it were only one."

Patrick Lewis, the protagonist of *In the Skin of a Lion*, is born somewhere in the northeastern reaches of Canada. His is a lonely life, and when he comes to Toronto in the early years of the twentieth century, he finds a city of immigrants—bustling with activity, filled with the sounds of languages he does not know. Yet, he feels comforted, as though he belongs with these people whose names are unfamiliar, whose food he cannot identify. Patrick finds that he *needs* them. In Patrick's desire for the friendship of immigrants, Ondaatje inverts the usual model of security and home. It is Patrick who feels alienated without his proximity to the Macedonians, Greeks, Finns, and Italians who run the bakeries, work in the meatpacking plants, fell the trees, tan the hides, and build the bridges and the waterworks of the young nation. He clings "like moss to strangers, to the nooks and fissures of their situations. He has always been alien, the third person in the picture. He is the one born in this country who knows nothing of the place" (156–57). Ondaatje's native-born Canadian has no privilege of birth, no entitlement of place. Without the immigrants, he is nothing: "when not aligned with another . . . he could hear the rattle within that suggested a space between him and community. A gap of love" (157). Just as Gilgamesh and Enkidu together were a complete person, so also, Ondaatje seems to suggest, Canada can be whole only when the gaps of love between its different groups of people are filled.

In writing about the European immigrants of early twentieth-century Canada, Ondaatje clearly claims North American history as his own. The story of North America is not the story of one people. Berger's words seem to be Ondaatje's promise to himself—that he will reveal the multitude of experiences and re-create the immense diversity of individuals whose intersecting stories make up the tumult of living.

Even so, there are noticeable absences in the novel—particularly that of non-Europeans. Chinese, Japanese, Indians, and blacks immigrated primarily to the western part of Canada in the early twentieth-century, so perhaps their absence can be attributed to the novel's eastern setting. But what about the Native Canadians or First Nations populations? There is not a single mention of them in the novel. Although the majority of Canada's First Nations tribes were in the West, they were not entirely absent from the East.[47] Perhaps they were invisible to the consciousness of Patrick Lewis. And maybe that is the point Ondaatje wishes to make. *That* particular gap of love—of acknowledging the First Nations peoples as being essential to Canada—cannot be bridged.

Announcing Presence

There are two ways that a group—as defined by any number of parameters, including ethnic, racial, religious, gender, sexual orientation, and political—can announce its presence on the socioliterary landscape of a nation and establish that it is here to stay. The most obvious strategy is for writers from that group to tell the stories of the group's experiences, and so require the world to pay attention to the desires, ambitions, and fears of its members. The second method of announcing presence is for writers to tell the narratives of *other* groups with whom they coexist, to show their engagement with these others' experiences. The latter approach signals that a group is already a part of the socioliterary landscape, because its members are interested in and have taken the time to understand the contours of other, unfamiliar lives. Authors who venture into the territory of writing what they are not often do so from an eagerness to learn about those who share the same civic space as themselves and to challenge themselves to imagine outside the bounds of familiarity. There are many ways to stimulate the imagination, of course, such as writing about ancient characters or aliens, but I am referring to those writers who are interested in contemporary social issues.

Writing about what one knows is the method of declaring presence that is most familiar to readers. South Asian American writers have contributed greatly to inserting the lives of South Asian Americans into the consciousness of other Americans. The honors granted and rave reviews accompanying Jhumpa Lahiri's *Interpreter of Maladies*, Chitra Divakaruni's *Arranged Marriage*, or Manil Suri's debut novel *The Death of Vishnu* have conferred visibility on South Asians in the United States. In addition, these positive recognitions make it easier for a South Asian American contemplating the serious pursuit of the writing life to believe that such a yearning is not without merit and viability.

Let me introduce a word of caution, however. In their excitement over this new literary visibility, South Asian Americans should not be lulled into forgetting that it is extremely easy to become trapped in expectations for a certain type of narrative. Gary Pak, a Korean American writer living in Hawai`i, bemoans that the dominant narrative among Chinese and Korean American women writers is that of the mother-daughter relationship; although he may exaggerate his irritation for dramatic effect, what he says is not without validity.[48] Judging from the spate of articles in the mainstream media on arranged marriages, there was a danger that this would become the expected theme for South Asian American writers. Another possible theme, in the words of Samir Dayal, is that "of picturesque poverty" set in South Asia.[49] Of course, I don't mean to suggest that South Asian American authors will end up writing to meet the expectations of the publishing industry or will create self-Orientalizing images; what I am pointing to is the limitations that South Asian Americans may place upon themselves as readers and potential writers in terms of the narratives that they envision for their communities.

In calling on writers to enter into a post-ethnic imaginative space, I am not suggesting that they abandon the ethnocentric literary endeavor. Ethnic self-gazing can be extremely gratifying and, more importantly, extremely empowering. Until recently, for South Asians living in the United States, there was little in print that spoke directly to their own histories here. Writers needed to emerge who could fill these gaps—who could imaginatively render the early histories of Sikh farmers in California's Pioneer Valley; tell the story of the first U.S. congressman of Indian descent; record the experiences of a boy entering the Arkansas school for the blind at age fourteen, then going on to Pomona College and Harvard University; relate what it is like to be a South Asian American gay man; describe the burgeoning sexuality of a young South Asian American woman; reflect on what it is like to be a cabdriver in New York City and why he would replicate the racism of the dominant culture by refusing to pick up black fares. These are the stories South Asian Americans needed to hear, because they were not being told, because no one else would tell them. These stories must continue to be told, because every story enriches the significance of the South Asian American presence here. Padmini Patwardhan, a doctoral student at the Southern Illinois University, Carbondale, recently unearthed the contributions of a Pulitzer Prize–winning Indian American science journalist, Gobind Behari Lal, who has all but disappeared from the consciousness of journalists in the United States.[50] Patwardhan's restorative research adds a new dimension to the lives of South Asians in the United States and fills in yet another blank space on the canvas of the South Asian American experience. These are critical interventions in a national narrative that is frequently fragmented and incomplete. For example, the very successful TV drama *ER*, about a hospital emergency room, did not until very recently have a South Asian doctor in its cast of characters. This omission is incomprehensible, given that a full 10 percent of doctors and residents in the United States are of South Asian descent. So narcissistic self-gazing is necessary, and old-style identity politics must still be practiced with vigilance.

The best that one could ask of a critical engagement with South Asian American literature is that South Asian Americans, both as writers and as readers, resist the seductive comfort of self-representation and open up their imaginations to the complicated nature of belonging in or arriving at a certain destination. I want to reiterate that I'm not advocating a departure from material focused exclusively on the South Asian American experience. I'm interested in the productive tension between writing stories that feature the South Asian or South Asian American experience and writing stories that take us to the edges of South Asian American communities where that experience enters the realms of other people's stories, lives, and communities. I see the tension as productive because I believe it liberates our imaginations to envision bold possibilities of living and participating in the civic spaces in which we make our homes.

Multiculturalism, as an outgrowth of the Civil Rights movement's demand for increased and legitimate participation by people of color in the U.S. body politic and structures of civic society, has been a remarkable force. But as a number of scholars in the last fifteen years have shown, it has rapidly become a phenomenon of mere window dressing—giving the appearance of rich variety without addressing the fundamental power dynamics that keep inequities in place. Writers from various disciplines, including Lisa Lowe, Peter McLaren, Abdul Jan Mohamed, and Vijay Prashad, have observed that as a movement promising radical alterations of power structures, multiculturalism has failed. Prashad goes even further, asserting that multiculturalism has propagated a false history of racial and ethnic purity, which posits that the cultures of disparate groups developed and should be encouraged to continue along separate lines and maintain their unique and distinctive components. In his book *Everybody Was Kung Fu Fighting*, Prashad advances an alternative narrative of polyculturalism as a more accurate and historically grounded way to explain and illuminate the cultural interaction among different racial and ethnic groups. Prashad contends that different ethnic groups constantly borrow from one another, that no group maintains its cultural isolation, and that there is invariably evidence of incorporation of cultural elements from groups not one's own. His argument is based on a historical analysis of Afro-Asian meldings in three sociopolitical locations: among the Dalits of India, the Rastafarians of Jamaica, and the Black Panthers of the United States. Prashad explains that the "theory of the polycultural does not mean that we reinvent humanism without ethnicity, but that we acknowledge that our notion of cultural community should not be built inside the high walls of parochialism and ethno-nationalism."[51] Prashad points to Robin Kelley's contention that our various cultures "have never been easily identifiable, secure in their boundaries, or clear to all people who live in or outside our skin We were multi-ethnic and polycultural from the get-go."[52]

Roshni Rustomji-Kerns, speaking of the pastiche of influences that characterizes the lives of many Asians in Latin America, notes that we need a more complex language to convey the sheer multitude of forces impinging on one another in the Latin American sociocultural context. Searching for an adequate vocabulary, she rejects the notion of a "palimpsest" because "a palimpsest is a . . . paradigm of domination that works on erasures, and the process of layering." She offers instead

a metaphor borrowed from the kind of weaving that produces a fabric known in South Asia as dhoop-chaun—the combination of bright sunlight and deep shade—in English termed as "shot" fabric and in Spanish as tornasolada. It is an iridescent fabric (often silk) of changeable and variegated colors because of the different colored warp and weft used in the weaving. Different colors come into prominence according to the way light falls on the fabric and the way it is moved for different viewings of it.[53]

Most cultures are like "shot" fabric, bled with the influences of multiple groups and peoples. Polyculturalism, it would appear, recognizes a world in which cultures not only exist side by side but also influence and are altered by one another. Although the reality of such cross-pollination has long been understood, over the past few years a deep immersion within a particular culture—undertaken as a corrective to decades and sometimes centuries of invisibility and silence surrounding the accomplishments of its people—has led to a preoccupation with questions of cultural authenticity and purity. And while no one would be so bold as to suggest that the time for such studied immersion in a particular ethnic or racial group has passed, it is nevertheless time to put the knowledge gained from that saturation to good use, for the benefit of other groups.

Vietnamese American playwright lê the diem thúy appears to have done precisely that. At a reading/performance at Wellesley College on November 12, 2001, thúy lê told the stories of her family's life in Vietnam before, during, and after the war; their passage as refugees to the United States; and the nature of their experiences in San Diego, in a community of other Vietnamese refugees. She developed this deeply autobiographical work because she found very little voicing of these experiences in the mainstream media or publishing world. But thúy lê did not present her work solely as a reclamation of the Vietnamese and Vietnamese American experience. Rather, she declared that it was an intervention in a time of war. Given that after the September 11 attacks people almost immediately started to speak about Afghanistan as though it were a potential "Vietnam," thúy lê began her performance by asserting that she is determined to position her work to inhibit such easy parallelism. "We cannot flatten an entire culture and its people by treating them as though they were merely a mirror for our concerns," she stated emphatically. She insists that neither Vietnam nor Afghanistan is merely a war.

A Question of Power, a Question of Humility, a Question of Genuine Interest

I began this chapter by asking under what conditions writers could responsibly undertake the task of crossing boundaries of race, gender, ethnicity, class, or sexual orientation. There is no formulaic set of acceptable conditions. We must engage with each work for the specificities of its narrative techniques, for the particularities of its crossings. We have seen how even within a single work a writer can cross boundaries with sensitivity in one instance and fail to observe the same nuanced technique in another. Creative freedom notwithstanding, writers practice their craft in a field of social, cultural, political, and economic forces. It is therefore disingenuous for any writer to believe that representations of racial, cultural, or gendered others will not stir up controversy, particularly when the author is from a group that is in a relationship of dominance over the group being represented. Acknowledgment of the possibility of controversy might lead an author to exercise care when engaging in these crossings. On the other hand, writers might argue that the exercise of their creativity cannot be constrained by political considerations, that if they were to ponder constantly the impact of their creative decisions, then they would never be able to write.

Most students of Asian American literature know about the tangle of events that led to the revocation of the Association for Asian American Studies' 1998 literary award for Lois Ann Yamanaka's novel *Blu's Hanging*. Even prior to the award, Yamanaka, a Japanese Hawaiian, had been accused of portraying her Filipino male characters in highly unfavorable terms—usually as sexual predators. Given the racial dynamics in Hawai`i, where those of Japanese descent enjoy greater economic power than Filipino Hawaiians or indigenous Hawaiians, Yamanaka's portrayal of Filipino males was seen as reinforcing stereotypical images of the Filipino Hawaiian community. Writers of color are not immune from considerations of the politics of representation; power differentials exist everywhere, and in Yamanaka's case her being of Japanese descent in Hawai`i placed her in the position of having her work be interpreted as an exercise of that power.

It is not only groups in power that are called upon to make responsible and sensitive artistic crossings. The representation of Sikhs in Bapsi Sidhwa's short story "Defend Yourself against Me" presents a particularly interesting case as it relates to the question of power and its impact on the reception of an author's work. (See Chapter 1 for a detailed consideration of this story.) Sidhwa is from the Parsi community. Because of their small numbers in South Asia during the Partition of 1947 (there are even fewer now), Parsis felt that their best chance for survival lay in remaining strictly neutral in the fierce hostilities among other communal groups. Therefore, I was intrigued when some Sikh readers remarked that Sidhwa's representation of the story's two Sikh men (who throw themselves at the feet of an old Muslim women and beg forgiveness for the horrific actions of their "fathers" during the Partition) is reductive and reinforces stereotypes of the Sikhs as violent. My initial reaction was to dismiss the observation as mere quibbling, but then I started to think about it with greater care.

In the two instances in which Sidhwa treats the Partition in her writing, she uses different narrators. In her novel devoted to the Partition events, *Cracking India* (first published under the title *Ice Candy Man*), her narrator is an eight-year-old Parsi girl. In the short story set in Houston, her narrator is a middle-aged Pakistani Christian woman. In order to address the issue of whether or not Sidhwa resorts to simple stereotypes in her representations of Sikhs, one would have compare "Defend Yourself against Me" with *Cracking India*, commenting on the two different narrative voices and determining the relationship between the narrators and the portrait of Sikhs that emerges. However, few readers are likely to have had the opportunity to see both texts in relation to one another. Thus, most readers of the short story would have to rely only on what was at hand to draw their inferences. The issue for me is not whether Sidhwa's representation of Sikhs in the short story is problematic; rather, the issue becomes the nexus of sociocultural and political forces that impinges on the reception of any text and the heightened complication of the interplay of these forces when portrayals cross ethnic and other boundaries. In the novel, there is a greater range of Sikh characters than in the short story; the reader has more evidence, therefore, with which to assess Sidhwa's representation of Sikhs. There is no denying, however, that even in the novel there are powerful images of Sikh violence.

Whether a writer has succeeded in a nuanced portrayal that avoids the pitfalls of simplification or essentializing may matter less than whether the text gives evidence of the writer's having struggled with the difficulties of crossing boundaries. Does the text reveal a genuine interest on the part of the writer to know about a dissimilar or unfamiliar group? Does the writer approach her/his subject matter with necessary humility, conceding that the imagination, though powerful, cannot envision every crevice of unfamiliar territory? I don't pose these questions as any kind of test to administer. But the experience of reading and writing are both enriched, I believe, when the exercise of venturing into unfamiliar experiences is not undertaken lightly but with full cognizance of the landmines strewn along the way.

What an author chooses to write about is an intensely personal decision. Like Mazumdar and Fan, I would hope that Asian American writers not limit themselves to rendering only the experiences of Asian Americans or of their particular ethnic subgroup. What narratives do we as South Asian Americans want to hear, and, more importantly, what narratives do we seek out? Because historically there has been such a dearth of images and stories about us, we want to hear about ourselves, about the lives we lead, about the lives we might lead. And while this longing is a powerful one and worthy of being fulfilled, it is also a longing that can insulate and isolate us from the very people among whom we wish to become more visible, from whom we desire greater understanding, and with whom we perhaps seek greater intimacy. I suggest that the act of self-illumination and self-representation must be accompanied by our implication in other groups' experiences, other communities' stories. I hesitate to use the word "must," because I'm the first to admit that creative energy cannot be coerced. But I use it to stress the urgency of our being able to go beyond the thirst for the South Asian American ethnic narrative to another kind of narrative—one that takes us to the edge of our realm and delineates the area of contact between South Asian Americans and those at the frontiers of our consciousness.

FIVE

Trust and Betrayal in the Idea of America

"ONE BOMB. THEN ANOTHER. Hiroshima. Nagasaki."[1] With these words, Michael Ondaatje invokes one manifestation of the United States: a bomb-dropping, power-wielding nation. At the opposite end of the continuum, solo performer Shishir Kurup declares that "Americans love[ ] to go streaking . . . and love[ ] double negatives: 'I didn't do nothin'": a fun-loving unsophisticated nation.[2] In truth, these positions are gross simplifications. I obscure the complexities of Ondaatje's and Kurup's presentations: Ondaatje's protagonist Kip misplaces blame for the bombing onto Britain, and Kurup's America is not all about laughs. In the errors of Kip's understanding and the humor of Kurup's clever phrases, and between the antipodal positions these texts occupy, lies a wealth of complicated narratives on the idea of America. This chapter addresses these representations and attempts to deepen and complicate the image of America and disrupt its self-mythologies. The texts I discuss hover in the space between adoration and condemnation, appreciation and rejection.

I make repeated reference in this chapter to the USA Patriot Act—Uniting and Strengthening America by Providing Appropriate Tools

Required to Intercept and Obstruct Terrorism Act. This legislative package, passed by Congress in October 2001, has had a devastating impact on the civil liberties of immigrants, particularly those from countries in the Middle East and South Asia, and is likely to alter dramatically the quality of immigrant life in the United States. It could also spell the end of civil liberties as we know them for all U. S. residents—immigrants and citizens alike—if its provisions are allowed to solidify and extend indefinitely. The works I discuss (with the exception of one) were written prior to the events of September 11, 2001, and the passage of the USA Patriot Act. My purpose in invoking this Act is not to undermine the literary texts by viewing them through the retroactive application of a draconian and arbitrarily wielded political frame. Rather, I seek to problematize and enrich our reception of these writings—to understand, for example, how hope, faith, promise, desire, and skepticism are influenced by the realities of historical, political, economic, and sociocultural forces.

In Ondaatje's *The English Patient*, four individuals sheltered (or so they believe) in their damaged villa in Italy learn to reenter humanity near the end of World War II. They gradually begin knitting together a community of friendship among themselves, but the delicate relationships they are cultivating suddenly shatter when the bombs fall on Japan. All through the novel, Ondaatje has attended carefully to each of the four characters, filling out their histories, excavating their memories, and creating among them the exchange of simple and not-so-simple gestures. After the bombs are dropped, in the novel's final pages Ondaatje's attention turns almost exclusively to Kip—Kirpal Singh—the Sikh sapper. During the war, Kip uses his expertise to defuse explosives—finding and disarming the mines the Germans place under bridges and toss into fields. In the waning months of the war, Kip painstakingly clears the mines whenever and wherever he finds them. The rhythms of life appear to be returning slowly to this odd conglomerate of four. That process is disrupted, however, when Kip hears about the bombing of Hiroshima and Nagasaki on his transistor radio, and everything changes for him. He becomes aware of his difference from the other three individuals with whom he shares the abandoned villa—a man recovering from severe burns, whom they have been calling the English patient; Hana, a young Canadian nurse, whom Kip loves; and Caravaggio, an Italian Canadian who makes his living as a thief. Kip feels betrayed. He knows that nothing will be the same again between him and his erstwhile companions. He closes his eyes and "sees the streets of Asia full of fire . . . roll[ing] across cities like a burst map, the hurricane of heat withering bodies as it meets them, the shadow of humans suddenly in the air." Kip knows that he will henceforth see "all those around him[ ] in a different light" (284). Kip's "education" about the true nature of the West is poignant, because he has until now refused to accept his brother's cynical warning never to trust Europeans. Caravaggio agrees with Kip's assessment that "[t]hey would never have dropped such a bomb on a white nation" (286).

However, Kip misplaces his anger onto the English: "When you start bombing the brown races of the world, you're an Englishman. You had King Leopold of Belgium and now you have fucking Harry Truman of the USA. You all learned it from the English" (286). He screams these words at the English patient and Caravaggio. In focusing his anger on the British, Kip overlooks the central role of the United States as the new world imperial power. In this view, he reinforces what Amy Kaplan describes as the "enduring assumption that the American struggle for independence from British colonialism makes U.S. culture inherently anti-imperialist." Further, Kaplan argues, "imperial politics denied at home are visibly projected onto demonic others abroad, as something only they do and we do not."[3] During the Cold War that followed World War II, U.S. foreign policy was almost entirely shaped by projecting imperial aspirations onto the Soviet Union; today, in a post–Cold War world, the demons—George W. Bush's "axis of evil"—are those nations that support terrorism. Kip must learn to move outside the ambit of his colonial experience with Britain and widen the sphere of his historical awareness to consider the United States as the current imperial power. It is not just Kip, however, who must learn to acknowledge the United States in its "new" avatar. Michael Ignatieff observes that Americans themselves fail to recognize their nation's imperialist tendencies: "A historian once remarked that Britain acquired its empire in 'a fit of absence of mind.' If Americans have an empire, they have acquired it in a state of deep denial."[4]

The imperialist agenda of the United States—whether articulated or denied—poses a danger not only for the peoples of other nations but also for U.S. residents. Donald E. Pease argues that a nation bent on imposing its vision of civic society on different cultures is not likely to entertain true heterogeneity of opinion or practice within its own borders: "The Persian Gulf War threatened to eclipse ... heterogeneous cultural histories with a monocultural image of the national identity predicated on the active suppression of the specificity of race, class, and gender relations as disruptive to this renewed synthesis of U.S. imperialism."[5] The repression of free speech, the roundups of Muslim men, the suspicions and hostilities directed at women wearing the hijab (head scarf), the egregious cuts in social welfare, and the relentless drumbeat of patriotism all testify to the impact of the U.S. global military mission on the domestic scene.

Read against Pease's dire assessment of the suppression of heterogeneity, Kurup's play *Assimilation* is positively carnivalesque—riotous, chaotic, and unpredictable. (*Assimilation* was written and first performed in 1994, so its creation occurred in less ominous times.) That the play is actually a solo performance—with the author performing all the characters—underscores the degree to which Kurup works to transport the individual voice into a multitude of registers, diverse languages, and modes of speech. Worlds are contained within a single physical body. (See Chapter 4 for a discussion of the disruptive impact that the body on stage can have upon the audience.) A cascade of words in English, Hindi, Malyalam, and Swahili tumbles from the performer's mouth. This is "assimilation," Kurup seems to suggest—first ingesting the heterogeneity of America and then releasing it from within in a torrent of language. His is the America of streaking and double negatives, the America that is "a veritable cornucopia of fast food joints" (342). His is the America in which immigrant mother, father, and child eat and eat and eat because they are happy and soon become "the fat family [that] ha[s] a combined weight equal to that of the Bulgarian Olympic weight-lifting team" (342). Kurup combines humor, cynicism, and satire. There's a bite to his words, but they are not corrosive. For instance, Kurup speaks as the character Mzee in Mombasa, Kenya, to comment on how the United States markets itself to the world. Notice how he combines sarcasm with fascination for the allure of America:

> The United States of America is a good place. Because there the black man is free ... and respected. Not like here. There a black man can be a film star like Mr. Jim Brown and Mr. Richard Roundtree "talking 'bout Shaft, John Shaft, he's a bad mother—shut your mouth" ... and Mr. Sidney Poitier, a great actor. And the women

here love their American accent. They think it's great. Not like our
African accent. (349; ellipses in original)

The shifts in mood and tone are rapid, creating the sense of an
America that's unrestrained and unpredictable. In the section of his
monologue titled "Siam," the scene ropes in Asian America, German
America, and African America. Siam is a Thai restaurant in Milwaukee.
Dahng, its motherly waitress, is married to a German American named
Kluss, so she is Dahng-Kluss. Dahng greets her customer with her usual
enthusiasm, ushering him in with her welcoming ritual—"'Come in,
come in. Sit down, sit down. It cold outside, huh? You cold, huh? Want
some spicy shrimp? Spicy shrimp and rice? It hot! Good for you! Warm
you up. I know, I know, I know. No M.S.G.'" (350). Then, suddenly, sadness enters into the conversation. Dahng's five-year-old adopted daughter, Susie, has just been sworn in as an American citizen. It should be a
happy day, but when the judge congratulated her, Susie's response was:
"'When I get my blue eyes?'" It is hard not to call to mind Toni
Morrison's novel *The Bluest Eye*: the shadow of Pecola's descent into
madness, wishing she could have Shirley Temple's blue eyes, hangs over
the scene.[6]

Not many South Asian American writers engage deeply with the
subject of whiteness in America. Susan Koshy examines South Asians'
complicated negotiation of the category "white" in the United States in
the early years of the twentieth century.[7] Responding to Sucheta
Mazumdar's criticism[8] of South Asians' racist attitudes—as evidenced by
cases filed in the courts by individuals who wished to be granted citizenship on the basis that Indians (pre-1947, the subcontinent was still
undivided into separate nations) were Aryans and, therefore, white—
Koshy notes that South Asians were merely trying to work within the
legal frameworks that were available to them: "The courtroom did not
provide a forum to mount an antiracist protest or to foster pan-ethnic
coalitions around the racist criteria for naturalization; in fact, the terms
of the law worked explicitly to undermine such possibilities, prompting
various litigants to prove their whiteness by declaring their dissimilarity
from other Asian groups or by disavowing their Asian-ness altogether"
(33). Thus, Koshy claims, to condemn them as racist does not take into
account the complexities of the situation. These historical complexities
may constitute one explanation for the minimal discussion on race in

Dalip Singh Saund's 1960 memoir *Congressman from India* (discussed below).

Chitra Divakaruni's Yuba City poems provide a glimpse of the impact of early twentieth-century immigration policies on the lives of Sikh farmers in California's Imperial Valley.[9] The Punjabi men who came from India in the first decades of the twentieth century could not bring their wives with them: immigration restrictions on entrants from Asia were meant to ensure that these men would return to their countries after a few years' sojourn. The United States wanted their labor but not their lives. In reality, however, the "sojourns" were permanent, and many men accommodated their lives to the immigration policies.[10] In "Yuba City Wedding," we learn of an impending marriage between Surdeep, a Sikh man, and Manuela, a Mexican American woman. On the eve of his wedding, Surdeep remembers the challenges he has had to face, including almost being knifed by Roberto, Manuela's cousin, when news of their relationship first became public. In his own community of Sikh farmers and railroad workers, some have tried to dissuade him from marrying Manuela: *"Be patient. Soon the laws will be changed and you can go back to your own village and marry. A fine girl, one who has never known a man."* But Surdeep "couldn't be like them, couldn't wait and wait while time burned through [his] flesh and left only trembling. So [he] filled his lungs with the smell of Manuela's cinnamon breath, the ripple of laughter deep in her throat, her fingers flying like wings over [his] body" (99). Surdeep will be married in a church and will be given a new name, Ysidro, which because it sounds a little like Surdeep will make him feel at home.

"The Brides Come to Yuba City" spotlights the wives who were forced to stay behind in India when their husbands left for California in the early 1900s; the women could not join them until the 1940s, when immigration restrictions were lifted. When they finally arrive and get off the train, the wives see their husbands, "[t]heir lined, / wavering mouths, their eyes like drowning lights," and they "cannot recognize a single face" (103). It has been thirty years since they have last seen their husbands. There are some "picture brides" among them—young women who are about to see their husbands in person for the first time.

For Asian Americanists, it is basic knowledge that the history of the Asian presence in the United States is marked by a series of restrictive immigration policies and exclusionary acts. From the bachelor Chinese societies of the West Coast in the late nineteenth and early twentieth centuries to the interethnic marriages described in "Yuba City Wedding," Asian American community demographics have been shaped by policies that marked the citizens of countries in Asia as undesirable. The cases of Bhagat Singh Thind and Takao Ozawa unequivocally established that whiteness was integral to the idea of America and who could be deemed "American."[11] The Naturalization Law of 1790 limited citizenship to "free white persons." (This law was amended in 1870 to extend citizenship to "aliens of African nativity or persons of African descent.) In 1922, Takao Ozawa, an immigrant from Japan, applied for citizenship on the grounds that he was "white." However, Justice George Sutherland of the U.S. Supreme Court deemed him ineligible on the grounds that "white" was synonymous with "Caucasian," and, being Japanese, Ozawa was not Caucasian. Bhagat Singh Thind, an immigrant from India, took this to mean that he would be eligible for citizenship because Indians belonged to "the Mediterranean branch of the Caucasian family." However, in 1923, the same Justice Sutherland declared that Thind could not be a citizen, because in the understanding of the common man he was not a white person, even though, technically, Caucasian was synonymous with white. (Valerie Babb's study of colonial America and the early Republic demonstrates the steady consolidation of whiteness as a sine qua non of complete citizenship.[12]) In practice, notwithstanding the Fourteenth Amendment and Civil Rights legislation, this sentiment continues to hold sway today. The USA Patriot Act, in its implementation, targets brown males for particular scrutiny and makes heightened demands for proof of worthiness to be considered American (more below on this set of legislations). Toni Morrison observes that in a multiracial society such as South Africa, one always has to qualify the term "South African" with "black," "white," or "colored," because "South African" includes all these different groups of citizens and there is no automatic application of the term to only one group of people. Not so with the term "American," she declares. When we say "American," implicit in that term is the notion of whiteness.[13]

Bharati Mukherjee, a strong apologist for the United States and the transformative possibilities it provides individuals, condemns Canada for its official policy of multiculturalism and its misguided approach to the issue (Mukherjee spent several years in Canada before settling in the United States). Jennifer Drake makes a persuasive link between Etienne

Balibar's critique of "neo-racism," which he describes as segregation based on culture/ethnicity (rather than race), and Mukherjee's distaste for Canada's response to the heterogeneity of its residents. Balibar, who bases his analysis on France's policy toward its immigrants, declares that neo-racism "centers upon the immigration complex" and is a "racism whose dominant theme is not biological heredity but the insurmount-ability of cultural differences, a racism which, at first sight, does not pos-tulate the superiority of certain groups of peoples in relation to others but 'only' the harmfulness of abolishing frontiers, the incompatibility of life-styles and traditions."[14] Thus, people become segregated not on the basis of race but on the basis of culture. This in itself may not constitute racism, Balibar implies; however, what makes this kind of attention to cultural difference pernicious is that it is accompanied by cultural hier-archy. Balibar argues that "the cultures supposed implicitly superior are those which appreciate and promote 'individual' enterprise, social and political individualism, as against those which inhibit these things."[15] Drake argues that Mukherjee's rejection of Canada's mosaic policy (acknowledging the diversity of its peoples and celebrating their distinc-tiveness from one another) is akin to Balibar's critique of neo-racism.[16]

In 1988, Canada officially enacted into law the Canadian Multiculturalism Act for "the preservation and enhancement of multi-culturalism in Canada." The Act stands as evidence that "Canada is com-mitted to a policy of multiculturalism designed to preserve and enhance the multicultural heritage of Canadians." In practical terms, what this means is that the government funds projects that enhance multicultural understanding, provides resources to "preserve and enhance the use of languages other than English and French," and funds scholarship that enhances the multicultural understanding of Canadian residents.[17] Such an approach, argues Mukherjee, marks and consolidates "difference" and ensures that people remain separate on the basis of distinct and discrete cultures. The United States, by comparison, allows her to become an integral part of a common social and cultural fabric, to "sing[ ] even in the seams of the dominant culture."[18]

While Mukherjee's criticism of cultural essentialism and uniqueness is not without legitimacy, her unquestioning embrace of the potential-ities of the U.S. model is highly problematic for two reasons. First, it does not recognize the direct impact of race, gender, and social class on opportunities for transformation. Being white, male, and Christian earn you the highest marks and, therefore, make you most likely to become the recipient of opportunities for transformation. Geographical location within the United States is also a key factor. Thus, while it may not be critical that one be Christian to run for political office in the Northeast or in California, it is a necessary condition in the South.[19] The second reason that Mukherjee's position is weak is that it does not address the limits of the laissez-faire multiculturalism practiced in the United States. By laissez-faire multiculturalism I mean a state of affairs in which people generally agree that recognizing diversity of cultural practices and experiences is a good thing but stop short of legislating diversity or supporting the use of government funds and resources to promote intercultural awareness. The problem with laissez-faire multiculturalism is that it is almost entirely dependent on the goodwill of individuals. Since nothing is expressly mandated and no monies are set aside for implementing multicultural practices, then nothing really gets done unless individuals take the initiative. Barry Kanpol and Peter McLaren, among others, argue that multiculturalism U.S. style pays mere lip service to differences among Americans while continuing to reinforce cultural and racial hierarchies.[20]

The events of September 11, 2001, have accentuated these hierarchies, particularly as they impinge on Muslim Americans and other brown-skinned peoples who physically resemble Arab Americans. Added to the racial profiling that now attends Arab Americans and South Asian Americans—who are learning what African Americans have had to endure for decades—is profiling by name. Muslim names are subject to particular scrutiny by airport security personnel, employers, and credit card companies. The rules of belonging have gotten stricter, the rules of entry quite arbitrary. Take the case of the arrival card that non-citizens are required to fill out when they enter the United States. A few hours before a flight arrives, passengers are handed immigration cards (for non-citizens) and customs cards (for citizens and non-citizens alike). The instructions for filling out the immigration card are thorough, and they are played on the video monitors in the aircraft so that there can be no confusion about what is required. Among the more unusual directions are those that concern penmanship. The numbers 1 and 7 come in for special mention. When filling out the form, the instructional voice intones, do not write the number one with an upstroke and do not put a horizontal bar across the number seven. On the face of it, this is a seemingly innocuous request; yet there is something distasteful about it. Two thoughts occur to me: Are the immigration officials in the United States so without basic intelligence that they cannot recognize a number one if written with an upstroke or a number seven with a horizontal bar across its middle? Or are passengers being reminded that they are entering a special region of the globe and therefore should learn right away that there are rules to be observed that will signal their worthiness to occupy the space of the United States? Mukherjee's public disparagement of her sister (see Chapter 4) and other immigrants from South Asian who do not become U.S. citizens but rather continue to cherish an attachment to the country of their birth suggests an unthinking embrace of U.S. nationalism and a rather outdated view of citizenship. The perception that she is an uncritical spokesperson for the United States is further reinforced by her recent inclusion in a U.S. government–sponsored collection of fifteen essays on what it means to be a writer in America. This publication, *Writers on America*, is intended for use outside the United States, to disseminate the image of a nation of diverse peoples with diverse opinions, valuing their freedom, democracy, and right to free speech. The other writers included in the collection are Elmaz Abinader, Julia Alvarez, Sven Birkerts, Robert Olen Butler, Michael Chabon, Billy Collins, Robert Creeley, David Herbert Donald, Richard Ford, Linda Hogan, Mark Jacobs, Charles Johnson, Naomi Shibab Nye, and Robert Pinsky.[21]

In her essay for the collection, "On Being an American Writer," Mukherjee addresses the charge often hurled at American writers that they pursue trivial subject matter and do not attend to global injustices. She acknowledges that critics have asked whether American fiction writers feel any responsibility "for countries that have been oppressed by colonial powers, war, pestilence, religious and tribal intolerance, corrupt police, judges, politicians and journalists, and for societies that are over-crowded, undereducated, unsanitary, and psychologically wounded." She admits the validity of the criticism, but offers a rather odd reason for the writers' lack of concern with issues of social justice. In the United States, the writer is confident that established institutional structures of redress can be counted on to deliver justice, leaving the writer free "to celebrate the impacted glories of individual consciousness." By her logic, the American writer's lack of attention to injustice becomes evidence of the United States' fairness. This attitude allows her to characterize the 2000 election as comedy: "What mad satirist thought up the 2000 election in which a poorly designed ballot played a pivotal role in determining the next American president? Is such a comic turn even conceivable anywhere else in the world? And what would have been its bloody consequence?" There is no interrogation on her part of the machinery that ratified an election that in any other country would have been declared fraudulent. She is incapable of conceiving that there may be flaws in the United States' vaunted system of participatory democracy.

Her confidence in the legal system indicates that she is either unaware of or unwilling to imagine the lengths to which the present administration will go to curtail civil liberties in the declared war on terrorism. She argues, "There is no history, there are no barriers, no taboos, no fatwa can be launched, and no secret police will knock on your door. (Or, anticipating the objections those colonial theorists will raise to such blanket assertions—if they knock on your door, and no one says they haven't in the past and will try it again—you at least have means of redress.)"

Not so, say legal scholars David Cole and Michael Avery. There is no redress today if you are an immigrant. Every legal protection has been sacrificed to the god of national security. Cole notes that to be an immigrant in the United States today is to be especially vulnerable. He observes that the reason that so little outrage has been expressed at the repressions of civil liberties in the post–September 11 period is that these legislations have all been targeted at immigrants, not citizens. "We'll take away *their* rights, so that you can be safe" is the implicit message of the administration, argues Cole.[22] Mukherjee's most problematic assertion comes at the close of her essay, when she suggests that Indian Americans (and one assumes she would extend her statement to apply to all South Asian Americans) have "not been called on to pay [their] dues" of suffering. It is true that the majority of immigration from South Asia took place after the Civil Rights era and the Vietnam War protests and that South Asians, therefore, have benefited from the struggles of others. But to suggest that somehow one should not expect full citizenship or hope to participate fully in the civic fabric of America until one has undergone suffering is to take the dangerous and morally untenable position of endorsing discriminatory practices as a test of one's mettle, as a rite of passage to share in the nation's founding ideals.[23]

Rule of Fear

Writers on America, which the U.S. State Department readied for distribution around the world, has as its objective the creation of trust in and fondness for the United States. Following the events of September 11, 2001, it became imperative in the minds of foreign policy bureaucrats that the United States respond quickly (and here I am talking about strategies that looked beyond the bombing of Afghanistan) in two ways: by understanding the underlying causes of certain people's hatred of the United States, and by taking measures to make them appreciate the openness of American life. *Writers on America* grew out of the second objective.

Art as marketing is not a new tactic at the State Department. Michael Berube reminds us that promotion of American culture and American democracy was common practice during the height of the Cold War. The Central Intelligence Agency carried out a "covert campaign," administered through the Congress for Cultural Freedom, which "published over twenty prestigious magazines, held art exhibits, . . . and rewarded musicians and artists with prizes and public performances" all for the purpose of enticing "the intelligentsia of western Europe away from its lingering fascination with Marxism and Communism towards a view more accommodating of 'the American way.'"[24]

In the war on terrorism, the most visible approach, at least at present, appears not to be one of encouraging people to appreciate American openness and freedom to dissent, but rather of wielding the arbitrary power of the Attorney General's office at home and displaying the full extent of U.S. military power abroad. John Brady Kiesling, a career diplomat in the American Foreign Service, resigned his post in Athens, Greece, on March 7, 2003 to protest the Bush administration's "fervent pursuit of war" and squandering of international goodwill. Kiesling's question to Secretary of State Colin Powell as to whether "oderint dum metuant" (let them hate as long as they fear) has become the motto of the United States points to an ominous turn in the exercise of power and an entrenchment of the policy of rule by fear.[25]

Fear is an emotion that African American women have known for generations: fear that their sons, husbands, or brothers can at any moment become the targets of suspicion or the victims of lynching, violent arrest, and imprisonment. Such a generalized and ever-present apprehension is, for the first time, becoming the experience of many Arab and South Asian women in the United States. The Arab and South Asian American communities are learning how to live with dread in a place that once was their home and in which they once felt reasonably comfortable. In the past, South Asian and Arab Americans who condemned racial profiling did so primarily on moral grounds. South Asian Americans, in particular, did not consider racial profiling to have anything to do with their lives; it was something that happened to other people. (Arab Americans have long been profiled as possible terrorists; with the passage of the USA Patriot Act, however, the profiling has taken on ominous proportions.) Now their condemnation of it has a visceral component, combining fear, sadness, anger, and a sense of betrayal.

Complicating this fear, however, are sentiments of the type expressed by one Arab American man in the weeks following September 11, 2001: he observed on WBUR Radio's "Connection" program that in most other places there would have been riots and Muslim communities would have become the target of angry mobs. People did become targets of hateful words and some people lost their lives to hateful retaliatory acts, but, according to him, the scale of vengeance was limited, and, in general, there was restraint. In contrast to this sentiment is that of Muneer Ahmad, who offers no such sanguine view of the aftermath. His indictment of the nation's indifference to the backlash killings of those who "look" Muslim is severe. According to him, these killings of brown people, of those who were deemed to "look like" the terrorists, were considered by many Americans as regrettable but not tragic. They have been rationalized as outbursts of passion motivated by love of country. Ahmad notes that whereas hate victims such as James Byrd and Matthew Shepard have become household names and their killings have been deemed incomprehensible,

the killings of Balbir Singh Sodhi, Waqar Hasan, and the others, while deplored as wrong, have been understood as the result of a displaced anger, that underlying anger being one with which the vast majority of Americans sympathize and agree. The perpetrators of these crimes, then, were guilty not of malicious intent, but of expressing a socially appropriate emotion in socially inappropriate ways. To borrow from criminal law, the hate crime killings before September 11 were viewed as crimes of moral depravity, while the hate killings since September 11 have been understood as crimes of passion.[26]

Ahmad's observations on the nation's general readiness to condone the killings of Muslim Americans (or those, such as Sikhs, who may be mistaken for the Taliban) may help us understand the astonishing rapidity with which Congress approved the USA Patriot Act, one of the most repressive pieces of legislation to have been assembled by the recently created Department of Homeland Security and the U.S. Attorney General's office. (On October 26, 2001, President Bush signed the act into passage. Many researchers and scholars observe that the Patriot Act carries to extremes laws that were already in place from earlier times of repression—the Palmer Raids, the FBI under J. Edgar Hoover, the McCarthy era. That a document of over 350 pages was assembled in a mere six weeks indicates that the practices it endorses were not constructed or imagined into existence after September 11, 2001; they were at hand and already in place.) Because this cluster of anti-terrorism measures is couched in the sophistication of legal language and presented as merely *incremental* increases to the scope of laws already on the books, its pernicious impact is disguised, its assault on certain communities presented as rational and necessary steps for a government to take. The USA Patriot Act evokes one idea of America—constitutionality, freedom, opportunity, tolerance—to justify policies that posit quite another idea of America: paranoia, discrimination, violence, power, self-righteousness.[27] Human rights scholar Winston Langley makes the point that by calling certain people "terrorists" and promising to pursue them no matter where they go, the United States mobilizes itself for the continuous condition of war that can be waged anywhere in the world.[28] Every country becomes a potential haven for terrorists, and thereby a potential site for battle. In this conception of the globe, all the world's a battlefield—including the United States. The USA Patriot Act is the weapon for domestic use, to be deployed against certain people within the country's borders.

A story that aired on February 21, 2003, on National Public Radio's *All Things Considered* caught my attention. The lead-in to the story noted

that it was the first in a series of occasional reports on the effects of the
USA Patriot Act on civil liberties. A rare acknowledgment by the media
that something is amiss as a result of the legislations accompanying the
creation of the Department of Homeland Security, the report began:
"September 11th, 2001, brought confrontation between law enforcement and American Muslims. Followers of Islam say the government is
alienating them with practices that amount to ethnic or religious profiling. In New Jersey, though, authorities and Muslims are reaching out to
each other." It was this sentence that piqued my interest, and I was eager
to see how the report would unfold. We were told about Joe Griffin, an
African American police officer who attends numerous Muslim functions and gatherings in an effort to increase contact between the community and law enforcement agents, and so to dispel their mutual suspicions. As a black man, Griffin says he understands what it is like to be
singled out as a community to be carefully monitored: "What the
Muslim community is going through now is just similar to the Civil
Rights movement. I mean, it's just a different time and a different place."
So far, the story was encouraging, but I wondered whether white police
officers would be equally empathetic, and whether members of the
Muslim community in Paterson would trust them as much as they
seemed to trust Griffin.

The report, though generally optimistic about the future of relations
among the New Jersey Muslim community, law enforcement officers,
and FBI officials, did not try to ignore the deep suspicions the groups
have of one another. What it failed to highlight, however, was the issue
of power: the government agents, at the state and federal levels, operate
with the comfort of power, a luxury that is not available to the Muslims.
The report included a rather telling instance of how fear creates and
exacerbates the large chasm between the FBI and the Muslim community. It illustrates perfectly the sanguine attitude that accompanies power,
the cheeriness and optimism that inhibit the person in power from recognizing and acknowledging the fear that grips those without power:

> The FBI's Ed Dixon [in the Newark, NJ office] insists counterter-
> ror efforts are not based on religious or ethnic profiling, and he feels
> fear of the government in many cases is overblown. Dixon says he
> was stunned and saddened after he spoke about the agency's work at

a recent Muslim gathering. A twelve-year-old boy came and asked him: "Does this mean that you're going to spy on my family?" In a strange way, though, Dixon sees the many complaints as a sign that relations between Arab Americans and law enforcement have improved.

The FBI agent is "stunned and saddened"; one gets the impression that even in his reaction, he is not able to step outside his own experiences. He is stunned and saddened that anyone would think ill of the agency. Not once does he concede that the Muslims may have cause for fear; nor does he consider how it might be to live with such fear as a constant aspect of one's life.[29]

The United States is both seductive and dangerous, alluring and fatally unpredictable. The nations and leaders we have befriended and then abandoned or turned against (for example, Iran, Iraq, El Salvador, General Manuel Noriega of Panama) have learned that to their peril. Yet, the United States succeeds in presenting itself as an injured innocent. John Carlos Rowe, for example, notes that "[t]he transnational imaginary of the early United States republic is significantly shaped by free-floating paranoia regarding wandering anarchists, dangerous foreigners, and murderous 'savages.' . . . [T]he remedy in both literary and geopolitical fictions seems to be the imposition of artificial borders to control such threatening foreignness."[30] Paul Giles, in a similar assessment, observes that although American culture is

> constitutionally empowered to incorporate diversity in unity, it reveals within itself traces of innumerable savage, intractable conflicts—conflicts involving Native Americans, from the seventeenth century onward; Great Britain (over the question of political independence), from the late-eighteenth century; Mexico, in the 1840s; Spain, Cuba, and the Philippines, in the 1890s; Korea, Vietnam, Iraq, Afghanistan, and many other countries in the twentieth and twenty-first centuries. The cradle of American literature, if one might be forgiven a Thoreauvian pun, is discord rather than Concord.[31]

Discord and, one might add, discrimination. The Civil War and the Civil Rights movement enabled the United States to coat itself with the

patina of uprightness. Both these critical moments in the nation's history made it possible for the United States to acknowledge its wrongdoing and moral shortcomings and demonstrate its capacity to move forward and do the right thing. The end of slavery and the end of legalized
segregation signaled both the death and the rebirth of American innocence. The ending of these horrific practices could not occur without
acknowledging that they had been an integral part of the national fabric; the sin had to be named and seized. But once it was named and officially stopped, the nation could rejoice in its having seen the true way.
One can almost see in this pattern of public admission of wrongdoing
and subsequent renewal a parallel to the meeting-house conversion ritual from sinner to saved. Herein lies the paradox of the United States'
self-perception: it can engage in the most ethically ambiguous actions
(dropping nuclear bombs on Hiroshima and Nagasaki, initiating regime
change in Guatemala, or engaging in arms sales to Iran, for example)
both at home and abroad even while maintaining belief in its essential
blamelessness.

In a sharp critique of post-apartheid South African theater, Mark
Gevisser dismisses the value of productions such as *Many Cultures, One
Nation* and *Sarafina!* Calling them empty "extravaganzas," "classic patri-
otic spectacle[s]," and "parade[s] of superficial cultural styles," Gevisser
argues that with their intense desire to present a democratic South Africa
as a nation in which once-opposed peoples are reconciled and ready to
build a new multiracial society, these theatrical spectacles do little to
address the enormous difficulties of forging accord from discord.[32]
Spectacles hypnotize and stun, he argues. They permit no interrogation,
and they reduce complexities to the level of entertainment.

Michael Rogin makes a similar claim in his analysis of U.S. foreign
policy. His examination of the American penchant for spectacle is particularly astute in that it presents spectacle in juxtaposition to secrecy.
Spectacle is so visible and so public that it gives the impression of total
transparency, of complete openness. Caught in the spell woven by spectacle, we cannot imagine that there may something covert, of which we
have no knowledge. "The thief hides the purloined letter in Edgar Allan
Poe's story, placing it in plain sight. His theft is overlooked because no
attempt is made to conceal it. The crimes of the postmodern American
empire . . . are concealed in the same way. Covert operations actually

function as spectacle."[33] I want to extend his analysis to apply not just to the "crimes" of "imperial politics" but also to a range of contexts in which the idea of America is constructed—for example, in the realms of power, freedom, opportunity, innocence, and justice.

If ever it were possible to speak of the ascendancy of spectacle in American politics, that moment would be now, while the nation is in the midst of the quagmire of bringing stability to the streets of Iraq and reconstructing the country so that basic amenities become available to the Iraqi people. In an eerily prescient utterance, Rogin outlines the legacy of the first President Bush:

> The Gulf war . . . did not save President Bush from the economic reality principle at home. Nonetheless, it allowed him to leave office orchestrating military raids abroad rather than sunk in domestic disgrace. It bequeathed to his successor . . . not only the dance of death in Iraq but also an imperial culture at home that may well resurface should the new president fail to ameliorate America's enormous internal troubles. (529)

Rogin's remarks about the mind-deadening power of spectacle have particular relevance to the drawn out process leading up to the November presidential election every four years. The debates preceding the primaries, the Democratic and Republican conventions, followed by the debates between the anointed candidates of the two parties, and the final election day hoopla—all richly orchestrated for televised transmission—make prime raw material for the construction of spectacle. The debates are the equivalent of gladiator sports, with candidates given brief opportunities to make their thrusts and parries, during which they seek to draw blood or seriously wound their opponents. Savants make their sage assessments as to winners and losers. Balloons, confetti, and other regalia are all integrated into the extravaganza. Thus, an activity central to a meaningful democracy is framed and offered as entertainment and easily absorbed meaning. In their capacity to seduce audiences, spectacles, Rogin notes, "shift attention from workers as producers [of meaningful participatory democracy, in this case] to spectators as consumers of mass culture. Spectacles colonize everyday life . . . and thereby turn domestic citizens into imperial subjects. . . . The society of the spectacle provides illusory unification and meaning" (507–8). In the first decade of the twenty-first century, a concerted effort is being made by the U.S. government to unite its citizens both through fear of an ever-present terrorist attack and through spectacles of U.S. power against and readiness to respond to terrorism.

The God of Large Things
(with apologies to Arundhati Roy)

The United States' displays of power and military might are secular expressions of a confidence bolstered by a bedrock of religious belief that the nation is blessed by God. (Sunaina Maira, with delightful acerbity, calls the United States of today "two nations under Ashcroft": one for citizens and one for immigrants.[34]) When John Winthrop first gave his sermon about the City on the Hill, he, too, was conscious of staging a spectacle for the consumption of his tired and weary fellow travelers and for God, who had blessed their journey so as to enable their safe arrival on the shores of the New World. A fundamental difference between those early settlers in pre-Revolutionary America and the citizens of the newly formed republic after 1776 lies in the attribute of pride. The New England Puritans were extremely attentive to self-pride; they guarded against displays or articulations that gave the impression that they were congratulating themselves for their achievements. Mary Rowlandson's 1682 captivity narrative and Jonathan Edwards's 1741 conversion narrative both record their protagonists' indebtedness to God at the same time that they carefully steer clear of sounding as though they are "chosen" by God to endure hardships and then enjoy reward. But that kind of self-doubt has become largely inaudible and invisible in promulgations of American greatness. (Perhaps one can trace the beginnings of such self-aggrandizing rhetoric to Benjamin Franklin, who declared in his autobiography that he had only himself to congratulate for his success and that he wished to share his methods with his fellow-citizens so that they might learn from his example.) It certainly is absent from the official government proclamations of U.S. power and superiority in recent years, particularly in the nation's insistent reminder during the days preceding and soon after the war against Iraq that victory is ours and that the United

States alone has the authority to decide who the key players will be in the reconstruction of Iraq. Such unquestioned pride comes from believing that God has blessed this nation and its ideologies. Why else, the thinking goes, would the Soviet Union and all its Communist minions have fallen, and why would the United States find itself in the position of being the sole economic and military superpower? God, by this view, is focused on the United States and is paving the way for its success.

Historian Garry Wills, in a recent essay, offers convincing proof that many American leaders and presidents in succession have invoked God as a justification for the nation's acts of aggression: the late seventeenth-century war between the New England settlers and the Native Americans (King Philip's War); the War of 1812; the Civil War; World War I; World War II; the Cold War; the first war against Iraq; and the war on terrorism, including the second war on Iraq. Wills notes with no little irony that "[t]he afflatus of becoming visible saints is intoxicating. It allows one to have great disdain for the manifest sinners who oppose our saintly will. This applies not only to outright enemies but to those (like the French) who do not join our crusade and even to those who dare criticize it."[35] Wills attributes George W. Bush's fierce conviction of the need to go to war against Iraq (despite international opposition) to the current president's faith that God requires this nation to rid the world of the evil force of Saddam Hussein. "The odd euphoria of war resembles the jubilant confession of sinfulness at the Great Awakening. We are afraid and exhilarated. The multiple items of population are drawn together in a People, God's People."[36] Chip Berlet of Political Research Associates refers to the "apocalyptic demonization" of the nation's enemies—they are evil and unless we rid the world of them, everything that we know and love will be destroyed—as a central component of the populist right-wing fundamentalism that underlies Bush's foreign policy, and Matthew Rothschild of *The Progressive* similarly speaks of the "messianic militarism" that informs the use of American power today.[37]

Clifford Krauss's article in the *New York Times* on the decline of religiosity in public life in Canada, read in conjunction with Wills's essay, suggests that the vaunted separation of church and state that is supposed to mark American political and public life exists more on the level of theory than practice in the United States. A recent survey by the Pew Research Center for the People and the Press in Washington revealed that "only 30 percent of Canadians said religion was very important to them compared with 59 percent of Americans." Krauss notes that "[i]n stark contrast with American presidents, Canadian prime ministers rarely, if ever, speak in religious terms. They even avoid being photographed attending church. It would be almost unthinkable for a prime minister to say 'God Bless Canada.'" He quotes sociologist Stephen A. Kent as saying, "Canada has never had a revolution or civil war or expansionist foreign policy . . . so there was no need to sanctify major political events."[38]

I turn now to three texts—the short stories "This Blessed House" and "Chagrin" and the play *Raisins Not Virgins*—that offer different types of counterpoint to the weightiness of the religious climate in the United States. In Jhumpa Lahiri's "This Blessed House," religion—in particular Christianity (more specifically Catholicism)—becomes an object of curiosity, a collector's item, and is thereby robbed of its power to exhort or even to punish. At the same time, however, Christianity is not dismissed. If anything, Lahiri's text seems to attest to its ubiquity, to the impossibility of ignoring it. I don't want to conflate the significant differences between Protestantism and Catholicism (or among the various denominations of Protestantism), but the story is less focused on investigating the Catholic-Protestant divide within Christianity than it is on exploring a sense of playfulness around faith.

The narrative unfolds within the context of a new marriage and a man's discovery of the various facets of his wife's unpredictable personality. In the closing lines of the story, Christianity and marriage converge in an image of gentle mockery. It may be that marriage is presented as a kind of faith—one to be taken both seriously and not too seriously in order to survive it. One may also read the wife as Lahiri's image of America: the husband, Sanjeev, is an immigrant from India and the wife, Twinkle, a woman who has grown up mostly in the United States. At first he is troubled by what he considers to be her eccentric desires; the development of the narrative is closely tied with his realization that in order to appreciate her he must learn not to view her with excessive gravity. Through her, Sanjeev's carefully planned and systematic life is infused with frivolity and unpredictability. Twinkle's self-indulgence annoys him initially, but eventually he succumbs to her allure.

While they are settling into their new home, Twinkle and Sanjeev discover an assortment of Christian bric-a-brac: a porcelain Jesus figure, a 3-D post card of St. Francis, a snow-filled dome containing a minia-ture Nativity scene, a paint-by-numbers picture of the Three Wise Men, and several other trinkets that Twinkle retrieves with sheer delight, while her slightly more staid husband watches with increasing alarm her pen-chant for displaying these ornaments on their mantel. "We're not Christians," he reminds her, to which she replies somewhat mockingly, "No, we're not Christian. We're good little Hindus."³⁹ The discoveries continue, and Sanjeev tolerates them until Twinkle finds "a larger-than-life-sized watercolor poster of Christ, weeping translucent tears the size of peanut shells and sporting a crown of thorns" (139). It's evident from the description that the narrative voice, while not ridiculing the poster, does nevertheless present it as an object of curiosity, devoid of religious significance. When Sanjeev firmly refuses to let her add the poster to the collection already on display in their living room, Twinkle insists on put-ting it up in her study. He is troubled by this exhibition of religious "souvenirs," perhaps believing that there ought to be a connection between one's faith and the decorative objects in one's home. Twinkle, on the other hand, sees them as conversation pieces, occasions for enter-tainment. Yet, unlike Sanjeev, who would happily have thrown away the objects, Twinkle believes that to discard them would be to undermine their importance to the previous owners of the home and perhaps even to be sacrilegious.

The paradox is that they are both simultaneously respectful and dis-missive of Christianity. Sanjeev, who is ready to trash the paraphernalia, feels that religious memorabilia should not be mere decorative additions to one's home; they must be articles of faith. Twinkle, who wishes to pre-serve the objects and honor them with her attention (and in so doing honor the religiosity of the previous owners), feels no compunction at treating them as spectacles to be consumed and dissected. Thus, she leads the guests at their housewarming party on a treasure hunt for more objects and, in the process, finds the biggest prize of all in the attic: "a solid silver bust of Christ, the head easily three times the size of [Sanjeev's]" (156), which she and the guests triumphantly adorn with someone's feather hat. The bust, we are told, weighs a good thirty pounds. Although Sanjeev agrees to let it occupy a prominent place on their mantel for only one night, he knows that it will remain there per-manently, "in the center of the mantel, flanked on either side by the rest of the menagerie," so that Twinkle could explain to any guest that came to their home "how she had found it, and they would admire her as they listened" (157).

Sanjeev sees these objects as Twinkle's occasion to shine—to exhibit herself, so to speak—and he is made slightly uncomfortable by her penchant for display. Ultimately, however, Sanjeev cannot resist her charms, particularly because he sees their effect on others: "He gazed at the crushed rose petals in her hair, at the pearl and sapphire choker at her throat, at the sparkly crimson polish on her toes. He decided that these were among the things that made Prabal think she was wow" (157). The story closes with Sanjeev "press[ing] the massive silver face to his ribs, careful not to let the feather hat slip, and follow[ing] her" (157). There is a kind of resignation to his acceptance of her hold on him. That he is careful not to let the hat on Jesus' head slip suggests perhaps that he recognizes the importance of a lighthearted approach to his marriage in this blessed house in America. The image of the massive silver face of Jesus crested by a feather hat reminds us, as well, that God, too, may have a sense of humor.

In *Raisins Not Virgins*, Sharbari Ahmed uses humor as a trenchant device to examine what it means to be a Muslim American after September 11. Ahmed boldly addresses non–Muslim Americans' (mis)understanding of Islam and the conflict that one Bangladeshi American woman feels about the religion of her birth. The play's title is explained in a particularly charged exchange between the protagonist, Sahar, and her lover, Rizwan. She's trying to make the case that Koranic scholars aren't to be trusted, that they have misinterpreted one of the holy book's most important teachings: "You know the section that states if one martyrs himself in the name of Allah, he will go to Paradise and receive the reward of two hundred virgins. . . . Well apparently, it's raisins, Rizwan, not virgins. . . . People are killing themselves because they think they are going to get laid and guess what? Instead, they're going to get an eternity's worth of raisins."[40]

The play has a traditional and perhaps predictable scaffolding—the protagonist's mother is anxious that she settle down with a "nice young" Muslim man and has arranged for Sahar to meet Rizwan. However, on this architectural frame hang a range of provocative issues—in addition to Sahar's interrogation of Koranic dictates, Ahmed explores the conversion of a European American man to Islam and the zeal with which he embraces his new religion. Sahar is defiant, independent, and feisty. She wants to infuse religiosity with a bit of imagination and humor:

> There could be a show on it: E's Holy Scriptures Makeovers. Meet the Koran, she's been around a long time and is stuck in a rut. Her friends, Torah and the King James Bible, think it's time for an E Holy Emergency makeover. In the next thirty minutes, watch as the Koran goes through from bland brimstone to kick ass profundity with the help of our renowned panel of religious and spiritual experts, the Dalai Lama, Deepak Chopra, Mother Theresa, and Madonna. (26)

Sahar's ironic humor is engaging, but she is also prone to smugness at her own perceived resistance to Islam's dictates. Through her, Ahmed makes the point that it is easy to absorb the mainstream culture's notions of the repressed status of women in Islam. Sahar attacks Maryam, Rizwan's sister, for her submissiveness: "What the hell's the matter with you? Don't you care about your life? Why should you let something as thankless as *religion* rule it?" (24). She tells Maryam that wearing the veil is un-American, impractical, and definitely not liberating: "I think it says that women are something repulsive and meant to be covered up, like the Elephant man or something" (25). Maryam, however, is quite equal to Sahar's assaults, and accuses her of being "naked and vulnerable." She reveals to Sahar that the interrogation and reinterpretation of the Koran has been going on for a long time, and that there is even a legal term for it—"ijthihad."

Rizwan reminds Sahar that "Muslims haven't cornered the market on religious zealotry" (15). Billy Graham believes that "Muslims should be driven out of Jerusalem. Because the Messiah is going to come there and he doesn't want any Muslims around" (14), Rizwan informs Sahar. She will not be convinced, however: "I don't care what you say, Rizwan Rahman. It's the Muslims who make the big gestures. Blowing every-thing up, taking people hostage" (15). Sahar's maturation doesn't come from her learning to embrace Islam—that would have been too obvious a trajectory to explore—but rather from her learning to understand the complexity of different Muslims' engagement with their faith.

Ahmed's examination of the complexity of Islam is not limited to the interaction between the play's Muslim characters. Some of the most darkly humorous exchanges take place between Sahar and Aaron, her Jewish photographer friend, as he tries to explain to her that "Islam is a metaphor for adolescence. It's still figuring itself out. I'm Jewish. We've been around a long time, we set the tone and we're stuck in our ways. The Christians are suffering from middle child syndrome" (32). Ultimately, Sahar decides that she "can live with trying to just work it out" because she doesn't have the time "to denounce an entire religion" (46). With characteristic irreverence she says, "I'll use what I need and make it up as I go along. That's what God does. As far as I can see, Allah always shoots from the hip" (47). However, Ahmed doesn't leave us with the neat ending of Sahar's satisfaction at having arrived at a reasonable approach to her faith. In the very last seconds of the play, Sahar's mother tells her to turn on the TV. We know what images Sahar will see (the play has been leading up to September 11, 2001); we are left to wonder whether Sahar will continue to hold on to her optimism about her relationship with Islam.

The America that emerges in her play is a complicated place: it's the home of Billy Graham, but also of mosques and synagogues. It's the place where it's possible to consider making a series of photographs of people "vomiting on symbols of American Imperialism like Shea Stadium, the big bull by the Stock Exchange." It's also the place where "fanatics . . . want to ban any mention of Darwin and the theory of evolution in schools" and "people murder abortion doctors." And it's the country where policies are made in support of Ariel Sharon's government in Israel. Ultimately, however, Ahmed's play portrays a United States that Sahar can embrace. In this United States, religious faith is fluid. A Muslim woman can fall in love with a Catholic man; he can convert to Islam, marry her, and outdo her in orthodoxy. One can be Jewish and still take a keen interest in Islam, Sufism, and Christianity. One can reject Muslim-ness in one breath and be willing to explore Islam in the next. Thus, the United States is presented as a rational place in which dissatisfaction, protest, and defiance can find expression within acceptable boundaries. In the Middle East—where Mohammed Chip, the converted Catholic, goes to fight for the cause of the Palestinian people—religious expression becomes irrational, lives are chaotic and incomprehensible. Sahar is perhaps stridently rebellious, almost as though she makes too much of a point of being the defiant Muslim female. Nevertheless, despite her fierce spirit and assertive interrogation of Islam, she is open to learning more about the religion. In the character of Sahar, Ahmed appears to be providing a model for the post–September 11 Muslim American woman—critical both of the United States and patriarchal Islam—who unequivocally declares her presence as an American.

In contrast to Ahmed's depiction of Sahar's overt and very obvious struggle with questions of faith, Tahira Naqvi in "Chagrin" explores with understated restraint the question of how to be an observant Muslim in the United States. The story, which is set in Connecticut, follows the Sunday routine of a Pakistani American family. The mother's announcement of "Islamic class today" barely rouses her three sons, who are watching Fred Flintstone on TV. When they reach the Brookfield Library, in whose recreation room the class is held, they notice the low attendance. Three young children study Arabic with Mr. Ismail; the older children and adults are guided in a reading and explication of the Koran (in English translation) by Mustafa, "a Pakistani electric engineer turned handyman."[41] In discussing the Koran and its directives about charity with the other adults, the narrator learns for the first time exactly how much of her income she is supposed to contribute to charity. But the adults wonder how one determines the worth of one's assets. Do stocks and bonds figure as part of one's merchandise? They consult the notes at the end of the translated text, but there is no explanation. They decide that they must refer to the hadith (the traditions of the Prophet Muhammad, which form an integral part of Islamic belief). What emerges from this conversation is that no one among them is so thoroughly steeped in knowledge of the Koran as to have a satisfactory interpretation.

Asghar, the narrator's son, continues to read aloud from the translated text, and he encounters the word "chagrin." On the way home, in the car, he asks his mother what it means. When she explains, he replies: "I never thought I'd see a word like this in the Koran." The narrator responds that "the Koran is full of words like this, ordinary, everyday words" (99). In a revised version of the story, the author adds right after these words the sentences: "We must teach, we must always teach. Especially when the children are listening."[42]

The story (in both versions) closes with the following passage: "as we travel on Route 133 toward home, late afternoon slowly turns into dusk. The horizon is shot with crimson and the thready limbs of tall dark leafless trees seem to be lifted up toward a darkening sky in postures of supplication. There's to be snow, I tell myself. Slowly, the children's voices gain momentum" (100). The image of the dark leafless trees lifting toward the sky "in postures of supplication" is one of the few embellishments of the story. Because the imagery in the story is so sparse, this casting of the leafless trees as ardent worshipers stands out. The narrator, one suspects, is drawing a parallel between the leafless trees and the not quite Koranically adept adults and children at the Islamic class. Regardless of the level of their expertise, they too are supplicants, the story suggests. Like the leafless trees, their knowledge of the Koran may be meager, but they are by no means without faith.

The word "chagrin" serves an almost paradoxical function. Although the word suggests disappointment, unease, and discomfort, it becomes the occasion for the narrator to overcome precisely these feelings. She has been vaguely uneasy that her husband and children aren't enthusiastic about the Sunday classes, and that they attend somewhat desultorily and as a matter of habit. Her son's encounter of the word, however, allows her to impress upon her children the Koran's relevance to their lives (a function made more explicit in the revised version of the story). Her explanation of the word allows her to mediate between the world of the Arabic Koran and the world of the children's lives in Connecticut. Because Asghar does not know what "chagrin" means and yet is curious enough to ask his mother, it reminds him that the Koran can have relevance to his life only if he makes the effort to search for the connection. Merely having the Koran available in English, the story seems to suggest, does not ensure that he will be a good Muslim.

The last line of the story in both versions reads: "Slowly, the children's voices gain momentum." The narrator understands that whatever she may do to deepen her faith in and practice of Islam, her children will find their own expressions of faith. She can bring the words of the Koran to them, but she cannot bring them the faith that they must find within themselves. Equally significant is the fact that Asghar's slow realization that Islam need not be entirely unconnected from the realities of his everyday life occurs in locations that have no intrinsic Islamic significance. The Islamic class is held in the Brookfield Library's recreation room, a space "which can be made to wear any disguise." For the Muslims, it is the Islamic Center, "for the girl scouts who meet here weekly, it's a den, for another group it's something entirely theirs" (96). The meaning of "chagrin" he learns in the car on the way home. One can be a good Muslim in America, the story suggests; in following one's faith, one need not experience "chagrin," which the narrator describes to Asghar as "a feeling of disappointment, or sadness, like someone put you down or embarrassed you" (99). Both the narrator and her son appear to come to an important realization, but with little fanfare. In the quiet interstices of reflection, the narrator in particular awakens to her relationship with Islam in the United States. The journey on Route 133 "toward home" thus signifies more than just a return to a residence.

Journeys of "Necessity," Journeys of "Extravagance" (with thanks to Maxine Hong Kingston and Sau-ling Wong)

Journeys, both voluntary and involuntary, are a particularly American motif: European settlers, Native Americans displaced from their lands, Africans sold into slavery, slaves sold down river to plantations in Louisiana, immigrants looking for economic opportunities, expatriate Americans in Europe, migrant farmworkers, Japanese Americans forced into internment camps, Vietnamese and Cambodian refugees fleeing the aftermath of wars of American involvement, Muslim Americans deported for suspected ties to terrorism. The history of the United States is filled with journeys undertaken with hope *and* those undertaken in despair.

In her analysis of Asian American literature, Sau-ling Wong uses Maxine Hong Kingston's opposition of necessity and extravagance to chart one axis of the journeys of Asian Americans: from those taken in response to coercion to those taken in response to choice. Wong observes that "[t]he terms *Necessity* and *Extravagance* signify two contrasting modes of existence and operation, one contained, survival-driven and conservation-minded, the other attracted to freedom, excess, emotional expressiveness, and autotelism. . . . *Necessity* usually appears with words like *force, demand,* or *constraint; Extravagance* with words like *urge, impulse,* or *desire.*[43]

Within the dialectic of necessity and extravagance, I consider another kind of journey—the intellectual and emotional journey of modifying one's perspective. I began this chapter with Kip's rapid journey of unlearning his trust in Europe in *The English Patient*. Kip has another journey to make, however: to learn that England is no longer the world power and that the United States has assumed that role. Some of us make journeys of gathering information, in which we seek to enlarge our reservoir of information; in the process, we journey to altered perspectives. Such a journey is an ongoing one, sometimes undertaken for extravagance, but usually for survival. Throughout this book, I have addressed this nation's general unwillingness to engage intimately with peoples in other lands, to step outside the boundaries of its national self and grasp other realities and other imperatives of living. (See Chapter 2 for a discussion of Asian American writers' attempts to take readers to these other locations in meaningful ways that go beyond mere voyeurism or sampling of difference.) In Chapter 4, I discuss the value of "writing what you're not," that is, making the bold move to imagine creatively in text the lives of those unlike oneself in race, gender, nationality, ethnicity, sexual orientation, or class, always mindful of the role of power in crossing boundaries. For some, such journeys outside familiar territory are matters of survival—for instance, Vietnamese American adolescents in some neighborhoods know that they must of necessity learn how to make connections with their African American counterparts; the same is true of Bangladeshi youth who establish links with Latino youth. Korean Americans and African Americans in South Central Los Angeles, New York City, and Chicago also know the urgency of journeying into each other's lives if they are to coexist meaningfully.[44]

Jhumpa Lahiri's story "The Third and Final Continent" interweaves two seemingly dissimilar journeys: the arduous and highly publicized journey of the Apollo 11 astronauts to the moon, and the journey of an immigrant to a new country. The narrator of this story renders a somewhat muted assessment of the astronauts' moon landing. Viewed against his own multiple migrations and length of stay in this new world of the United States, the protagonist sees the astronauts' achievement as slight: "While the astronauts, heroes forever, spent mere hours on the moon, I have remained in this new world for nearly thirty years." In that brief comparison, Lahiri's narrator reminds us that the act of emigrating from one's birth country and settling in a new place requires great courage and perseverance. By remembering with pride the small acts he has performed to arrive at and make for himself a life in the new destination, the narrator infuses the immigrant's experience with celebratory pride: "[T]here are times I am bewildered by each mile I have traveled, each meal I have eaten, each person I have known, each room in which I have slept. As ordinary as it all appears, there are times when it is beyond the imagination."[45]

One of the most puzzling persons the narrator encounters on first arriving in Boston is Mrs. Croft, his landlady. Lahiri's America, in the figure of Mrs. Croft, emerges as both a rather attractive location and an inexplicable challenge. The story allows for no easy allegiances or rejections. One way to read the narrator's recollections of his interactions with Mrs. Croft is to see him as too ingratiating. However, an alternate reading would be to see him as attentively sensitive to her extreme old age (she is 103 years old, having been born in 1866), an attitude of concern for the elderly that he displays in the care of his mother in India. Mrs. Croft is somewhat senile, particularly in her peremptory commands. For instance, she states on the phone that she only rents to Harvard and Tech (MIT) men. When the narrator first goes to Mrs. Croft's home, she says, "A flag on the moon, boy! I heard it on the radio! Isn't that splendid?" When the narrator agrees, she commands, "Say 'splendid'!" (179). Bewildered by her order, the narrator remains silent, until she bellows again, "Say 'splendid'!" When he complies, she orders him: "Go see the room!" (180). Once the narrator moves in, the ritual of intoning "Splendid" continues every night. In addition, he must follow a strict routine for paying the rent each month.

If one sees Mrs. Croft as symbolic of the nation, then it is not hard to see in her strange behavior a parallel to the arbitrary regulations to which an immigrant must adhere (for example, the exact instructions on how to write the numbers 1 and 7, discussed above). The story is neither a straightforward paean to immigrant resolve and adaptability nor an outright criticism of the arbitrary rules the immigrant is forced to observe. Through Mrs. Croft's senility, Lahiri introduces the idea of America as vulnerable, perhaps even prone to self-delusion. Although the narrator continues to do Mrs. Croft's bidding by repeating "splendid" whenever she raises the subject of the moon landing, he reminds us that he does so not because of any power that she wields over him but because he sees her as vulnerable and wishes to protect her. Although he knows full well that "[b]y then, of course, there was no flag on the moon [because] [t]he astronauts . . . had taken it down before flying back to Earth," he doesn't "have the heart to tell her" (183).

That Lahiri locates in a somewhat senile centenarian the protagonist's initial encounter with the mysteries of America enables us to consider age as a component of the idea of America. The United States, typically constructed as a young nation, or certainly as a constantly self-renewing nation, is seen to leave little room for an appreciation of the past and for revering the old. At the same time, however, longer life expectancy resulting from advances in medical technologies has led to a steady increase in the number of people over sixty-five over the past fifteen years. Senior citizens now make up a powerful voting bloc and wield considerable influence with elected officials. Lahiri's Mrs. Croft thus serves to remind us both of the power and the limitations of old age.

The narrator's initial reaction to Mrs. Croft's imperious yet quirky commands is one of discomfort and feeling insulted, but he gradually comes to admire her for her physical endurance and fierce will to control any situation. In contrast to his own mother—who retreated into a shell at the death of her husband and gradually lost her sanity—this American landlady is robust and vital. One could argue that in the contrast between the two mother figures, Lahiri sets up the opposition of tired East and energetic West and privileges the West by having the narrator see Mrs. Croft as inspiring. The narrator is "in awe of how many years she had spent on this earth" and therefore becomes attentive to the simple things he can do to make her life more comfortable: "At times I came downstairs before going to sleep, to make sure that she was sitting upright on the bench, or was safe in her bedroom. On Fridays I made sure to put the rent in her hands" (189). He closes his description of these simple gestures of assistance he offers her with an almost rueful reminder to himself that he is, after all, not her son. One gets the impression that perhaps there is a part of him that wishes he were.

The narrator comes to life, as it were, in Boston, through his interactions with Mrs. Croft. One could argue that Lahiri presents America as a site of rebirth. Her use of the phrase "third and final continent" for

North America underscores the distance—both physical and psychological—that the protagonist has traveled to arrive in the United States. He
leaves India for England; after a sojourn there for five years, he moves on
to Boston. Thus he journeys across Asia and Europe before settling finally in North America. Reinforcing the title's sense of an ultimate destination—beyond which there is no need to go, for one has arrived at the
best of all possible locations—the story uncovers, in Lahiri's unobtrusive
way, the protagonist's gradual understanding of himself as an emotional
being. It is in Boston that he moves from merely fulfilling duty to reacting as an independent human being, recognizing in himself the capacity
to feel sorrow and love. It is as though all his previous journeys were but
preparatory stages for his arrival and life in Boston, where by slow
degrees he grows out of his shell and matures.

The sensitivity that the narrator reveals in his meditations about Mrs.
Croft is almost entirely absent when he contemplates the arrival from
India of his new wife. He regards her arrival as he "would the arrival of
a coming month, or season—something inevitable, but meaningless at the
same time" (189). It is only when he and Mala go to visit Mrs. Croft that
the narrator is able to appreciate his wife. Listening to Mala respond to
Mrs. Croft's peremptory questions and commands—"Can you play the
piano?" "Then stand up!" (195)—the narrator feels for the first time an
empathy with his wife, whom he has up until this moment considered an
intrusion into his carefully ordered existence. "Like me, Mala had traveled
far from home, not knowing where she was going, or what she would
find, for no reason other than to be my wife. As strange as it seemed, I
knew in my heart that one day her death would affect me, and stranger
still, that mine would affect her" (195). And when Mrs. Croft declares that
Mala is a perfect lady, the couple share a first moment of quiet camaraderie—their eyes meet and they smile. The narrator observes, "I like to
think of that moment in Mrs. Croft's parlor as the moment when the distance between Mala and me began to lessen" (196).

It is problematic that the narrator's first awareness of his wife as an
individual whom it is possible for him to love and appreciate occurs in
the presence of, and is predicated by the acceptance of, the 103-year-old
woman who frames his first significant encounter with the United
States. It is hard not to see in the narrator's admiration for Mrs. Croft and
his desire for her validation of Mala a yearning for a new mother of

whom he can be proud (in contrast to his biological mother, who seems to have moved him to pity and embarrassment for her weakness). "Mrs. Croft's was the first death I mourned in America, for hers was the first life I had admired" (196), the narrator observes. The ambiguity of the closing clause—it is unclear whether hers was the first life he had admired anywhere or just in America—leaves unresolved the question of the intensity of the narrator's attachment to her. That he genuinely grieves her death is never in doubt. But whether one should read his fondness for her as a too ready willingness to declare his commitment to the United States or see it as nothing more than a young man's admiration for a life lived independently and stalwartly is not a question that can be easily answered.

The closing lines of the story, by juxtaposing the astronauts' landing on the moon against the immigrant's act of settling in a new land, serve to underscore the magnitude of the immigrant's achievement. The astronauts may remain "heroes forever," but so should the immigrant, the narrator suggests. Perhaps that is the text's ultimate gift: a reframing of the immigrant's journey as not ordinary but extraordinary. The narrator speaks of "the ambition that had first hurled [him] across the world" (197). Although the word "ambition" eclipses the unpleasant forces that propel individuals to travel thousands of miles from their original homes (economic servitude and slavery, for instance), the word "hurled" infuses the circumstance of displacement with the immigrant's power and strength. The astronauts' voyage may be hailed as "man's most awesome achievement" (179), but the immigrant's journey is no less one "beyond . . . imagination." The narrator has come to this realization thirty years after arrival in the United States. He knows now that voyages are of many kinds—the longevity and fortitude of Mrs. Croft, whose life spanned a century; the astronauts who made the moon landing; and his own journey of making a life in a new country—and they are all worthy of celebration.

Abraham Verghese's *My Own Country* admirably illustrates how some journeys cannot be easily identified as being either of necessity or of extravagance, because the distinction would be artificial and even detrimental. I have written elsewhere about this text's use of Western literary techniques even as it modifies them,[46] and in Chapter 4 I approach it for its value as a successful attempt at "writing what one is not." Here, I take up the other kinds of journeys it illuminates. Verghese himself, as a multiply displaced immigrant, has made many journeys: from Ethiopia where he was born to India, the birth-country of his parents, to England, and, finally, to the United States. Within the United States he has traveled from New York City to Boston to eastern Tennessee, where this memoir unfolds in the town of Johnson City, and finally to El Paso, Texas, where he works at the Texas Tech Health Sciences Medical Center. But the memoir is not primarily about Verghese's physical travels. It begins with his journey as an infectious disease specialist into the medical territory of his patients. Quickly, that journey leads to other journeys: through his "discovery" of the nature of their illness (AIDS), he and his patients make journeys in search of acceptance by the patients' families and the larger community. But this quest for acceptance must be paralleled by the journeys the families and the community ought to undertake to embrace their lost sons. (The majority of his patients are gay men who left Johnson City for urban locations more hospitable to same-sex relationships, but are now returning to be with their families when it is evident that they are very sick and near death.)

It is clear that some of the journeys are journeys of necessity: the homosexual men must leave Johnson City if they are to lead lives of pride and openness; by the same token, they feel the need to come home to die among family. Verghese must necessarily make the journey into his patients' lives to understand how and where they contracted AIDS and what he, as a doctor, can do to treat them and prevent the spread of AIDS in the region. He could, of course, gather all this information within the confines of his examination room. But he does not. One could argue that Verghese goes beyond necessity—he undertakes a journey of extravagance to become a friend, a confidant, a surrogate son and brother. He goes on journeys of friendship—making house calls, visiting the families of his patients, educating the larger community about the disease, and dispelling the fears associated with it. But, in Verghese's view, these are not add-on journeys, side trips he makes simply to think better of himself. To him they are urgent necessities. An attempted suicide by one of his patients convinces him of the kind of doctor he must be, the kinds of journeys he must make:

> Raleigh's suicide attempt shook me: . . . I had failed to appreciate what he was going through and perhaps underestimated the comfort I could have brought him in spheres of his life unrelated to the

virus. In the absence of a magic potion to cure AIDS, my job was to minister to the patient's soul, his psyche, pay attention to his family and his social and his social situation. I would have to make more home visits, make more attempts to understand the person I saw in the clinic, be sure to understand the family dynamics by meeting all its members. Some of this I was already doing as a matter of interest. I would now have to do it out of necessity. (219)

It is not just Verghese who must make these journeys of necessity, however. The memoir reveals that the entire nation, beginning with the politicians who construct its budget, must make the journey into the territory of AIDS to understand the urgent necessity for policies to fund research for cure and prevention. And then there is the necessity for the heterosexual person to make the journey to acceptance of, or at least a posture of neutrality toward, the homosexual life. James, one of Verghese's patients, draws a rather stark contrast between the willingness of homosexual men to travel (both physically and cognitively) and the limited aspirations of heterosexual men. Although his opposition is overdetermined and his conception of heterosexual men reductively monolithic (James is speaking for rhetorical effect and in a moment of unguarded anger at having had to live so much of his life in secrecy), its value lies in the spotlight it sheds on the heterosexual man's position of power vis-a-vis the homosexual man. James reminds us that for those in power the status quo is comfortable, "travel" not a necessity, and journeying to learn about other lives is an option they can very easily ignore:

> Most gay men have traveled to several countries, have seen the best shows, movies, plays, have taken an interest in art, in their clothes, in the way their house is decorated, have experienced more of this world than any heterosexual. To me, a heterosexual male is a slob. . . . His idea of a good time is to get a six-pack and park his truck on the side of the road with his buddy and drink. He might beat his wife, be mean to his kids and ultimately die where he was born having seen nothing, done nothing. But, by God, the one thing he knows is how he feels about queers! When he sees a queer he can look down on him, feel contempt, beat up a queer because it's justified. (204)

James's rant underscores the asymmetry of power. His fury and bitterness are expressed in words; the fury of heterosexual men, however, can and does translate into bodily violence against and economic disenfranchisement and social ostracism of gay men.

Verghese's several journeys—to Tennessee, then into his patients' lives, and then to the Iowa Writers' Workshop, where he refines his narrative and descriptive skills—has resulted in his charting the territory of a particular human condition within the borders of the United States. All are invited to enter this territory, to journey through its complex terrain, and then to arrive at a point of willingness to undertake similar voyages into other territories. That *My Own Country* was declared by *Time* magazine to be one of the best books of 1994 indicates that readers in the United States were willing to heed its call to journey into the domain of AIDS and understand the impact of the disease on families. The memoir's success has less to do with the average reader's interest in the immigrant doctor's story than with the compelling appearance of AIDS as an inevitable feature in our lives in the 1980s. That AIDS affected all types of families and crossed ethnic, racial, and class lines made this memoir everybody's business. That everyone is potentially vulnerable to the impact of AIDS—either directly by becoming infected or indirectly through caring for a loved one who has contracted the virus—makes the AIDS-awareness journey one of necessity.

Though the memoir focuses primarily on white families (one wonders whether he had patients of color and how the intersection of race and homosexuality affects family and societal reaction), Verghese's skillful and sensitive depiction of families from diverse socioeconomic backgrounds and their relationships to their gay sons, brothers, or husbands compensates in some small measure for the absence of families of color. Another compelling aspect of the memoir is that it features a caring and patient-centered physician—a lost figure in this day of insurance-run medical care; that yearning in each of us for a medical ministering to our body that is entwined with compassion and genuine interest in us as unique individuals makes reading this memoir akin to a self-indulgent wish fulfillment.

Verghese's immigrant medical memoir reflects a much-vaunted feature of the desirability of the American landscape—the possibilities of success available to the individual who comes here. It reinforces the idea that there are numerous ways to achieve renown and to become integrated into the national social fabric. The United States that emerges in his memoir is largely hospitable. Because he has made the journey into his patients' lives, and because they have needed him to do so to ease the pain of their emotional isolation and medical complications, he has felt welcomed into America. At the close of his memoir, on the road from Tennessee to Iowa, where he has enrolled in the prestigious creative writing program, Verghese declares his deep passion for this country with Whitmanesque expansiveness and lyricism:

> I look up at the stars. I feel connected: legs to earth, shoulders to sky. I squint my eyes and see the lines that link stars to make constellations, feel their umbra extend down to me, connecting me with this parcel of land that I stand on. Everything is united: my children, the clouds, God, the moon, the mother of my children, . . . Under this sky I am connected to all that I left behind in Tennessee, all the friends and the patients who wished me luck. (347)

These are the words of a man who feels he has arrived at home. He has claimed his own country.

Blinded by Success, Sighted through Humility

A similar optimism about the United States pervades the earlier memoirs of two South Asian Americans—Dalip Singh Saund's *Congressman from India* (1960) and Ved Mehta's *Sound-Shadows of the New World* (1985). Saund was the first American of Asian descent to become a U.S. congressman, a position he held for two terms (1956–60). Mehta, blind since an illness in his infancy, entered the United States to attend the Arkansas School for the Blind (ASB) at the age of fifteen. Both memoirs record their narrators' immense achievements in spite of a variety of obstacles and in the process underscore the opportunity for success in the United States, whatever the nature of an individual's handicap.

In Saund's text, the United States, viewed against the colonizer Britain, stands as the champion of freedom and individual rights. "Lincoln changed the entire course of my life" (31), observes Saund. The

Gettysburg Address with its reinscription of a "government of the people, by the people, and for the people" holds special meaning for Saund
as a college student in India in 1919. Thus, although his family wants him
to join the service of the British Government in India, Saund is determined to make his way to America.

Saund pursues his opportunities in the United States with seemingly indefatigable and irrepressible drive. An illustrative moment in his
memoir concerns his efforts to become a U.S. citizen at a time (in the
years prior to and during World War II) when peoples of Asian descent
were deemed to be ineligible for citizenship. Saund evokes the American
spirit of self-reliance in deciding that "[i]nstead of crying or complain-
ing about the situation [he] would do something about it" (73). It is not
only the "lives of great Americans in the past" to which he turns for
inspiration, but also the examples of his neighbors, Sikh farmers from
India in California's Imperial Valley, "who had started life in the desert
against serious handicaps." His undeterred pursuit of what must have
seemed a near unthinkable move—getting a special bill passed in
Congress that would allow Asians to obtain citizenship—may seem too
idealistic to be true, steeped as we are today in cynicism about the common people's power to effect change. Saund, on the other hand, "had
great faith in the American sense of justice and fair play and the righteousness of [his] cause" (73). He mobilizes Indians in New York and
friends of India to contact influential members of Congress to urge them
to introduce the bill. We get some intimation of the difficulties preceding the passage of the Luce-Celler bill (the legislation that ultimately lifted the ban on citizenship), but there is a curious and tantalizing gap at
precisely the point where we expect details of why and how the bill was
finally accepted and the immigration ban lifted. Note the deus ex
machina intervention of President Harry S. Truman in Saund's account:

> The law . . . prohibited not only natives of India, but natives of all
> countries in Asia, from becoming American citizens. Opponents of
> the bill feared the reaction of other countries in Asia, particularly the
> Philippine Islands, if the ban was lifted for natives of India only.
> These questions raised serious matters of policy and there was a
> sharp division over the Luce-Celler bill in congressional circles.
> Chances for its passage were further handicapped because there was

no one particularly powerful force to push it through. Suddenly the
chances for our success brightened when, at the beginning of 1946,
President Truman took a special interest in its passage. After four
years of long waiting and hard effort the Luce-Celler bill was finally passed by both houses of Congress and signed by President
Truman on July 3, 1946. (75)

The absence of detail is not limited to the circumstances surrounding the passage of the bill. What is perhaps more surprising is that Saund
makes no critique of the circumstances and attitudes that necessitated
the special bill in the first place. There is little interrogation of the United
States' anti-Asian attitude, little discussion of California's Alien Land Law
that prohibited noncitizens from owning land. One gets the impression
that Saund sees these inherent injustices as aberrations, not features
endemic to the social and political fabric of America. Or perhaps he sees
them as tests he is required to pass to demonstrate to himself and others
his worthiness to belong. His attitude seems to suggest that he has only
earned his rights if he can prove he is capable of fighting for them.
Another reading of Saund's resolve may be to see it as evidence of the
individual's power in the United States. Saund's faith in his ability to
challenge even the judicial system strikes one today as remarkably bold.
    In 1957, the year after being elected to his first term to the U.S.
House of Representatives, Saund made an official trip to Asia, during
which he visited Japan, Taiwan, Hong Kong, Singapore, Vietnam,
Indonesia, the Philippines, India, and Pakistan. In Japan he was asked
about the battles against segregation in Little Rock, Arkansas, and questioned pointedly about U.S. nuclear testing on the Bikini Islands (an atoll
that lies between Japan and Hawai`i). As a U.S. congressman, Saund not
surprisingly presents the nation as working in the best interests of both
its own people and all the peoples of the world. On the events in Little
Rock, he responds to a question by a professor in Sendai by stressing that
"segregation was limited to one part of the country where its roots are
deep and will take some time to dig up" (157). He then deflects attention from racism in the United States by turning the audience's attention toward a generalized inhumanity of man to man. Saund's rendition
of what he said reads more like an exhortatory speech than an actual
memory. It is almost as though he uses the occasion of writing his mem-

oir to mount a new campaign, or as though he wishes always to be seen as the mouthpiece of America to the peoples of Asia:

> My friends, no matter where we live, whether it be in Japan, in India, or the United States of America, there exists in one form or another injustice of man toward man. And the people of the United States full well recognize they are faced with a very difficult race problem in their midst. They are trying to do the best they can, and I shall urge to my friends in Japan, and to people wherever I go, to try to understand this difficult problem of the people of the United States, just as they would want other people to study and understand their problems. Instead of finding fault with each other, it should be the duty of civilized men everywhere to resolve these injustices of man toward man. (157)

Saund presents himself as the champion of the United States. He urges the nations he visits to choose freedom and democracy and cautions them against turning to the Soviet Union and Communism. Saund takes very seriously the role that he believes he must play in Asia: to serve as "a living example of American democracy in practice" (152). He concludes that the immense interest that the various nations of Asia have shown in his visit to that part of the world could only have one reason: "The people of India and the Asiatic world knew the story of my election to the United States Congress in 1956 and were proud of the fact that a man born in India had been elected to that high office" (183). Then, in a quick move to deflect attention from himself, he adds, "[P]eople are not proud of something they don't respect and love. I could only conclude that there is a great reservoir of respect and affection for the United States of America and its people in that part of that world, but we must husband that treasure carefully and see that it grows and flourishes" (183). The last clause indicates that Saund is cognizant of the need for the United States to keep in mind the welfare of other nations even as it focuses on its own welfare. Read in light of current events, Saund's articulation, despite its exuberant faith in the United States' sense of justice and fairness, strikes one as balanced. In placing upon the United States the responsibility for ensuring that it does not lose the goodwill of other nations—"we must husband that treasure

carefully and see that it grows and flourishes"—Saund reveals a fundamental humility in his conception of the U.S. role in global politics.
Thus, although his own enthusiastic embrace of the United States as a
person of color may seem, in a post–Civil Rights and postmodern era,
naive and misguided, his awareness of the United States' dependency on
the trust of other nations complicates a reading of him as unequivocally
and uncritically jingoistic.

Ved Mehta's memoir, published in the period of intensifying multiculturalism, engages the issue of survival, but not primarily within the
context of race and ethnicity. Mehta's blindness introduces disability into
the discussion, but because most of the memoir is set in the Arkansas
School for the Blind, where Mehta spent four years (1949–53) among
other blind students, we do not get an extensive discussion of the ways
in which his brownness complicates his blindness in the wider sighted
world. We do see how it affects his reception by at least one student,
Wayne, at ASB. Wayne, who is not blind or partially sighted but suffers
from a condition called nystagmus, in which the involuntary movement
of the eyeball leads to varying degrees of visual loss, questions Mehta's
presence at ASB, a school for white blind children.

Mehta writes from the perspective of a fourteen-to-eighteen-year
old; this point of view frees him from having to interrogate deeply the
subject of race even in those instances when he calls attention to it. I
would argue that Mehta's near elision of race is perhaps meant to suggest that color is not of fundamental importance to those who cannot
see. More urgent issues are at stake. That it is always Wayne, the one student in the school with the least loss of vision, who brings up race indicates that sightedness is unfortunately accompanied by moral blindness.

Yet, certain silences on and dismissals of the subject of race are too
noticeable, even if we make allowances for the narrow interests of a fourteen-
year-old boy. The young Ved is clearly capable of complex thought,
particularly when it comes to the subject of India's independence or the
newly liberated country's friendship with the Soviet Union. Therefore,
his perfunctory discussion of race strikes one as deliberate and pointed.
We learn that in India, Mehta and his family had "worried whether the
school [he] was going to might be for Negroes" (43), but they had not
wanted to risk his admission or create bad feelings by inquiring. Not to
give us any explanation—particularly one appropriate to a fourteen-

year-old blind boy from India—for the distaste he and his family exhib-it for "Negroes" (for instance, did his father acquire his prejudice during his sojourn as a medical student in the United States or come by it through the British, or is the sentiment an expression of Indians' gener-al unfavorable attitude toward people of African descent?) underscores a certain level of indifference, if not callousness, to the condition of being black. Such a reading is bolstered by Mehta's comment that in many of his classes "little real work got done. Much of the time was spent argu-ing about things that had little to do with . . . studies, like the perennial subjects of Negroes and religion" (92). Yet Mehta's indifference cannot be divorced from the context in which it occurs and is reinforced. Most importantly, the teacher Miss Harper, in whose English class the discus-sion becomes particularly heated during the study of *Tom Sawyer*, con-tributes to Mehta's indifference when she declares that she is switching to teaching *Jane Eyre* because "'[t]here are no Negroes in this book'" (92) to disrupt the peace and quiet of the classroom.

Mehta is not without sensitivity, however. One of the most signifi-cant reflective moments in the book occurs when he is attempting to understand his place in the universe of racial hierarchy:

> Some people thought that the blind lived in darkness, but that was nonsense. The point was that the blind had no perception of light or darkness. Perhaps darkness was like the quiet of night. I wondered how dark I was, how much I looked like a Negro, and what my kin-ship with the Negro was—where I fitted into the social puzzle. I wanted somehow or other to find out where I stood in the shading from white to black, to connect myself to the rest of the world. (74)

For the most part, *Sound-Shadows of the New World* records Mehta's extraordinary resourcefulness and resolve in the face of blindness. In this approach, it underscores the courage and determination that supposedly mark the American character. Although we learn about the other stu-dents at ASB, the text is one individual's narrative, one individual's dec-laration that he counts in the sighted world.

Mehta's acute consciousness of how the blind are perceived by the sighted makes his survival in the sighted world truly remarkable. Unlike many of his classmates, who desire to spend their life in a sheltered environment among other blind individuals, Mehta opts for the sighted world, despite knowing that to that world, the blind are considered "donkeys—beasts of burden, scorned and undervalued, even condemned to compete with natural prancers and jumpers" (164–65). The awareness that one is perceived this way, Mehta says, is the ultimate pain: "we were worse off than jackasses, because they at least had no consciousness, no idea that they were deficient in gait or in mane. Would that we had their innocence!" (165).

All three memoirs—Verghese's, Saund's, and Mehta's—privilege individual effort over collective achievement, but to varying degrees. In an essay on Verghese, I have explored more fully the ways in which his memoir negotiates between Augustinian and Rousseauvian traditions of Western autobiography.[47] Augustine's *Confessions*, although a document of his arrival at the knowledge of God, is nevertheless meant for the reassurance of a collectivity that has as its highest moral imperative the belittling of self. On the other hand, as John Sturrock points out, Nietzsche in *Ecce Homo*, going further even than Rousseau, presents the self as unique, "an 'entity' writing in order to proclaim his superiority over a population of nonentities."[48] The three male South Asian American memoirs just discussed call attention to the ways in which the *individual* succeeds in the United States, provided that he is willing to persevere.

By contrast, Meena Alexander's memoir *Fault Lines* (1993) foregrounds not the resolve of the individual but the influences of the various communities to which the individual is connected. In an interview with Deepika Bahri and Mary Vasudeva, Alexander articulates the difference between American autobiography and her memoir: "this focus on the self is very peculiar to the culture of North America, . . . A constant attempt to vivify what one thinks of as identity by redefining oneself is a very American project. . . . I'm interested in how one's relationship to others defines where one is. . . . My story is only one among the many others that connect with it."[49] Lavina Shankar observes that Alexander's poetry, fiction, and prose "resist. . . a stable, unified sense of self or home in America."[50] The many components of her identity coexist in complex interaction: the communities of her childhood in Kerala in India; the schoolchildren among whom she grew up in the Sudan; the intellectuals at the university in Khartoum, and then in England; and the many women of color with whom she makes common cause in the

United States. "There are so many strands all running together in a bright snarl of life," says Alexander. "My job is to evoke it all, altogether. For that is what my ethnicity requires, that is what America with its hot-shot present tense compels me to."[51] She will not be overpowered by the emphasis on the present, and in a deliberate act of resistance against what she perceives is the United States' privileging of the here and the now, Alexander turns to the many theres and thens that constitute her life. "The whole issue of what it means to speak out is occasioned . . . by the pressure of living in America . . . looking at myself and how I fit in rela-tion to others," she observes.[52]

Her emergence as a writer is inextricably linked to other people. Erika Duncan notes that Alexander was first published in Khartoum in Arabic. At the university there, she showed her friends the poems she had been writing. One of her friends translated a few of them and they appeared in Khartoum's Arabic newspaper. Of her debut as a published writer in Arabic, Alexander says, "It made a lot of sense to me that my first poems were published in a language I couldn't read."[53] In that remark, Alexander reveals that her poetry is for others as much as it is for herself; that her work has an existence beyond her crafting of it. In a manner of speaking, her poetic self becomes dependent on the voices of others to exist. Living in New York, Alexander is acutely aware of the many different communities of people that live there. New York, she observes, makes her conscious of her diasporic history; she has come here after many wanderings, and in the diverse peoples she encounters on its streets, she is reminded of the many geographical locations that have made her who she is: "In Manhattan it is hard to make the bits and pieces hold together. Things are constantly falling apart. The city is dis-persing itself, jolting, juggling its parts. There is no ideal of poise in its construction, just the basting together of bits" (*Fault Lines* 177).

In Chapter 2, I discussed Alexander as a writer deeply engaged in the project of social justice. This impulse is directly linked to her under-standing of herself as stitched with other people. She writes, "The strug-gle for social justice, for human dignity, is for each of us. Like ethnicity, like the labor of poetry, it is larger than any single person, or any single voice. It transcends individualism" (203). Alexander writes with passion of injustice and the resistance to it, both in the United States and beyond. Her connections are many, and the subjects she takes on are wide ranging—for example, police brutality, art, social protest, rape, eviction, war, migrant labor, fantasy, memory, legend, ethnic conflict, rehabilitation, healing, and birth. The globe is her field of vision, the United States merely the place from which she looks out on it.

Here in the United States, she is made aware of her brownness: "I can make myself up and this is the enticement, the exhilaration, the compulsive energy of America. But only up to a point. And the point, the sticking point, is my dark female body. I may try the voice-over bit, the textual pyrotechnic bit, but my body is here now and cannot be shed" (202). Here she is made aware of how she must repress her knowledge of multiple tongues—Malayalam, Arabic, Hindi, Marathi—to speak English; she is cognizant of the ways in which her brown body limits the transformative possibilities available to her in America; and she is reminded that since the events of September 11, 2001, she and others who look like her can at any moment become the targets of hate and abuse. But here, too, is where she finds comfort and energy among the other women who agitate, create, and preserve communities. Alexander's idea of America is complex. Her bardic voice speaks out with urgency on what matters, or should matter, to us, and she urges us to observe an America that is large with paradoxes.

Conclusion: Just Reading

South Asian American literature, too, is large with paradoxes. I began this book by speaking of the need to approach this body of writing as more than just an act of reading. Reading this literature should be a just act, I said, paying attention to the multiple histories, contexts, and urgencies informing the works. To reinforce the importance of resisting quick conclusions and convenient interpretations, I turn to two stories: Himani Bannerjee's "The Moon and My Mother" and Jhumpa Lahiri's "The Interpreter of Maladies."[54]

"The Moon and My Mother" is set almost exclusively in India. The story presents an opposition between a scientific-minded atheist daughter and her mother, who is immersed in traditional beliefs of ancestors, gods, and the afterlife. The time is 1969, and the global news is full of the Americans' imminent moon landing. The mother is eager to hear what the astronauts will find there. What she learns disturbs her greatly: "They landed, came out of their aeroplane and walked on the moon, and they didn't find anything," she says bleakly, bitter that the holy books have lied to her; she had placed so much trust in them and they had led her to believe in "a celestial sphere of the ancestors, where we all go after death" (191). Her sudden loss of spiritual faith fills her with such deep fear that at the time of her death she is convinced that all there is on the other side is "[a]n immense great darkness. . . . There is nothing there. No ancestors, nobody. . . . On the other side of death, there is death" (195). When she dies, the daughter is thousands of miles away in North America. As the daughter watches the moon, she recalls her mother: "The moon seemed to be looking at me as well. It spoke to me of my mother, of a time long ago, of when I was a young woman, when my mother was active and alive. But most of all it had become one with my mother, a very private and personal moon, populated with memories of hope and horror, with a parable of faith and its loss. It was not empty, that moon, I thought. The Americans were wrong" (196).

At a superficial level, this story sets up the rather predictable dichotomy of scientific America and spiritual India. The daughter's initial impatience with her mother's extreme distress at the emptiness of the moon is also illustrative of the typical chasm between a Westernized daughter and an orthodox parent. But the story does not play out as anticipated. Distraught at her mother's deathbed fear, the daughter tries to revive her mother's faith in God, crying out to her, "And God? Isn't there God, on the other side? Will it not be to us as we believe? And if we believe . . ." (195), only to be told by her mother that such belief is foolishness. The daughter's realization that her mother "had become like the dead moon, lit by the false glow of a sun about to withhold its light from her" (195), gives us a compelling metaphor for the influence of the United States' actions on belief systems in other parts of the world. That the promise of science—or in this case, the achievement of the United States—is characterized as a "false glow" indicates that the daughter has begun to question her own earlier uncritical acceptance of all things modern and Western. That this "sun" is about to withhold its light from her mother in these final moments reveals that the daughter has begun to understand that the allures of the United States may not always be salutary, that they may in fact be intensely damaging. Knowledge, in this instance, results in spiritual darkness for the mother.

And yet, the story does not ultimately rest with a position of devaluing science. In its closing lines, the moon (whose illumination is, after all, spurious, reflecting as it does the sun's light) becomes the daughter's link to her mother, the conduit of her appreciation for what her mother has suffered in the acquisition of knowledge and the realization of scientific truth. The daughter has acquired knowledge as well, albeit of a different kind. Hers is the knowledge of human emotion and of her mother's ultimate courage in facing the loss of her faith in an afterlife. Perhaps the most significant knowledge the daughter acquires, however, is that "[t]he Americans were wrong." Wrong, perhaps, to define success in terms of their conquest of space and arrival on the moon; wrong perhaps to observe only the surface details of the moon's barrenness. The daughter is hungry for connection with her mother and, in the context of her loss, the moon becomes the repository of her memories of her mother. The story does not privilege either the scientific or the religious worldview. Rather, it suggests that there are different types of knowledge and that all types of knowledge do not have the same effect on all people. The mother knows on her deathbed that her previous belief in an afterlife graced by her ancestors will no longer serve to ease her mind; she has accepted the knowledge of science, which has displaced her faith. The daughter labels her mother's prescientific attitude (prior to her knowing of the moon's barrenness) as "hope" and "faith" and her later attitude as "horror" and "loss [of faith]." These terms may help explain the cause of the mother's suffering: *she couldn't accommodate both types of knowledge—scientific and religious.* So the mother falls prey to a bipolar vision and is too quick to subordinate herself to the pronouncements of the American astronauts and scientists. Knowledge, the story seems to suggest, is neither entirely about the hard evidence of science nor the unprovable tenets of one's faith. The success of the moon landing does not establish the United States as the last word on knowledge or living.

Lahiri's "Interpreter of Maladies," which was selected for inclusion in the 1999 collections of *O. Henry Award* choices and *Best American Short Stories*, offers a complex treatment of the allures and disappointments of interpretation. The narrative is set entirely in India. Mr. Kapasi is a tour guide who, because of his knowledge of English, is regularly assigned the task of driving foreign tourists to sites of interest. On this particular day, his client is an Indian American family of five (Mr. and Mrs. Das and their three children). Like other Western tourists, Mr. Das (Raj) has prepared for this trip by consulting a tour book, in all likelihood published in the United States. Both he and his wife, Mina, were born in the United States, and they are visiting India to see their parents, who live a retired life here. Raj and Mina are young—barely thirty, perhaps.

Mr. Kapasi serves as a tour guide on Fridays and Saturdays only. During the week, he has a job as an interpreter at a doctor's office. It is this job that arouses Mina's curiosity. Until she hears of his unusual occupation, Mina has been bored and disaffected by the trip and not that interested in the sights or her family. "What does a doctor need an interpreter for?" she asks Mr. Kapasi. He explains that the doctor has many Gujarati patients; because the doctor doesn't speak Gujarati, he relies on Mr. Kapasi to describe the patients' symptoms accurately so that he can diagnose the ailment and prescribe the correct medications. Mina is enthralled by Mr. Kapasi's role, which she sees as somewhat romantic. She observes that in a way the patients are more dependent on Mr. Kapasi than on the doctor. *He* holds their good health in his hands. If he misrepresented their symptoms, neither the doctor nor the patients would ever know.

Mr. Kapasi has never thought of his job in grandiose terms; to him it is an economic necessity. In fact, he came by it when he first bartered his services as a translator to the doctor as payment for treatment of his son's illness. The narrator informs us that to Mr. Kapasi the interpretation of maladies was a thankless occupation: "He found nothing noble in . . . assiduously translating the symptoms of so many swollen bones, countless cramps of bellies and bowels, spots on people's palms that changed color, shape, or size" (51). His aspirations for his linguistic ability had been higher, for he had considered himself a global soul. "He had dreamed of being an interpreter for diplomats and dignitaries, resolving conflicts between people and nations, settling disputes of which he alone could understand both sides" (52). The job with the doctor is a continuous reminder of his failing.

When Mina exhibits interest in his work and calls it romantic, Mr. Kapasi is intoxicated by her attention and stirred to imagine an intimate relationship between them. Every gesture, word, and act of hers becomes a text in which he reads her fascination for him. When she asks for his address so that they can send him the photograph they've taken of him, he anticipates pleasurably the letters he will receive from her that over time would begin to hold her deepest secrets: "She would write to him, asking him about his days interpreting at the doctor's office, and he would respond eloquently, choosing only the most entertaining anecdotes, ones that would make her laugh out loud as she read them in her house in New Jersey. In time she would reveal the disappointment of her marriage, and he his. In this way, their friendship would grow, and flourish" (55).

That Mr. Kapasi is more comfortable in the world of texts than in the world of material realities is evident in his remembering that years ago he used to experience "a mild and pleasant shock . . . when, after months of translating with the aid of a dictionary, he would finally read a passage from a French novel, or an Italian sonnet, and understand the words, one after another, unencumbered by his own efforts" (56–57). When he thinks about receiving letters from Mina, he is filled with the same feeling. He imagines that in the letters he will explain things about India and she about America. "In his own way this correspondence would fulfill his dream, of serving as an interpreter between nations" (59).

Mina's interest in his interpretive skills has a much narrower application, however. She wishes a remedy for her malaise of spirit. When she is alone with him (Raj and the children having gone to look at sites she has no interest in seeing), she reveals to Mr. Kapasi that Raj is not the biological father of one of the children, and that he is ignorant of her betrayal. She gives him a list of her symptoms: "I feel terrible looking at my children, and at Raj, always terrible. I have terrible urges, Mr. Kapasi, to throw things away. One day I had the urge to throw everything I own out the window, the television, the children, everything. Don't you think it's unhealthy?" (65). When he doesn't respond immediately, she appeals to him, "Mr. Kapasi, don't you have anything to say? I thought that was your job" (65). Initially baffled that she would expect him to "interpret" her illness in the absence of any language barrier, he then feels insulted that she would look to him to "interpret her common, trivial little secret" (66). He asks Mina to consider whether it is pain she feels or just guilt. With that sharp analysis, he destroys forever any chance of a friendship, real or imagined, with Mina.

There are two primary disappointments in this story—Mr. Kapasi's and Mina's. Believing that Mr. Kapasi's ability to translate from one language to another has given him insight into the human condition, Mina expects that he will be able to minister to her spirit. Mr. Kapasi assumes that Mina's interest in his interpretive skills stems from her appreciation of the lofty aspirations he holds. He believes that she will enhance the limited quality of his life. Each misreads the other.

While the drama of misinterpretation between Mina and Mr. Kapasi unfolds, another and more urgent drama is taking place. A group of monkeys has circled Bobby, the child that is not Raj's. About a dozen of the animals pull at his shirt, while one monkey rhythmically beats the boy with a stick. When they come upon the scene, Mina screams for Mr. Kapasi to do something. He succeeds in shooing away the monkeys and brings the boy back to his parents.

The story's closing lines warn against romanticized readings and ungrounded imaginings. They suggest that a proper ironic perspective is key to sound understanding. When Mina opens her bag to retrieve a hairbrush to straighten Bobby's hair, the slip of paper with Mr. Kapasi's address falls out and flutters away in the wind. No one but Mr. Kapasi notices the paper's disappearance; he had placed so much hope earlier in this slip of paper, but he is wiser now. He watches the monkeys as they sit in the trees and look down on the Das family united in its desire to leave the site of Bobby's recent adventure. "Mr. Kapasi observed it [the scene below] too, knowing that this was the picture of the Das family he would preserve forever in his mind" (69). He sees what the monkeys see. Does that mean that like the monkeys he only sees but does not and cannot understand? Or are we to surmise that the monkeys' presence reminds him of his own earlier folly in chasing a useless fantasy? Or does the juxtaposing of the image of the monkeys in the tree against the family on the ground fussing over the injured Bobby impress upon Mr. Kapasi that like Bobby, he, too, has escaped with a minor "injury"?

Lahiri seems to suggest that interpretation is neither a mere matter of literally translating meaning from one language to another (or one context to another), as Mr. Kapasi does in his role in the doctor's office; nor is it an elaborate flight of fantasy whose connection to the "original text" is at best minimal, as are Mr. Kapasi's imaginings upon learning of Mina's interest in his work. Making meaning, as translation theorists have shown, is a delicate process involving the "source text" and the multiplicity of meanings it engenders, and the translator's attitude to and methodology in the act of translating or making meaning.[55] Mr. Kapasi's awakening to the allurements and entrapments of conferring meaning should also be ours.

NOTES

CHAPTER 1

1. For a comprehensive history of Canada's settlement and immigration policy, see Ninette Kelley and Michael Trebilcock, *The Making of the Mosaic: A History of Canadian Immigration Policy* (Toronto: University of Toronto Press, 1998). For the United States, see William Bradford, *Of Plymouth Plantation: 1620–1647* (New York: Modern Library, 1981); Perry Miller, ed., *The American Puritans: Their Prose and Poetry* (New York: Anchor Books, 1956); Albert Hurtado and Peter Iverson, *Major Problems in American Indian History* (Lexington, MA: D. C. Heath, 1994); Gary Okihiro, *Common Ground: Reimagining American History* (Princeton: Princeton University Press, 2001); Ronald Takaki, *Strangers from a Different Shore: A History of Asian Americans* (Boston: Little Brown, 1989); Sucheng Chan, *Asian Americans: An Interpretive History* (New York: Twayne, 1991).

2. See Joan Jensen, *Passage from India: Asian Indian Immigrants in North America* (New Haven: Yale University Press, 1988); Peter W. Ward, *White Canada Forever: Popular Attitudes and Public Policy toward Orientals in British Columbia* (Montreal: McGill-Queen's University Press, 1990).

3. I am indebted to Jennifer Drake for directing me to Etienne Balibar's very fine essay "Is There a Neo-Racism?" in *Race, Nation, Class: Ambiguous Identities,* ed. Etienne Balibar and Immanuel Wallerstein (London: Verso, 1991), 17–28. Balibar argues that overemphasizing the distinctiveness of different cultures and ethnicities and working to preserve their unique characteristics amounts to a segregation akin to that based on race.

4. See Stuart Hall's characterization of the black experience as a diaspora experience in "New Ethnicities," in *Stuart Hall: Critical Dialogues in Cultural Studies*, ed. David Morley and Kuan-Hsing Chen (New York: Routledge, 1996), p. 447.

5. Ibid., 470.

6. See the editors' introduction, "Cosmopolitanisms," in *Cosmopolitanism*, ed. Carol A. Breckenridge, Sheldon Pollock, Homi K. Bhabha, and Dipesh Chakrabarty (Durham, NC: Duke University Press, 2002), 11.

7. See Lavina Dhingra Shankar and Rajini Srikanth, eds., *A Part, Yet Apart: South Asians in Asian America* (Philadelphia: Temple University Press, 1998), esp. 1–22.

8. Stuart Hall, "On Postmodernism and Articulation: An Interview with Stuart Hall," *Journal of Communication Inquiry* 10, no. 2 (Summer 1986): 53.

9. I take the phrase from the title of Deepika Bahri's essay, "With Kaleidoscope Eyes: The Potential (Dangers) of Identitarian Coalitions," in *A Part, Yet Apart*, pp. 25–48.

10. Laura Hyun Yi Kang, *Compositional Subjects: Enfiguring Asian/American Women* (Durham, NC: Duke University Press, 2002), 20.

11. Jane Singh, "Interview with Nand Kaur Singh: Gadar Indian Nationalist Poetry in America," in *Blood into Ink: South Asian and Middle Eastern Women Write War*, ed. Miriam Cooke and Roshni Rustomji-Kerns (Boulder, CO: Westview Press, 1994), 175–78.

12. Una Chaudhuri, "Theater and Cosmopolitanism: New Stories, Old Stages," in *Cosmopolitan Geographies: New Locations in Literature and Culture*, ed. Vinay Dharwadker (New York: Routledge, 2001), 175.

13. Indran Amirthanayagam, "Not Much Art," in *The Elephants of Reckoning* (New York: Hanging Loose Press, 1993), 44, 45.

14. Vinay Dharwadker, "Introduction: Cosmopolitanism in Its Time and Place" in *Cosmopolitan Geographies: New Locations in Literature and Culture*, ed. Vinay Dharwadker (New York: Routledge, 2001), 7. In her 1994 essay "Patriotism and Cosmopolitanism," Martha Nussbaum makes an identical point. Nussbaum's essay, which appeared in the October/November issue of *Boston Review*, was accompanied by a vigorous debate. There were twenty-nine replies to her essay, eleven of which are collected, along with her essay, in *For Love of Country: Debating the Limits of Patriotism*, ed. Joshua Cohen (Boston: Beacon Press, 1996).

15. Kwame Anthony Appiah, "Cosmopolitan Reading," in Dharwadker, *Cosmopolitan Geographies*, 202 (emphasis added).

16. Amitav Ghosh, "The Diaspora in Indian Culture," *Public Culture* 2, no. 1 (1989): 78.

17. Particularly in his analysis of the fascist use of the visual, Benjamin underscores the ways in which the nondiscursive can repress careful thought: "Through its peculiar way of capturing monster rallies, fascist cinematography wants to freeze both its human referent and the spectator in the hopes of disempowering possible unrest and scrambling rational judgments." Lutz Koepnick, *Walter Benjamin and the Aesthetics of Power* (Lincoln: University of Nebraska Press, 1999), 120.

18. Iain Chambers, "Citizenship, Language, and Modernity," *Publications of the Modern Language Association of America* 117, no. 1 (January 2002): 28.

19. Amitava Kumar, *Passport Photos* (Berkeley: University of California Press, 2000), 3.

20. Ibid., 3–4.

21. Gayatri Chakravorty Spivak, "Reading the World: Literary Studies in the Eighties," in *In Other Worlds: Essays in Cultural Politics* (New York: Routledge, 1988), 95.

22. Kumar, *Passport Photos,* 17. See also Kumar's chapter titled "Language," 16–34.

23. Pheng Cheah, "Given Culture: Rethinking Cosmopolitical Freedom in Transnationalism," in *Cosmopolitics: Thinking and Feeling Beyond the Nation,* ed. Pheng Cheah and Bruce Robbins (Minneapolis: University of Minnesota Press, 1998), 299.

24. Elaine Scarry, "The Difficulty of Imagining Other People," in Cohen, *For Love of Country,* 104.

25. Ibid., 103.

26. Ibid., 105.

27. Steven Knapp, *Literary Interest: The Limits of Anti-Formalism* (Cambridge: Harvard University Press, 1993), 100–102.

28. Amartya Sen's speech was titled "On Reporting and Interpreting." Full text of the speech is available on the web site of the Global Equity Initiative Program at Harvard's Kennedy School of Government: http://www.ksg.harvard.edu/gei/publications.htm#sen_pubs.

29. Ibid.

30. Paul Wong, Meera Manvi, and Takeo Hirota Wong, "Asiacentrism and Asian American Studies?" *Amerasia Journal* 21, nos. 1 and 2 (1995): 145.

31. Part of my apprehension in evoking this mythical story stems from the use of Hinduism today by right-wing communalists in India to desecularize the nation and declare it a Hindu state. That I narrate the story despite my apprehension is my way of resisting the agenda of religious extremists.

32. Rebecca Saunders, "The Agony and the Allegory: The Concept of the Foreign, the Language of Apartheid, and the Fiction of J. M. Coetzee," *Cultural Critique* 47 (Winter 2001): 217.

33. Margaret Talbot, "Other Woes," *New York Times Magazine,* November 18, 2001, 23–24.

34. Appiah, "Cosmopolitan Patriots," in Cheah and Robbins, *Cosmopolitics,* 111.

35. Ibid., 94.

36. Thomas McCarthy, "On Reconciling Cosmopolitan Unity and National Diversity," *Public Culture* 11, no. 1 (1999): 180.

37. Sidhwa's story first appeared in 1990 in the collection *Colours of a New Day: Writing for South Africa,* ed. Sarah Lefanu and Stephen Hayward (New York: Pantheon, 1990).

38. Sidhwa has been faulted by some readers for her portrayal of Sikh men. I discuss this matter in Chapter 4.

39. The issue of the Korean comfort women continues to play an active role in Japan–Korea relations. The apologies that have been issued thus far by successive Japanese governments are seen to be inadequate by some of the former comfort women.

40. Peter Marks, "For Tony Kushner, an Eerily Prescient Return," *New York Times,* November 25, 2001, sec. 2, pp. 1, 20.

41. Amy Barrett, "The Way We Live Now: 10-07-01: Questions for Tony Kushner; Foreign Affairs," *New York Times,* October 7, 2001, sec. 6, p. 230.

42. Marks, "For Tony Kushner," pp. 1, 20.

43. Ibid. I saw *Homebody/Kabul* performed by the Trinity Repertory Company in Providence, R.I., on April 19, 2002. The performance was magnificent; it is impossible to convey the effect of Kushner's eerily accurate predictions of what was about to happen to the West. In this context, it is noteworthy that two recently staged plays whose scripts use the September 11 attacks as their backdrop treat that day in significantly different ways from one another and from Kushner's *Homebody/Kabul*. Israel Horowitz's play *Speaking Well of the Dead* focuses inward, turning its attention to a family and the relationships within it—a woman's desperate attempt to hold on to memories of her husband who died in the World Trade Center attack and her daughter's struggle with whether to reveal that her father was about to leave her mother for a younger woman before he died in the attack. Frank Pugliese's play *The Crazy Girl* turns outward, raising questions of how the United States' "ideological and economic exploitation of other people" might be linked to September 11. However, the character who forces a consideration of such issues is a "crazy girl" who is institutionalized because she believes she can hear the screams of victims (of both the World Trade Center bombings and the American bombing of Afghanistan), almost as though the playwright were uncomfortable about placing such views in the mouth of someone recognizably "normal." See Ed Siegel, "Two Stirring Plays Take Divergent Paths to Post-9/11 Realities," *Boston Globe,* July 30, 2002, E1, E5.

44. Bruce Robbins, "The Village of the Liberal Managerial Class," in *Cosmopolitan Geographies: New Locations in Literature and Culture,* ed. Vinay Dharwadker (New York: Routledge, 2001), 24.

45. Arundhati Roy, "The End of Imagination," *Frontline,* August 6, 1998, 2–15.

46. National Public Radio's *Morning Edition,*" hosted by Michael Sullivan, broadcast a special report on May 15, 2001, on the call center business in India. The business is worth $1 billion now and is expected to reach $5 billion by 2008.

47. Rustom Bharucha, in his essay "Somebody's Other: Disorientations in the Cultural Politics of Our Times" (in *The Intercultural Performance Reader,* ed. Patrice Pavis [New York: Routledge, 1996], 196–212), rails against the invasion of Western images in the Third World: "This invasion of images—more often than not, context-less but not value-free—is of critical significance because, for the first time in our cultural history, we are seeing the homogenization of western cultures into a very consolidated and alluring image . . . a liberal, capitalist, sexually enticing market of a world—in relation to which we can now see and compare ourselves in the so-called 'third world' with greater deference than ever before" (205). In this context, actor and dancer Arjun Raina's solo performance *A Terrible Beauty Is Born* (which I saw on November 23, 2003, at the Massachusetts Institute of Technology in Boston) explores with great sensitivity both the psychological ravages and the possibilities of emotional connection attending call center work. The two characters he portrays are a male call center worker in India and an elderly woman in the United States distraught that she does not know what has become of her daughter after the September 11, 2001 destruction of the World Trade Center buildings. Raina's performance foregrounds the human element of an economic phenomenon.

48. See Walt Whitman, *Leaves of Grass,* ed. Sculley Bradley and Harold W. Blodgett (New York: Norton, 1973), 711–12.

49. Bradford, *Of Plymouth Plantation,* 331.

50. Deborah L. Madsen, *American Exceptionalism* (Jackson: University Press of Mississippi, 1998), 22; Miller and Johnson, *The Puritans*, 186; Williams quoted in Miller and Johnson, *The Puritans*, 216.

51. Seymour Martin Lipset places the United States and Japan at two ends of the spectrum of social behavior, with the United States being the most individualistic culture among societies and Japan the most group-oriented. See Lipset, *American Exceptionalism: A Double-Edged Sword* (New York: Norton, 1996), esp. 211–30.

52. See Robert Penn Warren, *The Legacy of the Civil War: Meditations on the Centennial* (New York: Random House, 1961).

53. See *Truth v. Justice: The Morality of Truth Commissions*, ed. Robert I. Rotberg and Dennis Thompson (Princeton: Princeton University Press, 2000), 99–121.

54. For diametrically opposed analyses of the causes and repercussions of the September 11 attacks, see Howard Zinn, *Terrorism and War* (New York: Seven Stories Press, 2002); and Dinesh D'Souza, *What's So Great about America?* (Washington, DC: Regnery Publishing, 2002). *New York Times* reporter Thomas Friedman's Pulitzer Prize–winning book *Longitudes and Attitudes: Exploring the World after September 11* (New York: Farrar, Straus and Giroux, 2002) provides a centrist perspective. Arundhati Roy, "The Algebra of Infinite Justice," *The Guardian*, September 29, 2001, provides a fierce critique of President Bush's declaration of war against terrorism.

55. Amitav Ghosh, *In an Antique Land: History in the Guise of a Traveler's Tale* (New York: Vintage, 1992), 13.

56. See my essay, "The *Komagata Maru*: Memory and Mobilization among the South Asian Diaspora in North America," in *Re/Collecting Early Asian America: Essays in Cultural History*, ed. Josephine Lee, Imogene Lim, and Yuko Matsukawa (Philadelphia: Temple University Press, 2002), 78–94, for a discussion of early twentieth-century transnationalism encompassing India, Hong Kong, Japan, and Canada.

57. The holdings of the Peabody Essex Museum in East India Square in Salem, Massachusetts, give ample evidence of the trade links between the American colonies and India in the seventeenth and eighteenth centuries.

58. I quote at length a remarkable passage in Saki, *Making History: Karnataka's People and Their Past*, vol. 1 (Bangalore, India: Vimukthi Prakashana, 1998), 515: "In his lifetime Tipu was also witness to the success of the American War of Independence from the clutches of British colonialism. Benjamin Franklin, a leader of the American struggle for liberation . . . in his campaign to mobilize financial support for the struggle, issued advertisements in French newspapers on his visit to that country. MV Kamath says that Tipu who read one such advertisement sent his contributions from the 'Kingdom of Mysore' with a letter to the American leaders hailing them of success in their mission against British colonialism. In this letter he is reported to have stated: '*Every blow that is struck in the cause of American liberty throughout the world, in France, India and elsewhere and so long as a single insolent savage tyrant remains the struggle shall continue.*'" I am indebted to K. C. Prashanth of the Department of History, Mangalore University, for leading me to Saki's text. Saki quotes Kabir Kausar, in whose book *Secret Correspondence of Tipu Sultan* (New Delhi: Light and Life Publishers, 1986) the letter believed to be written by Tipu is excerpted. Finally, I wish to thank K. S. Govindaraj for first having raised the subject of Tipu's letter to Bejamin Franklin in a conversation that he and I had almost eight years ago.

59. See especially Werner Sollors's introduction to *Beyond Ethnicity: Consent and Descent in American Culture* (New York: Oxford University Press, 1986), 3–20, where he articulates the attributes of American culture, a cluster of values to which those who live in the country either willingly give or are required to give their consent.

60. See Inderpal Grewal, "The Postcolonial, Ethnic Studies, and the Diaspora: The Contexts of Ethnic Immigrant/Migrant Cultural Studies in the US," *Socialist Review* 24, no. 4 (1994): 45–73.

61. Kenneth Mostern, "Postcolonialism after W. E. B. Du Bois," in *Postcolonial Theory and the United States: Race, Ethnicity, and Literature*, ed. Amritjit Singh and Peter Schmidt (Jackson: University Press of Mississippi, 2000), 259.

62. Ibid., 270.

63. Ibid., 271.

CHAPTER 2

1. Jhumpa Lahiri, "When Mr. Pirzada Came to Dine," in *The Interpreter of Maladies* (Boston: Houghton Mifflin, 1999), 23.

2. Elaine Kim, "Home Is Where the *Han* Is: A Korean American Perspective on the Los Angeles Upheavals," in *Asian American Studies: A Reader*, ed. Jean Wu and Min Hyoung Song (New Brunswick, NJ: Rutgers University Press, 2000), 272.

3. See Wen Ho Lee and Helen Zia, *My Country versus Me: The First-Hand Account by the Los Alamos Scientist Who Was Falsely Accused* (New York: Hyperion, 2002). Lee was accused in December 1999 of espionage and indicted on fifty-nine counts. His civil liberties suspended for a year, which he spent under the most mortifying conditions in jail, Lee was ultimately vindicated when a judge found that there was nothing to substantiate the government's charges against him.

4. See Deborah N. Misir, "The Murder of Navroze Mody: Race, Violence, and the Search for Order," *Amerasia Journal* 22, no. 2 (1996): 55–76. For details on the savage beating of Rishi Maharaj in Ozone Park, see Somini Sengupta, "Racial Motive Is Seen in Beating of Indian-American Man," *New York Times*, September 22, 1998, D1, D6; and Somini Sengupta and Vivian S. Toy, "United Ethnically and by an Assault; Two Groups of East Indians Are Brought Closer, for Now," *New York Times*, October 7, 1998, B1, B4.

5. Kandice Chuh, "Transnationalism and Its Pasts," *Public Culture* 9 (1996): 93.

6. Luis Francia, "Inventing the Earth: The Notion of 'Home' in Asian American Literature," in *Across the Pacific: Asian Americans and Globalization*, ed. Evelyn Hu-Dehart (New York: Asia Society; Philadelphia: Temple University Press, 1999), p. 213. Irish Americans, too, invest in property in Ireland; these homes become summer-vacation destinations and are frequently referred to in language that underscores their value as refuge and haven, despite the secure position of Irish Americans in the U.S. body politic. Diasporic Irish feel the same kind of interest in the affairs of their ancestral homeland as a postcolonial nation as do South Asian, Filipino/a, Korean, and Vietnamese Americans. While South Asian Americans fall under the census category "Asian American," the issue of South Asian membership within Asian America in the popular imagination is by no means completely resolved. That

debate is taken up in extensive terms in Lavina Dhingra Shankar and Rajini Srikanth, eds., *A Part, Yet Apart: South Asians in Asian America* (Philadelphia: Temple University Press, 1998). That the issue continues to be a contested matter is evident in the invitations I receive to speak about it: most recently, in September 2003, at Harvard University and, in April 2002, at Yale University. My stand on this issue is that the extent to which South Asian Americans feel or desire to be a part of Asian America is context-specific. "Asian America" itself is by no means a non-problematic label, for it encompasses populations as diverse as fifth-generation Chinese Americans and relatively recent refugees from Vietnam and Cambodia. All Asian Americans, despite their many differences from one another, share the condition of being outsiders in the United States, and that outsider status can be conferred on them with startling speed in certain situations. Whether Arab Americans may be considered Asian Americans presents an interesting dilemma, as well. There is a move among some scholars to speak of the Middle East as West Asia. Deepika Bahri reminds us that even the region "Asia" is a constructed category, a nomenclature given by the West to lands that lay east of some imaginary boundary denoting the limit of Europe.

7. Taken from the unpublished manuscript of Najmi's talk, "Aftershocks of 9/11: Terrorism, War, and Racial Profiling," delivered in November 2001 at Wheaton College in Norton, Massachusetts.

8. For example, see Corey Killgannon, "All American? U.S. Says No; Teenager May Be Deported, but Pakistan Isn't Home," *New York Times*, Metro Desk, April 19, 2003, D1, D4. David Rohde, "U.S.-Deported Pakistanis: Outcasts in Two Lands," *New York Times*, January 20, 2003, A1. For Canada's role as a haven for Pakistanis fleeing the United States, see Gaiutra Bahadur, "Fear Shakes Immigrant Enclave," *Philadelphia Inquirer*, August 18, 2003, http://www.philly.com/mld/inquirer/6556864.htm.

9. Rajini Srikanth, "Unsettling Asian American Literature: When More Than America Is in the Heart," in *Beyond the Borders: American Literature and Post-Colonial Theory*, ed. Deborah L. Madsen (London: Pluto Press, 2003), 92–110.

10. Frank Chin, Jeffrey Chan, Lawson Inada, and Shawn Wong, eds., *Aiiieeeee! An Anthology of Asian-American Writers* (Washington, DC: Howard University Press, 1974), vii.

11. For example, see Helen C. Toribio, "We Are Revolution: A Reflective History of the Union of Democratic Filipinos (KDP)," *Amerasia Journal* 24, no. 2 (Summer 1998): 155–77. Toribio notes that the activist organization Katipunan ng mga Demokratikong Pilipino was made up primarily of young Filipino Americans who came together around anti-imperialist and anti-racist causes. Between 1973 and 1986, the organization was "in the forefront of protests against the Marcos regime" (155).

12. Lisa Lowe, "Heterogeneity, Hybridity, Multiplicity: Asian American Differences," in *Immigrant Acts* (Durham, NC: Duke University Press, 1996), 66.

13. Cynthia Sau-ling Wong, "Denationalization Reconsidered: Asian American Cultural Criticism at a Theoretical Crossroads," *Amerasia Journal* 21, nos. 1 and 2 (1995): 1–27.

14. Pheng Cheah, "Given Culture: Rethinking Cosmopolitical Freedom in Transnationalism," in *Cosmopolitics: Thinking and Feeling beyond the Nation*, ed. Pheng Cheah and Bruce Robbins (Minneapolis: University of Minnesota Press, 1998), 312.

15. See Joseph E. Stiglitz, *Globalization and its Discontents* (New York: Norton, 2002). Although Stiglitz is generally positive about the function of the World Bank and the IMF and believes that globalization has created many opportunities for developing nations, he is also critical of the pressure that these institutions exert on governments to implement policies that guarantee debt payment over essential social services such as public health care and education.

16. "Asians for Mumia" is a collection of Asian American activists who have come together largely through the internet. Their statement of purpose reads, in part, "Asians for Mumia is part of a united front effort to galvanize diverse forces to free Mumia. Mumia Abu-Jamal speaks not only for the Black community but also for the marginalized and oppressed people around the world. We will not allow this revolutionary 'voice of the voiceless' to be silenced. The 'voiceless' of the Asian and Pacific Islander communities are found in abundance in sweatshops, restaurants, farms, and factories, forced to work overtime in unsafe conditions without pay or benefits. The 'voiceless' are Asian and Pacific Islander women working as live-in domestic workers in homes where there is little protection from harassment, abuse and exploitation. The 'voiceless' are the unheard victims of police brutality and anti-Asian violence. The 'voiceless' are the men and women who are incarcerated in maximum security prisons for the 'crime' of trying to work for exploitative wages. They are the people who are incarcerated without due process under secret evidence rules. The 'voiceless' are the countless numbers of undocumented people who are unable to speak out against the systemic abuse they face because of the vicious nature of the INS." For the political efforts of young South Asian Americans, see the special issue of *Amerasia Journal* 25, no. 3 (Winter 1999), guest edited by Vijay Prashad and Biju Mathew.

17. Roger Sanjek, *The Future of Us All: Race and Neighborhood Politics in New York City* (Ithaca, NY: Cornell University Press, 1998), 295–99.

18. Nirav Desai, "Forging Political Identity: South Asian Americans in American Policy Making," *The Subcontinental: A Journal of South Asian American Political Identity* 1, no. 1 (Spring 2003): 7.

19. Jinqi Ling, *Narrating Nationalisms: Ideology and Form in Asian American Literature* (New York: Oxford University Press, 1998), 164.

20. Ibid.

21. Sucheta Mazumdar, "Afterword," in *Contours of the Heart: South Asians Map North America*, ed. Sunaina Maira and Rajini Srikanth (New York: Asian American Writers Workshop, 1996), 465.

22. Roshni Rustomji-Kerns with Rajini Srikanth and Leny Mendoza Strobel, eds., *Encounters: People of Asian Descent in the Americas* (Boulder, CO: Rowman & Littlefield, 1999). See also *Asians in the Americas: Transculturations and Power*, special issue of *Amerasia Journal* 28, no. 2 (2002), guest edited by Lane Ryo Hirabayashi and Evelyn Hu-Dehart.

23. Roshni Rustomji, *The Braided Tongue* (Toronto: TSAR Publications, 2003), 19.

24. Andrew X. Pham, *Catfish and Mandala: A Two-Wheeled Voyage through the Landscape and Memory of Vietnam* (New York: Picador USA, 2000).

25. E. San Juan, Jr., Introduction to *On Becoming Filipino: Selected Writings of Carlos Bulosan* (Philadelphia: Temple University Press, 1995), 16.

26. Bulosan, *On Becoming Filipino*, 212.

27. For a more extended treatment of the transnational impulse in Vietnamese and Filipino/a American writing, see my essay "Unsettling Asian American Literature." For the Philippine-American War and colonization of the Philippines, see, e.g., *Amerasia Journal* 24, no. 2 (1998), and 24, no 3 (1998), special issues on "Essays into American Empire in the Philippines"; Eric Gamalinda, "Myth, Memory, Myopia: Or, I May Be Brown But I Hear America Singin'," in *Flippin': Filipinos on America*, ed. Eric Gamalinda and Luis Francia (New York: Asian American Writers Workshop, 1996); Luis Francia, "The Other Side of the American Coin," also in *Flippin'*; Thomas Peyser, *Utopia and Cosmopolis: Globalization in the Era of American Literary Realism* (Durham, NC: Duke University Press, 1998), esp. 142–51; Daniel B. Schirmer, *Republic or Empire: American Resistance to the Philippine War* (Cambridge, MA: Schenkman, 1972); Ephraim K. Smith, "William McKinley's Enduring Legacy: The Historiographical Debate on the Taking of the Philippine Islands," in *Crucible of Empire: The Spanish-American War and Its Aftermath*, ed. James C. Bradford (Annapolis, MD: Naval Institute Press, 1993); Richard E. Welch, Jr., *Response to Imperialism: The United States and the Philippine-American War, 1899–1902* (Chapel Hill: University of North Carolina Press, 1979); Marilyn Blatt Young, ed., *American Expansionism: The Critical Issues* (Boston: Little Brown, 1973); *Mark Twain's Weapons of Satire: Anti-Imperialist Writings on the Philippine-American War*, ed. Jim Zwick (Syracuse, NY: Syracuse University Press, 1992).

28. Arjun Appadurai, *Modernity at Large: Cultural Dimensions of Globalization* (Minneapolis: University of Minnesota Press, 1996), 171.

29. Agha Shahid Ali, "Snow on the Desert," in *A Nostalgist's Map of America* (New York: Norton, 1991), 101–5.

30. Ali, "In Search of Evanescence," in *A Nostalgist's Map of America*, 41. See also Lavina Dhingra Shankar and Rajini Srikanth, "South Asian American Literature: 'Off the Turnpike' of Asian America," in *Postcolonial Theory and the United States: Race, Ethnicity, and Literature*, ed. Amritjit Singh and Peter Schmidt (Jackson: University Press of Mississippi, 2000), 370–88.

31. Ali, "I See Chile in My Rearview Mirror," in *A Nostalgist's Map of America*, p. 96.

32. Agha Shahid Ali, "Some Vision of the World Cashmere," in *The Country Without a Post Office* (New York: Norton, 1997), 35.

33. Ali, "The Correspondent," in *The Country Without a Post Office*, 54–55.

34. Ali, "A Footnote to History," in *The Country Without a Post Office*, 69–70.

35. Indran Amirthanayagam, *The Elephants of Reckoning* (New York: Hanging Loose Press, 1993), 45.

36. Amirthanayagam, "How Politics Becomes Language," *New England Review* 22, no. 1 (Winter 2001): 56.

37. Indran Amirthanayagam, "Elegy for Neelan Tiruvechalam," *Catamaran: South Asian American Writing* 1, no. 1 (2003): 17–18.

38. Amitav Ghosh, 2001 interview with Nimathi Rajasingham of Tehelka's online newspaper, http://www.tehelka.com/channels/literary/2001/aug/20/printable/lr082001ghosh_intpr.htm.

39. See Michael Watkins and Susan Rosegrant, *Breakthrough International Negotiation: How Great Negotiators Transformed the World's Toughest Post-Cold War Conflicts* (San

Francisco: Jossey-Bass, 2001), especially their discussion of the Oslo accords and the Norwegians' role as facilitators rather than mediators. For a consideration of third-party intervention in Sri Lanka specifically, see William Weisberg and Donna Hicks, "Overcoming Obstacles to Peace: An Examination of Third-Party Processes," in *Creating Peace in Sri Lanka: Civil War and Reconciliation*, ed. Robert I. Rotberg (Washington, DC: Brookings Institution Press, 1999), 143–56.

40. Michael Hardt and Antonio Negri, *Empire* (Cambridge: Harvard University Press, 2000).

41. Jayadeva Uyangoda, "A Political Culture of Conflict," in *Creating Peace in Sri Lanka: Civil War and Reconciliation*, ed. Robert I. Rotberg (Washington, DC: Brookings Institution Press, 1999), 166.

42. See also David A. Crocker, "Truth Commissions, Transitional Justice, and Civil Society," in *Truth v. Justice: The Morality of Truth Commissions*, ed. Robert I. Rotberg and Dennis Thompson (Princeton: Princeton University Press, 2000), 99–121.

43. Meena Alexander, "An Honest Sentence," in *The Illiterate Heart* (Evanston, IL: Northwestern University Press, 2002), 53.

44. Meena Alexander, *River and Bridge* (Toronto: TSAR Publications, 1996), 27.

45. Ibid., 36.

46. Meena Alexander, *The Shock of Arrival: Reflections on Postcolonial Experience* (Boston: South End Press, 1996), 78.

47. See, for instance, Shilpa Davé, "Nampally Road," in *A Resource Guide to Asian American Literature*, ed. Sau-ling Cynthia Wong and Stephen H. Sumida (New York: Modern Language Association, 2001), 13–20. Davé takes up the question of how Alexander's novel *Nampally Road*, set entirely in India, could be approached as an Asian American literary text.

48. Alexander, *Shock of Arrival*, 89, 91.

49. Ibid., 87.

50. Ibid., 121.

51. Representative texts include Bruce Robbins, *Feeling Global: Internationalism in Distress* (New York: New York University Press, 1999); R. Radhakrishnan, *Diasporic Mediations: Between Home and Location* (Minneapolis: University of Minnesota Press, 1996); Cheah, and Robbins, eds., *Cosmopolitics*; Rey Chow, *Writing Diaspora: Tactics of Intervention in Contemporary Cultural Studies* (Bloomington: Indiana University Press, 1993).

52. Alexander, *Shock of Arrival*, 6–7.

53. Robbins, "The Village of the Liberal Managerial Class," in *Cosmopolitan Geographies*, 24.

54. The same spirit of transnational collaboration has manifested itself in the search to isolate and understand the virus causing Severe Acute Respiratory Syndrome (SARS), a mysterious global illness that made its appearance in March 2003.

55. Amitav Ghosh, *The Calcutta Chromosome* (New York: Avon Books, 1997), 57–58.

56. Amitav Ghosh, *The Glass Palace* (New York: Random House, 2001), 9.

57. Salil Tripathi, "Personal Journal: An Indian Novelist's Journey," *The Asian Wall Street Journal*, October 26, 2000.

58. Sameer Parekh, *Stealing the Ambassador* (New York: Free Press, 2002), 181.

59. Peyser, *Utopia and Cosmopolis*, 18.

60. Evelyn Hu-DeHart, "Introduction: Asian American Formations in the Age of Globalization," in *Across the Pacific: Asian Americans and Globalization*, ed. Evelyn Hu-Dehart (New York: Asia Society; Philadelphia: Temple University Press, 1999), 19.

CHAPTER 3

Acknowledgments: I am greatly indebted to Gautam Premnath for his meticulous and astute reading of this chapter. His observations and suggestions were invaluable in strengthening critical arguments and conclusions.

1. Zia Jaffrey, *The Invisibles: A Tale of the Eunuchs of India* (New York: Pantheon, 1996), 19.
2. See, for instance, Amy Waldman, "Loss of the Shuttle: The Call of Space; For a Resolute Girl, Traditions of India Imposed No Limits," *New York Times*, February 3, 2003, A1, A4. Waldman's article followed the breakup of the Columbia space shuttle and the deaths of the seven astronauts aboard it. While she celebrates Indian American astronaut Kalpana Chawla's achievements, she cannot resist referring to the conditions that Chawla had to overcome as a woman in India—a society in which female fetuses are routinely killed, and women are denied opportunity. Waldman writes, "In the early narrative of Dr. Chawla's truncated life, there is a disquieting undercurrent of the girl who was often told no, simply because she was a girl." Of the state of Haryana in which Chawla grew up, Waldman observes, "Statistics suggest that the state has taken the cruel art of sex selection, in which female fetuses are aborted, to new heights. Among children under 6, it has 820 girls for every 1,000 boys, according to the 2001 census." Waldman's article set off a lively string of responses from members of the South Asian Journalists Association (SAJA), with heavy exchange of e-mail comments.
3. Jaffrey, *The Invisibles*, 10.
4. Jaffrey's book combines several types of text: her personal anthropological memoir detailing her search for the "real story" of the Hijra community; historical documents and mythological narratives providing evidence of eunuchs; and medical reports on incidents of castration. It's an unusual study of an ancestral homeland by a diasporic offspring. Typically, U.S.-born Indian Americans provide us with narratives of self-discovery against the backdrop of a discovery of the land of "heritage." See, for example, Vineeta Vijayaraghavan's novel *Motherland* (New York: Soho Press, 2001).
5. Lloyd Schwartz, conversation with author, January 29, 2003.
6. Leti Volpp, "Feminism versus Multiculturalism," *Columbia Law Review* 101, no. 5 (June 2001): 1185.
7. See also Leti Volpp, "Blaming Culture for Bad Behavior," *Yale Journal of Law and the Humanities* 12, no. 89 (2000): 89–116; and Volpp, "(Mis)identifying Culture: Asian Women and the 'Cultural Defense,'" *Harvard Women's Law Journal* 17 (1994): 57–101.
8. For a rich and engaging recapitulation of the changes in and impulses underlying the genre of the gothic novel from its beginnings in the eighteenth century to its current manifestations, see Terry Castle, "The Gothic Novel," in *Boss Ladies, Watch Out! Essays on Women, Sex, and Writing* (New York: Routledge, 2002), 73–107. Castle's essay

ends with the claim that unlike most practitioners of the genre, who were interested in horror as a distraction from the concerns of day-to-day life, Jane Austen, Mary Shelley, and Charlotte Bronte turned the reader's attention to horrors located "in the uncanny purlieus of the everyday" (102). In this context, Charlotte Perkins Gilman's story "The Yellow Wallpaper" is also a critical text. In another context, Mootoo's treatment of the Ramchandin home may also be compared to the symbol of home as it operates in V. S. Naipaul's *A House for Mr. Biswas*, set in Trinidad. Mr. Biswas longs for a place of his own in which he can assert his independence and demonstrate control over the course of his life. His success is equivocal.

9. Such a construction has little basis in reality. For details on the conservative sexual laws of Trinidad and Tobago, see M. Jacqui Alexander, "Redrafting Morality: The Postcolonial State and the Sexual Offences Bill of Trinidad and Tobago," in *Third World Women and the Politics of Feminism*, ed. Chandra Talpade Mohanty, Ann Russo, and Lourdes Torres (Bloomington: Indiana University Press, 1991), 133–53. Although Mootoo does not outright declare that Lantacamara is the fictional counterpart of Trinidad and Tobago, one cannot ignore the parallels of colonial history and its legacy.

10. See Anne Fausto-Sterling, "How to Build a Man," in *The Gender/Sexuality Reader*, ed. Roger N. Lancaster and Micaela di Leonardo (New York: Routledge, 1997), 244–49; Diep Khan Tran, Bryan, and Rhode, eds., "Transgender/Transsexual Roundtable," in *Q & A: Queer in Asian America*, ed. David Eng and Alice Hom (Philadelphia: Temple University Press, 1998), 227–44; Deirdre McCloskey, *Crossing: A Memoir* (Chicago: University of Chicago Press, 1999); Sheila Kirk, *Feminizing Hormonal Therapy for the Transgendered* (Pittsburgh, PA: Together Lifeworks, 1999); and Mildred Brown and Chloe Ann Rounsley, *True Selves: Understanding Transsexualism— For Families, Friends, Coworkers, and Helping Professionals* (San Francisco: Jossey-Bass, 1996).

11. See especially the chapter on mimicry in Homi K. Bhabha's *The Location of Culture* (New York: Routledge, 1994), 85–92. Relevant to Chandin Ramchandin's case are Bhabha's observations that "mimicry is at once resemblance and menace" and "colonial mimicry is the desire for a reformed recognizable Other, as a subject of a difference that is almost the same, but not quite" (86). Chandin imagines himself to be so much an Englishman that he becomes infatuated with Lavinia Thoroughly and has to be reminded by her parents that though they may wish to make him a Christian Englishman, there are certain boundaries he cannot cross.

12. See Viranjani Munasinghe, "Redefining the Nation: The East Indian Struggle for Inclusion in Trinidad," *Journal of Asian American Studies* 4, no. 1 (February 2001): 1–34; Shalini Puri, "Canonized Hybridities, Resistant Hybridities: Chutney Soca, Carnival, and the Politics of Nationalism," in *Caribbean Romances: The Politics of Regional Representation*, ed. Belinda J. Edmondson (Charlottesville: University Press of Virginia, 1999), 12–39; Vijay Prashad, *Everybody Was Kung Fu Fighting : Afro-Asian Connections and the Myth of Cultural Purity* (Boston: Beacon, 2001), especially 70–97.

13. Puri, "Canonized Hybridities, Resistant Hybridities," 25.

14. Ibid., 32.

15. Shani Mootoo, "Out on Main Street," in *Out on Main Street and Other Stories* (Vancouver: Press Gang Publishers, 1993), 45–57.

16. Lavina Shankar and Rajini Srikanth, "South Asian American Literature: 'Off the Turnpike' of Asian America," in *Postcolonial Theory and the United States: Race, Ethnicity, and Literature*, ed. Amritjit Singh and Peter Schmidt (Jackson: University Press of Mississippi, 2000), 370–87.

17. Ginu Kamani, e-mail exchange with author, February 3, 2003.

18. Ginu Kamani, "Preface to 'Just Between Indians,'" in *Contours of the Heart: South Asians Map North America*, ed. Sunaina Maira and Rajini Srikanth (New York: Asian American Writers Workshop, 1996), 353. See also Naheed Islam, "Naming Desire, Shaping Identity: Tracing the Experiences of Indian Lesbians in the United States," in *Patchwork Shawl: Chronicles of South Asian American Women in America*, ed. Shamita Das Dasgupta (New Brunswick, NJ: Rutgers University Press, 1998), 72–93. Islam records her interview subjects as feeling that while they appreciated the opportunity to live their life as lesbians in the West, they found too isolating the Western idea that a lesbian identity and lifestyle were about following one's individual desires and giving up the emotional reliance on family and community. They were not willing to do this, and several of them opted to keep their sexual orientation hidden from their families. Islam quotes a personal ad in the gay and lesbian California-based magazine *Trikone* that shows the degree to which South Asian gays and lesbians are unwilling to sever ties from family and community: "'Twenty-four year old lesbian/bisexual woman is searching for a gay South Asian man settled in the United States with whom to enact matrimonial rituals to dissuade harried parents from aging prematurely while drowning in her guilt. Friendly, supportive, seeking same. Is this a laugh or what?'" (89). A similar sentiment of consideration for one's parents' feelings is expressed in Cristy Chung, Aly Kim, Zoon Nguyen, and Trinity Ordona, with Arlene Stein, "In Our Own Way: A Roundtable Discussion," in *Asian American Sexualities: Dimensions of the Gay and Lesbian Experience*, ed. Russell Leong (New York: Routledge, 1996), 91–100. These participants reject the view that there is only one way of "coming out" and asserting one's sexual orientation to one's parents and families.

19. Kamani, "Preface to 'Just Between Indians,'" 354.

20. Ginu Kamani, "Just Between Indians," in *Junglee Girl* (San Francisco: aunt lute, 1995), 156 (ellipses in original).

21. Ginu Kamani, "Goddess of Sleep," in *Bold Words: A Century of Asian American Writing*, ed. Rajini Srikanth and Esther Y. Iwanaga (New Brunswick, NJ: Rutgers University Press, 2001), 260.

22. See Edward Soja, *Postmodern Geographies: The Reassertion of Space in Critical Social Theory* (London: Verso, 1989), 133–37.

23. Le Corbusier quoted in Anthony Vidler, "Bodies in Space/Subjects in the City: Psychopathologies of Modern Urbanism," *Differences: A Journal of Feminist Cultural Studies* 5, no. 3 (1993): 42.

24. De Fleury quoted in ibid., 43.

25. Ibid., 32.

26. Arjun Appadurai, "Spectral Housing and Urban Cleansing: Notes on Millennial Mumbai," in *Cosmopolitanism*, ed. Carol A. Breckenridge, Sheldon Pollock, Homi K. Bhabha, and Dipesh Chakrabarty (Durham, NC: Duke University Press, 2002), 65–66. Mumbai was previously known as Bombay.

27. Michele Janette made this comment on March 8, 2002, in a conversation with me at a conference she organized at Kansas State University in Manhattan, Kansas. The conference, *Late Modern Planet: Globalization, Modernity, and Cultural Studies*, was held March 7–9, 2002, and featured Ginu Kamani and Joel Barraquiel Tan, among others, as keynote speakers.

28. Ginu Kamani, "MSM Messenger," *MAN'S World* 2, no. 10 (December 2001): 98–99.

29. Ibid., 98.

30. Gary Okihiro, *Margins and Mainstreams: Asians in American History and Culture* (Seattle: University of Washington Press, 1994), 148–75.

31. Gayatri Gopinath, "Funny Boys and Girls: Notes on a Queer South Asian Planet," in *Asian American Sexualities: Dimensions of the Gay and Lesbian Experience*, ed. Russell Leong (New York: Routledge, 1993), 119–27.

32. M. Jacqui Alexander, "Erotic Autonomy as a Politics of Decolonization: An Anatomy of Feminist and State Practice in the Bahamas Tourist Economy," in *Feminist Genealogies, Colonial Legacies, and Democratic Futures*, ed. M. Jacqui Alexander and Chandra Talpade Mohanty (New York: Routledge, 1997), 63.

33. Lavina Shankar is engaged in a book-length study of the impact of Uday Shankar's appearances in England and the United States.

34. Una Chaudhari, "Theater and Cosmopolitanism: New Stories, Old Stages," in *Cosmopolitan Geographies: New Locations in Literature and Culture*, ed. Vinay Dharwadker (New York: Routledge, 2001), 174.

35. Josephine Lee, *Performing Asian America: Race and Ethnicity on the Contemporary Stage* (Philadelphia: Temple University Press, 1997), 7.

36. I saw Sharif perform an excerpt from "Afghan Woman" at the East of California conference in November 2002, organized by the Asian American Studies program at the University of Illinois Urbana-Champaign.

37. Deborah Geis, "Wordscapes of the Body: Performative Language as Gestus in Marie Irene Fornes's Plays," in *Feminist Theatre and Theory*, ed. Helene Keyssar (New York: St. Martin's Press, 1996), 168–88.

38. Elin Diamond, "Brechtian Theory / Feminist Theory: Toward a Gestic Feminist Theory," *TDR: A Journal of Performance Studies* 32, no. 1 (Spring 1988): 89.

39. See comments made by Bina Sharif at the University of Hawai'i, where she gave a performance of excerpts from "Afghan Woman," archived at http://pidp. eastwestcenter.org/pireport/2003/January/12-31-eww.htm#5.

40. Leila Ahmed, *Women and Gender in Islam* (New Haven: Yale University Press, 1992), 160–64.

41. Ibid., 166–67.

42. See my interview, "Chitra Bannerjee Divakaruni: Exploring Human Nature under Fire," *The Asian Pacific American* 5, no. 2 (Fall/Winter 1996): 94–101, in which I ask about the dissatisfaction of many Indian American male readers at her negative portrayal of their group. Divakaruni talks of the need to acknowledge the unpleasant aspects of the South Asian community, even as she points to several male characters that are sensitive and caring. Divakaruni's perspective is perhaps shaped by her being a founding member of a women's help center in the Bay State area.

43. Amitava Kumar, *Passport Photos* (Berkeley: University of California Press, 2000), 190, 191.

44. Aaron Donovan, "Losing Spouse, and Maybe a Country: Dependents of 9/11 Victim Search for Ways to Stay in the U.S.," *New York Times*, July 23, 2002, A20.

45. Meena Alexander, "Preface," in *Blood into Ink: South Asian and Middle Eastern Women Write War*, ed. Miriam Cooke and Roshni Rustomji-Kerns (Durham, NC: Duke University Press, 1994), xvii. That the woman can find strength in the most horrific situations, at the moment when her body has been most brutalized, is seen in the Indian writer Maheshweta Devi's story "Draupadi," in *In Other Worlds: Essays in Cultural Politics*, ed. and trans. Gayatri Chakravorty Spivak (New York: Routledge, 1988), 179–96. In the story, a young peasant woman is taken prisoner for her resistance to government forces; she is tortured, raped, and humiliated in every possible way. At the very end, the police official who authorizes these deeds upon her body comes into her cell, where he expects to find her covered in cloth that his lackeys have supplied her so that she may be respectably clothed when he arrives. What he encounters, instead, is a woman who seizes the moment of her body's most objectified condition to turn it into a weapon, flaunting the totality of her objectification and flinging it into the eyes of the perpetrator so that she will not give him the satisfaction of her shame. "You can strip me, but how can you clothe me again? Are you a man?" she says, challenging the official. "There isn't a man here that I should be ashamed. I will not let you put my cloth on me. What more can you do?" (196). In that final question, one understands that Draupadi's strength paradoxically comes from the moment of greatest vulnerability. The final line of the story suggests the possibility of a changed man: "Draupadi pushes Senanayak with her two mangled breasts, and for the first time Senanayak is afraid to stand before an unarmed *target*, terribly afraid."

46. Shamita Das Dasgupta and Sayantani Dasgupta, "Bringing Up Baby: Raising a Third World Daughter in the First World," in *Dragon Ladies*, ed. Sonia Shah (Boston: South End Press, 1997), 190, 195.

47. Nalini Natarajan, "Introduction: Reading Diaspora" in *Writers of the Indian Diaspora*, ed. Emmanuel Nelson (Westport, CT: Greenwood Press, 1993), xiii–xix.

48. Rajini Srikanth, "Gender and the Image of Home in the Asian American Diaspora: A Socio-Literary Reading of Some Asian American Works," *Critical Mass: A Journal of Asian American Cultural Criticism* 2, no. 1 (Winter 1994): 161.

49. Saleem Peeradina, "Sisters," in *Group Portrait* (Madras: Oxford University Press, 1992), 21–22.

50. From an unpublished manuscript by Saleem Peeradina and Rajini Srikanth.

51. Gautam Premnath, conversation with author, March 2003.

52. See Iqbal Akhund, *Trial and Error: The Advent and Eclipse of Benazir Bhutto* (Oxford: Oxford University Press, 2000); see also http://womenshistory. about.com/gi/dynamic/offsite.htm?site=http%3A%2F%2Fwwics.si. edu%2FWHATSNEW%2FNEWnews%2Fbhutto2.htm for Benazir Bhutto's acknowledgements of the mistakes she made in her two terms as prime minister.

53. Ayub Khan's victory in 1965 was widely seen as a fraud. He manipulated a political and election machinery that he himself had put in place during his 1958–62 presidency of martial law. Although popular sentiment was against him, he was elected by a system of "basic democracies," which were government councils that functioned as electoral colleges, which he shrewdly manipulated. See Rafique Afzal, *Pakistan: History and Politics 1947–1971* (Oxford: Oxford University Press, 2002).

54. See U.S. Government Census 2000 websites http://www.census.gov/prod/ 2002pubs/c2kbr01-16.pdf (for population by specific Asian ethnic group) and http://www.census.gov/population/cen2000/phc-t08/tab05.pdf (for age break-down of Asian category). The age categories between 20 and 40 have the largest population figures; South Asian Americans, one would assume, reflect this general Asian American trend.

55. See Kalpana Sharma, "September 11 and the Yellow Cabs," *The Hindu* (online edition), May 19, 2002, http://www.hindu.com/thehindu/mag/2002/05/19/ stories/2002051900260300. This article is of particular interest in that it gives the perspective of an Indian female reporter on a second-generation Indian American woman. See also A. P. Kamath, "The Protest Generation Has No Time for Remix Parties and Silicon Valley," *Rediff on the Net*, May 11, 1999, http://www.rediff.com/ news/1999/may/11us.htm.

56. Monami Maulik, "Organizing in Our Communities Post September 11," *Manavi Newsletter* 12, no. 3 (Winter 2001), http://www.research.att.com~krishnas/ manavi/NEWSLETTER/newsletter.htm.

57. A significant amount of literature on this phenomenon has been published. Texts that have a specific reference to Asian American families include Nazli Kibria, *Family Tightrope: The Changing Lives of Vietnamese Americans* (Princeton: Princeton University Press, 1993); Pyong Gap Min, *Changes and Conflicts: Korean Immigrant Families in New York* (Needham Heights, MA: Allyn and Bacon, 1998); and Pyong Gap Min, ed. *The Second Generation: Ethnic Identity Among Asian Americans* (Boulder, CO: Rowman and Littlefield, 2002).

58. Premnath, conversation with author, March 2003.

CHAPTER 4

1. Trinh T. Minh-ha, *Woman, Native, Other: Writing Postcoloniality and Feminism* (Bloomington: Indiana University Press, 1989), 30. The title of this chapter is modified from Katherine Mayberry, ed., *Teaching What You're Not: Identity Politics in Higher Education* (New York: New York University Press, 1996).

2. Sucheta Mazumdar, "Afterword," in *Contours of the Heart: South Asians Map North America*, ed. Sunaina Maira and Rajini Srikanth (New York: Asian American Writers Workshop, 1996), 469.

3. For a good survey of the changes to the American literary landscape, see A. Lavonne Brown Ruoff, ed., *Redefining American Literary History* (New York: Modern Language Association, 1990).

4. Christopher Fan, "Step out of the Frame," *Ten Magazine* (Winter 2001): 8–9.

5. Ibid., 11.

6. Gayatri Chakravorty Spivak, in an interview with Howard Winant, "Gayatri Spivak on the Politics of the Subaltern," *Socialist Review* 20, no. 3 (July–September 1990): 93.

7. See Laura Browder, *Slippery Characters: Ethnic Impersonators and American Identities* (Chapel Hill: University of North Carolina Press, 2000); Henry Louis Gates, "

'Authenticity,' or the Lesson of Little Tree," *New York Times Book Review*, November 24, 1991, 26; John Henrik Clarke, *William Styron's Nat Turner: Ten Black Writers Respond* (Boston: Beacon Press, 1968). Styron, who was heavily attacked by African Americanists for speaking for a slave in *The Confessions of Nat Turner* (1968), was again criticized in 1979 for *Sophie's Choice*, a novel about a female Polish Holocaust survivor—this time for exploiting the trauma of an ethnic group not his own.

8. See Viranjani Munasinghe, "The East Indian Struggle for Inclusion in Trinidad," *Journal of Asian American Studies* 4, no. 1 (February 2001): 1–34; Brij Lal, "Fiji Indians and the Politics of exclusion: Some Thoughts and Reflections," in *The Coolie Connection: From the Orient to the Occident*, ed. Mahin Gosine (New York: Windsor Press, 1992), 84–104; Parminder Bhachu, *Twice Migrants: East African Sikh Settlers in Britain* (London: Routledge and Kegan Paul, 1985).

9. Mazumdar, "Afterword," 464.

10. Stanley Hoffman, "America Goes Backward," *New York Review of Books* 50, no. 10 (June 12, 2003), 74–75, 78–80; Jack Beatty, On Point News Analyst, "The U.S. Role in the World," On Point Radio, April 10, 2003.

11. Shelby Steele made these comments in an article published in the *Wall Street Journal*, September 17, 2001, and on October 24, 2001, on "On Point," WBUR's radio program on the impact of the September 11, 2001, attacks.

12. Deborah Gewertz and Frederick Errington, "We Think, Therefore They Are? On Occidentalizing the World," in *Cultures of United States Imperialism*, ed. Amy Kaplan and Donald E. Pease (Durham, NC: Duke University Press, 1993), 640.

13. Tahira Naqvi, "Thank God for the Jews," in *Dying in a Strange Country* (Toronto: TSAR Publications, 2001), 17–28.

14. James Agee's lyrical description of Depression-era Alabama sharecroppers forms the text of *Let Us Now Praise Famous Men*, which includes the famous Walker Evans photographs of the families with whom he and Agee lived. Agee, a privileged reporter, found writing about these sharecropping families enormously difficult. His searching questions about his inability to fathom the basic rhythms of their lives constitutes the best of self-aware documentary.

15. Vivek Bald, "Taxi Meters and Plexiglass Partitions," in *Contours of the Heart: South Asians Map North America*, ed. Sunaina Maira and Rajini Srikanth (New York: Asian American Writers Workshop, 1996), 67.

16. James Clifford, *Routes: Travel and Translation in the Late Twentieth Century* (Cambridge: Harvard University Press, 1997).

17. Kamala Visweswaran, *Fictions of Feminist Ethnography* (Minneapolis: University of Minnesota Press, 1994), 104.

18. Patti Lather, "Postbook: Working the Ruins of Feminist Ethnography," *Signs: Journal of Women in Culture and Society* 27, no. 1 (2001): 201. See also George Marcus, "Critical Cultural Studies as One Power/Knowledge like, among, and in Engagement with Others," in *From Sociology to Cultural Studies: New Perspectives*, ed. Elizabeth Long (London: Blackwell, 1997), 399–425; and Marcus, "What Comes (Just) after 'Post'? The Case of Ethnography," in *The Handbook of Qualitative Research*, ed. Norman Denzin and Yvonna Lincoln (Thousand Oaks, CA: Sage Publications, 1994), 563–74.

19. I don't wish to go into a discussion here of the limitations of language as a medium of representation—a sentiment central to the concerns of feminist ethnographers, who note that acknowledging the failure to speak for and of others is a more ethical mode of study than an anthropology that presumes to represent the complexity of others. See Lather, "Postbook"; Marcus, "Critical Cultural Studies" and "What Comes (Just) after 'Post'?"

20. Monique Truong, "The Reception of Robert Olen Butler's *A Good Scent from a Strange Mountain*: Ventriloquism and the Pulitzer Prize," in *Not a War: American Vietnamese Fiction, Poetry and Essays*, ed. Dan Duffy (New Haven: Yale University Council on Southeast Asia Studies, 1997), 75–94.

21. See Rajini Srikanth, "Ventriloquism in the Captivity Narrative: White Women Challenge European American Patriarchy," in *White Women in Racialized Spaces: Imaginative Transformation and Ethical Action in Literature*, ed. Samina Najmi and Rajini Srikanth (Albany: State University of New York Press, 2002), 85–103.

22. Anna Deavere Smith, *Twilight: Los Angeles, 1992* (New York: Anchor, 1994), xxv.

23. Quoted in ibid., 255.

24. Anna Deavere Smith, interview with author, February 2001. The interview focused on the process of gathering the information for *Twilight, Los Angeles, 1992*.

25. Jonathan Kalb, "Documentary Solo Performance: The Politics of the Mirrored Self," *Theater* 31, no. 3 (2001): 18.

26. For a poetic rendition of this sentiment, see especially Meena Alexander, "Lost Language," *River and Bridge* (Toronto: TSAR Publications, 1996), 29–30.

27. Naheed Islam, "Race Markers Transgressors: Mapping a Racial Kaleidoscope within an (Im)migrant Landscape," in *Encounters: People of Asian Descent in the Americas*, ed. Roshni Rustomji-Kerns (Boulder, CO: Rowman and Littlefield, 1999), 239–54.

28. See Clifford, *Routes*, esp. the chapter titled "Spatial Practices: Fieldwork, Travel, and the Disciplining of Anthropology," 52–91.

29. Smith, interview with author, February 2001.

30. Minh-ha, *Woman, Native, Other*, 68, 76.

31. Dayanita Singh is featured in the film *Three Women and a Camera* (1998), directed by Sabeena Gadihoke.

32. Andrew X. Pham, *Catfish and Mandala: A Two-Wheeled Voyage through the Landscape and Memory of Vietnam* (New York: Picador USA, 2000).

33. David Mura, *Turning Japanese: Memoirs of a Sansei* (Boston: Atlantic Monthly Press, 1991).

34. Pico Iyer, *The Lady and the Monk: Four Seasons in Kyoto* (New York: Vintage, 1992), 4–5.

35. Iyer made these remarks at a reading in California a few years ago; his comments were reported to me by Iyer enthusiast Meherwan Najmi.

36. See Rajini Srikanth, ""Ethnic Outsider-ism as the Ultimate Insider-ism: The Paradox of Verghese's *My Own Country*," *MELUS* (forthcoming).

37. See Lavina Melwani, "Call of the Country," *India Today International*, September 14, 1998, 24c.

38. See Srikanth, "Abraham Verghese Doctors Autobiography in His Own Country," in *Asian American Literature: Form, Confrontation, and Transformation*, ed. Xiaojing Zhou and Samina Najmi (University of Washington Press, forthcoming).

39. Carmen Wickramagamage, "Relocation as Positive Act: The Immigrant Experience in Bharati Mukherjee's Novels," *Diaspora: A Journal of Transnational Studies* 2, no. 2 (1992): 171–200.

40. Abha Dawesar spoke at a reading at Wellesley College, Wellesley, Massachusetts, in November 2001.

41. Cynthia Sau-ling Wong, *From Necessity to Extravagance: Reading Asian American Literature.* Princeton: Princeton University Press, 1993), 54. Another fine analysis of Mukherjee's writings is Jennifer Drake, "Looting American Culture: Bharati Mukherjee's Immigrant Narratives," *Contemporary Literature* 40, no. 1 (Spring 1999): 60–84. Drake addresses the criticism that scholars make of Mukherjee's perspective—that it elides the difficulties of transforming and adapting to a new place—and offers a persuasive reading of the nuances in her work.

42. Some criticisms of Mukherjee's work include Inderpal Grewal, "Reading and Writing the South Asian Diaspora: Feminism and Nationalism in North America," in *Our Feet Walk the Sky: Women of the South Asian Diaspora*, ed. The Women of South Asian Descent Collective (San Francisco: aunt lute books, 1993), 226–36; and Alpana Sharma Knippling, "Toward an Investigation of the Subaltern in Bharati Mukherjee's *The Middleman and Other Stories* and *Jasmine*," in *Bharati Mukherjee: Critical Perspectives*, ed. Emmanuel S. Nelson (New York: Garland Publishing, 1993), 143–59. For favorable readings of Mukherjee, see Wong, *From Necessity to Extravagance*, 54; Jennifer Drake, "Looting American Culture."

43. Bharati Mukherjee, "Two Ways to Belong in America," *New York Times*, September 22, 1996, sec. 4, p. 13.

44. Kwame Anthony Appiah, "Giving Up the Perfect Diamond: Woman Reaches Out to Woman in Bharati Mukherjee's Novel: Around the World and Across Three Centuries" (review of *Holder of the World*), *New York Times Book Review*, October 10, 1993, 7.

45. A less charitable reading is offered by Gita Rajan in her essay "Fissuring Time, Suturing Space: Reading Bharati Mukherjee's *The Holder of the World*," in *Generations: Academic Feminists in Dialogue*, ed. Devoney Looser and E. Ann Kaplan (Minneapolis: University of Minnesota Press, 1997), 288–308. Mukherjee, says Rajan, renders Hannah voiceless and "uncover[s] her heroine's body by entombing her agency" (290).

46. See N. K. Sandars's edition of *The Epic of Gilgamesh* (Harmondsworth, U.K.: Penguin, 1965), especially 94–119.

47. See *The Making of the Mosaic*, especially 3–20, 112, 143-146.

48. Gary Pak, "In That Valley Beautiful Beyond," in *Bold Words: A Century of Asian American Writing*, ed. Rajini Srikanth and Esther Y. Iwanaga (New Brunswick, NJ: Rutgers University Press, 2001), 133–39.

49. Samir Dayal made this comment to me in response to a discussion that followed a reading by Manil Suri from his novel in January 2001 in the Boston area.

50. Padmini Patwardhan, "Gobind Behari Lal: The Gentle Indian Firebrand of American Science Journalism," *American Journalism* 20 (Winter 2003): 33–55.

51. Vijay Prashad, *Everybody Was Kung Fu Fighting: Afro-Asian Connections and the Myth of Cultural Purity* (Boston: Beacon, 2001), 65. For more on the African-Asian connection, see the *Journal of Asian American Studies* 4, no. 3 (October 2001). The articles in this issue are developed from papers delivered at a conference titled "Blacks

and Asians: Revisiting Racial Formations," organized by Vijay Prashad of Trinity College and Sudhir Venkatesh of Columbia University, November 9–10, 2000.

52. Kelley quoted in Prashad, *Everybody Was Kung Fu Fighting*, 65.

53. Roshni Rustomji-Kerns, "Introduction," in *Encounters: People of Asian Descent in the Americas*, ed. Roshni Rustomji-Kerns with Rajini Srikanth and Leny Mendoza Strobel (Boulder, CO: Rowman and Littlefield, 1999), 6.

CHAPTER 5

1. Michael Ondaatje, *The English Patient* (New York: Vintage, 1992), 296.

2. Shishir Kurup, "Assimilation," in *Bold Words: A Century of Asian American Writing*, ed. Rajini Srikanth and Esther Y. Iwanaga (New Brunswick, NJ: Rutgers University Press, 2001), 341.

3. Amy Kaplan, "'Left Alone with America': The Absence of Empire in the Study of American Culture," in *Cultures of United States Imperialism*, ed. Amy Kaplan and Donald E. Pease (Durham, NC: Duke University Press, 1993), 12, 13. See also Maureen Dowd, "Hypocrisy and Apple Pie," *New York Times*, April 30, 2003, A31. Dowd observes that "America is a furtive empire, afraid to raise its flag or linger too long or even call things by their real names. The U.S. is having a hard time figuring out how to wield its colonial power, how to balance collegiality with coercion, how to savor the fruits of imperialism without acknowledging its imperial hubris."

4. Michael Ignatieff, "The Burden," *New York Times Magazine*, January 5, 2003, 22.

5. Donald E. Pease, "New Perspectives on U.S. Culture and Imperialism," in *Cultures of United States Imperialism*, 23.

6. In *The Bluest Eye*, Pecola Breedlove, a young black girl, so desperately longs to look like Shirley Temple that at the novel's end she actually believes herself to have blue eyes. Morrison's first novel is a powerful indictment of white notions of beauty that devalue the self-worth of young black female children.

7. Susan Koshy, "South Asians and the Complex Interstices of Whiteness: Negotiating Public Sentiment in the United States and Britain," in *White Women in Racialized Spaces: Imaginative Transformation and Ethical Action in Literature*, ed. Samina Najmi and Rajini Srikanth (Albany: State University of New York Press, 2002), 29–50.

8. Sucheta Mazumdar, "Race and Racism: South Asians in the United States," in *Frontiers of Asian American Studies: Writing, Research, and Commentary*, ed. Gail M. Nomura et al. (Pullman: Washington University Press, 1989), 25–38.

9. Chitra Divakaruni, *Leaving Yuba City* (New York: Anchor, 1997).

10. See Karen Isaksen Leonard, *Making Ethnic Choices: California's Punjabi Mexican Americans* (Philadelphia: Temple University Press, 1992), especially 62–79, for the legal and social climate under which Punjabi men married Mexican American women. California's antimiscegenation laws prohibited them from marrying white women. Leonard's explanation for why the Punjabi men did not typically marry black women bears out the validity of Koshy's argument that South Asians' avoidance of blacks had less to do with racist attitudes than with their awareness of whites' deep seated hostility toward and fear of blacks. Leonard poses the question:

"Why ally themselves with a group hated by whites, when the Punjabis had similar problems and could fight them better alone?" (69).

11. S. Chandrasekhar, "A History of United States Legislation with Respect to Immigration from India," in *From India to America: A Brief History of Immigration; Problems of Discrimination; Admission and Assimilation*, ed. S. Chandrasekhar (La Jolla, CA: Population Review, 1982), 19–20.

12. Valerie Babb, *Whiteness Visible: The Meaning of Whiteness in American Literature and Culture* (New York: New York University Press, 1998).

13. Toni Morrison, *Playing in the Dark: Whiteness and the Literary Imagination* (New York: Vintage, 1993), 47.

14. Etienne Balibar, "Is There a 'Neo-Racism'?" in *Race, Nation, Class: Ambiguous Identities*, ed. Etienne Balibar and Immanuel Wallerstein (London: Verso, 1991), 21.

15. Ibid., 25.

16. Jennifer Drake, "Looting American Culture: Bharati Mukherjee's Immigrant Narratives," *Contemporary Literature* 40, no. 1 (Spring 1999): 60–84.

17. See Linda Hutcheon and Marion Richmond, *Other Solitudes: Canadian Multicultural Fictions* (Toronto: Oxford University Press, 1990); the full text of the act is printed in the book's conclusion. The Act is also available online at http://www.pch.gc.ca/progs/multi/policy/act_e.cfm.

18. Bharati Mukherjee, *Darkness* (New York: Fawcett Crest, 1985), xv.

19. In 1994, Ram Uppuluri ran for the congressional seat in the U.S. House of Representatives from Tennessee's third district. Uppuluri, whose mother is Japanese and father Indian, told me in a conversation in August 1998 that had he not formally adopted Unitarianism he could not have run for political office in the South. Uppuluri's father was Hindu and his mother is Buddhist. See my essay "Identity and Admission into the Political Game: The Indian American Community Signs Up," *Amerasia Journal* 25, no. 3 (1999–2000): 59–80.

20. See Barry Kanpol and Peter McLaren, *Critical Multiculturalism: Uncommon Voices in a Common Struggle* (Bergin and Garvey, 1995).

21. George Clack, ed., *Writers on America*, available at http://usinfo.state.gov/products/pubs/writers/

22. David Cole and Michael Avery made these comments at the conference "War on Terrorism or Assault on Human Rights?" at the University of Massachusetts Boston, May 3, 2003. See also "Reforming Immigration," special issue of *The Subcontinental: A Journal of South Asian American Political Identity* 1, no. 3 (Autumn 2003).

23. Mukherjee's essay is available at http://usinfo.state.gov/products/pubs/writers/mukherjee.htm.

24. Frances Saunders, quoted in Michael Berube, "American Studies without Exceptions," *Publications of the Modern Language Association of America* 118, no. 1 (January 2003): 105.

25. For the text of Kiesling's letter, see *New York Times* (International Section), February 27, 2003; also available at http://www.nytimes.com/2003/02/27/international/27WEB-TNAT.html?ex=1051156800&en=491d3368f46380ac&ei=5070.

26. Muneer Ahmad, "Homeland Insecurities: Racial Violence the Day after September 11," *Social Text* 72 20, no. 3 (Fall 2002): 108.

27. See David Cole, James X. Dempsey, and Carole E. Goldberg, *Terrorism and the Constitution: Sacrificing Civil Liberties in the Name of National Security* (New York: New Press, 2002); Nancy Chang and Howard Zinn, *Silencing Political Dissent: How Post–Sept. 11 Anti-Terrorism Measures Threaten Our Civil Liberties* (New York: Seven Stories Press, 2002). Cole's *Enemy Aliens* (New York: New Press, 2003) focuses specifically on the status of immigrants or foreign nationals.

28. Langley was the moderator for a forum titled "Teaching During the War," held at the University of Massachusetts Boston, April 18, 2003.

29. See the explosive play by Amiri Baraka (formerly Leroi Jones), *Dutchman* (New York: William Morrow, 1964), which both depicts and critiques the remarkable arsenal at the disposal of those in power. *Dutchman* is brilliant in revealing the psychological framework within which power is exercised. It is a bleak portrayal of the black man's fate in a United States controlled and structured by whiteness.

30. John Carlos Rowe, "Nineteenth-Century United States Literary Culture and Transnationality," *Publications of the Modern Language Association of America* 118, no. 1 (January 2003): 80.

31. Paul Giles, "Transnationalism and Classic American Literature," *Publications of the Modern Language Association of America* 118, no. 1 (January 2003): 65.

32. Mark Gevisser, "Truth and Consequences in Post-Apartheid Theater," *Theater* 25, no. 3 (1995): 10.

33. Michael Rogin, "'Make My Day!' Spectacle as Amnesia in Imperial Politics," in *Cultures of United States Imperialism,* edited by Amy Kaplan and Donald E. Pease, 499.

34. Maira made this comment at the conference "War on Terrorism or Assault on Human Rights?" at the University of Massachusetts Boston, May 3, 2003.

35. Garry Wills, "With God on His Side," *New York Times Magazine,* March 30, 2003, 29.

36. Ibid.

37. See Matthew Rothschild, "Bush, the Gunslinger," *The Progressive,* March 18, 2003, available at http://www.progress.org; Berlet made the comment at the conference "War on Terrorism or Assault on Human Rights?" at the University of Massachusetts Boston, May 3, 2003.

38. Clifford Krauss, "In God We Trust . . . Canadians Aren't So Sure," *New York Times,* March 26, 2003, A4.

39. Jhumpa Lahiri, "This Blessed House," in *The Interpreter of Maladies* (Boston: Houghton Mifflin, 1999), 137.

40. Sharbari Ahmed, *Raisins Not Virgins,* 14. Ahmed's play is still in manuscript form. It had several staged readings in New York and was performed at the Producer's Club II in New York City, July 3–13, 2003.

41. Tahira Naqvi, "Chagrin," in *Dying in a Strange Country* (Toronto: TSAR Publications, 2001), 96. Subsequent page citations in the text are to this version of the story.

42. Tahira Naqvi, "Chagrin" in *Bold Words: A Century of Asian American Writing,* ed. Rajini Srikanth and Esther Yae Iwanaga (New Brunswick, NJ: Rutgers University Press, 2001), 284.

43. Cynthia Sau-ling Wong, *From Necessity to Extravagance: Reading Asian American Literature* (Princeton: Princeton University Press, 1993), 13. Wong constructs her theoretical framework from two passages in Maxine Hong Kingston's *Woman Warrior* (New York: Vintage, 1977): "My mother told me once and for all the useful parts [of the no name woman's story]. She will add nothing unless powered by Necessity, a riverbank that guides her life. She plants vegetables rather than lawns; she carries the odd-shaped tomatoes home from fields and eats food left for the gods" (6). "Adultery is extravagance. Could people who hatch their own chicks and eat the embryos and the heads for delicacies and boil the feet in vinegar for party food, leaving only the gravel, eating even the gizzard lining, could such people engender a prodigal aunt?" (ibid.).

44. See Kwang Chung Kim, *Koreans in the Hood: Conflict with African Americans* (Baltimore: Johns Hopkins University Press, 1999). See also Roberta Uno, "Asian American Theater Awake at the Millennium," in *Bold Words: A Century of Asian American Writing*, ed. Rajini Srikanth and Esther Yae Iwanaga (New Brunswick, NJ: Rutgers University Press, 2001), 323–32. Uno relates a conversation she had with solo performer Brenda Wong Aoki about a performance of Aoki's play *Obake* in a public high school in New Orleans. Many Vietnamese American students walked out of *Obake*, which uses many traditional Japanese ghost stories. Aoki had doubted the wisdom of performing the play at the school. Later, says Aoki, one Vietnamese girl came up to her and said, "'Miss Aoki, we don't mean to be dissin' you, but this is N'ahlins (New Orleans). Here we don't got to be Vietnamese. We got to be Black'" (326).

45. Jhumpa Lahiri, "The Third and Final Continent," in *The Interpreter of Maladies* (Boston: Houghton Mifflin, 1999), 198.

46. Srikanth, Rajini. "Abraham Verghese Doctors Autobiography in His Own Country," in *Asian American Literature: Form, Confrontation, and Transformation*, ed. Xiaojing Zhou and Samina Najmi (Seattle: University of Washington Press, forthcoming).

47. Ibid.

48. John Sturrock, *The Language of Autobiography: Studies in the First Person Singular* (Cambridge: Cambridge University Press, 1993), 13.

49. Deepika Bahri and Mary Vasudeva, "Observing Ourselves among Others: Interview with Meena Alexander," in *Between the Lines: South Asians and Postcoloniality*, ed. Deepika Bahri and Mary Vasudeva (Philadelphia: Temple University Press, 1996), 36–38.

50. Lavina Dhingra Shankar, "Postcolonial Diasporics 'Writing in Search of a Homeland': Meena Alexander's *Manhattan Music, Fault Lines* and *The Shock of Arrival*," *LIT: Literature, Interpretation, Theory* 12, no. 3 (2001): 287.

51. Meena Alexander, *Fault Lines* (New York: Feminist Press, 1993), 198.

52. Bahri and Vasudeva, "Observing Ourselves among Others," 37.

53. Erika Duncan, "A Portrait of Meena Alexander," *World Literature Today* 73 no. 1 (1999): 26.

54. Himani Bannerjee, "The Moon and My Mother," in *Contours of the Heart: South Asians Map North America*, ed. Sunaina Maira and Rajini Srikanth (New York: Asian

American Writers Workshop, 1996), 188–96; Lahiri, "The Interpreter of Maladies," in *The Interpreter of Maladies*, pp. 43–70.

55. See Maria Tymoczko and Edwin Gentzler, eds., *Translation and Power* (Amherst: University of Massachusetts Press, 2002); and Anthony Pym, *Method in Translation History* (Manchester, U.K.: St. Jerome Publishing, 1998).

BIBLIOGRAPHY

Ahmad, Muneer. "Homeland Insecurities: Racial Violence the Day after September 11." *Social Text 72* 20, no. 3 (Fall 2002): 101–16.

Ahmed, Leila. *Women and Gender in Islam*. New Haven: Yale University Press, 1992.

Alexander, M. Jacqui. "Erotic Autonomy as a Politics of Decolonization: An Anatomy of Feminist and State Practice in the Bahamas Tourist Economy." In *Feminist Genealogies, Colonial Legacies, and Democratic Futures*, edited by M. Jacqui Alexander and Chandra Talpade Mohanty, 63–101. New York: Routledge, 1997.

———. "Redrafting Morality: The Postcolonial State and the Sexual Offences Bill of Trinidad and Tobago." In *Third World Women and the Politics of Feminism*, edited by Chandra Talpade Mohanty, Ann Russo, and Lourdes Torres, 133–53. Bloomington: Indiana University Press, 1991.

Alexander, Meena. *Fault Lines*. New York: Feminist Press, 1993.

———. "Foreword: Translating Violence: Reflections after Ayodhya." In *Blood into Ink: South Asian and Middle Eastern Women Write War*, edited by Miriam Cooke and Roshni Rustomji-Kerns, xi–xviii. Durham, NC: Duke University Press, 1994.

———. *The Illiterate Heart*. Evanston, IL: Northwestern University Press, 2002.

———. *River and Bridge*. Toronto: TSAR Publications, 1996.

———. *The Shock of Arrival: Reflections on Postcolonial Experience*. Boston: South End Press, 1996.

Ali, Agha Shahid. *The Country without a Post Office*. New York: Norton, 1997.

———. *A Nostalgist's Map of America*. New York: Norton, 1991.

Amirthanayagam, Indran. *The Elephants of Reckoning*. New York: Hanging Loose Press, 1993.

————. "How Politics Becomes Language." *New England Review* 22, no. 1 (Winter 2001): 54–56.

Appadurai, Arjun. *Modernity at Large: Cultural Dimensions of Globalization.* Minneapolis: University of Minnesota Press, 1996.

————. "Spectral Housing and Urban Cleansing: Notes on Millennial Mumbai." In *Cosmopolitanism,* edited by Carol A. Breckenridge, Sheldon Pollock, Homi K. Bhabha, and Dipesh Chakrabarty, 54–81. Durham: Duke University Press, 2002.

Appiah, Kwame Anthony. "Cosmopolitan Patriots." In *Cosmopolitics: Thinking and Feeling beyond the Nation,* edited by Pheng Cheah and Bruce Robbins, 91–114. Minneapolis: University of Minnesota Press, 1998.

————. "Cosmopolitan Reading." In *Cosmopolitan Geographies: New Locations in Literature and Culture,* edited by Vinay Dharwadker, 197–227. New York: Routledge, 2001.

————. "Giving Up the Perfect Diamond: Woman Reaches Out to Woman in Bharati Mukherjee's Novel, Around the World and Across Three Centuries." *New York Times Book Review,* October 10, 1993, 7.

Babb, Valerie. *Whiteness Visible: The Meaning of Whiteness in American Literature and Culture.* New York: New York University Press, 1998.

Bahri, Deepika. "With Kaleidoscope Eyes: The Potential (Dangers) of Identitarian Coalitions." In *A Part, Yet Apart: South Asians in Asian America,* edited by Lavina Dhingra Shankar and Rajini Srikanth, 25–48. Philadelphia: Temple University Press, 1998.

Bahri, Deepika, and Mary Vasudeva. "Observing Ourselves among Others: Interview with Meena Alexander." In *Between the Lines: South Asians and Postcoloniality,* edited by Deepika Bahri and Mary Vasudeva, 35–54. Philadelphia: Temple University Press, 1996.

Bald, Vivek. "Taxi Meters and Plexiglass Partitions." In *Contours of the Heart: South Asians Map North America,* edited by Sunaina Maira and Rajini Srikanth, 66–73. New York: Asian American Writers Workshop, 1996.

Balibar, Etienne. "Is There a 'Neo-Racism'?" In *Race, Nation, Class: Ambiguous Identities,* edited by Etienne Balibar and Immanuel Wallerstein, 17–28. London: Verso, 1991.

Bannerjee, Himani. "The Moon and My Mother." In *Contours of the Heart: South Asians Map North America,* edited by Sunaina Maira and Rajini Srikanth, 188–96. New York: Asian American Writers Workshop, 1996.

Barrett, Amy. "Questions for Tony Kushner; Foreign Affairs." *New York Times,* October 7, 2001, sec. 6, p. 23.

Becker, Elizabeth. "U.S. Ties Military Aid to Peacekeepers' Immunity." *New York Times,* August 10, 2002, A1, A4.

Berube, Michael. "American Studies without Exceptions." *Publications of the Modern Language Association of America* 118, no. 1 (January 2003): 103–13.

Bhabha, Homi K. *The Location of Culture.* New York: Routledge, 1994.

Bharucha, Rustom. "Somebody's Other: Disorientations in the Cultural Politics of Our Times." In *The Intercultural Performance Reader,* edited by Patrice Pavis, 196–212. New York: Routledge, 1996.

————. *Theatre and the World: Performance and the Politics of Culture.* New York: Routledge, 1993.

Bradford, William. *Of Plymouth Plantation: 1620–1647.* New York: Modern Library, 1981.

Brown, Wesley, and Amy Ling, eds. *Imagining America: Stories from the Promised Land.* New York: Persea Books, 1991.

Bulosan, Carlos. *On Becoming Filipino: Selected Writings of Carlos Bulosan*, edited by E. San Juan, Jr. Philadelphia: Temple University Press, 1995.

Castle, Terry. "The Gothic Novel." In *Boss Ladies, Watch Out! Essays on Women, Sex, and Writing*, 73–107. New York: Routledge, 2002.

Chambers, Iain. "Citizenship, Language, and Modernity." *Publications of the Modern Language Association of America* 117, no. 1 (January 2002): 24–31.

Chan, Sucheng. *Asian Americans: An Interpretive History*. New York: Twayne Publishers, 1991.

Chandrasekhar, S. "A History of United States Legislation with Respect to Immigration from India." In *From India to America: A Brief History of Immigration; Problems of Discrimination; Admission and Assimilation*, edited by S. Chandrasekhar, 11–29. La Jolla, CA: Population Review, 1982.

Chang, Nancy, Howard Zinn, and the Center for Constitutional Rights. *Silencing Political Dissent: How Post–Sept. 11 Anti-Terrorism Measures Threaten Our Civil Liberties*. New York: Seven Stories Press, 2002.

Chaudhuri, Una. "Theater and Cosmopolitanism: New Stories, Old Stages." In *Cosmopolitan Geographies: New Locations in Literature and Culture*, edited by Vinay Dharwadker, 171–95. New York: Routledge, 2001.

Cheah, Pheng. "Given Culture: Rethinking Cosmopolitical Freedom in Transnationalism." In *Cosmopolitics: Thinking and Feeling beyond the Nation*, edited by Pheng Cheah and Bruce Robbins, 290–328. Minneapolis: University of Minnesota Press, 1998.

Chow, Rey. *Writing Diaspora: Tactics of Intervention in Contemporary Cultural Studies*. Bloomington: Indiana University Press, 1993.

Chuh, Kandice. "Transnationalism and Its Pasts." *Public Culture* 9 (1996): 93–112.

Chung, Cristy, Aly Kim, Zoon Nguyen, and Trinity Ordona, with Arlene Stein. "In Our Way: A Roundtable Discussion." In *Asian American Sexualities: Dimensions of the Gay and Lesbian Experience*, edited by Russell Leong, 91–100. New York: Routledge, 1996.

Clifford, James. *Routes: Travel and Translation in the Late Twentieth Century*. Cambridge: Harvard University Press, 1997.

Cole, David, James X. Dempsey, and Carole E. Goldberg. *Terrorism and the Constitution: Sacrificing Civil Liberties in the Name of National Security*. New York: New Press, 2002.

Cooke, Miriam, and Roshni Rustomji-Kerns, eds. *Blood into Ink: South Asian and Middle Eastern Women Write War*. Durham, NC: Duke University Press, 1994.

Coomaraswamy, Radhika. "Violence, Armed Conflict, and the Community." In *Women in Post-Independence Sri Lanka*, edited by Swarna Jayaweera, 79–98. Thousand Oaks, CA: Sage Publications, 2002.

Crocker, David. "Truth Commissions, Transitional Justice, and Civil Society." In *Truth v. Justice: The Morality of Truth Commissions*, edited by Robert I. Rotberg and Dennis Thompson, 99–121. Princeton: Princeton University Press, 2000.

Das Dasgupta, Shamita, and Sayantani Dasgupta. "Bringing Up Baby: Raising a Third World Daughter in the First World." In *Dragon Ladies*, edited by Sonia Shah, 192–200. Boston: South End Press, 1997.

Davé, Shilpa. "Nampally Road." In *A Resource Guide to Asian American Literature* edited by Sau-ling Cynthia Wong and Stephen H. Sumida, 13–20. New York: Modern Language Association, 2001.

Dawesar, Abha. *Miniplanner*. San Francisco: Cleis Press, 2000.

Desai, Nirav S. "Forging Political Identity: South Asian Americans in American Policy Making." *The Subcontinental: A Journal of South Asian American Political Identity* 1, no. 1 (Spring 2003): 7–13.

Devi, Mahesweta. "Draupadi." In *In Other Worlds: Essays in Cultural Politics* edited and translated by Gayatri Chakravorty Spivak, 179–96. New York: Routledge, 1987.

Dharwadker, Vinay. "Introduction: Cosmopolitanism in Its Time and Place." In *Cosmopolitan Geographies: New Locations in Literature and Culture*, edited by Vinay Dharwadker, 1–13. New York: Routledge, 2001.

Diamond, Elin. "Brechtian Theory/Feminist Theory: Toward a Gestic Feminist Theory." *TDR: A Journal of Performance Studies* 32, no. 1 (Spring 1988): 82–94.

Dirlik, Arif. "Asians on the Rim: Transnational Capital and Local Community in the Making of Contemporary Asian America." In *Across the Pacific: Asian Americans and Globalization*, edited by Evelyn Hu-DeHart, 29–60. New York: Asia Society; Philadelphia: Temple University Press, 1999.

Divakaruni, Chitra Bannerjee. *Arranged Marriage*. New York: Anchor, 1993.

———. *Leaving Yuba City*. New York: Anchor, 1997.

Donovan, Aaron. "Losing Spouse, and Maybe a Country: Dependents of 9/11 Victim Search for Ways to Stay in the U.S.," *New York Times*, July 23, 2002, A20.

Drake, Jennifer. "Looting American Culture: Bharati Mukherjee's Immigrant Narratives." *Contemporary Literature* 40, no. 1 (Spring 1999): 60–84.

Duncan, Erika. "A Portrait of Meena Alexander." *World Literature Today* 73 no. 1 (1999): 23–28.

Dutt, Ela. "The Immigrant Experience and Other Stories." *India Abroad*, March 12, 1999, 35.

Espiritu, Augusto. "The 'Pre-History' of an 'Asian American' Writer: N.V.M. Gonzalez' Allegory of Decolonization." *Amerasia Journal* 24, no. 3 (1998): 126–41.

Fan, Christopher. "Step out of the Frame." *Ten Magazine* (Winter 2001): 8–11.

Fanon, Frantz. *Black Skin, White Masks*. New York: Grove, 1967.

Fausto-Sterling, Anne. "How to Build a Man." In *The Gender/Sexuality Reader*, edited by Roger N. Lancaster and Micaela di Leonardo. 244–49. New York: Routledge, 1997.

Francia, Luis. "Inventing the Earth: The Notion of 'Home' in Asian American Literature." In *Across the Pacific: Asian Americans and Globalization*, edited by Evelyn Hu-DeHart, 191–218. New York: Asia Society; Philadelphia: Temple University Press, 1999.

Geis, Deborah. "Wordscapes of the Body: Performative Language as Gestus in Marie Irene Fornes's Plays." In *Feminist Theatre and Theory*, edited by Helene Keyssar, 168–88. New York: St. Martin's Press, 1996.

Gevisser, Mark. "Truth and Consequences in Post-Apartheid Theater." *Theater* 25, no. 3 (1995): 9–18.

Gewertz, Deborah, and Frederick Errington. "We Think, Therefore They Are? On Occidentalizing the World." In *Cultures of United States Imperialism*, edited by Amy Kaplan and Donald E. Pease, 635–55. Durham, NC: Duke University Press, 1993.

Ghosh, Amitav. *The Calcutta Chromosome*. New York: Avon Books, 1997.

———. "The Diaspora in Indian Culture." *Public Culture* 2, no. 1 (1989): 73–78.

———. *The Glass Palace*. New York: Random House, 2001.

———. "Imperial Temptation." *The Nation*, May 27, 2002, 24.

———. *In an Antique Land: History in the Guise of a Traveler's Tale*. New York: Vintage, 1992.

Giles, Paul. "Transnationalism and Classic American Literature." *Publications of the Modern Language Association of America* 118, no. 1 (January 2003): 62–77.

Gopinath, Gayatri. "Funny Boys and Girls: Notes on a Queer South Asian Planet." In *Asian American Sexualities: Dimensions of the Gay and Lesbian Experience*, edited by Russell Leong, 119–27. New York: Routledge, 1993.

Grewal, Inderpal. "The Postcolonial, Ethnic Studies, and the Diaspora: The Contexts of Ethnic Immigrant/Migrant Cultural Studies in the US." *Socialist Review* 24, no. 4 (1994): 45–73.

Hall, Stuart. "New Ethnicities." In *Stuart Hall: Critical Dialogues in Cultural Studies*, edited by David Morley and Kuan-Hsing Chen, 441–50. New York: Routledge, 1996.

———. "On Postmodernism and Articulation: An Interview with Stuart Hall." *Journal of Communication Inquiry* 10, no. 2 (Summer 1986): 45–60.

———. "What Is This 'Black' in Black Popular Culture?" In *Stuart Hall: Critical Dialogues in Cultural Studies*, edited by David Morley and Kuan-Hsing Chen, 465–76. New York: Routledge, 1996.

Hardt, Michael, and Antonio Negri. *Empire*. Cambridge: Harvard University Press, 2000.

Hoffman, Stanley. "America Goes Backward." *New York Review of Books* 50, no. 10 (June 12, 2003): 74–75, 78–80.

Hu-DeHart, Evelyn. "Introduction: Asian American Formations in the Age of Globalization." In *Across the Pacific: Asian Americans and Globalization*, edited by Evelyn Hu-DeHart, 1–28. New York: Asia Society; Philadelphia: Temple University Press, 1999.

Hurtado, Albert L., and Peter Iverson, eds. *Major Problems in American Indian History*. Lexington, MA: D. C. Heath, 1994.

Hutcheon, Linda. "Multicultural Furor: The Reception of *Other Solitudes*." In *Cultural Difference and the Literary Text: Pluralism and the Limits of Authenticity in North American Literatures*, edited by Winfried Siemerling and Katrin Schwenk, 10–18. Iowa City: University of Iowa Press, 1996.

Hutcheon, Linda, and Marion Richmond, eds. *Other Solitudes: Canadian Multicultural Fictions*. Toronto: Oxford University Press, 1990.

Ignatieff, Michael. "The Burden." *New York Times Magazine*, January 5, 2003, 22–27, 50–54.

Iqbal, Anwar. "U.S. Image-Maker for Muslims Quits." *Washington Times*, March 3, 2003, online at http://www.washtimes.com/upi-breaking/20030303-034403-5777r.htm.

Islam, Naheed. "Naming Desire, Shaping Identity: Tracing the Experiences of Indian Lesbians in the United States." In *Patchwork Shawl: Chronicles of South Asian American Women in America*, edited by Shamita Das Dasgupta, 72–93. New Brunswick, NJ: Rutgers University Press, 1998.

———. "Race Markers Transgressors: Mapping a Racial Kaleidoscope within an (Im)migrant Landscape." In *Encounters: People of Asian Descent in the Americas*, edited by Roshni Rustomji-Kerns, 239–54. Boulder, CO: Rowman and Littlefield, 1999.

Ismail, Qadri. "A Flippant Gesture Towards Sri Lanka: A Review of Michael Ondaatje's *Anil's Ghost*," *Pravada* 6, nos. 9 and 10 (2000): 24–29. Published by the Social Scientists Association. Colombo, Sri Lanka.

Iyer, Pico. *The Global Soul: Jet Lag, Shopping Malls, and the Search for Home*. New York: Vintage, 2000.

———. *The Lady and The Monk: Four Seasons in Kyoto*. New York: Vintage, 1992.

———. *Video Night in Kathmandu: And Other Reports from the Not-So-Far East*. New York: Vintage, 1989.

Jaffrey, Zia. *The Invisibles: A Tale of the Eunuchs of India*. New York: Pantheon, 1996.

Jensen, Joan M. *Passage from India: Asian Indian Immigrants in North America*. New Haven: Yale University Press, 1988.

Juan, E. San. "Introduction." In *On Becoming Filipino: Selected Writings of Carlos Bulosan*, edited by San E. Juan, 1–44. Philadelphia: Temple University Press, 1995.

Kalb, Jonathan. "Documentary Solo Performance: The Politics of the Mirrored Self."
    Theater 31, no. 3 (2001): 13–29.
Kamani, Ginu. "Goddess of Sleep." In *Bold Words: A Century of Asian American Writing*,
    edited by Rajini Srikanth and Esther Y. Iwanaga, 260–64. New Brunswick, NJ:
    Rutgers University Press, 2001.
———. *Junglee Girl*. San Francisco: aunt lute, 1995.
———. "MSM Messenger." *MAN'S World* 2, no. 10 (December 2001): 96–100.
———. "Preface to 'Just Between Indians.'" In *Contours of the Heart: South Asians Map
    North America*, 353–55. New York: Asian American Writers Workshop, 1996.
Kanaganayagam, Chelva. *Configurations of Exile: South Asian Writers and Their World*.
    Toronto: TSAR Publications, 1995.
Kang, Laura Hyun Yi. *Compositional Subjects: Enfiguring Asian/American Women*. Durham,
    NC: Duke University Press, 2002.
Kaplan, Amy. "'Left Alone with America': The Absence of Empire in the Study of
    American Culture." In *Cultures of United States Imperialism*, edited by Amy Kaplan
    and Donald E. Pease, 3–21. Durham, NC: Duke University Press, 1993.
Kelley, Ninette, and Michael Trebilcock. *The Making of the Mosaic: A History of Canadian
    Immigration Policy*. Toronto: University of Toronto Press, 1998.
Kibria, Nazli. "College and Notions of 'Asian American': Second Generation Chinese
    and Korean Americans Negotiate Race and Identity." *Amerasia Journal* 25, no. 1
    (Spring 1999): 29–51.
Kim, Elaine H. "Home Is Where the *Han* Is: A Korean American Perspective on the Los
    Angeles Upheavals." In *Asian American Studies: A Reader*, edited by Jean Wu and Min
    Hyoung Song, 270–89. New Brunswick, NJ: Rutgers University Press, 2000.
Knapp, Steven. *Literary Interest: The Limits of Anti-Formalism*. Cambridge: Harvard
    University Press, 1993.
Koepnick, Lutz. *Walter Benjamin and the Aesthetics of Power*. Lincoln: University of
    Nebraska Press, 1999.
Koshy, Susan. "South Asians and the Complex Interstices of Whiteness: Negotiating
    Public Sentiment in the United States and Britain." In *White Women in Racialized
    Spaces: Imaginative Transformation and Ethical Action in Literature*, edited by Samina
    Najmi and Rajini Srikanth, 29–50. Albany: State University of New York Press,
    2002.
Krauss, Clifford. "In God We Trust . . . Canadians Aren't So Sure." *New York Times*, March
    26, 2003, A4.
Krupat, Arnold. "Native American Autobiography and the Synecdochic Self." In
    American Autobiography: Retrospect and Prospect, edited by Paul John Eakin, 171–94.
    Madison: University of Wisconsin Press, 1991.
Kumar, Amitava. *Passport Photos*. Berkeley: University of California Press, 2000.
Kurup, Shishir. "Assimilation." In *Bold Words: A Century of Asian American Writing*, edited
    by Rajini Srikanth and Esther Y. Iwanaga, 340–51. New Brunswick, NJ: Rutgers
    University Press, 2001.
Lahiri, Jhumpa. *The Interpreter of Maladies*. Boston: Houghton Mifflin, 1999.
Lather, Patti. "Postbook: Working the Ruins of Feminist Ethnography." *Signs: Journal of
    Women in Culture and Society* 27, no. 1 (2001): 199–227.
Lee, Josephine. *Performing Asian America: Race and Ethnicity on the Contemporary Stage*.
    Philadelphia: Temple University Press, 1997.
Lee, Wen Ho, with Helen Zia. *My Country versus Me: The First-Hand Account by the Los
    Alamos Scientist Who Was Falsely Accused*. New York: Hyperion, 2002.

Leonard, Karen Isaksen. *Making Ethnic Choices: California's Punjabi Mexican Americans.* Philadelphia: Temple University Press, 1992.

Ling, Jinqi. *Narrating Nationalisms: Ideology and Form in Asian American Literature.* New York: Oxford University Press, 1998.

Lipset, Seymour Martin. *American Exceptionalism: A Double-Edged Sword.* New York: Norton, 1996.

Lowe, Lisa. *Immigrant Acts.* Durham: Duke University Press, 1996.

Madsen, Deborah L. *American Exceptionalism.* Jackson: University Press of Mississippi, 1998.

Maira, Sunaina Marr. *Desis in the House: Indian American Youth Culture in New York City.* Philadelphia: Temple University Press, 2002.

Marcus, George. "Critical Cultural Studies as One Power/Knowledge like, among, and in Engagement with Others." In *From Sociology to Cultural Studies: New Perspectives,* edited by Elizabeth Long, 399–425. London: Blackwell, 1997.

———. "What Comes (Just) after 'Post'? The Case of Ethnography." In *The Handbook of Qualitative Research,* edited by Norman Denzin and Yvonna Lincoln, 563–74. Thousand Oaks, CA: Sage Publications, 1994.

Marks, Peter. "For Tony Kushner, an Eerily Prescient Return." *New York Times,* November 25, 2001, sec. 2, pp. 1, 20.

Mazumdar, Sucheta. "Afterword." In *Contours of the Heart: South Asians Map North America,* edited by Sunaina Maira and Rajini Srikanth, 461–69. New York: Asian American Writers Workshop, 1996.

McCarthy, Thomas. "On Reconciling Cosmopolitan Unity and National Diversity." *Public Culture* 11, no. 1 (1999): 175–208.

McEvoy-Levy, Siobhán. *American Exceptionalism and U.S. Foreign Policy: Public Diplomacy at the End of the Cold War.* New York: Palgrave, 2001.

Mehta, Ved. *Sound-Shadows of the New World.* New York: Norton, 1985.

Messmer, Marietta. "Toward a Declaration of Interdependence; or, Interrogating the Boundaries in Twentieth-Century Histories of North American Literature." *Publications of the Modern Language Association of America* 118, no. 1 (January 2003): 41–55.

Miller, Perry, and Thomas H. Johnson, eds. *The Puritans. Volume 1.* New York: Harper and Row, 1963.

Minh-ha, Trinh T. *Woman, Native, Other: Writing Postcoloniality and Feminism.* Bloomington: Indiana University Press, 1989.

Mootoo, Shani. *Cereus Blooms at Night.* New York: Grove Press, 1996.

———. *Out on Main Street and Other Stories.* Vancouver: Press Gang Publishers, 1993.

Morrison, Toni. *Playing in the Dark: Whiteness and the Literary Imagination.* New York: Vintage, 1993.

Mostern, Kenneth. "Postcolonialism after W.E.B. Du Bois." In *Postcolonial Theory and the United States: Race, Ethnicity, and Literature,* edited by Amritjit Singh and Peter Schmidt, 258–76. Jackson: University Press of Mississippi, 2000.

Mukherjee, Bharati. *Darkness.* New York: Fawcett Crest, 1985.

———. *The Holder of the World.* New York: Knopf, 1993.

———. *The Middleman and Other Stories.* New York: Fawcett Crest, 1988.

———. "Two Ways to Belong in America." *New York Times,* September 22, 1996, sec. 4, p. 13.

Munasinghe, Viranjani. "Redefining the Nation: The East Indian Struggle for Inclusion in Trinidad." *Journal of Asian American Studies* 4, no. 1 (February 2001): 1–34.

Naqvi, Tahira. *Attar of Roses and Other Stories of Pakistan*. Boulder, CO: Three Continents, 1997.

———. "Chagrin." In *Bold Words: A Century of Asian American Writing*, edited by Rajini Srikanth and Esther Yae Iwanaga, 280–85. New Brunswick, NJ: Rutgers University Press, 2001.

———. *Dying in a Strange Country*. Toronto: TSAR Publications, 2001.

Natarajan, Nalini. "Introduction: Reading Diaspora." In *Writers of the Indian Diaspora*, edited by Emmanuel Nelson, xiii–xix. Westport, CT: Greenwood Press, 1993.

Nussbaum, Martha C. "Patriotism and Cosmopolitanism." In *For Love of Country: Debating the Limits of Patriotism*, edited by Joshua Cohen, 2–17. Boston: Beacon Press, 1996.

Okihiro, Gary. *Common Ground: Reimagining American History*. Princeton: Princeton University Press, 2001.

———. *Margins and Mainstreams: Asians in American History and Culture*. Seattle: University of Washington Press, 1994.

Ondaatje, Michael. *Anil's Ghost*. New York: Knopf, 2000.

———. *The English Patient*. New York: Vintage, 1992.

———. *In the Skin of a Lion*. New York: Knopf, 1987.

Pak, Gary. "In That Valley Beautiful Beyond." In *Bold Words: A Century of Asian American Writing*. Edited by Rajini Srikanth and Esther Y. Iwanaga, 133–39. New Brunswick, NJ: Rutgers University Press, 2001.

Parekh, Sameer. *Stealing the Ambassador*. New York: Free Press, 2002.

Pease, Donald E. "New Perspectives on U.S. Culture and Imperialism." In *Cultures of United States Imperialism*, edited by Amy Kaplan and Donald E. Pease, 22–37. Durham, NC: Duke University Press, 1993.

Peeradina, Saleem. *Group Portrait*. Madras: Oxford University Press, 1992.

Peyser, Thomas. *Utopia and Cosmopolis: Globalization in the Era of American Literary Realism*. Durham, NC: Duke University Press, 1998.

Pham, Andrew X. *Catfish and Mandala: A Two-Wheeled Voyage through the Landscape and Memory of Vietnam*. New York: Picador USA, 2000.

Pollock, Sheldon, Homi K. Bhabha, Carol A. Breckenridge, and Dipesh Chakrabarty, eds. *Cosmopolitanism*. Durham, NC: Duke University Press, 2002.

Prashad, Vijay. *Everybody Was Kung Fu Fighting: Afro-Asian Connections and the Myth of Cultural Purity*. Boston: Beacon, 2001.

———. *The Karma of Brown Folk*. Minneapolis: University of Minnesota Press, 2000.

Puri, Shalini. "Canonized Hybridities, Resistant Hybridities: Chutney Soca, Carnival, and the Politics of Nationalism." In *Caribbean Romances: The Politics of Regional Representation*, edited by Belinda J. Edmondson, 12–39. Charlottesville: University Press of Virginia, 1999.

Radhakrishnan, R. *Diasporic Mediations: Between Home and Location*. Minneapolis: University of Minnesota Press, 1996.

Rajan, Gita. "Fissuring Time, Suturing Space: Reading Bharati Mukherjee's *The Holder of the World*." In *Generations: Academic Feminists in Dialogue*, edited by Devoney Looser and E. Ann Kaplan, 288–308. Minneapolis: University of Minnesota Press, 1997.

Robbins, Bruce. *Feeling Global: Internationalism in Distress*. New York: New York University Press, 1999.

———. "The Village of the Liberal Managerial Class." In *Cosmopolitan Geographies: New Locations in Literature and Culture*, edited by Vinay Dharwadker, 15–32. New York: Routledge, 2001.

Rogin, Michael. " 'Make My Day!': Spectacle as Amnesia in Imperial Politics." In *Cultures of United States Imperialism*, edited by Amy Kaplan and Donald E. Pease, 499–534. Durham, NC: Duke University Press, 1993.

Roos, Sigmund J. "Keep a Close Eye on This Man." *Boston Globe*, August 9, 2002, A14.

Rowe, John Carlos. "Nineteenth-Century United States Literary Culture and Transnationality." *Publications of the Modern Language Association of America* 118, no. 1 (January 2003): 78–89.

Roy, Arundhati. "The End of Imagination." *Frontline*, August 6, 1998, 2–15.

Rustomji, Roshni. *The Braided Tongue*. Toronto: TSAR Publications, 2003.

Rustomji-Kerns, Roshni, with Rajini Srikanth and Leny Mendoza Strobel, eds. *Encounters: People of Asian Descent in the Americas*. Boulder, CO: Rowman and Littlefield, 1999.

Sandars, N. K, ed. *The Epic of Gilgamesh*. Harmondsworth, U.K.: Penguin, 1960.

Sanjek, Roger. *The Future of Us All: Race and Neighborhood Politics in New York City*. Ithaca: Cornell University Press, 1998.

Saund, Dalip Singh. *Congressman from India*. New York: Dutton, 1960.

Saunders, Frances Stonor. *The Cultural Cold War: The CIA and the World of Arts and Letters*. New York: New Press, 2000.

Saunders, Rebecca. "The Agony and the Allegory: The Concept of the Foreign, the Language of Apartheid, and the Fiction of J. M. Coetzee." *Cultural Critique* 47 (Winter 2001): 215–64.

Scarry, Elaine. "The Difficulty of Imagining Other People." In *For Love of Country: Debating the Limits of Patriotism*, edited by Joshua Cohen, 98–110. Boston: Beacon Press, 1996.

Schwenk, Katrin. "Introduction: Thinking about 'Pure Pluralism.'" In *Cultural Difference and the Literary Text: Pluralism and the Limits of Authenticity in North American Literatures*, edited by Winfried Siemerling and Katrin Schwenk, 1–9. Iowa City: University of Iowa Press, 1996. 1–9.

Selvadurai, Shyam. *Funny Boy*. New York: William and Morrow, 1994.

Sen, Amartya. "On Reporting and Interpreting." Full text of speech available on the web at Harvard's Kennedy School of Government's Global Equity Initiative Program site: http://www.ksg/harvard.edu/gei/publications.htm#sen_pubs.

Shankar, Lavina Dhingra. "Postcolonial Diasporics 'Writing in Search of a Homeland': Meena Alexander's *Manhattan Music, Fault Lines* and *The Shock of Arrival*." *LIT: Literature, Interpretation, Theory* 12, no. 3 (2001): 285–312.

Shankar, Lavina Dhingra, and Rajini Srikanth. "South Asian American Literature: 'Off the Turnpike' of Asian America." In *Postcolonial Theory and the United States: Race, Ethnicity, and Literature*, edited by Amritjit Singh and Peter Schmidt, 370–87. Jackson: University Press of Mississippi, 2000.

Shinebourne, Jan Lo. "Soho, Southhall, Brixton: Chinatown in New York." In *Encounters: People of Asian Descent in the Americas*, edited by Roshni Rustomji-Kerns with Rajini Srikanth and Leny Mendoza Strobel, 258–62. Boulder, CO: Rowman and Littlefield, 1999.

Sidhwa, Bapsi. *Cracking India*. Minneapolis: Milkweed, 1991.

———. "Defend Yourself against Me." In *Contours of the Heart: South Asians Map North America*, edited by Sunaina Maira and Rajini Srikanth, 401–20. New York: Asian American Writers Workshop, 1996.

Siegel, Ed. "Two Stirring Plays Take Divergent Paths to Post-9/11 Realities." *Boston Globe*, July 30, 2002, E1, E5.

Singh, Amritjit, and Peter Schmidt. "On the Borders between U.S. Studies and Postcolonial Theory." In *Postcolonial Theory and the United States: Race, Ethnicity, and Literature*, edited by Amritjit Singh and Peter Schmidt, 3–69. Jackson: University Press of Mississippi, 2000.

Slack, Jennifer Daryl. "The Theory and Method of Articulation in Cultural Studies." In *Stuart Hall: Critical Dialogues in Cultural Studies*, edited by David Morley and Kuan-Hsing Chen, 112–27. New York: Routledge, 1996.

Smith, Anna Deavere. *Twilight: Los Angeles, 1992*. New York: Anchor, 1994.

Soja, Edward. *Postmodern Geographies: The Reassertion of Space in Critical Social Theory*. London: Verso, 1989.

Sollors, Werner. *Amiri Baraka / LeRoi Jones: The Quest for a "Populist Modernism."* New York: Columbia University Press, 1978.

Spivak, Gayatri Chakravorty. "Reading the World: Literary Studies in the Eighties." In *In Other Worlds: Essays in Cultural Politics*, 95–102. New York: Routledge, 1987.

Srikanth, Rajini. "Abraham Verghese Doctors Autobiography in His Own Country." In *Asian American Literature: Form, Confrontation, and Transformation*, edited by Xiaojing Zhou and Samina Najmi. Seattle: University of Washington Press, (forthcoming).

———. "Chitra Bannerjee Divakaruni: Exploring Human Nature Under Fire." *Asia Pacific American Journal* 5, no. 2 (Fall/Winter 1996): 94–101.

———. "Ethnic Outsider-ism as the Ultimate Insider-ism: The Paradox of Verghese's *My Own Country*." *MELUS* (forthcoming).

———. "Gender and the Image of Home in the Asian American Diaspora: A Socio-Literary Reading of Some Asian American Works." *Critical Mass: A Journal of Asian American Cultural Criticism* 2, no. 1 (Winter 1994): 147–81.

———. "Identity and Admission into the Political Game: The Indian American Community Signs Up." *Amerasia Journal* 25, no. 3 (1999–2000): 59–80.

———. "The *Komagata Maru*: Memory and Mobilization among the South Asian Diaspora in North America." In *Re/Collecting Early Asian America: Essays in Cultural History*, edited by Josephine Lee, Imogene Lim, and Yuko Matsukawa, 78–94. Philadelphia: Temple University Press, 2002.

———. "Unsettling Asian American Literature: When More Than America Is in the Heart." In *Beyond the Borders: American Literature and Postcolonial Theory*, edited by Deborah L. Madsen, 92–110. London: Pluto Press, 2003.

———. "Ventriloquism in the Captivity Narrative: White Women Challenge European American Patriarchy." In *White Women in Racialized Spaces: Imaginative Transformation and Ethical Action in Literature*, edited by Samina Najmi and Rajini Srikanth, 85–103. Albany: State University of New York Press, 2002.

Stiglitz, Joseph E. *Globalization and Its Discontents*. New York: Norton, 2002.

Sturrock, John. *The Language of Autobiography: Studies in the First Person Singular*. Cambridge: Cambridge University Press, 1993.

Takaki, Ronald. *Strangers from a Different Shore: A History of Asian Americans*. Boston: Little Brown, 1989.

Talbot, Margaret. "Other Woes." *New York Times Magazine*, November 18, 2001, 23–24.

Toribio, Helen C. "We Are Revolution: A Reflective History of the Union of Democratic Filipinos (KDP)." *Amerasia Journal* 24, no. 2 (Summer 1998): 155–77.

Tripathi, Salil. "Personal Journal: An Indian Novelist's Journey." *Asian Wall Street Journal*, October 26, 2000.

Truong, Monique T. D. *The Book of Salt*. Boston and New York: Houghton Mifflin, 2003.

———. "The Emergence of Voices: Vietnamese American Literature 1975–1990." *Amerasia Journal* 19, no. 3 (1993): 27–50.

————. "The Reception of Robert Olen Butler's *A Good Scent from a Strange Mountain*: Ventriloquism and the Pulitzer Prize." In *Not a War: American Vietnamese Fiction, Poetry and Essays*, edited by Dan Duffy, 75–94. New Haven:Yale University Council on Southeast Asia Studies, 1997.

Uno, Roberta. "Asian American Theater Awake at the Millennium." In *Bold Words: A Century of Asian American Writing*, edited by Rajini Srikanth and EstherYae Iwanaga, 323–32. New Brunswick, NJ: Rutgers University Press, 2001.

Uyangoda, Jayadeva. "A Political Culture of Conflict." In *Creating Peace in Sri Lanka: Civil War and Reconciliation*, edited by Robert I. Rotberg, 157–68. Washington, DC: Brookings Institution Press, 1999.

Verghese, Abraham. *My Own Country: A Doctor's Story of a Town and Its People in the Age of AIDS*. New York: Simon and Schuster, 1994.

Vidler, Anthony. "Bodies in Space / Subjects in the City: Psychopathologies of Modern Urbanism." *Differences: A Journal of Feminist Cultural Studies* 5, no. 3 (1993): 31–51.

Visweswaran, Kamala. *Fictions of Feminist Ethnography*. Minneapolis: University of Minnesota Press, 1994.

Volpp, Leti. "Feminism versus Multiculturalism." *Columbia Law Review* 101, no. 5 (June 2001): 1181–1218.

Waldman, Amy. "Loss of the Shuttle: The Call of Space; For a Resolute Girl, Traditions of India Imposed No Limits." *New York Times*, Feburary 3, 2003, pp. A1, A4.

Ward, Peter W. *White Canada Forever: Popular Attitudes and Public Policy toward Orientals in British Columbia*. Montreal: McGill-Queen's University Press, 1990.

Weisberg, William, and Donna Hicks. "Overcoming Obstacles to Peace: An Examination of Third-Party Processes." In *Creating Peace in Sri Lanka: Civil War and Reconciliation*, edited by Robert I. Rotberg, 143–56. Washington, DC: Brookings Institution Press, 1999.

Wells, Jennifer. "Big Bucks Won't Buy Respect for 'Brand America.'" *Toronto Star*, March 5, 2003, A6.

Whitman, Walt. *Leaves of Grass*. Edited by Sculley Bradley and Harold W. Blodgett. New York: Norton, 1973.

Wickramagamage, Carmen. "Relocation as Positive Act: The Immigrant Experience in Bharati Mukherjee's Novels." *Diaspora: A Journal of Transnational Studies* 2, no. 2 (1992): 171–200.

Wills, Garry. "With God on His Side." *New York Times Magazine*, March 30, 2003, 26–29.

Winant, Howard. "Gayatri Spivak on the Politics of the Subaltern: Interview by Howard Winant." *Socialist Review* 20, no. 3 (July–September 1990): 82–97.

Wong, Cynthia Sau-ling. "Denationalization Reconsidered: Asian American Cultural Criticism at a Theoretical Crossroads." *Amerasia Journal* 21, nos. 1 and 2 (1995): 1–27.

————. *From Necessity to Extravagance: Reading Asian American Literature*. Princeton: Princeton University Press, 1993.

Wong, Paul, Meera Manvi, and Takeo Hirota Wong. "Asiacentrism and Asian American Studies?" *Amerasia Journal* 21, nos. 1 and 2 (1995): 137–48.

INDEX